India and International Family Law

A PRACTICAL GUIDE

Stutee Nag

ABA
AMERICAN BAR ASSOCIATION
Family Law Section

Cover design by Sara Wadford/ABA Design

Printed in the United States of America.

30 29 28 27 26   5 4 3 2 1

ISBN 978-1-63905-812-9

A catalog record for this book is available from the Library of Congress.

To those navigating the messy middles

Contents

About the Author

Stutee Nag is an attorney admitted to practice in India, New York, and New Jersey. She specializes in international family law. Her practice focuses on complex cross-border matrimonial and custody disputes, particularly matters involving India and the United States. She is among the very few tri-qualified attorneys from India practicing in this field. She appears as an expert in matters involving international family law, including issues concerning international child abduction, jurisdictional conflicts, and recognition of foreign judgments. Stutee is a Steering Group Member of the American Bar Association's International Family Law Committee and a former Fellow of the New York State Bar Association Family Law Section. She frequently speaks and writes on international family law issues and is the author of several publications addressing cross-border family disputes and international parental child abduction.

She lives in New Jersey with her husband and six-year-old child. Having lived internationally herself, she brings both professional and personal perspectives to the evolving challenges faced by families navigating legal systems across borders.

Preface

We Indians often joke, *"Indians and potatoes are found everywhere,"* because we have found homes in almost every country in the world. It is lighthearted, but it reflects a profound demographic truth. Few communities have dispersed as widely, as quickly, and as successfully as Indians have over the last half-century.

But the comparison breaks down at one important point. Potatoes, wherever they are found, retain a clear home jurisdiction. Indians do not.

We migrate. We build careers across continents. We marry abroad. We raise children in countries we did not grow up in. We hold U.S. passports, green cards, H-1B visas, OCIs, and sometimes a combination of all of them within the same household. Yet Indian family law is structured in a way that allows Indian courts to continue asserting jurisdiction over us long after we have physically left, sometimes indefinitely.

Nowhere is this more striking than when Indian family law collides with the family law systems of the United States.

Take custody first. Under the Uniform Child Custody Jurisdiction and Enforcement Act, a U.S. state court may retain continuing and exclusive jurisdiction so long as statutory conditions are satisfied. The architecture is deliberate. It is designed to prevent forum shopping and conflicting orders within the United States. Indian law does not mirror that structure. At the same time, India has its own form of continuing jurisdiction, but it often attaches to marriage itself. Under statutes such as the Hindu Marriage Act and the Special Marriage Act, Indian courts may continue to exercise divorce jurisdiction even after spouses have relocated and rebuilt their lives abroad. The inversion is striking. The United States may retain custody jurisdiction after a child has left; India may retain divorce jurisdiction after the couple has.

The differences deepen.

India remains largely fault-based in its statutory divorce framework. There is no comprehensive, uniform no-fault dissolution regime across personal laws. Asset division presents another sharp contrast. While Indian courts have, over time, stretched maintenance doctrines in pursuit of equitable outcomes, there is no statutory matrimonial property regime comparable to equitable distribution or community property. Many Indians, lawyers included, assume that Indian law provides for division of marital assets upon divorce. When I practiced exclusively in India nearly a decade ago, I did not fully appreciate the structural distinction between a codified property division system and judicially expanded maintenance intended to approximate fairness. In cross-border disputes, that distinction becomes decisive.

Immigration adds another layer of complexity. According to World Bank data, the United States, Germany, Saudi Arabia, Russia, and the United Kingdom are among the top destination countries for migrants, while India ranks among the largest origin countries in the world. We are not a marginal diaspora. We are one of the largest transnational communities globally. Family law systems drafted for geographically stable populations now regulate marriages and children that span oceans, time zones, and immigration regimes.

India's statutory landscape itself is evolving. The Code of Criminal Procedure has been replaced by the Bharatiya Nagarik Suraksha Sanhita. The Indian Penal Code has been replaced by the Bharatiya Nyaya Sanhita. Reform is underway. Yet family disputes continue to operate within overlapping personal laws, legacy frameworks, and an overburdened judiciary. Conflicting high court decisions coexist. Supreme Court clarification does not always arrive swiftly. Gendered provisions, religious distinctions, and procedural asymmetries continue to shape outcomes in ways that cannot be ignored.

For a family law attorney trained entirely outside India, this terrain can be disorienting. An Indian client may appear as a single, discrete matter. More often, that first case becomes a gateway to many more. Diaspora networks are real. Word travels quickly. One Indian client often leads to a thousand others.

This book is shaped by lived experience. I am trained in India and qualified in India, New York, and New Jersey. I have spent years practicing at the intersection of Indian and U.S. family law, handling custody disputes, anti-suit injunction battles, recognition challenges, service complications, and the full spectrum of cross-border matrimonial issues. I have appeared as an expert on Indian family law in U.S. proceedings, translating doctrines such as ordinary residence, section 13 of the Code of Civil Procedure, maintenance jurisprudence, and personal law distinctions into frameworks that American courts can apply coherently. I am also a parent raising a child in a transnational family and part of an Indian couple building a life in the United States. The professional and personal inevitably intersect in this field.

I am also firmly of the view that India should accede to the Hague Convention on the Civil Aspects of International Child Abduction. The absence of a treaty-based return framework has real consequences for children, parents, and courts on both sides of the ocean. Much of the confusion, delay, and human cost I have witnessed stems not from malice, but from structural incompatibility between legal systems.

Law school, bar admissions across jurisdictions, expert testimony, migration, parenthood, and sustained immersion in India–United States disputes have placed me in a position to guide the reader through what can be a frustrating, but navigable, maze. This book is written for lawyers who suddenly find themselves handling Indian matters, for judges confronting unfamiliar legal terrain, and for families caught in the legal limbo globalization so often creates.

The goal is not to oversimplify the law. It is to make sense of it. Clearly. Honestly. Practically.

CHAPTER 1

Indian Diaspora

1.1. Scope of the Chapter

Q. I live in the United States, but I am an Indian citizen. Does American law even apply to me?

Q. My child is an American citizen. Doesn't U.S. law apply to him no matter where he lives?

Q. International parental abduction is not even an offense in India. If I let my child visit India, am I risking permanent separation? Can't the American Embassy in India secure my child's return if my spouse refuses to bring him back?

Q. Can two courts in two different countries have parallel divorce and custody jurisdiction? If I file first in one country, can my spouse still file in another?

Q. I will never consent to a divorce; can my spouse still get it? Can't I file for restitution of conjugal rights in India?

Q. I am dependent on my spouse's immigration status in the United States. Can he make me leave the country if I file for divorce?

Q. I am the mother. Doesn't that entitle me to preferential custody rights over my child?

Q. I am the father. My personal law grants me sole custody. Will a U.S. court recognize this?

Q. My spouse is having an extramarital affair. Shouldn't that entitle me to sole custody?

Q. Will an Indian court view relocation to the United States as abandonment of family values?

Q. Will a U.S. court view extended family involvement as interference or control?

Q. Where will I fare better financially in a divorce—India or the United States?

Q. Is my U.S. divorce valid in India? Is my Indian divorce valid in the United States?

Q. Does gender matter? Does religion matter? Does nationality matter?

Q. What if I do everything "right" in one country and still lose in another?

Q. Why are the laws of these two countries so different?

And the list goes on.

These questions do not arise in a vacuum.

They arise because Indian families in the United States do not live within a single legal system. They build careers, buy homes, raise children, and participate fully in American civic life. At the same time, they maintain property in India, support parents abroad, preserve inheritance rights, hold Overseas Citizen of India (OCI) cards, travel frequently, and sustain dense extended-family ties. Their lives are not divided; they are layered.

This layered existence produces what may be called a dual legal consciousness. Indian-origin couples often make decisions—where to marry, where to give birth, how to title property, whether to sign a prenuptial agreement, whether to return to India for a period of time—with an awareness that two legal systems hover in the background. Even in stable marriages, the questions linger quietly: If something goes wrong, which court will decide? Which country's law will apply? Will a divorce granted in one jurisdiction be recognized in the other? Where would custody be determined? Where would financial relief be greater, or more limited?

These are not strategic questions asked only at the point of breakdown. They shape behavior long before litigation begins. They influence immigration choices, career sacrifices, and decisions about where children are educated. They affect whether extended family involvement is viewed as support or interference, whether relocation is opportunity or abandonment, and whether return to India feels like homecoming or retreat.

Visibility and success do not eliminate this tension. Indian Americans are deeply embedded in American professional and civic life. Yet migration history, visa dependency, family obligations abroad, and shifting political climates create a persistent awareness that belonging can be secure and contingent at the same time. For some families, that awareness strengthens ties to India; for others, it intensifies commitment to permanence in the United States. For many, it produces careful hedging across both systems.

When relationships fracture, the transnational architecture of family life becomes legally decisive. Assets are spread across jurisdictions. Children hold multiple citizenships. Custody proceedings may be filed in parallel. Religious law, personal law, and secular statutes intersect. What once felt like flexibility becomes a jurisdictional puzzle.

The purpose of this chapter is therefore not demographic description for its own sake. It is to explain why the questions posed at the outset are structurally inevitable. The Indian diaspora's scale, selectivity, education profile, economic stability, and transnational orientation make cross-border family disputes predictable rather than exceptional. Understanding these disputes requires understanding the social and legal ecosystem from which they emerge.

Only against that backdrop can the legal analysis that follows, involving jurisdiction, divorce recognition, custody, relocation, and enforcement, be properly understood.

1.2. The Indian Diaspora as a Global Phenomenon

Indian migration is not a byproduct of modern globalization; it is a defining feature of India's engagement with the world across centuries. Long before contemporary debates about borders, visas, and citizenship, Indians moved across regions and empires as traders, laborers, scholars, administrators, and professionals. These movements were shaped by commerce, colonial rule, education, and opportunity, producing overseas communities that long predate the modern nation-state.

During the colonial period, Indian mobility followed imperial pathways that linked South Asia to East Africa, the Caribbean, Southeast Asia, and parts of Europe. Merchants established trading networks, while indentured laborers were transported to plantations across the British Empire. Although these early migrations were often coerced or constrained, they laid the foundation for enduring diasporic communities with deep historical roots.

Following independence, Indian migration took on a different character. Post-1947 movements were increasingly driven by professional opportunity and educational aspiration. Doctors, engineers, academics, and scientists left India to train or work abroad, particularly in the United Kingdom and, later, North America. These migrants were typically English-proficient, highly educated, and oriented toward long-term settlement. Their departure reflected both global demand for skilled labor and domestic constraints within India, where opportunities for elite professionals remained limited.

The most recent phase of Indian migration emerged alongside economic liberalization, technological integration, and the globalization of higher education. Since the 1990s, Indian students, technology workers, entrepreneurs, and families have moved through increasingly complex legal pathways, often combining temporary visas with aspirations for permanence. Unlike earlier migrants, this cohort sustains constant, real-time ties to India through travel, communication, investment, and caregiving. Migration no longer implies rupture; it enables simultaneity.

What distinguishes the Indian diaspora is not simply its size, but its selectivity. Despite being the world's largest source of emigrants in absolute numbers, India has a remarkably low rate of emigration relative to its population. Only a small fraction of Indians live outside the country. Those who do are disproportionately drawn from educated, urban, and professionally mobile segments of society. Indian migration is therefore best understood as strategic and opportunity-driven rather than mass displacement.

This selectivity has profound implications. Migrants carry with them not only skills and credentials, but expectations about family life, education, marriage, and intergenerational obligation. These expectations shape how Indian families live abroad and how they engage with legal systems when relationships cross borders.

1.3. India as a Country of Emigration

India's position in the global migration system is that of a sending state. Outward migration has become normalized within many Indian families as a pathway to education, professional advancement, and long-term security. Students leave to pursue degrees abroad, professionals relocate to specialized labor markets, and families reunite through marriage and sponsorship. These movements are embedded in law, policy, and social expectation.

Economic considerations play a central role, but they are rarely reducible to poverty or desperation. Many Indian migrants are responding to relative opportunity rather than absolute need. Intense competition for elite educational and professional positions within India, combined with global demand for skilled labor, has long incentivized outward mobility among the middle and upper-middle classes. In certain regions, unemployment among educated youth further accelerates this trend, even as overall economic indicators remain strong.

Remittances illustrate the structural nature of Indian emigration. Funds sent by Indians abroad constitute one of the largest remittance inflows received by any country in the world.[1] These transfers support education, healthcare, property acquisition, and entrepreneurship, reinforcing transnational family strategies rather than merely addressing short-term need. For many households, migration and remittances are part of long-range planning across generations.

At the same time, India does not conceive of itself as a country of immigration. Citizenship law remains restrictive, long-term residence for foreigners is relatively uncommon, and legal frameworks are not designed to absorb large numbers of permanent settlers.[2] This outward orientation contrasts sharply with countries such as the United States, where immigration is built into the legal and cultural architecture of the state.

1. World Bank, *Remittances Slowed in 2023, Expected to Grow Faster: Migration and Development Brief 40*, at vi (Dec. 2024), https://documents1.worldbank.org/curated/en/099714008132436612/pdf/IDU1a9cf73b51fcad1425a1a0dd1cc8f2f3331ce.pdf.

2. Organisation for Economic Co-operation and Development (OECD), *International Migration Outlook 2022* (2022), https://www.oecd.org/content/dam/oecd/en/publications/reports/2022/10/international-migration-outlook-2022_140ace0e/30fe16d2-en.pdf; Simranjeet, *"Foreigners Cannot Claim Right to Reside and Settle in India as per Article 19(1)(e), Their Rights Limited to Article 21"; Delhi HC Dismisses Petition Against Illegal Detention*, SCC Online (Jan. 17, 2024), https://www.scconline.com/blog/post/2024/01/17/foreigners-cannot-claim-right-to-reside-settle-in-india-their-rights-limited-to-article-21-legal-news/; The Citizenship Act, 1955, §§ 5–6 (India), https://indiankanoon.org/doc/305990/.

This asymmetry, between a country structured to send people and one structured to receive them, lies at the heart of many Indo-American legal complexities. Indian families moving between these systems encounter fundamentally different assumptions about permanence, belonging, and jurisdiction.

1.4. The United States as a Country of Immigration: The Structural Inverse of India

Where India is organized around outward mobility, the United States is organized around inward migration. Immigration is not peripheral to the American project; it is foundational. From its earliest constitutional commitments to its evolving statutory framework, the United States has defined itself as a destination for people from elsewhere. While immigration policy has oscillated between openness and restriction, the underlying premise, that newcomers will arrive, settle, and eventually belong, has remained intact.

This structural orientation distinguishes the United States sharply from India. Indian law and political culture do not presume permanent inward migration as a feature of national life. By contrast, American legal institutions have long been tasked with integrating immigrants into civic, economic, and social systems. Citizenship, labor markets, public education, and family law all operate on the assumption that migrants will not merely pass through, but will put down roots.

The modern shape of Indian migration to the United States is inseparable from the Immigration and Nationality Act of 1965. That legislation dismantled national-origins quotas that had systematically excluded Asian migrants and replaced them with a framework emphasizing family reunification and employment-based admissions.[3] For Indian migrants, many of whom were English-proficient, highly educated, and professionally trained, this shift was transformative. It aligned U.S. immigration law with India's growing output of engineers, physicians, scientists, and academics.

The result was not a sudden influx, but a steady and compounding demographic change. Indian migration accelerated gradually, then dramatically, as professional pipelines matured. Educational migration fed employment migration; employment migration enabled family reunification; family reunification laid the groundwork for intergenerational settlement. Over time, Indians came to occupy a distinctive position within the American immigration landscape: legally admitted, economically successful, and increasingly permanent.

Citizenship philosophy further reinforces this divergence. The United States confers citizenship by birth on its soil, embedding children of immigrants fully within the national community from the moment of birth. India, by contrast, grounds citizenship more heavily in descent and does not have the concept of

3. History, Art & Archives, U.S. House of Representatives, *Historical Highlights: Immigration and Nationality Act of 1965*, https://history.house.gov/Historical-Highlights/1951-2000/Immigration-and-Nationality-Act-of-1965/.

dual nationality.[4] These differing approaches shape family decision-making in subtle but powerful ways. Where children are born, which passports they hold, and which courts exercise authority over them are not abstract questions for Indian families; they are foundational considerations.

This structural inversion, *India as a sender state and the United States as a receiver state*,[5] creates predictable friction when families operate across both systems. Legal expectations about residence, permanence, parental authority, and jurisdiction diverge. When marriages falter, parents separate, or families relocate, those divergences surface in ways that courts must ultimately resolve.

1.5. Indians as the World's Largest Immigrant Group

Indian migration must also be understood in global terms. Indians today constitute the largest emigrant population in the world, with nearly 18 million people born in India residing abroad.[6] This figure exceeds that of any other country and reflects the extraordinary geographic reach of Indian mobility. Indian migrants live across the Gulf states, North America, Europe, Africa, and Southeast Asia, occupying roles that range from temporary labor to permanent professional settlement.

This global dispersion is not uniform. In the Gulf, Indian migrants often reside on temporary contracts with limited pathways to citizenship. In Western democracies, by contrast, migration is more likely to result in long-term residence, naturalization, and family formation. These divergent migration regimes produce different legal realities for Indian families depending on destination.

Remittances provide a window into the durability of these connections. India has, for years, been the world's largest recipient of remittance inflows, receiving well over 100 billion dollars annually through formal channels. These funds are not merely symbolic ties to the homeland. They finance education, healthcare, real estate, and business ventures, reinforcing transnational family structures that endure across decades.

Yet the scale of Indian emigration should not obscure its selectivity. Only a small percentage of Indians live outside the country. Migration is not the norm; it is an option exercised by those positioned to pursue it. This reality differentiates Indian migration from that of populations driven primarily by conflict, displacement, or economic collapse. *Indian migrants tend to arrive with credentials, capital, and expectations of stability, factors that shape how they engage with legal systems abroad.*

Within this global picture, the United States occupies a distinctive position. It is not the largest destination numerically, but it is the most consequential legally. Migration to the United States is more likely to culminate in citizenship,

4. The Citizenship Act § 3 (India).

5. World Bank, *supra* note 1, at vi.

6. Ruchi Singh, *Origin of World's Largest Migrant Population, India Seeks to Leverage Immigration*, Migration Policy Institute (Mar. 9, 2022), https://www.migrationpolicy.org/article/india-migration-country-profile.

property ownership, and intergenerational continuity. It is therefore within the American context that the legal dimensions of Indian migration are most fully realized.

1.6. Indians in the United States: Size, Growth, and Geographic Concentration

As of the early 2020s, nearly three million immigrants born in India resided in the United States.[7] When U.S.-born individuals who identify as Indian are included, the Indian-origin population exceeds five million people.[8] Indians are now the second-largest immigrant group in the country and the second-largest Asian-origin population overall.[9] This growth has been sustained, substantial, and accelerating.

The demographic trajectory of Indian migration reflects the cumulative effects of post-1965 immigration law, global labor demand, and educational mobility. The greatest expansion occurred after 2000, as technology-driven industries expanded and U.S. universities increasingly drew international students from India. Over time, these students transitioned into the workforce, sponsored family members, and established permanent communities.

Indian Americans are not evenly distributed across the United States; rather, they are highly concentrated in certain states whose economic structures align with skilled migration. As of the early 2020s, roughly half of the Indian American population lived in four states, California, Texas, New Jersey, and New York, with California alone accounting for approximately one-fifth of the total.[10] Texas has emerged as a second major hub, reflecting the growth of technology, healthcare, and energy sectors, while New Jersey and New York continue to attract Indian families through dense professional networks, educational institutions, and established immigrant infrastructure.

This concentration is not merely demographic but socio-economic: Indian American households in these states report median incomes well above national and Asian American averages, reinforcing patterns of suburban settlement, homeownership, and long-term permanence.

New York provides a particularly instructive case study. Immigrants comprise nearly a quarter of the state's population and more than a quarter of its labor force.[11] Indian immigrants and Indian Americans are embedded within this broader immigrant ecosystem, participating in sectors ranging from

7. Madeleine Greene & Jeanne Batalova, *Indian Immigrants in the United States*, Migration Policy Institute (Nov. 8, 2024), https://www.migrationpolicy.org/article/indian-immigrants-united-states.

8. Carolyne Im, *Facts About Indians in the U.S.*, Pew Research Center (May 1, 2025), https://www.pewresearch.org/race-and-ethnicity/fact-sheet/asian-americans-indians-in-the-u-s/.

9. *Id.*

10. Pew Research Center, *Indian Americans: A Survey Data Snapshot*, https://www.pewresearch.org/2024/08/06/indian-americans-a-survey-data-snapshot/.

11. American Immigration Council, *Immigrants in New York*, https://map.americanimmigrationcouncil.org/locations/new-york/.

healthcare and technology to entrepreneurship and education. The density of Indian-origin families in the New York metropolitan area means that family courts in this region routinely confront cases involving international marriages, overseas assets, and cross-border parenting arrangements.

Geographic concentration also increases the likelihood that disputes will be litigated rather than resolved informally. Dense professional communities, high asset values, and overlapping legal obligations make formal adjudication more likely when relationships break down. The result is a disproportionate representation of Indian-origin families in complex family law proceedings within certain jurisdictions.

1.7. Education and Professional Pathways

Education occupies a central place in the migration narrative of the Indian diaspora. Indian Americans are among the most highly educated populations in the United States, with levels of educational attainment that far exceed national averages.[12] This pattern is visible across generations and reflects both selection at the point of migration and sustained investment after arrival.

For many Indian families, education is not merely a means of economic mobility but a cultural imperative. Competitive examinations, elite institutions, and credential-based advancement are deeply familiar features of life in India, particularly for the urban middle class from which many migrants originate. These norms travel with migrants and are often reinforced in the diaspora, where education functions as both protection and proof—protection against economic uncertainty and proof of legitimacy in a new society.

Educational migration has played a particularly important role in shaping Indian presence in the United States. Indian students have become one of the largest international student populations in American higher education, especially at the graduate level.[13] Programs in engineering, computer science, medicine, and business have long drawn applicants from India, creating a pipeline that links Indian secondary education to American professional labor markets. For many students, study in the United States is followed by employment, permanent residence, and eventual citizenship.

This educational pathway has legal consequences. Students often arrive on temporary visas that limit employment options and create dependence on institutional sponsorship. Transitioning from student status to professional employment frequently involves navigating complex visa regimes, including employer sponsorship and lengthy backlogs for permanent residence. These constraints shape family decisions in subtle but powerful ways, influencing when and

12. Sumitra Badrinathan et al., *Social Realities of Indian Americans: Results from the 2020 Indian American Attitudes Survey*, Carnegie Endowment for International Peace (June 2021), https://assets.carnegieendowment.org/static/files/files__Vaishnav_etal_IAASpt3_Final.pdf.

13. Sakshi Venkatraman, *Indians Become Biggest International Student Group in U.S., Surpassing Chinese for First Time Since 2009*, NBC News (Nov. 19, 2024), https://www.nbcnews.com/news/asian-america/indian-students-surpass-chinese-largest-international-group-rcna180783.

where marriages occur, whether children are born in the United States, and how long families remain geographically mobile.

Professional outcomes mirror educational attainment. Indian Americans are heavily concentrated in high-skilled occupations, including technology, medicine, engineering, finance, academia, and management.[14] They are disproportionately represented in industries that reward specialization, credentialing, and continuous professional development. Over time, Indian Americans have also emerged as entrepreneurs and corporate leaders, founding companies, managing large workforces, and contributing to innovation across sectors.[15]

At the same time, professional success does not guarantee legal security. Many highly skilled Indian professionals remain on temporary or conditional immigration status for extended periods. Employment-based immigration pathways can stretch over decades, leaving families legally vulnerable despite economic stability. This tension between professional integration and legal precarity is a recurring feature of Indian American life and a critical backdrop to later family law disputes.

1.8. Undocumented Indians

Although Indian Americans are overwhelmingly represented in lawful, skilled, and family-based immigration streams, a smaller and often underreported subset of the population has entered or remained in the United States without authorization. In recent years, U.S. Customs and Border Protection data has recorded a sharp increase in encounters with Indian nationals at U.S. borders, particularly following the pandemic. These encounters, nearly 97,000 in the 2023 fiscal year, reflect a dramatic rise from pre-2020 levels, though they remain modest when compared with undocumented migration from neighboring regions.[16] Importantly, such figures capture border encounters rather than the settled population size, and they do not displace the broader reality that undocumented Indians constitute a relatively small share of the overall unauthorized immigrant population in the United States.

The recent increase in irregular Indian migration is also geographically patterned. A significant proportion of undocumented Indian migrants originate from northern India, particularly the states of Punjab and Haryana, regions with long-standing histories of overseas migration and dense transnational networks.[17] In these areas, migration has become a normalized, sometimes expected, pathway to mobility, reinforced by family connections abroad and community-level success stories.

14. Greene & Batalova, *supra* note 7.

15. Indo American Chamber of Commerce, U.S.A., *The Rising Tide: Indian Americans Reshape the U.S. Business Landscape*, https://iaccus.org/blog/blog2.

16. Gil Guerra & Sneha Puri, *Indian Migrants at the U.S. Border: What the Data Reveals*, Niskanen Center (Sep. 16, 2024), https://www.niskanencenter.org/a-data-guide-to-indian-migrants-at-the-border/.

17. *Id.*

Structural factors such as limited local employment opportunities for educated youth, agricultural instability, prolonged visa backlogs for lawful migration, and perceptions of political or social marginalization have contributed to a willingness to pursue high-risk routes. Migrants from these regions often undertake complex, multi-country journeys facilitated by smuggling networks, arriving at U.S. borders through southern or northern routes rather than traditional ports of entry.[18]

In addition to irregular entry at land borders, a subset of undocumented Indian migrants enter the United States lawfully on temporary visas, most commonly tourist visas, and subsequently overstay their authorized period of stay. This pattern has been observed particularly among migrants from western India, including parts of Gujarat, where overseas mobility has long been embedded in community and family strategies.[19] Others seek to regularize their presence through asylum applications or enter into marriages that are later scrutinized by immigration authorities for lack of bona fides. While such pathways reflect a range of individual circumstances, they underscore the limited availability of timely lawful migration options for those without immediate access to employment-based or family-sponsored visas.

Once in the United States, undocumented Indian migrants often occupy economic niches that allow for relative financial stability despite legal precarity. Many find work as long-haul truck drivers, convenience store and gas station operators, motel owners, or small business employees within co-ethnic networks. These occupations can be physically demanding and socially isolating, yet they frequently provide incomes that exceed what migrants could earn in India. As a result, some undocumented Indian migrants achieve a degree of economic success while remaining socially and legally peripheral, living outside formal institutions, avoiding interaction with the state, and limiting mobility due to fear of enforcement. This combination of financial viability and legal invisibility distinguishes their experience from both the professionalized Indian American mainstream and other undocumented populations.

1.9. Income, Wealth, and Class Position

Indian Americans occupy a distinctive socio-economic position within the United States. On average, Indian-headed households report median incomes significantly higher than those of the general population.[20] Poverty rates among Indian Americans are comparatively low, and rates of labor force participation are high. These indicators place Indian Americans firmly within the upper tiers of the American income distribution.

18. Matt Rivers & Doc Louallen, *Smuggler Reveals Migration Routes to US for Indian Migrants*, ABC News (Feb. 12, 2025), https://abcnews.go.com/International/smuggler-reveals-migration-routes-us-indian-migrants/story?id=118481540.

19. Suhasini Raj, *India, a Big Source of Illegal Migration, Hopes to Navigate the Trump Storm*, N.Y. Times (Jan. 26, 2025), https://www.nytimes.com/2025/01/26/world/asia/india-illegal-immigration-trump.html.

20. Im, *supra* note 8.

This economic profile is the cumulative product of selective migration, educational attainment, and professional concentration. Indian migrants often arrive with credentials that command immediate market value or acquire such credentials shortly after arrival. Over time, stable employment in high-paying sectors facilitates asset accumulation, homeownership, and long-term financial planning.

Yet aggregate success can obscure internal diversity. The Indian American population is not monolithic. Differences in caste, religion, region, language, and class shape individual experiences and outcomes. While many Indian Americans occupy professional and managerial roles, others work in service industries, small businesses, or caregiving sectors. Economic inequality exists within the community, even as overall indicators remain strong.

Moreover, wealth and income do not always align neatly. High earnings may coexist with limited liquidity, particularly for families navigating visa restrictions or supporting relatives abroad. Assets may be spread across jurisdictions, with property, investments, and obligations in both the United States and India. These transnational financial arrangements complicate family law proceedings, particularly in divorce and inheritance disputes, where questions of valuation, jurisdiction, and enforcement arise.

Economic stability also enables mobility. Indian American families are more likely than many others to contemplate international relocation for career advancement, education, or family reasons. This mobility, while advantageous, introduces legal complexity when spouses disagree about relocation or when children's ties to multiple countries must be weighed.

1.10. Marriage Formation and Marital Patterns

Marriage remains a central institution within the Indian diaspora, though its form and timing vary across generations. Indian Americans, particularly those who are foreign-born, have high marriage rates, reflecting cultural norms that link marriage to adulthood, stability, and family responsibility. These patterns coexist with increasing diversity in how marriages are formed and sustained in the United States.

Marriage formation within the diaspora follows multiple pathways. Some unions are arranged or facilitated through family networks that span continents, while others are self-selected partnerships formed through education, work, or social life. Many marriages occupy a middle ground, combining individual choice with varying degrees of family involvement. These hybrid forms reflect adaptation to American social norms rather than a wholesale abandonment of inherited expectations.

Cross-border marriages remain common among first-generation immigrants. Individuals may marry partners residing in India or elsewhere and later pursue family-based immigration pathways to reunite in the United States. Such marriages often involve complex negotiations over residence, career sacrifice, and cultural adjustment. Immigration status can introduce dependency within the marital relationship, shaping power dynamics and decision-making long before any legal dispute arises.

Generational differences are pronounced. U.S.-born Indian Americans tend to marry later and are significantly more likely to enter interracial, interfaith, or intercultural marriages, reflecting broader American patterns of family formation. These unions may bring additional considerations related to extended family involvement, religious practice, and geographic ties, particularly where relatives remain abroad.

Divorce, while historically stigmatized in many Indian communities, has become more visible within the diaspora. Greater economic independence, exposure to American legal norms, and shifting social attitudes have contributed to this change. At the same time, stigma persists, and families may attempt to manage marital breakdown privately or strategically across jurisdictions, sometimes delaying formal separation or initiating parallel proceedings. These dynamics often complicate resolution and foreshadow the legal challenges addressed in later chapters.

1.11. Marriage to U.S. Citizens and Mixed-Status Families

Marriage to U.S. citizens, both of Indian origin and otherwise, has played a significant role in Indian migration to the United States and continues to shape family formation within the diaspora. While endogamy remains common among foreign-born Indian Americans, particularly through marriages to partners from India, intermarriage is substantially more prevalent among the U.S.-born.[21] These marriages increasingly reflect ordinary patterns of American family life rather than migration strategy alone, even as they intersect with immigration law in important ways.

From a family law perspective, marriages involving U.S. citizens frequently give rise to mixed-status families whose legal lives are shaped by overlapping immigration and domestic-relations regimes. Marriage to a U.S. citizen may provide a pathway to lawful permanent residence, but such cases are subject to heightened scrutiny by immigration authorities, particularly where the noncitizen spouse entered on a temporary visa or has prior immigration complications.[22] Immigration dependency can affect bargaining power within the marriage, influence decisions about when or whether to separate, and complicate litigation strategy if the relationship breaks down.

In intermarriages, differences in cultural expectations, family involvement, and geographic attachment may further shape disputes over residence, parenting, and relocation. Even where both spouses ultimately hold U.S. citizenship, the transnational origins of the marriage and the continued presence of extended family abroad often surface in custody disputes, forum selection, and enforcement questions. These marriages thus illustrate how immigration

21. Badrinathan et al., *supra* note 12.

22. *"Marriage Not Enough for Green Card": US Immigration Attorney Warns Couples*, NDTV World (Jan. 1, 2026), https://www.ndtv.com/world-news/marriage-not-enough-for-green-card-us-immigration-attorney-warns-couples-10176963.

history can continue to influence family law outcomes long after formal status issues appear to be resolved.

1.12. Children, Parenting, and Intergenerational Life

Children occupy a central place in the Indian American family structure. A significant share of the Indian American population consists of U.S.-born children of immigrants, many of whom grow up in households shaped by both Indian cultural norms and American legal frameworks. These children are typically citizens by birth, anchoring families legally even as emotional and cultural ties extend abroad.[23]

Parenting within the diaspora reflects strong emphasis on education, discipline, and upward mobility. Families invest heavily in schooling, extracurricular activities, and residential choices aligned with high-performing school districts. Language retention, religious education, and cultural participation often accompany these investments, producing children who navigate multiple identities with relative ease.

Intergenerational arrangements are also common. Elderly parents may live with adult children or rotate between countries depending on health, visa status, and caregiving needs. Grandparents often play significant roles in childcare, particularly in households where both parents pursue demanding professional careers. These arrangements blur conventional distinctions between nuclear and extended families and introduce additional legal considerations related to dependency, residence, and healthcare decision-making.

Children raised in transnational households often develop strong ties to more than one country. Visits to India, relationships with extended family, and exposure to multiple languages and traditions shape their sense of belonging. At the same time, their legal identities are firmly grounded in the United States. This duality becomes especially salient when parents separate or disagree about relocation, education, or custody.

1.13. Why the Indian Diaspora Matters for Family Law

The Indian diaspora's scale, selectivity, educational attainment, economic integration, and sustained transnational ties make it uniquely consequential for family law. Indian-origin families appear with disproportionate frequency in disputes involving international marriage, competing custody proceedings, relocation, jurisdictional conflict, and recognition or enforcement of foreign decrees. These cases are not aberrations or edge scenarios; they are the foreseeable byproduct of lives constructed across borders. Families that are professionally mobile, legally layered, and economically established in more than one country will inevitably encounter legal systems that were not designed for such complexity.

---

23. Arpan Jhaveri, *Asian-Indian Immigrants and Their Children in America*, Boston University, https://people.bu.edu/prothero/ia_immigrants.htm.

Understanding these disputes therefore requires more than doctrinal literacy. It requires recognition of the migration histories, immigration dependencies, extended family structures, asset dispersion, and dual legal consciousness that shape decision-making long before litigation begins. The Indian diaspora is not merely background context; it is the structural source of the legal conflicts that follow.

With that foundation in place, the chapters ahead turn to doctrine. They examine how Indian and U.S. courts assert and decline jurisdiction, recognize and refuse foreign divorces, determine custody and relocation, and enforce financial obligations across borders. The demographic and social realities described in this chapter explain why those doctrinal questions arise, and why their answers so often diverge.

CHAPTER 2

Overview of Indian Family Law

2.1. Scope of the Chapter

This chapter explains how Indian family law is structured, who decides what, and why no single statute or court provides the full answer. It begins with the historical layering that still defines the system today: pre-colonial personal law traditions, colonial judicialization of religion-based norms, post-independence constitutional restructuring, the Hindu Code reforms of the 1950s, and the eventual creation of specialized family courts in 1984. Unlike the largely unified domestic-relations systems familiar to American practitioners, India operates a plural regime in which the substantive law governing marriage, divorce, maintenance, guardianship, and succession often depends on the parties' religious identity unless they opt into a secular statute such as the Special Marriage Act. That structural pluralism is not peripheral; it drives jurisdiction, remedies, enforceability, and litigation strategy.

The chapter then maps the judicial architecture. It situates the Supreme Court, high courts, district courts, and family courts within a vertically integrated system in which appellate courts exercise not only review but meaningful administrative supervision over trial courts. It explains the establishment, jurisdiction, and functioning of family courts under the Family Courts Act, 1984, including their conciliatory mandate, procedural flexibility, and statutory emphasis on settlement. It contrasts this welfare-driven institutional design with New York's adversarial but specialized framework, including the bifurcation between Supreme Court and family court and the integrated approach adopted in the *Integrated Domestic Violence* (IDV) Parts. It also addresses the reality that, despite statutory exclusivity, Indian matrimonial disputes frequently unfold across multiple forums simultaneously: family courts, magistrates under the Domestic Violence Act, summary maintenance proceedings under the criminal procedure framework, and criminal prosecutions under the *Bharatiya Nyaya Sanhita* (the Indian Penal Code), creating parallel tracks that materially influence leverage and timing.

Substantively, the chapter provides a detailed account of divorce law across India's personal law systems. It explains the grounds for divorce under the Hindu Marriage Act, including cruelty, desertion, adultery, conversion, mental disorder, venereal disease, renunciation, and presumption of death, as well as the development of irretrievable breakdown jurisprudence through the Supreme Court's exercise of constitutional powers. It analyzes divorce under the Special Marriage Act, which mirrors many Hindu Marriage Act grounds but operates as a secular regime. It addresses Christian divorce under the Indian Divorce Act, including statutory grounds and historical asymmetries that have been judicially corrected. It explains Parsi divorce under the Parsi Marriage and Divorce Act, including the distinctive procedural framework involving community delegates. It discusses Muslim divorce in its various forms—*talaq, khula, mubarat*—judicial dissolution under the Dissolution of Muslim Marriages Act, and the constitutional invalidation of instantaneous triple talaq, while clarifying the continued interaction between uncodified personal law and statutory intervention. Throughout, the chapter emphasizes that although doctrinal grounds may appear familiar to U.S. lawyers, their evidentiary thresholds, judicial interpretation, and interaction with personal law produce different strategic outcomes.

The financial dimension of matrimonial litigation is treated as a central structural feature rather than an ancillary issue. The chapter explains the fragmented maintenance regime: interim and permanent alimony under matrimonial statutes; independent maintenance rights under personal laws; summary maintenance under criminal procedure; financial relief under the Domestic Violence Act; and the Supreme Court's effort in *Rajnesh v. Neha* to impose uniform financial-disclosure standards across forums. It highlights a defining difference from U.S. law: India has no comprehensive statutory matrimonial property regime. There is no community property system and no codified equitable-distribution framework. Property disputes between spouses are often resolved through title-based analysis, trust principles, *stridhan* claims, or limited statutory maintenance, rather than through a holistic redistribution of marital assets. The chapter addresses prenuptial agreements, noting their limited and context-dependent enforceability, the absence of a robust statutory framework governing them, and the cultural and judicial skepticism that often surrounds them.

The chapter further addresses unmarried partners and live-in relationships, explaining the absence of a comprehensive cohabitation property regime, the conditional recognition of domestic violence protections for women in relationships "in the nature of marriage," and the limited avenues for financial relief outside formal marriage. It situates these developments within evolving constitutional jurisprudence while underscoring the practical limits of nonmarital claims compared to the structured rights available within statutory marriage.

Custody and guardianship are analyzed both structurally and comparatively. The chapter explains the Guardians and Wards Act, the welfare principle as the "paramount consideration," the distinction between guardianship and custody, the statutory tender years preference under Hindu law, and the conceptual separation of *hizanat* and *wilayat* under Muslim law. It contrasts India's open-textured, judge-developed welfare standard with the multi-factor best interests analyses typical of U.S. jurisdictions. It also examines India's non-accession to the Hague Abduction Convention, the resulting reliance on habeas corpus and guardianship proceedings in international child-return disputes, and the Supreme Court's prioritization of welfare over comity in cross-border custody cases.

Finally, the chapter underscores the systemic realities that shape practice: uneven geographic implementation of family courts, significant delays despite statutory mandates for expeditious resolution, the Supreme Court's structural interventions to standardize maintenance and streamline procedure, and the strategic implications of parallel civil and criminal proceedings. It emphasizes that in Indian matrimonial litigation, forum selection, personal law identity, and procedural posture are not peripheral considerations; they are often determinative.

In sum, this chapter provides American lawyers with the structural literacy necessary to understand how Indian divorce, financial relief, custody, religious personal law, and judicial hierarchy interact in practice. It does not present India as an outlier, nor as a mirror image of U.S. family law, but as a sophisticated, plural, judge-shaped system in which historical layering, constitutional values, and statutory fragmentation converge, particularly in cross-border disputes involving the Indian diaspora.

2.2. Court and Statutory Structure

2.2.1. Historical Overview

India's contemporary family law system is the product of layered legal development spanning pre-colonial personal law traditions, colonial codification, and post-independence constitutional and statutory reform. Understanding this progression is essential for practitioners dealing with Indian parties because modern adjudication in matrimonial and child-related cases cannot be understood without reference to these historical layers.

A. Pre-Colonial Personal Law Traditions

Before British intervention, family relations in the Indian subcontinent were governed almost entirely by community-specific religious and customary systems. "Personal law" determined issues of marriage, divorce (where permissible), maintenance, succession, guardianship, legitimacy, and adoption.[1] For Hindus, these matters were shaped by Dharmashastric texts and regional custom;[2] for Muslims, by the Hanafi school of Islamic jurisprudence as interpreted through Qaza courts;[3] for Christians[4] and Parsis,[5] by ecclesiastical and customary norms. None of these systems operated through a unified territorial court structure. Instead, adjudication occurred through community institutions, caste councils,

1. Bhatt & Joshi Associates, *Booklet on Family Laws in India* 14 (2024), https://bhattandjoshiassociates.s3.ap-south-1.amazonaws.com/booklets+%26+publications/Family+Law+in+India+--+Marriage%2C+Divorce+%26+Inheritance+Laws.pdf.

2. *Id.*

3. *Id.*

4. *Id.*

5. Nandini Chatterjee, *Religious Change, Social Conflict, and Legal Competition: The Emergence of Christian Personal Law in Colonial India* 1171–72 (Department of History, University of Plymouth 2010), https://ore.exeter.ac.uk/ndownloader/files/56710919.

religious courts, and informal dispute-resolution mechanisms. The pluralistic, decentralized nature of these norms meant that jurisdiction over family matters was closely tied to religious identity, kinship networks, and localized customs.

B. Early British Administration and the Introduction of Personal Law as Judicially Applied Law (1772–1860)

The modern trajectory of India's family law system began with Warren Hastings's judicial plans in 1772–1774, which introduced the principle that colonial courts would adjudicate matters of inheritance, marriage, caste, and other religious usages according to the parties' respective religious laws.[6] This policy entrenched personal law pluralism into the formal judicial system. For Hindus and Muslims, British judges relied on translations and digests of religious texts prepared by colonial scholars such as Henry Colebrooke.[7] Because religious texts did not always address modern matrimonial issues, British courts developed a large body of case law interpreting personal law principles, often modifying traditional doctrines.

Two consequences of this colonial approach continue to shape Indian family litigation today:

1. Courts, not clergy, became the interpreters of religious personal law. Even though the substantive rules were religious, their application became judicial and precedential.
2. Personal law identity became legally determinative. The question of whether a party was Hindu, Muslim, Christian, or Parsi became central to matters of jurisdiction and applicable law, a feature that persists in modern statutes.

C. Codification and Expansion of Colonial-Era Statutory Family Law (1860–1947)

Beginning in the mid-19th century, colonial administrators gradually codified areas of personal law to address perceived gaps and inconsistencies. Key enactments included:

- Indian Divorce Act, 1869, establishing grounds for divorce among Christians[8]
- Special Marriage Act, 1872, permitting civil marriage across religions for a limited class of persons (replaced by Special Marriage Act, 1954)[9]

6. Geetanjali Srikantan, *A Forgotten Chapter in the History of Hindu Law? James Henry Nelson and 19th Century Madras High Court Jurisprudence*, Canopy Forum (Mar. 10, 2022), https://canopyforum.org/2022/03/10/a-forgotten-chapter-in-the-history-of-hindu-law-james-henry-nelson-and-19th-century-madras-high-court-jurisprudence/.

7. H.T. Colebrooke was a prominent orientalist and judge who, following Sir William Jones, compiled and translated key digests of Hindu law, most notably the *Digest of Hindu Law on Contracts and Successions* (1798) and *Two Treatises on the Hindu Law of Inheritance* (1810).

8. The Indian Divorce Act, 1869 (India), https://indiankanoon.org/doc/806295/.

9. The Special Marriage Act, 1872 (Special Marriage Act, 1872, was repealed and replaced by Special Marriage Act, 1954, https://indiankanoon.org/doc/4234/) was India's first civil marriage law, introduced by the British to facilitate inter-religious or inter-caste marriages, initially requir-

- Guardians and Wards Act, 1890, creating a uniform statutory framework for guardianship and custody applicable regardless of religion[10]
- Parsi Marriage and Divorce Act, 1936, codifying Parsi matrimonial law[11]
- Child Marriage Restraint Act, 1929, establishing minimum marriage ages (since repealed, superseded by the Prohibition of Child Marriage Act, 2006)[12]

These statutes did not displace religious personal law but supplemented it, creating a hybrid regime in which matrimonial and custody matters could depend simultaneously on statutory text, personal law principles, and judge-made precedent. The judicial structure during this period consisted of the federal court (from 1937), high courts established in major presidencies (Calcutta, Bombay, Madras), district courts, and subordinate civil courts.[13]

D. Post-Independence Constitutional Transformation (1947–1950)

Upon gaining independence in 1947, India retained the colonial legal system but adopted a new Constitution in 1950, which reorganized judicial power and reaffirmed personal law pluralism.[14] The Constitution created a Supreme Court of India as the final appellate authority; high courts for each state; district and subordinate courts; and (in time) provisions empowering states and Parliament to legislate on marriage, divorce, guardianship, adoption, and succession.[15]

The Constitution did not mandate a uniform family law system. Instead, personal laws were preserved under Articles 25–26 (freedom of religion)[16] and through legislative practice, while the Directive Principles (Article 44) called for a Uniform Civil Code as a future aspiration.[17] To this day, India continues to operate a plural family law regime where the applicable substantive law

ing parties to renounce their faith; it was later amended to allow Hindus, Sikhs, Buddhists, and Jains to marry within these communities without renunciation.

10. The Guardians and Wards Act, 1890 (India), https://indiankanoon.org/doc/1874830/.

11. The Parsi Marriage and Divorce Act, 1936 (India), https://indiankanoon.org/doc/122564/.

12. The Child Marriage Restraint Act, 1929 (India), https://indiankanoon.org/doc/323064/. The Child Marriage Restraint Act, 1929 (also known as the Sarda Act) was a significant law in British India that aimed to prevent child marriages by setting minimum ages (initially 18 for males, 14 for females) and penalizing those who arranged or solemnized them, though implementation was weak; it was a precursor to modern anti-child marriage laws in India and Bangladesh, later raising the age to 21 for boys and 18 for girls, and criminalizing adult perpetrators.

13. Sri Swami Dayal, *Origin and Growth of the High Court* (Allahabad High Court, India), https://www.allahabadhighcourt.in/event/OriginAndGrowthOfHighCourtSDayal.html.

14. Supreme Court of India, *History*, https://www.sci.gov.in/about-department/history/.

15. Supreme Court of India, *Constitution*, https://www.sci.gov.in/constitution/.

16. Articles 25 and 26 of the Constitution of India guarantee the right to freedom of religion, with Article 25 ensuring freedom of conscience, practice, and propagation for individuals (subject to public order, health, and morality). Article 26 grants religious denominations the right to manage their own religious affairs, establish institutions, and own/administer property. Key cases interpreting these articles include *The Commr, Hindu Religious Endowments v. Sri Lakshmindra Thirtha Swamiar of Sri Shirur Mutt*, 1954 AIR 282, and *Durgah Committee, Ajmer v. Ali*, AIR 1961 SC 1402.

17. Shalina A. Chibber, *Charting a New Path Toward Gender Equality in India: From Religious Personal Laws to a Uniform Civil Code*, 83 Indiana Law Journal 695, 700 (2008), https://www.repository.law.indiana.edu/ilj/vol83/iss2/10.

depends on the parties' religious identity unless they opt into a secular statute such as the Special Marriage Act.

E. The Hindu Code Bills and the Emergence of Modern Matrimonial Statutes (1954–1956)

One of the most significant legal reforms in Indian family law occurred between 1954 and 1956 when Parliament enacted a series of statutes collectively referred to as the "Hindu Code Bills":[18]

- Special Marriage Act, 1954 (in its modern form), creating a fully secular marriage and divorce regime
- Hindu Marriage Act, 1955, governing marriage, divorce, restitution of conjugal rights (RCR), and maintenance for Hindus, Buddhists, Jains, and Sikhs
- Hindu Succession Act, 1956, reforming inheritance rules
- Hindu Minority and Guardianship Act, 1956, establishing guardianship principles
- Hindu Adoptions and Maintenance Act, 1956, addressing adoption and spousal/child maintenance

These enactments modernized family law for the majority population and provided, for the first time, statutory grounds for divorce and judicial separation in Hindu law. Although a uniform matrimonial code was not adopted for all communities, the Hindu Code Bills reflected a shift toward statutory consolidation and judicial oversight.

F. Parallel Development of Muslim, Christian, and Parsi Family Law

Muslim personal law remained uncodified in most areas except provision of maintenance under section 125 of the Code of Criminal Procedure (CrPC)[19] and the Dissolution of Muslim Marriages Act, 1939.[20] Christian matrimonial law continued under the Indian Divorce Act, 1869,[21] supplemented by amendments and case law. Parsi matrimonial law remained governed by the 1936 statute.[22]

This meant that after independence, India's family law system consisted of four parallel personal law tracks, each with distinct rules on marriage, divorce, adoption, maintenance, succession, and custody, alongside secular statutes applicable to interfaith or civil marriages.

---

18. Rina Verma Williams, Reform and Codification of Hindu Personal Law: The Hindu Code Bills, 1948–57, *in Postcolonial Politics and Personal Laws: Colonial Legal Legacies and the Indian State* 96 (Oxford Academic 2006), https://doi.org/10.1093/acprof:oso/9780195680140.003.0004; Wikipedia, *Hindu Code Bills*, https://en.wikipedia.org/wiki/Hindu_code_bills.

19. Khan v. Begum, AIR 1985 SC 945 (India), https://indiankanoon.org/doc/823221/.

20. The Dissolution of Muslim Marriages Act, 1939 (India), https://indiankanoon.org/doc/1458498/.

21. Indian Divorce Act.

22. Parsi Marriage and Divorce Act.

G. Rise of Judicial Precedent and the Supreme Court's Expanding Role (1950–1980)

Beginning in the 1950s, the Supreme Court of India developed a substantial body of jurisprudence interpreting family statutes and personal law. Key doctrinal developments included:

- Defining the scope of the "welfare of the child" principle under the Guardians and Wards Act[23]
- Interpreting the grounds for divorce, cruelty, and desertion[24]
- Harmonizing conflicts between statutory text and traditional personal law[25]
- Developing evidentiary and procedural standards for matrimonial litigation[26]
- Determining the enforceability of foreign matrimonial decrees[27]

---

23. Jacob v. Chakramakkal, AIR 1973 SC 2090, https://indiankanoon.org/doc/270778/. Although the principle of child welfare was established well before 1973, notably by the Privy Council in *Besant v. Narayaniah*, (1914) 41 IA 314, which characterized parental guardianship as a "sacred trust" revocable in the child's best interest. This was later affirmed by the Supreme Court in *Begum v. Suggi*, AIR 1960 SC 93, where the Court held that the child's interest is the "sole and predominant criterion" in custody matters; however, these precedents were only truly expanded in *Jacob* in 1973.

24. Sailesh v. Sreenivasan, Transfer Petition (Civil) No. 1118 of 2014 (India) (interpreting irretrievable breakdown of marriage as a ground for divorce under Article 142 of the Constitution), https://indiankanoon.org/doc/37623680/; Narendra v. Meena, AIR 2016 SC 4599 (holding that groundless efforts to separate a husband from his parents constitute mental cruelty), https://indiankanoon.org/doc/130314186/; Rao v. Deepa, AIR 2013 SC 2176 (India) (ruling that filing false criminal complaints against a spouse amounts to mental cruelty), https://indiankanoon.org/doc/14713882/; Ghosh v. Ghosh, AIR Online 2007 SC 347 (India) (providing an exhaustive illustrative list of behaviors constituting mental cruelty), https://indiankanoon.org/doc/766894/; Pandey v. Pandey, AIR 2002 SC 591 (India) (defining desertion as total repudiation of marital obligations), https://indiankanoon.org/doc/325522/; Dastane v. Dastane, AIR 1975 SC 34 (India) (establishing the "reasonable apprehension" test for mental cruelty), https://indiankanoon.org/doc/198827109/; Kiriplani v. Meena, AIR 1964 SC 40 (India) (discussing the impact of insincere offers to return on the period of desertion), https://indiankanoon.org/doc/1376469/; Shah v. Prabhawati, AIR 1957 SC 176 (India) (defining the dual requirements of *factum* and *animus deserendi* for desertion), https://indiankanoon.org/doc/1131783/.

25. *Khan*, AIR 1985 SC 945; Abhilasha v. Parkash, AIR 2020 SC 4355 (India), https://indiankanoon.org/doc/150712885/; Bano v. Union of India, AIR 2017 SC 4609 (India), https://indiankanoon.org/doc/115701246/; Mudgal v. Union of India, AIR 1995 SC 1531 (India), https://indiankanoon.org/doc/733037/; Roy v. State of Kerala, AIR 1986 SC 1011 (India), https://indiankanoon.org/doc/1143189/.

26. Rajnesh v. Neha, AIR 2021 SC 569 (India) (mandating comprehensive asset disclosure affidavits and uniform maintenance commencement from the date of filing), https://indiankanoon.org/doc/117541087/; Garg v. Neha, S.L.P. (Civil) No. 2115 of 2021 (India) (addressing the admissibility of surreptitious digital recordings versus privacy rights); Bhowmick v. Chakraborty, Civil Appeal No. 5167 of 2012 (India) (holding that protracted litigation exceeding 20 years constitutes objective evidence of mental cruelty), https://indiankanoon.org/doc/87331682/.

27. Satya v. Singh, AIR 1975 SC 105 (India) (ruling that foreign decrees obtained by misrepresenting jurisdictional facts are unenforceable), https://indiankanoon.org/doc/1774034/; Rao v. Lakshmi (*Y. Narasimha Rao*), AIR Online 1991 SC 10 (India) (establishing that a foreign court's jurisdiction must be recognized by the law under which the marriage was solemnized and the

Thus, over the span of seven decades, the Supreme Court's constitutional powers somewhat allowed it to shape family law through public interest litigation, appeals, and transfer jurisdiction, ensuring nationwide uniformity of interpretation even within a plural legal system.

H. Enactment of the Family Courts Act, 1984: Structural Reorganization of Matrimonial Adjudication

The most significant institutional reform in modern Indian family litigation was the Family Courts Act, 1984, enacted in response to recommendations by the Law Commission of India and women's rights advocates.[28] The Family Courts Act sought to:

1. Create specialized courts for matrimonial, custody, and maintenance matters.
2. Promote conciliation and settlement through counselors and mediation.
3. Reduce procedural rigidity by relaxing strict application of the Civil Procedure Code and Evidence Act.
4. Centralize jurisdiction by giving family courts exclusive jurisdiction over a defined set of matters.

Under the Family Courts Act, the state governments are required to establish a family court in every city or town with a population exceeding one million and, as of August 2025, a total of 953 family courts are functional across India.[29]

I. Post-1990 Developments: International Mobility and Cross-Border Litigation

The liberalization of India's economy in the 1990s and the rapid growth of the Indian diaspora led to a surge in cross-border matrimonial disputes. Courts began confronting complex issues such as recognition of foreign divorce decrees; conflicting custody orders from foreign courts; international relocation disputes; abductions involving Indian minors abroad; enforcement of foreign financial orders; forum non conveniens in matrimonial proceedings; and anti-suit injunctions restraining parallel proceedings in foreign jurisdictions.

As discussed throughout this book, the high courts and the Supreme Court issued a series of landmark judgments on these issues, shaping a sophisticated but sometimes unpredictable framework for international family litigation. Largely, the judicial reasoning emphasized the welfare of the child, the

decree must be granted on grounds available under that personal law), https://indiankanoon.org/doc/989920/.

28. Poornima Advani, *Working of Family Courts in India*, National Judicial Academy 1, https://nja.gov.in/Concluded_Programes_2015-16/P-957_PPTs/1.%20Working%20of%20Family%20courts%20in%20India.pdf; Law Commission of India, *Fifty-Ninth Report on Hindu Marriage Act, 1955 and Special Marriage Act, 1954*, at 13 (Mar. 1974), https://cdnbbsr.s3waas.gov.in/s3ca0daec69b5adc880fb464895726dbdf/uploads/2022/08/2022080562.pdf; The Family Courts Act, 1984 (India), https://indiankanoon.org/doc/373687/.

29. Advani, *supra* note 28.

continuance of matrimonial ties to India, and skepticism toward foreign ex parte decrees.

J. India's Non-Accession to the Hague Abduction Convention

As discussed in Chapter 3, India has not acceded to the Hague Convention on the Civil Aspects of International Child Abduction. As a result,

- international child-return disputes must be resolved through the Guardians and Wards Act or habeas corpus petitions;
- Indian courts are not bound by the Convention's habitual-residence or prompt-return framework; and
- foreign return orders are treated as persuasive, not binding.

Supreme Court judgments such as *Raghavan* (2017)[30] and *Sakhamuri* (2019)[31] solidified India's position that the welfare of the child outweighs comity considerations. This approach significantly impacts U.S.–India custody disputes.

K. Contemporary Trends and Ongoing Reform Debates

In recent decades, Indian family law has continued to evolve, with courts expanding the grounds for divorce through judicial interpretation and increasingly recognizing irretrievable breakdown of marriage even without formal statutory amendment.[32] The Indian Law Commission in its 71st report (1978)[33] and 217th report (2009)[34] recommended the inclusion of irretrievable breakdown as a specific statutory ground for divorce, highlighting the need for legislative action to align the law with judicial trends.

The period has also seen significant reforms to maintenance provisions and domestic violence protections, along with a growing judicial insistence on institutional enforcement of statutory rights, most notably under the Protection of Women from Domestic Violence Act, 2005. In *We the Women of India v. Union of India*, the Supreme Court directed all states and union territories to designate protection officers, empanel service providers, notify shelter homes, and widely publicize the act, acknowledging its uneven implementation and mandating time-bound compliance to secure effective access to protection, shelter, medical aid, and free legal services for aggrieved women.[35] The Court's intervention reflects a broader acknowledgement of the need for uniform procedural

30. Raghavan v. State of NCT of Delhi, Criminal Appeal No. 972 of 2017 (India), https://indiankanoon.org/doc/53310178/.

31. Sakhamuri v. Kodali, AIR 2019 SC 2881 (India), https://indiankanoon.org/doc/75878380/.

32. *Ghosh*, AIR Online 2007 SC 347; Kohli v. Kohli, AIR 2006 SC 1675 (India), https://indiankanoon.org/doc/1643829/; *Rao*, AIR 2013 SC 2176; *Sailesh*, Transfer Petition (Civil) No. 1118 of 2014.

33. Law Commission of India, *Seventy-first Report on The Hindu Marriage Act, 1955—Irretrievable Breakdown of Marriage as a Ground of Divorce* (Apr. 1978), https://cdnbbsr.s3waas.gov.in/s3ca0daec69b5adc880fb464895726dbdf/uploads/2022/08/2022080518.pdf.

34. Law Commission of India, *217th Report on Irretrievable Breakdown of Marriage—Another Ground for Divorce* (Mar. 2009), https://indiankanoon.org/doc/117804397/.

35. We the Women of India v. Union of India, Writ Petition (C) No. 1156 of 2021 (2025) (India), https://www.sci.gov.in/view-pdf/?diary_no=204132021&type=o&order_date=2025-05-20&from=latest_judgements_order; The Protection of Women from Domestic Violence Act, 2005,

standards and functional infrastructure across states to translate substantive family law rights into practical relief.

Family courts continue to face challenges, including heavy caseloads, delays, shortage of counselors, and limited specialization in some jurisdictions. Nonetheless, they remain the primary forum for matrimonial and custody litigation nationwide.

L. Practical Significance for International Practitioners

For U.S. attorneys and other foreign practitioners, understanding this historical trajectory is essential for predicting how an Indian court is likely to treat a foreign divorce decree, identifying the personal law regime applicable to each party, and anticipating the jurisdictional challenges that routinely arise in Indian matrimonial and custody litigation. It also provides critical insight into the supervisory and corrective roles played by the high courts and the Supreme Court in transfer petitions and habeas matters, informs advice regarding the enforceability of foreign custody or support orders, and enables practitioners to prepare clients for the significant procedural differences between Indian family courts and their U.S. counterparts.

Because Indian family law evolved through religious personal law, colonial codification, statutory reform, and judicial innovation, every modern dispute (especially cross-border ones) is influenced by historical layers.

2.2.2. Organization of the Courts

India's judiciary is a unified national system structured in multiple layers established by the Constitution of India, with a vertical appellate hierarchy and a mixture of general and specialized courts. Within this system, family law adjudication is distributed across several levels, with specialized family courts serving as the primary trial forum for matrimonial and child-related disputes. Understanding the structure, hierarchy, and interlocking jurisdictions is essential for practitioners navigating Indian family law, especially in cases with cross-border implications.

A. The Constitutional Framework and Judicial Hierarchy

The Constitution of India (1950) establishes the formal judicial structure and allocates jurisdiction among the Supreme Court, high courts, and subordinate courts. Article 124 creates the Supreme Court; Articles 214–231 establish high courts; and Article 233 and related provisions empower states to create subordinate courts. These provisions create a unified yet federal judicial architecture. In practice, the judiciary functions as a single integrated hierarchy, even though legislative powers over family law rest with both Parliament and state legislatures.

§§ 6–11, 9(1)(d) (India), https://indiankanoon.org/doc/542601/; The Legal Services Authorities Act, 1987 (India), https://www.indiacode.nic.in/bitstream/123456789/1925/1/198739.pdf.

1. Supreme Court of India

The Supreme Court is the apex court with final appellate authority over all civil, criminal, constitutional, and family matters. It exercises appellate jurisdiction under Articles 132–136 of the Constitution of India, possesses transfer jurisdiction under section 25 of the Code of Civil Procedure (CPC) and Article 139A, and holds original writ jurisdiction under Article 32 for the enforcement of fundamental rights.[36]

In family law, the Supreme Court routinely hears appeals from high court judgments, including divorce proceedings, custody matters, maintenance disputes, and jurisdictional conflicts. The Court's decisions bind all other courts under Article 141. Its jurisprudence on child welfare, recognition of foreign decrees, transfer petitions, and statutory interpretation shapes national family law practice.

2. High Courts

Each state or union territory has a high court, which exercises appellate jurisdiction over family courts and district courts, original jurisdiction in certain matters depending on the state, constitutional writ jurisdiction under Articles 226–227, and supervisory control over subordinate courts.[37]

In family law, high courts function as the appellate forum for family court decisions under section 19 of the Family Courts Act, the supervisory authority reviewing interlocutory orders through writ petitions, the transfer authority for inter-district matrimonial disputes, and the administrative body responsible for appointing family court judges in coordination with state governments. High courts frequently intervene in family litigation to address allegations of violations of natural justice, delay, procedural irregularities, or jurisdictional defects, ensuring oversight and corrective supervision of the lower judiciary.

3. District Judiciary and Subordinate Civil Courts

Beneath high courts lie the district courts, which form the backbone of the judicial system. District judges preside over civil and criminal matters, including family disputes where family courts have not been established. Subordinate civil courts (senior civil judges, civil judges, munsifs) also handle family matters in the absence of family courts, particularly guardianship under the Guardians and Wards Act.

Before the Family Courts Act (1984), all matrimonial litigation was handled by district courts under personal law statutes. Even today, in districts lacking family courts, district judges retain jurisdiction over matrimonial and guardianship matters, applying personal law statutes and the Guardians and Wards Act.

B. The Family Courts System Under the Family Courts Act, 1984

In 1984, the Family Courts Act created a specialized, socially oriented, and conciliatory system exclusively for family disputes. Parliament enacted the statute

---

36. Supreme Court of India, *Jurisdiction*, https://www.sci.gov.in/jurisdiction/.

37. *Id.*

in response to findings by the Law Commission of India and the Committee on the Status of Women in India that family disputes required a forum focused on welfare, privacy, and settlement rather than adversarial civil litigation.

By contrast, New York's family court system developed earlier and along different institutional lines. The New York Family Court was created in 1962 following a constitutional amendment reorganizing the state's court structure. Its establishment was driven less by a conciliatory social welfare philosophy and more by a desire to centralize and professionalize the handling of juvenile delinquency, child protection, support, and custody matters that had previously been dispersed among various lower courts. Divorce jurisdiction, however, remained with the Supreme Court (New York's court of general jurisdiction), resulting in a bifurcated system that persists today: family courts handle custody, support, paternity, and family offense proceedings, while the Supreme Court retains exclusive authority over matrimonial actions.

Unlike India's Family Courts Act, 1984, which expressly embeds conciliation, informality, and settlement as statutory objectives, New York's family court operates within a conventional adversarial framework. Judges are neutral arbiters applying established procedural and evidentiary rules, and while settlement conferences and mediation are common, they are not structurally mandated as a defining feature of the court's design. Representation by counsel is standard, and proceedings generally follow formal litigation norms.

In short, whereas India's 1984 reform reflected a legislative judgment that family disputes required a distinct, socially oriented and conciliatory forum, New York's earlier reform focused primarily on judicial efficiency and specialization within an adversarial system. The result is that India's family court model is normatively welfare-driven in its statutory architecture, while New York's is institutionally specialized but procedurally aligned with mainstream civil adjudication.

1. Establishment of Family Courts

Section 3 of the act authorizes state governments, in consultation with high courts, to establish family courts "for every area in the State comprising a city or town whose population exceeds one million," or in any other area deemed necessary.[38] Despite this statutory mandate, implementation varies significantly across the country: some states, such as Maharashtra, Karnataka, and Kerala, have established family courts in nearly all districts; others, including Uttar Pradesh and Bihar, have far more uneven coverage; and certain smaller states or rural districts continue to rely on general district courts in the absence of dedicated family courts.

The result is a mixed system where litigants' access to specialized forums depends on geographic location.

38. Family Courts Act § 3.

2. Exclusive Jurisdiction of Family Courts

Section 7 of the act grants family courts exclusive jurisdiction over matrimonial causes, including divorce, nullity, judicial separation, and restitution, along with matters involving the legitimacy of children, civil and certain criminal maintenance applications, custody, guardianship, and access, as well as suits between spouses relating to property when connected to matrimonial relief and injunctions arising out of marital relationships.[39]

Once a family court is established in a district, this exclusive jurisdiction displaces that of the district courts for all matters within the scope of the act.[40]

3. Emphasis on Conciliation and Counseling

A defining feature of family courts is their statutory obligation to promote settlement, with section 9 requiring judges to make every effort to assist and persuade parties to arrive at a compromise.[41] To fulfill this mandate, courts may appoint counselors, refer matters to mediation, conduct in-camera discussions where appropriate, and adopt flexible procedures designed to facilitate conciliatory outcomes rather than adversarial escalation.

In this regard, the Supreme Court in *Bhandari v. Bhandari* made the following observations:

> Under Section 9 of the Family Courts Act, 1984, the Court has a duty to make an endeavour to assist and persuade the parties in arriving at a settlement. Unlike many other legislations, the Legislature has cast a duty on the Court in that regard. The jurisdiction is not just to decide a dispute, on the contrary, the court also has to involve itself in the process of conciliation/mediation between the parties for assisting them not only to settle the disputes but also to secure speedy settlement of disputes. Such timely intervention of the court will not only resolve the disputes and settle the parties peacefully but also prevent sporadic litigations between the parties.[42]

This conciliatory ethos represents a deliberate departure from adversarial litigation and aligns more closely with therapeutic and social-justice models of family adjudication.

Unlike the Indian model, New York does not conceptualize the family court as a reconciliation-centered institution with a legislatively imposed duty to actively engineer compromise. Although judges in both family court and the Supreme Court routinely encourage negotiated resolutions, particularly in custody and parenting disputes, their role remains adjudicative rather than facilitative in a statutory sense. Settlement is promoted as a matter of sound judicial administration, not as an affirmative legal obligation embedded in the court's jurisdiction.

---

39. *Id.* § 7.
40. *Id.* § 8(a).
41. *Id.* § 9.
42. Bhandari v. Bhandari, AIR 2018 SC (Supp) 440, ¶ 14 (India), https://indiankanoon.org/doc/193461849/.

New York's framework therefore reflects a more conventional conception of judging: the court provides structure, manages the case, and determines disputed issues under established procedural and evidentiary rules if settlement fails. Mediation programs and settlement conferences operate alongside litigation, but they do not redefine the judge's institutional function. In this respect, the Indian Family Courts Act represents a more explicit normative shift toward therapeutic engagement, whereas New York maintains a clearer boundary between adjudication and conciliation.

4. Procedure and Evidence

Family courts are not strictly bound by the CPC or the Indian Evidence Act, and specifically sections 10 and 14 of the Family Courts Act permit them to adopt flexible procedures so long as they remain consistent with principles of natural justice.[43] In practice, courts may receive affidavit evidence, relax cross-examination requirements, rely on counselor reports, conduct informal hearings, and hold in-camera proceedings to protect privacy. This relaxed procedural framework makes family courts more accessible to self-represented litigants and supports more expedited and less adversarial resolution of disputes.

By contrast, New York courts do not operate under a comparably relaxed evidentiary or procedural regime. Proceedings in both family court and the Supreme Court are governed by established procedural statutes and court rules, and the ordinary rules of evidence apply. While judges retain discretion in managing hearings—particularly in custody matters—there is no statutory departure from evidentiary standards akin to sections 10 and 14 of the Family Courts Act. Affidavits may supplement testimony in certain contexts, but fact-finding hearings generally require live testimony subject to cross-examination.

That said, New York courts do employ certain child-sensitive mechanisms. Lincoln hearings (in-camera interviews of children), forensic evaluations, and court-appointed attorneys for children are common features in custody litigation. These practices aim to protect privacy and safeguard the child's interests, yet they function within a structured adversarial framework rather than as part of a legislatively relaxed procedural model. Self-represented litigants are common in family court, but the procedural expectations remain aligned with formal adjudication.

Accordingly, while both systems recognize the need for privacy and flexibility in family disputes, India's statutory design expressly authorizes procedural informality to advance welfare objectives, whereas New York maintains traditional evidentiary safeguards and adversarial structure, modifying them only at the margins for child-sensitive concerns.

C. Interaction Between Family Courts and Other Forums

Despite their exclusive jurisdiction, family courts operate within a larger ecosystem of civil, criminal, and administrative forums.

43. Family Courts Act §§ 10(c), 14.

1. Criminal Courts and Maintenance

Section 125 of the CrPC, 1973 (now section 144 of the Bharatiya Nagarik Suraksha Sanhita, 2023[44] (BNSS)), provides a summary, quasi-criminal remedy for maintenance to wives, children, and parents.[45] Family courts can hear section 125 applications when they exist, but in many districts criminal courts continue to adjudicate these matters. This dual structure creates parallel litigation streams for the same parties.

A comparable overlap is less pronounced in New York. While different courts exercise jurisdiction over distinct categories of family-related disputes—family court for support, custody, paternity, and family offenses, and the Supreme Court for divorce—maintenance and child support are generally handled within a unified civil framework rather than through a quasi-criminal mechanism. Spousal maintenance is determined within the matrimonial action in the Supreme Court, and child support is addressed either in family court or incorporated into the divorce proceeding. The remedies are civil in nature, and enforcement typically proceeds through income withholding, money judgments, or contempt proceedings, rather than through a summary criminal process.

As a result, although New York does maintain a bifurcated jurisdictional structure between family court and the Supreme Court, the risk of parallel quasi-criminal and civil maintenance proceedings for the same parties is comparatively reduced. The system is more procedurally streamlined in that support determinations and enforcement mechanisms operate within a consolidated civil scheme, rather than through overlapping criminal and family adjudicatory tracks.

2. Magistrates Under the Domestic Violence Act

The Protection of Women from Domestic Violence Act, 2005, authorizes magistrate courts, rather than family courts, to issue protection orders, residence orders, monetary relief, temporary custody orders, and compensation.[46]

As a result, many matrimonial disputes proceed simultaneously under multiple statutory frameworks, including the Family Courts Act for divorce and custody issues, section 125 of the CrPC for maintenance, the Protection of Women from Domestic Violence Act for protection and residence orders, and section 498A of the Indian Penal Code, 1860 (now sections 85 and 86 of the Bharatiya Nyaya Sanhita, 2023[47]), for allegations of cruelty, creating a multidimensional and often overlapping litigation landscape.

New York has attempted to address fragmentation in domestic violence-related matters through the creation of the IDV Part, which consolidates a single family's criminal, family, and matrimonial proceedings before one judge when the underlying issue is domestic violence. The IDV model is premised on coordinated adjudication rather than parallel litigation. One judge presides over

44. BNSS, 2023, § 144 (India), https://indiankanoon.org/doc/91117739/.
45. CrPC, 1973, § 125 (India), https://indiankanoon.org/doc/1056396/.
46. Protection of Women from Domestic Violence Act.
47. Bharatiya Nyaya Sanhita, 2023, §§ 85–86 (India), https://indiankanoon.org/doc/149679501/.

related criminal charges, custody disputes, orders of protection, and divorce proceedings, thereby reducing inconsistent rulings and promoting informed, holistic decision-making.

The stated mission of the IDV court emphasizes efficiency, victim safety, offender accountability, and elimination of conflicting orders. Cases are calendared sequentially to minimize litigants' time in court, and the model integrates legal representation and social services, including supervised visitation, substance testing, and parenting programs. In this respect, while India's dual structure can generate parallel maintenance and criminal proceedings across different forums, New York's IDV Part represents a structural effort to streamline overlapping domestic violence matters into a coordinated, single-judge system.

3. Guardianship and Adoption Authorities

While family courts adjudicate custody and guardianship under personal law statutes, adoption of orphans or abandoned children is governed by the Juvenile Justice (Care and Protection of Children) Act, 2015, with orders issued by district Child Welfare Committees and magistrates.[48] The Central Adoption Resource Authority (CARA) administers inter-country adoption under the Hague Adoption Convention, but family courts may intervene in related guardianship matters.[49]

D. Specialized Tribunals and Parallel Jurisdictions Affecting Family Matters

Although not "family courts," several specialized forums impact matrimonial and child-related litigation.

1. Juvenile Justice Boards and Child Welfare Committees

These bodies, established under the Juvenile Justice Act, determine child protection issues, custody of children in need of care, and matters involving rehabilitation and foster placement, and their decisions often influence assessments of custody, guardianship, or parental suitability in concurrent matrimonial litigation.[50]

2. Women's Commissions and Legal Services Authorities

State Commissions for Women investigate complaints of domestic abuse, provide advocacy support, and coordinate with police and courts, while Legal Services Authorities offer mandatory free legal aid to eligible women under the Legal Services Authorities Act, 1987.[51] Although neither body is adjudicatory,

48. The Juvenile Justice (Care and Protection of Children) Act, 2015, § 29 (India), https://indiankanoon.org/doc/9677640/.

49. Ministry of Women & Child Development, Government of India, *Central Adoption Resource Authority: About CARA*, https://cara.wcd.gov.in/about/about_cara.html.

50. Juvenile Justice Act §§ 4, 27.

51. Legal Services Authorities Act § 12; The National Commission for Women Act, 1990, § 10(f) (India), https://indiankanoon.org/doc/131273063/.

both play an important role in shaping the procedural landscape surrounding family disputes.

3. Legal Standing of Personal Law Religious Tribunals

In some Muslim communities, nonbinding religious bodies ("Sharia councils") issue opinions on marital status. However, the Indian Supreme Court has stated that such religious courts have "no legal status. Such courts are bereft of any legal pedigree and have no sanction in laws of the land. They are not part of the corpus juris of the State."[52] Although, it can be argued that such religious bodies may influence party behavior.

A similar position applies across other religious communities. In Sikh practice, for example, disputes may be addressed informally within gurdwara committees or community bodies, but these have no adjudicatory authority recognized by the state. Sikh marriages are governed by the Anand Marriage Act, 1909 (as amended), yet dissolution and related relief must be pursued before civil courts under applicable matrimonial statutes. Religious opinion may shape community perception, but it does not displace judicial authority. Comparable dynamics exist within Jewish communities in New York, where rabbinical courts (*batei din*) may issue religious divorces (*gets*) affecting religious status, but civil dissolution and ancillary relief require recognition by state courts.

In this respect, India's position parallels that of jurisdictions such as New York, where religious tribunals, including rabbinical courts or other faith-based bodies, may resolve disputes consensually, often through arbitration agreements, but derive legal effect only if their determinations are incorporated into or enforced by civil courts. Absent such recognition, their authority remains religious or moral rather than juridical.

E. The Role of High Courts in Shaping Family Court Functioning

High courts supervise family courts in both judicial and administrative capacities.[53] Judicially, they hear appeals under section 19 of the Family Courts Act, decide writ petitions challenging interim orders, intervene in cases involving delay, denial of natural justice, or jurisdictional error, and issue contempt directions to secure compliance with family court orders. Administratively, under section 4 of the act, the high courts oversee the recruitment, training, and evaluation of family court judges, manage their transfers within the state, and coordinate the establishment of new family courts. High courts also issue practice directions aimed at improving efficiency, such as requirements for mandatory mediation, standardized case management, or digital filing, which significantly influence the functioning of family courts.

This model contrasts sharply with the structure in New York and many U.S. jurisdictions, where family court judges are not institutionally supervised by appellate courts in an administrative capacity. In New York City, for example,

52. Madan v. Union of India, AIR 2014 SC 2957 (India), https://indiankanoon.org/doc/22464727/.

53. Family Courts Act §§ 4, 19.

family court judges are appointed by the mayor for fixed terms, subject to confirmation and reappointment processes, rather than being recruited, transferred, or administratively evaluated by the judiciary itself.[54] As a result, while appellate courts in New York exercise judicial review over family court decisions, they do not play a comparable role in shaping the internal administration, staffing, or operational design of family courts. The Indian framework thus reflects a centralized and court-driven model of institutional control, blurring the line between judicial oversight and administrative governance in a manner largely unfamiliar to the U.S. family court system.

F. The Supreme Court's Structural and Policy Influence

The Supreme Court has profoundly shaped the development and functioning of family courts, particularly in cross-border matters. It articulates national standards for child welfare, determines the enforceability of foreign decrees, resolves conflicting interpretations issued by different high courts, exercises its transfer powers to consolidate disputes arising across states, and monitors delays and systemic deficiencies within the family justice system. In the absence of India's accession to the Hague Child Abduction Convention, the Supreme Court's judgments effectively operate as a national framework for handling international custody disputes.

G. Geographic Variations, Judicial Delays, and Systemic Challenges

Family court access varies significantly across the country. Urban centers often have multiple family courts equipped with specialized judges, mediation centers, counselor support, and stronger digital infrastructure, whereas many rural districts lack dedicated family courts altogether and continue to rely on general district courts with limited family law resources.

Although family courts were intended to reduce delay through conciliation-oriented and flexible procedures, high caseloads, shortages of counselors, limited infrastructure, and the pressure of simultaneous criminal and civil proceedings have contributed to substantial delays in many jurisdictions.

In the landmark case of *Singh v. Meena*, the Supreme Court of India delivered a stern critique of the systemic delays in family courts, emphasizing that such procrastination subverts the very purpose of social welfare legislation.[55] In particular it stated:

> The Family Courts have been established for adopting and facilitating the conciliation procedure and to deal with family disputes in a speedy and expeditious manner. . . . Procrastination is the greatest assassin of

---

54. New York Family Court Act § 123 (McKinney 2024) (providing for appointment of New York City Family Court judges by the mayor); *see also* N.Y. Const. art. VI, § 13(b) (authorizing legislative determination of the method of selection of family court judges).

55. Singh v. Meena, AIR 2014 SC 2875 (India), https://indiankanoon.org/doc/34330243/.

[matrimonial litigation]. It not only gives rise to more family problems but also gradually builds unthinkable [] bitterness.[56]

Access to counsel also remains uneven: while legal aid is mandated, many litigants appear without representation, requiring judges to explain procedure, manage evidence, and facilitate settlement themselves, which increases judicial workload and prolongs proceedings. The coexistence of criminal complaints, particularly under the Domestic Violence Act and section 498A of the Indian Penal Code, further complicates matrimonial litigation by creating overlapping factual inquiries, opportunities for forum shopping, and inconsistent interim orders across different forums.

H. Significance for International Family Law Practice

For U.S. family lawyers handling transnational disputes involving Indian parties, understanding the organization of India's courts is essential for advising on where an action may be filed, which court will take priority when multiple proceedings arise, whether the relevant Indian forum is specialized or a general civil court, and how to interpret transfer petitions, writs, and appeals within the Indian system. It is also critical for assessing how parallel criminal and civil proceedings may influence custody or divorce strategy, and for evaluating how delays in family courts may strengthen or weaken forum non conveniens arguments abroad.

India's judicial structure is more fragmented, multi-layered, and procedurally diverse than family court systems in the United States, and this complexity can be strategically leveraged only through a careful mapping of jurisdictional rules, venue options, and available remedies.

2.2.3. Judges: Selection and Jurisdiction

Family court judges in India are part of the state judicial service system and are appointed under a combination of the Family Courts Act, state recruitment rules, and constitutional provisions governing the appointment, control, and service conditions of the subordinate judiciary. Their qualifications, selection pathways, and jurisdictional powers are essential for practitioners, particularly when evaluating the court's expertise, procedural approach, or potential appellate issues.

56. Some Indian judicial decisions, particularly older ones, may not include uniform paragraph numbering or pagination across publicly available sources. Accordingly, pinpoint citations (by page or paragraph) are not always feasible. In such instances, relevant portions of the judgment are identified through quotations to assist the reader. For ease of access, this book primarily relies on publicly available versions of decisions (including Indian Kanoon), which are widely used but may differ in formatting from official court copies. Where paragraph numbering is available, it has been included.

A. Constitutional and Statutory Framework for Appointment

Articles 233–235 of the Constitution govern the recruitment, posting, and discipline of judges in the subordinate judiciary.[57] Under these provisions, the governor of the state formally appoints district judges, including those designated to preside over family courts, while the high court plays a central supervisory and consultative role in setting selection standards and overseeing transfers, postings, disciplinary proceedings, and assessments of suitability.

The Family Courts Act, 1984, supplements this constitutional framework. Section 4 provides that a family court judge must either be a district judge or qualified for appointment as one, possess at least seven years of experience in family law practice, or be a judicial officer or legal academic with expertise in social welfare, counseling, or family dispute resolution, though this last category is seldom used in practice.[58] Despite the statute's preference for judges with specialized family law or social science backgrounds, Indian states overwhelmingly appoint career judicial officers drawn from the civil judicial services.

B. Selection Pathways

As mentioned in the previous section, there are three principal pathways through which a judge may come to preside over a family court. The first is direct recruitment from the bar, permitted in some states for advocates with seven years of standing. Those selected may be posted to family courts based on administrative needs or demonstrated specialization, bringing valuable practical matrimonial-litigation experience, though their numbers remain comparatively small. The second, and by far the most common, is promotion from the civil judiciary, where judges progress from the Junior Division to the Senior Division and ultimately to the district judge cadre based on written examinations, annual confidential reports, seniority, and high court evaluations. Judges promoted through this channel are frequently assigned to family courts, sometimes without prior specialization in matrimonial or custody matters, resulting in notable variation in judicial approach across districts.

Third, in states with staffing shortages, high courts may transfer existing district judges to family courts temporarily. Such transfers may occur for administrative convenience, caseload rebalancing, or to fill vacancies.

C. Qualifications and Desired Expertise

Section 4(4)(a) of the Family Courts Act provides that judges should be individuals "*committed to the need to protect and preserve the institution of the family.*"[59] Section 4(4)(b) states that *preference shall be given to women* in the appointment of family court judges to ensure a gender-sensitive approach to disputes.[60]

Theoretically, it is preferred that the appointee possesses qualifications in psychology, social work, child development, or family law. In practice, however,

57. India Const. arts. 233–235, https://indiankanoon.org/doc/237570/.
58. Family Courts Act § 4.
59. *Id.*
60. *Id.*

most appointees do not have formal interdisciplinary training. To address this gap, high courts increasingly require family law refresher courses, training on domestic violence legislation, modules on child psychology, mediation certification, and exposure to international child custody jurisprudence, particularly in cases involving non-resident Indians (NRIs). Both the National Judicial Academy and various State Judicial Academies now offer substantial training programs tailored specifically to family law.[61]

D. Jurisdictional Powers of Family Court Judges

The jurisdiction of family court judges flows primarily from section 7 of the Family Courts Act, which grants exclusive authority over matrimonial and child-related matters; section 8, which ousts the jurisdiction of civil courts once a family court is established; section 10, which provides procedural flexibility; section 11, which authorizes (private) in-camera proceedings; and section 12, which permits the court to seek assistance from counselors, medical professionals, and welfare agencies. Within this framework, family court judges exercise a blend of civil, criminal, and equitable powers.

On the civil side, they adjudicate divorce, nullity, judicial separation, RCR, maintenance and alimony, custody, guardianship, visitation, legitimacy, paternity, suits between spouses concerning property, and injunctions arising out of marital relationships. To do so, judges may record oral and affidavit evidence, issue interim orders, direct the production of documents, order psychological evaluations, and modify custody arrangements according to the welfare of the child.

In their criminal or quasi-criminal capacity, family courts may hear maintenance applications under section 125 of the CrPC, proceedings that are technically criminal but resemble civil summary trials, allowing judges to issue maintenance orders enforceable by fine or imprisonment, modify orders based on changed circumstances, and coordinate with magistrate courts handling parallel domestic violence or cruelty cases.

Beyond these defined powers, family court judges also exercise inherent and equitable authority to promote settlement, conduct conciliation, refer parties to mediation, obtain counselor reports, reduce adversarial intensity, and protect children's welfare even where statutory text offers limited guidance. These broad discretionary powers enable holistic decision-making but contribute to jurisdictional and procedural variation across different courts.

E. Limits on Family Court Jurisdiction

A recent Supreme Court decision underscores that family courts, although vested with exclusive jurisdiction over matters connected to matrimonial proceedings, lack jurisdiction where the underlying dispute is not connected to a

61. National Judicial Academy, *Refresher Course for Family Courts: Programme Report* (Nov. 2020), https://nja.gov.in/Concluded_Programmes/2020-21/P-1229%20Programme%20Report.pdf.

marital relationship.[62] In *Rathinam,* the Court held that while section 7 of the Family Courts Act confers exclusive jurisdiction on family courts over suits or proceedings seeking a declaration as to the legitimacy of a person, such jurisdiction cannot be invoked in the absence of a claim arising out of a marital relationship. The Court further clarified that the jurisdiction of family courts is confined to the settlement of issues arising out of matrimonial causes, which essentially relate to the rights and obligations flowing from the marital relationship between a husband and wife.

Accordingly, family courts do not adjudicate all disputes involving spouses. Civil courts retain jurisdiction over property disputes not directly linked to matrimonial causes, tort claims such as defamation or civil assault, contract disputes between spouses, and matters of probate and succession governed by separate statutes.

This jurisdictional fragmentation is compounded by the absence of any statutory matrimonial property regime in India. Unlike jurisdictions that recognize community property or equitable distribution as a matter of substantive law, Indian matrimonial law does not define or regulate "marital property" as a distinct legal category. As a result, property disputes between spouses often fall into an uneasy gap between general civil jurisdiction and family court jurisdiction. Where such disputes, such as disputes concerning the property of the parties or either of them, are connected to matrimonial proceedings, family courts may assert jurisdiction under section 7(1)(c). Even in such cases, however, the practical scope of family court adjudication over property disputes remains limited.

By contrast, New York and most U.S. states treat marital property as a statutorily defined legal category and vest exclusive jurisdiction over its division in the court hearing the matrimonial action.[63] This integrated substantive–procedural framework avoids the jurisdictional ambiguity that characterizes the Indian system, ensuring that all financial incidents of marriage, title, ownership, valuation, and distribution are resolved within a single forum as part of the divorce proceeding.

2.2.4. Family Court Practice in India: Structure, Terminology, and Comparative Practical Implications

Indian family law employs a blend of statutory language, common-law concepts, and personal law vocabulary, making mastery of terminology essential for understanding the nature of proceedings, available remedies, and jurisdictional boundaries. Misinterpreting even a single term can significantly alter case strategy, particularly in cross-border matters where U.S. practitioners may expect uniform terminology that simply does not exist in India.

---

62. Rathinam v. Joseph, Criminal Appeal No. 413 of 2025, ¶¶ 54–58 (India), https://api.sci.gov.in/supremecourt/2018/20907/20907_2018_3_1501_58757_Judgement_28-Jan-2025.pdf.

63. N.Y. Dom. Rel. Law § 236(B) (McKinney 2024) (defining "marital property" and mandating equitable distribution upon dissolution of marriage); *see also* Brett R. Turner, *Equitable Distribution of Property* § 1:1 (4th ed. 2023) (noting that the vast majority of U.S. jurisdictions follow equitable-distribution principles, while a minority follow community property regimes, and that in both systems marital property is statutorily defined and divided within the matrimonial action).

A. "Matrimonial Causes": The Indian Equivalent of the American Concept of "Domestic Relations"

The expression "matrimonial causes" is a broad category that includes all actions relating to marital status, such as divorce, nullity, judicial separation, RCR, and declarations of marital validity or invalidity. Originating in English matrimonial law, it appears in the Hindu Marriage Act, Special Marriage Act, Parsi Marriage and Divorce Act, and Christian matrimonial statutes. Correctly classifying a case as a matrimonial cause determines the applicable personal law, the appropriate forum, the scope of appellate review, and whether a family court has exclusive jurisdiction.

While the expression "matrimonial causes" is deeply rooted in English law and continues to structure family law jurisdiction in India, U.S. law does not employ this terminology as a formal doctrinal category. Instead, American family law organizes marital litigation through the concept of "domestic relations" jurisdiction, a broad umbrella encompassing divorce, annulment, legal separation, child custody, child support, and spousal maintenance. In the United States, classification of a matter as a "domestic relations" case serves a function closely analogous to that of "matrimonial causes" in India: it determines subject-matter jurisdiction (typically vested in state trial courts of general or family jurisdiction), triggers specialized procedural rules, and activates the federal "domestic relations exception," which largely excludes such matters from federal court jurisdiction.[64] Thus, although the U.S. system avoids the historically English label of "matrimonial causes," it performs the same gatekeeping role through jurisdictional doctrines and court structures that segregate marital and family disputes from ordinary civil litigation.

B. "Maintenance" and "Alimony": Distinguished from the U.S. Perspective

Indian family law does not offer a single codified definition of either *alimony* or *maintenance*. Instead, these concepts emerge functionally (rather than definitionally) across a fragmented statutory landscape. In the absence of a unified legislative formulation, a useful conceptual distinction may nonetheless be drawn: all alimony is maintenance, but not all maintenance is alimony (a foundational yet frequently blurred line in both practice and discourse). This terminological overlap is particularly disorienting for foreign lawyers, as "maintenance" in India performs functions that, in other jurisdictions, are distributed among spousal support, child support, and, at times, even property-distribution regimes.

This complexity is further compounded by the fact that maintenance and alimony in India are shaped not only by general civil statutes but also by criminal-law remedies and religion-based personal laws, which continue to govern marital rights and obligations for different communities.[65]

64. Ankenbrandt v. Richards, 504 U.S. 689, 703–04 (1992); Elk Grove Unified Sch. Dist. v. Newdow, 542 U.S. 1, 12–13 (2004); N.Y. Const. art. VI, § 13; New York Family Court Act § 115 (McKinney 2025).

65. The Hindu Marriage Act, 1955, §§ 24–25 (India), https://indiankanoon.org/doc/590166/ (interim maintenance and permanent alimony); Bharatiya Nyaya Suraksha Sanhita § 144 (replacing CrPC § 125); Parsi Marriage and Divorce Act §§ 39–40; Indian Divorce Act §§ 36–37; The

Maintenance is the broader and more pervasive concept. It refers to the continuing obligation to provide financial support to dependents, including spouses, children, and in some cases parents, and operates as a pluralistic, multi-domain institution cutting across various frameworks.[66] Maintenance may be claimed during the subsistence of a marriage, during the pendency of matrimonial proceedings, or independently of divorce, including through summary proceedings under criminal law.[67] Importantly, maintenance claims are not defeated by the mere pendency of parallel matrimonial litigation, and courts routinely entertain maintenance petitions lis pendens to ensure immediate financial relief while the underlying marital dispute remains unresolved. Maintenance thus reflects a welfare-oriented, status-based conception of familial obligation rather than one tethered exclusively to marital breakdown.[68]

Alimony, by contrast, is a narrower, divorce-linked concept, primarily concerned with financial support awarded to a spouse upon or following dissolution of marriage, and is most prominently codified in personal law statutes such as the Hindu Marriage Act. While interim alimony may be awarded pendente lite, permanent alimony is structurally tied to the adjudication of marital status and reflects a postmarital economic adjustment between spouses rather than a generalized duty of familial support.

In this sense, permanent alimony is the closest analogue in Indian law to the division of marital assets in the United States, in that it seeks to account for economic disparity arising from the marital relationship at its termination. Yet, it remains fundamentally different in both form and extent: Indian alimony is typically framed as a support obligation rather than as a true redistribution of marital property, and it lacks the comprehensive, asset-based recalibration characteristic of American equitable distribution regimes.

By contrast, in the United States, the concept most closely analogous to Indian alimony is "spousal support" or "alimony," but American law does not recognize a freestanding concept equivalent to India's broad notion of maintenance. U.S. alimony is procedurally and conceptually tethered to divorce or legal separation proceedings and does not exist as an independent support mechanism during an intact marriage outside formal separation.[69] While American courts may award temporary spousal support pendente lite, such relief remains strictly ancillary to a pending matrimonial action rather than a

Muslim Women (Protection of Rights on Divorce) Act, 1986, §§ 3–4 (India), https://indiankanoon.org/doc/1933289/.

66. The Hindu Adoptions and Maintenance Act, 1956, § 20 (India), https://indiankanoon.org/doc/17630/; Guardians and Wards Act § 24; The Maintenance and Welfare of Parents and Senior Citizens Act, 2007, §§ 4–5 (India) (parental maintenance), https://indiankanoon.org/doc/118724005/.

67. Bharatiya Nyaya Suraksha Sanhita § 144 (replacing CrPC § 125).

68. Pallavi Tayal Chadha, *Shaping Quantum: The Supreme Court of India on Maintenance and Alimony*, Bar and Bench (Jan. 12, 2026), https://www.barandbench.com/view-point/shaping-quantum-the-supreme-court-of-india-on-maintenance-and-alimony.

69. N.Y. Dom. Rel. Law § 236(B)(5)(a), (6) (McKinney 2024) (authorizing maintenance only in connection with matrimonial actions); Cal. Fam. Code §§ 4300–4339 (West 2024) (spousal support authorized incident to dissolution or legal separation).

parallel, standalone claim as in India, and is not criminally enforceable in the manner of India's summary maintenance remedies.[70] Moreover, U.S. law strictly segregates spousal support from child support, each governed by distinct statutory frameworks and policy objectives.[71] Thus, whereas Indian maintenance functions as a multi-purpose familial safety net, American alimony remains a remedial adjunct of divorce, shaped primarily by equitable distribution principles and postmarital economic adjustment rather than by a generalized duty of familial support.[72]

Lastly, Indian family law also employs a distinct financial vocabulary alongside alimony and maintenance, reflecting its pluralist personal law structure. Courts and statutes routinely engage with concepts such as stridhan, denoting a Hindu woman's absolute property in gifts and assets received at or around marriage,[73] and *mahr* or *dower*, referring to the financial obligation owed by a Muslim husband to his wife as an incident of marriage.[74] These concepts are not forms of spousal support as such, but they frequently intersect with maintenance claims in practice and are critical to understanding the overall financial consequences of matrimonial litigation in India.

C. Custody and Guardianship in India Versus Physical and Legal Custody in the United States

Custody, guardianship, and the welfare principle stem primarily from the Guardians and Wards Act, 1890, which centers jurisdiction on the child's ordinary residence and requires courts to prioritize the "welfare of the child" above all else.[75] Guardianship is broader than custody, encompassing legal decision-making authority, control of property, and long-term parental responsibility.[76]

Several other Indian statutes also define the term "guardian" in ways that reflect their distinct regulatory purposes. The Juvenile Justice (Care and Protection of Children) Act, for example, adopts a welfare-centered understanding of guardianship that emphasizes care and control over the child rather than management of the child's estate, consistent with the act's child-protective

70. N.Y. Dom. Rel. Law § 236(B)(5)(a) (temporary maintenance during pendency of matrimonial action); Cal. Fam. Code § 3600 (temporary spousal support "during the pendency of any proceeding for dissolution or legal separation"); 24A Am. Jur. 2d *Divorce and Separation* § 623 (2024) ("Spousal support generally arises only upon dissolution of marriage or legal separation and is not available in intact marriages absent statutory separation proceedings."); *compare* N.Y. Dom. Rel. Law § 245 (civil enforcement mechanisms for support orders), *with* 18 U.S.C. § 228 (criminalization limited to interstate nonpayment of child or spousal support, post-order, and not as a primary support-granting mechanism).

71. N.Y. Dom. Rel. Law §§ 236(B)(5)(a) (maintenance), 240(1)(b) (child support); Cal. Fam. Code §§ 4050–4076 (child support), 4300–4339 (spousal support).

72. *See* N.Y. Dom. Rel. Law § 236(B)(5)(a), (c) (maintenance factors tied to equitable distribution and postmarital standard of living); Turner, *supra* note 63, § 1:2.

73. The Hindu Succession Act, 1956, § 14 (India), https://indiankanoon.org/doc/685111/.

74. Muslim Women (Protection of Rights on Divorce) Act § 3.

75. Guardians and Wards Act §§ 7, 9, 17 (vesting jurisdiction based on ordinary residence and mandating that the court be guided by the welfare of the minor).

76. *Id.* § 4(2).

orientation.[77] By contrast, education legislation such as the Tamil Nadu Elementary Education Act employs a broader, functional conception of guardianship that extends to any person who has lawfully assumed or been entrusted with the care, nurture, or custody of a child.[78]

Personal law traditions introduce further nuance: under Hindu law, guardianship formally follows a hierarchical structure in which the father is designated as the natural guardian of a minor's custody and property, with the mother succeeding him; however, this ordering is expressly qualified by the statutory "tender years doctrine," under which custody of a child below five years of age is ordinarily to be with the mother, reflecting a legislative preference grounded in early-childhood welfare rather than parental hierarchy.[79]

Muslim law distinguishes between hizanat (physical custody) and wilayat (legal guardianship). Unlike Hindu law, where guardianship is statutorily codified, Muslim law's distinction between custody and wilayat guardianship remains uncodified and derives from classical personal law, as judicially recognized rather than legislatively enacted.

Suffice it to say, custody and guardianship in Indian family law broadly correspond to what American law describes as physical custody and legal custody, respectively, even though the doctrinal origins and statutory structures of the two systems differ significantly. In India, custody primarily concerns the child's day-to-day care and residence, while guardianship entails broader legal authority over the child and, in some cases, the child's property. By contrast, U.S. family law expressly bifurcates custody into physical custody, referring to where and with whom the child resides, and legal custody, denoting decision-making authority over the child's education, healthcare, religion, and general welfare.[80]

Notably, unlike Indian law, which statutorily recognizes a maternal preference for children of tender years, the United States has rejected any tender years doctrine or gender-based custodial presumptions, instead mandating gender-neutral, best interests determinations irrespective of the parents' sex. As a result, while the Indian and American systems deploy conceptually analogous categories, the American framework is structurally more symmetrical and formally detached from parental hierarchy or age-based presumptions.

77. Juvenile Justice Act § 2(j).

78. The Tamil Nadu Elementary Education Act, 1994, § 2(6) (India), https://indiankanoon.org/doc/131832016/.

79. The Hindu Minority and Guardianship Act, 1956, §§ 4(b), 6 (India) (defining "natural guardian" and enumerating categories of natural guardians under Hindu law), https://indiankanoon.org/doc/76168618/.

80. In New York, "legal custody" refers to decision-making authority over a child's education, healthcare, religion, and general welfare, while "physical custody" concerns where and with whom the child resides on a day-to-day basis. *See* N.Y. Dom. Rel. Law § 240(1)(a) (McKinney 2024); Weiss v. Weiss, 52 N.Y.2d 170, 175–76 (1981). California similarly distinguishes between legal custody (the right and responsibility to make decisions relating to the child's health, education, and welfare) and physical custody (the right and responsibility to have the child reside with a parent), and expressly authorizes joint or sole allocations of each. *See* Cal. Fam. Code §§ 3003–3004 (West 2024); *In re* Marriage of Burgess, 13 Cal. 4th 25, 31–32 (1996).

D. *Standard of the Best Interests of the Child: A Comparative Analysis (India and the United States)*

1. The Best Interests Standard as a Unifying Principle

Across jurisdictions, the "best interests of the child" functions as the dominant (often dispositive) standard governing custody and parenting determinations. Despite differences in statutory formulation and procedural architecture, both Indian and U.S. family law systems treat the child's welfare as paramount, subordinating parental rights, marital fault, and forum convenience to the child's present and future well-being. That shared vocabulary, however, masks meaningful divergences in how the standard is articulated, operationalized, and applied in practice, particularly in cross-border disputes.

In India, the best interests principle is deeply entrenched in guardianship jurisprudence and constitutional interpretation, often framed as the child's "paramount consideration." In the United States, by contrast, "best interests" operates as a multi-factor balancing test, *explicitly codified in many states* and structured to constrain judicial discretion. These differences have significant implications for international custody, relocation, and return proceedings.

2. India: Welfare as the "Paramount Consideration"

a. Best Interest/Welfare Definition and Determinative Factors

Indian law (especially in context of the statutes governing the issues covered in this book) does not statutorily define either "welfare of the minor" or "best interest of the child."[81] Instead, Indian courts operate with an open-textured welfare standard whose content has been developed almost entirely through judicial interpretation. The governing statutes deliberately employ broad, value-laden language, leaving courts with wide discretion to assess the child's physical, emotional, psychological, moral, educational, and social well-being on the facts of each case. In practice, Indian courts frequently use the expressions "welfare of the child," "welfare of the minor," and "best interests of the child" interchangeably, without treating them as distinct doctrinal tests.

Multiple Indian statutes invoke variations of the welfare formulation without defining it. The Guardians and Wards Act, 1890, directs courts to treat the "welfare of the minor" as the paramount consideration in guardianship determinations. The Hindu Minority and Guardianship Act, 1956, similarly elevates

81. While Indian custody jurisprudence generally relies on a judge-developed welfare standard, it bears noting that the phrase "best interest of the child" is statutorily defined in a different legislative context. Section 2(9) of the Juvenile Justice (Care and Protection of Children) Act defines the "best interest of the child" as the basis for any decision taken to ensure fulfillment of the child's basic rights and needs, identity, social well-being, and physical, emotional, and intellectual development. This definition, however, is confined to the child-protection and care framework governing children in need of care and protection or in conflict with law, and does not control custody or guardianship determinations under the Guardians and Wards Act, or matrimonial statutes. Accordingly, while the Juvenile Justice Act reflects a comprehensive, rights-based articulation of child welfare, Indian courts in custody disputes continue to apply a broader, open-textured welfare analysis developed through case law rather than importing the Juvenile Justice Act's statutory definition wholesale.

the child's welfare above parental rights when appointing or declaring a natural guardian. The Hindu Marriage Act, 1955, authorizes custody orders having regard to the "welfare of the children," while the Family Courts Act, 1984, reinforces a child-centric approach through specialized jurisdiction, without articulating a substantive definition. Across these enactments, the statutory choice is consistent: welfare is the controlling principle, but its content is left to judicial elaboration rather than legislative enumeration.

Although the welfare standard remains undefined in statute, the Supreme Court has articulated guiding considerations through case law. In *Sakhamuri v. Kodali*, the Supreme Court of India articulated specific considerations that guide the inquiry of the welfare of the children, observing:

> The crucial factors which have to be kept in mind by the Courts for gauging the welfare of the children equally for the parent's can be inter alia, delineated, such as (1) maturity and judgment; (2) mental stability; (3) ability to provide access to schools; (4) moral character; (5) ability to provide continuing involvement in the community; (6) financial sufficiency and last but not the least the factors involving relationship with the child. . . .[82]

In *Nagpal v. Nagpal*, the Supreme Court held that the term "welfare" must be interpreted in its "widest sense," encompassing not only physical comfort and financial security but also moral, emotional, educational, and psychological well-being.[83] The Court expressly rejected any presumption that biological or legal parenthood alone determines custodial entitlement.[84]

Similarly, in *Kundu v. Kundu*, the Court clarified that the child's welfare must be assessed in light of "moral and ethical" values, and the child's environment, even if that assessment cuts against a parent's legal claim.[85] The Court cautioned against mechanical reliance on statutory hierarchies or personal law presumptions.[86] The Supreme Court of India has repeatedly emphasized that welfare is not merely one factor among many, but the overriding consideration, eclipsing parental entitlements or formal legal rights.

By contrast, U.S. family law, while also acknowledging that "best interests of the child" resists rigid definition, has moved toward explicit statutory articulation and factorization. All U.S. states require courts to consider the child's best interests in custody and placement decisions, and many jurisdictions codify detailed, nonexclusive factor lists to guide that inquiry.[87] These statutes commonly enumerate considerations such as the child's safety, emotional ties,

82. *Sakhamuri*, AIR 2019 SC 2881, ¶ 49.

83. Nagpal v. Nagpal, AIR 2009 SC 557, ¶ 43 (India), https://indiankanoon.org/doc/929793/.

84. *Id.* ¶ 40.

85. Kundu v. Kundu, Civil Appeal No. 4960 of 2008, ¶ 56 (India), https://indiankanoon.org/doc/687286/.

86. *Id.*

87. Child Welfare Information Gateway, U.S. Department of Health & Human Services, *Determining the Best Interests of the Child* 1 (2013), https://www.govinfo.gov/content/pkg/GOVPUB-HE23_1200-PURL-gpo88013/pdf/GOVPUB-HE23_1200-PURL-gpo88013.pdf.

stability, parental capacity, history of abuse, and the child's expressed preferences, thereby constraining discretion and promoting analytical transparency.[88] The American approach thus contrasts with India's more discretionary, judge-developed welfare doctrine, even though the underlying substantive concerns, child safety, stability, and well-being, largely overlap.

b. Constitutional Overlay and Parens Patriae Jurisdiction

Indian courts frequently invoke their constitutional parens patriae jurisdiction in custody matters, particularly in transnational disputes. In *Sakhamuri*, the Supreme Court reiterated that habeas corpus jurisdiction in child custody cases is not limited to unlawful detention, but extends to an independent welfare inquiry, even where foreign custody orders exist.[89]

This approach was further reinforced in *Raghavan v. State of NCT of Delhi*, where the Court declined to summarily return a child to the United Kingdom, holding that the child's welfare in India, rather than automatic deference to foreign courts, was determinative.[90] The Court expressly rejected any presumption of return based solely on habitual residence, underscoring India's non-signatory status to the Hague Abduction Convention.[91] While the Hague Abduction Convention was referenced, it bears noting that the Convention does not require a prior foreign return or custody order as a precondition to its application. Neither is the Convention's concept of "habitual residence" analogous to the "home state" framework under U.S. law, nor to the concept of "ordinary residence" as traditionally understood in U.K. family law.

Taken together, these cases illustrate that Indian courts treat best interests as a substantive, fact-intensive inquiry, largely unconstrained by rigid statutory factors or international comity considerations.

3. United States: Best Interests as a Structured, Factor-Based Inquiry

Although many U.S. states prescribe statutory best interest factors, New York law frames the best interests analysis as a holistic but factor-driven inquiry, developed through common law rather than a single codified checklist. In *Eschbach v. Eschbach*, the New York Court of Appeals articulated a non-exhaustive set of considerations, including the stability of each parent's home, past parental performance, the child's emotional bonds, and each parent's ability to foster the child's relationship with the other parent.[92] Subsequent cases have refined this framework. In *Friederwitzer v. Friederwitzer*, the court emphasized continuity and stability, warning against unnecessary disruption absent compelling reasons.[93] More recently, New York courts have given significant weight

88. *See* Mich. Comp. Laws § 722.23 (2025); Fla. Stat. § 61.13 (2025); Va. Code Ann. § 20-124.3 (2025); N.J. Stat. Ann. § 9:2-4 (West 2025) (enumerating statutory factors guiding best interest determinations).

89. *Sakhamuri*, AIR 2019 SC 2881, ¶ 39.

90. *Raghavan*, Criminal Appeal No. 972 of 2017, ¶ 33.

91. *Id.*

92. Eschbach v. Eschbach, 56 N.Y.2d 167 (1982).

93. Friederwitzer v. Friederwitzer, 55 N.Y.2d 89 (1982).

to factors such as parental cooperation, history of domestic violence, and the child's expressed preferences (where age-appropriate), while maintaining a gender-neutral posture. Importantly, New York strictly segregates custody determinations from marital fault and financial disputes, reinforcing the child-centered nature of the inquiry.

On the other hand, the State of California provides one of the most explicit statutory articulations of the best interests standard. California Family Code section 3011 requires courts to consider factors including the child's health, safety, and welfare; any history of abuse; the nature of the child's contact with both parents; and habitual or continual substance abuse.[94]

Like many other U.S. states, California law expressly rejects any gender-based presumptions and places heightened emphasis on protecting children from domestic violence, reflected in mandatory consideration of restraining orders and abuse findings.[95] Unlike India, California courts operate within a tightly regulated statutory framework that cabins discretion and prioritizes predictability and uniformity.

4. Key Comparative Divergences

a. Structure Versus Discretion

The most striking difference lies in structure. Indian courts exercise broad discretionary authority under the welfare principle, often invoking constitutional powers to reach equitable outcomes. U.S. courts, by contrast, operate within articulated statutory or common-law factors designed to channel discretion and promote consistency.

b. International Comity and Return Expectations

In cross-border disputes, U.S. courts, particularly in Hague Convention cases, approach best interests as distinct from jurisdictional return inquiries, reserving welfare determinations for the court of habitual residence. Indian courts, by contrast, frequently merge jurisdictional and welfare analyses, conducting an independent best interests review even where foreign proceedings are pending or concluded.

c. Presumptions and Neutrality

While Indian law has moved away from rigid parental hierarchies, vestiges of doctrines such as "tender years" continue to influence outcomes in practice. U.S. jurisdictions have formally repudiated such presumptions, mandating gender-neutral assessments grounded in individualized evidence.

5. Practical Implications for Cross-Border Practice

For practitioners handling India–U.S. custody disputes, these doctrinal differences are not merely academic. Evidence that carries decisive weight in one

94. Cal. Fam. Code § 3011(a)(1)–(5) (West 2025).
95. *Id.* § 3040(a)(1).

system (such as stability in India post-removal) may be treated as legally irrelevant or even problematic in another. Likewise, Indian welfare assessments may lack the factor-specific rigor expected by U.S. courts, while U.S. custody evaluations may appear unduly formalistic to Indian judges.

Understanding how each system conceptualizes and applies the best interests standard is therefore essential to managing client expectations, framing evidence, and anticipating enforcement or recognition challenges across borders.

E. Joint Parenting, Shared Custody, and Visitation: A Comparative Perspective (India and the United States)

Indian family law does not recognize joint parenting or equal parenting time as a presumptive outcome. Although courts increasingly acknowledge the importance of a child maintaining meaningful relationships with both parents, custody determinations in India continue to be framed around identifying a primary custodial parent, with visitation or access rights granted to the other. The governing statutory framework (principally the Guardians and Wards Act, 1890, and personal law enactments) does not contemplate structured shared-time or joint physical custody models analogous to those routinely employed in the United States.

Recent Supreme Court jurisprudence reinforces this orientation. In *Sahu v. State of Rajasthan*, the Court emphasized that custody and access arrangements must preserve the child's bond with both parents and expressly recognized the child's right to "love, affection, company, [and] protection of both parents."[96] Yet even while expanding access rights and criticizing token visitation, the Court did not endorse joint physical custody or equal time-sharing as a normative model. Instead, it reaffirmed a welfare-based approach centered on stability and continuity, typically achieved through a single primary residence.

As regards, the state of visitation rights in India, the Supreme Court stated: "The concept of visitation rights is not fully developed in India. Most courts while granting custody to one spouse do not pass any orders granting visitation rights to the other spouse."[97]

Similarly, in *Sharma v. Sharma*, the Court clarified the "tender years" principle and underscored the primacy of maternal custody for young children, subject always to welfare considerations.[98] While the decision tempered rigid parental hierarchies, it remained firmly anchored in a primary-custodian framework rather than a shared-parenting paradigm. Even where Indian courts encourage "shared parenting," the concept is generally operationalized through expanded visitation and structured access, not through near-equal division of custodial time. This structural asymmetry is particularly evident in several Indian cases involving parents living in different countries, where shared parenting arrangements are often impractical or legally complex.

96. Sahu v. State of Rajasthan, AIR 2020 SC 577, ¶ 19 (India), https://indiankanoon.org/doc/144083733/.

97. *Id.* ¶ 20.

98. Sharma v. Sharma, AIR 2015 SC 2232, ¶ 13 (India), https://indiankanoon.org/doc/68807480/.

By contrast, particularly in cases where both parents live in close proximity to each other, U.S. family law has evolved toward a functional norm of joint parenting and such posture is more pronounced, even in the absence of a formal 50/50 presumption. In New York, courts routinely award joint legal custody and increasingly approve shared physical custody where parents demonstrate the ability to cooperate and place the child's interests above interparental conflict. In *Matter of Granger v. Misercola*, the court of appeals reaffirmed that custody determinations must focus on maximizing the child's relationship with both parents, with parental cooperation serving as a critical determinant.[99] More recently, appellate courts have upheld shared-custody arrangements that approximate equal time where stability and parental fitness are shown, even over one parent's objection.

California's statutory and decisional law reflects an even clearer structural commitment to joint parenting. California Family Code section 3020 declares the state's public policy of assuring "frequent and continuing contact" with both parents, and courts regularly implement this policy through shared physical custody arrangements. In *In re Marriage of LaMusga*, while addressing relocation, the California Supreme Court underscored the centrality of maintaining substantial contact with both parents and recognized shared custody as a common baseline from which relocation disputes are assessed.[100] Subsequent decisions have normalized parenting plans that divide custodial time in roughly equal proportions, provided no safety or welfare concerns exist.

When parents reside in different countries, (much like Indian courts) both New York and California courts recognize that equal or near-equal physical custody is usually impracticable, even where both parents are fit and actively involved. In such cases, courts recalibrate the best interests analysis away from mathematical parity and toward functional parenting arrangements that preserve stability, schooling, and continuity for the child. However, such an arrangement is more explicitly structured and formally articulated in the United States, where typically one parent is designated as the primary physical custodian, while joint legal custody is often maintained so long as the parents can meaningfully participate in shared decision-making. The non-resident parent is commonly awarded extended blocks of parenting time during school vacations and holidays, supplemented by regular virtual contact, with detailed provisions governing international travel, passports, and allocation of travel costs. Geographic separation alone is not treated as disqualifying, as courts focus on crafting realistic, enforceable parenting plans that preserve the child's relationship with both parents while accounting for the practical constraints of international distance.

The divergence between the systems is therefore not semantic but structural. Indian courts remain oriented toward identifying a primary custodian in service of stability, with access serving as a supplementary mechanism. U.S. courts, by contrast, increasingly conceive of custody as an allocation of parental

99. *Matter of* Granger v. Misercola, 21 N.Y.3d 86 (2013).
100. *In re* Marriage of LaMusga, 32 Cal. 4th 1072 (2004).

time and responsibility, with shared parenting often treated as the starting point rather than the exception. This difference has significant cross-border implications: parenting arrangements that appear routine and child-centered in U.S. courts may seem disruptive or impractical to Indian courts, while Indian primary-custodian models may appear inconsistent with U.S. expectations of joint parental involvement.

F. "In-Camera Proceedings"

Section 11 of the Family Courts Act allows proceedings to be held in camera, meaning closed to the public.[101] This approach is commonly used in matters involving allegations of cruelty or adultery, sensitive custody disputes, and cases involving domestic or sexual violence.

While this confidentiality framework serves an important protective function, it has practical implications in international cases. For foreign practitioners, private proceedings can significantly affect access to judicial records, including certified transcripts, orders, and counselor reports that may be required for use in parallel proceedings abroad. In practice, obtaining such materials often requires specific court directions or party consent, and delays are not uncommon. Counsel handling cross-border matters should therefore anticipate these access constraints early and proactively address documentary needs when coordinating litigation or enforcement across jurisdictions.

G. Limits of Mediation and Conciliatory Measures: Reciprocity and Enforcement in Cross-Border Indian Family Disputes

Indian statutory framework governing matrimonial and family disputes is intentionally settlement-driven. Mediation and conciliation are embedded as core features of the process, reflecting a policy preference for preserving family relationships and achieving timely resolution rather than defaulting to adversarial litigation.

The Family Courts Act, 1984, places an affirmative duty on family courts to make every reasonable effort to assist and persuade parties to reach a settlement, including by adjourning proceedings to facilitate conciliation.[102] This approach is reinforced by the Hindu Marriage Act, 1955, which requires courts, as a threshold matter, to attempt reconciliation before granting substantive relief,[103] while allowing for adjournments to enable such efforts.[104]

The Mediation Act, 2023, further strengthens this framework by formally integrating mediation into the dispute-resolution system. It permits voluntary pre-litigation mediation and authorizes courts to refer matters to mediation at any stage of the proceedings, signaling a clear legislative shift toward resolving family disputes outside the courtroom whenever possible.[105]

---

101. Family Courts Act § 11; Hindu Marriage Act § 22.
102. Family Courts Act § 9.
103. Hindu Marriage Act § 23(2).
104. *Id.* § 23(3).
105. The Mediation Act, 2023 (India), https://indiankanoon.org/doc/177697739/.

Family courts incorporate counselors and mediation into the judicial process, and the terminology carries specific meanings. Counselors (often trained social workers or psychologists) assist the court in promoting settlement, evaluating parties, and preparing welfare assessments that may strongly influence custody determinations. Conciliation refers to settlement efforts conducted within the court process, whereas mediation involves referral to external or court-annexed mediators.

From a practitioner's perspective, India's settlement-oriented family law framework, while well-intentioned, requires careful handling in international cases. Mediation and court-annexed counseling are frequently approached with an underlying assumption that reconciliation is the optimal outcome. In cross-border custody, relocation, and abduction disputes, this reconciliation bias can be misaligned with the legal realities of international family law, where time sensitivity, habitual residence, and the rights of the left-behind parent are central considerations. In practice, extended mediation efforts may inadvertently delay judicial determination, allowing factual circumstances on the ground to change in ways that complicate eventual enforcement or return decisions.

Practitioners should also be alert to qualitative and structural limitations in counselor-driven processes when cases involve foreign jurisdictions. Welfare assessments and mediation reports in India often reflect localized social expectations and may not engage with concepts commonly examined in international custody disputes, such as parental alienation dynamics, cross-cultural child development, or coercive bargaining power between parties. As a result, these reports, while influential domestically, may carry limited persuasive value before foreign courts assessing best interests through a different evidentiary and methodological lens. Counsel advising clients in cross-border matters should therefore treat mediation outcomes as one component of a broader strategy, rather than as determinative.

Finally, enforceability and strategic timing are recurring practical concerns. Mediated settlements reached in India, particularly through community or informal mechanisms, may not translate cleanly into enforceable outcomes abroad, creating uncertainty and, at times, "limping" family statuses across jurisdictions. Mandatory or court-encouraged mediation can also be leveraged tactically in international disputes to delay proceedings, consolidate a child's presence in India, or limit financial transparency that would otherwise be required in foreign litigation. Practitioners representing internationally mobile families should proactively assess whether mediation will meaningfully advance resolution, or whether early judicial intervention is necessary to preserve jurisdictional integrity and cross-border enforceability.

2.2.5. Jurisdiction, Generally

Jurisdiction in Indian family law is defined by a combination of personal law, statutory text, and territorial nexus. Unlike the unified subject-matter jurisdiction in many U.S. family courts, Indian courts determine jurisdiction based on multiple layers: the relevant personal law statute, residence of parties, situs of marriage, the child's ordinary residence, and the presence or absence of a family court within the district. There is no defined residential requirement in Indian family law comparable to the durational residency or domicile thresholds commonly imposed in U.S. jurisdictions; instead, jurisdiction may be founded on a range of connecting factors, including ordinary residence, last cohabitation, place of marriage, or the child's location, depending on the governing statute and the nature of the relief sought.

A. Statutory Foundations for Matrimonial Jurisdiction

The principal matrimonial statutes, the Hindu Marriage Act (1955),[106] Special Marriage Act (1954),[107] Parsi Marriage and Divorce Act (1936),[108] and Indian Divorce Act (1869),[109] each define territorial jurisdiction based on:

1. Place where the marriage was solemnized
2. Place where the parties last resided together
3. Place where the petitioner currently resides
4. Place where the respondent resides (varies by statute)

These rules attach jurisdiction to concrete geographical markers and differ subtly by statute. For example, under the Hindu Marriage Act, the petitioner's place of residence is a valid basis for jurisdiction even if the respondent resides outside the district or outside India. Under the Special Marriage Act, residence of either party creates jurisdiction. Because these statutes are distinct, determining jurisdiction generally requires identifying the personal law of the parties.

B. Custody and Guardianship Jurisdiction: The "Ordinary Residence"

Custody and guardianship jurisdiction in India is primarily governed by the Guardians and Wards Act, 1890, which vests authority in the court within whose territorial limits the minor "ordinarily resides."[110] The statute does not define "ordinary residence," leaving the content of the term to judicial interpretation. Indian courts have consistently construed ordinary residence as the child's settled, regular, and normal place of living, determined on the facts of each case rather than by reference to legal domicile or the unilateral intentions of a parent. The inquiry is child-centric and focuses on lived reality, schooling, caregiving arrangements, social environment, and continuity, rather than on a residence created through a fleeting, casual, or strategic stay.

The Supreme Court of India has provided authoritative guidance on this question, particularly in transnational custody disputes. In *Majoo v. Majoo*, the Court held that ordinary residence cannot be equated with mere physical presence and must reflect a place where the child is "normally expected to live," cautioning that jurisdiction cannot be artificially created through unilateral

106. Hindu Marriage Act § 19.
107. Special Marriage Act § 31.
108. Parsi Marriage and Divorce Act § 29.
109. Indian Divorce Act § 3(3).
110. Guardians and Wards Act § 9(1).

parental conduct.[111] The Court emphasized that the determination of ordinary residence is a mixed question of law and fact, requiring scrutiny of the child's degree of permanence and integration in the place asserted as the jurisdictional forum. This principle was reinforced in *Sakhamuri*, where the Court rejected jurisdictional claims founded solely on parental relocation divorced from the child's settled life, underscoring that custody jurisdiction must align with the child's welfare rather than forum advantage.[112]

Notably, Indian law imposes no minimum durational residency requirement before custody jurisdiction may attach. Unlike jurisdictions that condition jurisdiction on a fixed period of residence, Indian courts retain flexibility to assume jurisdiction once a child is found to ordinarily reside within their territorial limits. While this open-textured approach enables courts to respond swiftly to welfare concerns, it also creates scope for misuse in international child abduction and relocation cases. An abducting parent may seek to invoke Indian jurisdiction shortly after relocating the child, particularly by demonstrating school enrollment or familial integration, even where the child's connection to the forum is recent. Although the Supreme Court has increasingly scrutinized such conduct, the absence of a statutory bright-line threshold continues to distinguish Indian custody jurisdiction from time-bound international models.

By contrast, custody jurisdiction in the United States is governed by the Uniform Child Custody Jurisdiction and Enforcement Act (UCCJEA), which adopts a structured, durational framework. Under the UCCJEA, a child's "home state," typically defined as the state in which the child lived with a parent for at least six consecutive months immediately preceding the commencement of proceedings, has primary jurisdiction.[113] Temporary absences do not interrupt home-state status, and emergency jurisdiction is narrowly confined to situations involving abandonment or immediate risk of harm. This time-based requirement is designed to prevent forum shopping and ensure that custody determinations are anchored in established stability rather than recent relocation.

The divergence between India's flexible "ordinary residence" standard and the UCCJEA's durational "home state" rule has significant cross-border implications. Conduct insufficient to confer jurisdiction in a U.S. court may nonetheless ground custody proceedings in India, requiring Indian courts to engage directly with custody merits at an earlier stage. For practitioners navigating India–U.S. disputes, understanding this jurisdictional asymmetry is critical to anticipating parallel proceedings, managing forum contests, and mitigating the strategic misuse of jurisdiction in international child abduction cases.

C. *Exclusive Jurisdiction of Family Courts*

Once a family court is established in a district, section 7 of the Family Courts Act grants it exclusive jurisdiction over all matrimonial causes, civil and certain

111. Majoo v. Majoo, AIR 2011 SC 1952, ¶¶ 31–33 (India), https://indiankanoon.org/doc/637664/.

112. *Sakhamuri*, AIR 2019 SC 2881, ¶¶ 52–55.

113. UCCJEA § 201(a)(1) (Unif. L. Comm'n 1997).

criminal maintenance matters, custody, guardianship and access, property disputes between spouses arising out of the marital relationship, questions of legitimacy and paternity, and injunctions connected to marriage.[114] Under section 8, civil courts are divested of authority over these subjects.[115] This exclusivity carries particular importance in cross-border disputes, as a foreign decree cannot displace the family court's independent jurisdiction unless (under extremely limited circumstances in international divorces and custody disputes) it satisfies the requirements for conclusiveness set out in section 13 of the CPC.[116]

D. Jurisdiction and NRI/Foreign-Resident Parties

Jurisdiction remains intact even when the respondent resides abroad, the parties last lived together outside India, or the child is living in another country. The Supreme Court has repeatedly held that Indian courts may adjudicate matrimonial and guardianship matters whenever any domiciliary nexus exists, such as the petitioner's residence in India, or either party's Indian domicile (in many cases), regardless of where the marriage was centered or where the family last cohabited. This principle has significant implications for U.S.–India cases, as an Indian spouse who returns to India can initiate proceedings there even when the marital home was located in the United States.

2.2.6. Jurisdiction by Referral from Higher Courts

A. High Court Transfer Powers (Inter-District)

Under section 24 of the CPC and Articles 226–227 of the Constitution, high courts may transfer a case from one family court to another within the state, withdraw a matter to themselves, consolidate related proceedings filed in different districts, or direct expedited hearings. Transfers are commonly granted when the petitioner faces financial hardship that makes travel impracticable, alleges harassment or safety risks, has minor children residing with them, or is simultaneously prosecuting criminal proceedings in their home district. Consistent with Supreme Court guidance, high courts generally prioritize the convenience of the wife in matrimonial matters.

B. Supreme Court Transfer Powers (Inter-State)

Under section 25 of the CPC and Article 139A of the Constitution, the Supreme Court may transfer cases between family courts located in different states, consolidate inter-state matrimonial disputes, and intervene to prevent conflicting judgments arising from parallel proceedings. The Court frequently directs that

---

114. Family Courts Act § 7 (conferring exclusive jurisdiction on family courts over matrimonial causes, custody and guardianship, maintenance proceedings (including matters under Chapter IX of the CrPC), property disputes between spouses arising out of the marital relationship, questions of legitimacy and paternity, and injunctions connected with marriage).

115. *Id.* § 8 (divesting civil courts of jurisdiction in respect of matters over which family courts have exclusive authority once such a court is established in the district).

116. CPC, 1908, § 13 (setting out the conditions under which foreign judgments are conclusive, including exceptions for lack of jurisdiction, violation of natural justice, fraud, or inconsistency with Indian law).

cases be heard in the forum most convenient for the wife or custodial parent, emphasizing both the welfare of the child and the need to avoid undue economic or logistical hardship.

C. Extraordinary Jurisdiction and Referral in Child Custody Cases (Limitations)

Both the Supreme Court and the high courts may assume direct custody jurisdiction through habeas corpus or other writ proceedings, or by exercising their parens patriae authority. In appropriate cases, these courts may direct the production of the child, override or stay interim orders of a family court, transfer proceedings to another state, or require the family court to adjudicate the matter within a specified timeframe.

In international custody disputes, high courts are frequently approached where a child has been brought into India from abroad, where a foreign court has issued a return order, or where an urgent welfare determination is sought. Often, however, the left-behind parent is directed to pursue substantive custody relief before the appropriate family court by initiating (or participating in) a de novo proceeding, particularly where the taking parent has already invoked family court jurisdiction by filing a custody action shortly after relocation, capitalizing on the absence of any defined residency requirement for custody proceedings under Indian law.

2.2.7. Venue (Often Treated as Jurisdiction in Indian Family Law)

Venue refers to the appropriate geographical forum for instituting a matrimonial or custody proceeding, and while it is closely related to jurisdiction, the two concepts are analytically distinct. Jurisdiction concerns a court's power to adjudicate a particular class of disputes, whereas venue determines which court among multiple competent courts is the proper forum based on territorial or connecting factors.

In Indian family law, however, this distinction is frequently blurred. Statutes such as the Guardians and Wards Act, 1890, articulate territorial criteria in language that appears jurisdictional, directing that proceedings be instituted before the court within whose territorial limits the minor "ordinarily resides," even though the provision functions primarily to allocate forum rather than to confer subject-matter authority.[117] As a result, provisions that are conceptually concerned with venue are often described, both in pleadings and judgments, as questions of jurisdiction.

Indian courts have tended to tolerate imprecise usage, treating compliance with territorial filing requirements as a condition for the proper institution of proceedings rather than as a jurisdictional bar in the strict sense.

The Supreme Court addressed this dynamic squarely in *Majoo v. Majoo*, where it framed the inquiry under section 9(1) of the Guardians and Wards Act, 1890, as one turning primarily on factual determination rather than abstract

117. Guardians and Wards Act § 9(1) (providing that an application for guardianship shall be made to the court having jurisdiction in the place where the minor ordinarily resides).

jurisdictional competence.[118] Observing that section 9(1) merely identifies the court competent to entertain a guardianship application based on where the minor "ordinarily resides," the Court emphasized that ordinary residence is fundamentally a question of intention and lived reality, and therefore at best a mixed question of law and fact. Unless the jurisdictional facts are admitted, the issue cannot be resolved as a pure question of law without an inquiry into the factual matrix surrounding the child's residence:

> Section [9(1) of the Guardians and Wards Act] identifies the court competent to pass an order for the custody of the persons of the minor. . . . It says: "9. Court having jurisdiction to entertain application—(1) If the application is with respect to the guardianship of the person of the minor, it shall be made to the District Court having Jurisdiction in the place where the minor ordinarily resides."
>
> It is evident from a bare reading of the above that the solitary test for determining the jurisdiction of the court under Section 9 of the Act is the "ordinary residence" of the minor. The expression used is "Where the minor ordinarily resides". *Now whether the minor is ordinarily residing at a given place is primarily a question of intention which in turn is a question of fact. It may at best be a mixed question of law and fact, but unless the jurisdictional facts are admitted it can never be a pure question of law, capable of being answered without an enquiry into the factual aspects of the controversy* [emphasis added].

While this approach promotes procedural flexibility and access to justice, it also creates analytical ambiguity, particularly in cross-border custody disputes, where territorial filing rules may be invoked strategically to anchor proceedings in a preferred forum.[119]

A. Venue in Matrimonial Actions

Venue in matrimonial cases is determined by statute and typically depends on one or more of the following: the place where the marriage was solemnized, the place where the parties last resided together, the place where the petitioner resides at the time of filing, or depending on the statute the place where the respondent resides. Among these, the "last residence together" frequently becomes the most contested basis, particularly in cases where spouses lived abroad and later separated.

B. Venue in Custody and Guardianship

For custody and guardianship matters, the Guardians and Wards Act assigns venue to the court within whose territorial limits the minor ordinarily resides. Indian courts consistently reject attempts to establish venue by bringing a child

118. *Majoo*, AIR 2011 SC 1952.

119. *Id.* (emphasizing that territorial criteria relating to a child's residence cannot be mechanically or strategically invoked to manufacture forum advantage).

into a district solely for the purpose of initiating litigation, emphasizing that ordinary residence must reflect a genuine and settled connection.

C. Transfers for Convenience, Safety, or Child Welfare

High courts routinely order venue transfers to accommodate financial hardship, the presence of minor children, allegations of harassment, medical limitations, significant travel burdens, or credible risks of domestic violence. In cross-border disputes, courts also take into account the practical ability of a foreign-resident party to participate in proceedings, and frequently permit virtual appearances to ensure fairness and access to justice.

2.2.8. Appeals

Appeals from family court decisions follow a distinct appellate regime created by the Family Courts Act, 1984, read with the Constitution. Under section 19, an appeal lies to the high court from every judgment or order of a family court, other than interlocutory orders, within the period of limitation prescribed by the applicable procedural law.[120] In practice, the limitation period for family court appeals is shorter and more streamlined than under general civil statutes: appeals are ordinarily required to be filed within 30 days, reflecting the legislative intent that family disputes (particularly those involving custody, maintenance, or access) be resolved expeditiously.[121] This contrasts with matrimonial or guardianship proceedings instituted in districts where no family court exists, which continue to be governed by the CPC, 1908, or the relevant personal law statute, often allowing a longer limitation period (commonly 90 days) for first appeals.[122] The Family Courts Act thus represents a conscious departure from ordinary civil appellate timelines in favor of speed and finality.

In reviewing appeals from family courts, high courts exercise a limited but substantive appellate jurisdiction. Errors of law, misapplication or misinterpretation of personal law, procedural irregularities, violations of natural justice, and factual findings resting on a clear misreading of evidence are all reviewable. In custody and guardianship matters, however, appellate courts are particularly cautious: while findings of fact are not immune from scrutiny, high courts generally defer to the family court's assessment of evidence unless the decision is shown to be perverse, manifestly unreasonable, or demonstrably inconsistent with the child's welfare. Custody appeals are often taken up on a priority or expedited basis, recognizing the time-sensitive nature of child-related determinations and the risk of harm caused by prolonged uncertainty.

Interim orders issued by family courts, such as temporary custody, visitation schedules, or interim maintenance, are not ordinarily appealable under section 19, as they are treated as interlocutory. Such orders are instead challenged

120. Family Courts Act § 19(1).

121. *Id.* § 19(3).

122. CPC § 96 (providing for first appeals from original decrees); The Limitation Act, 1963, art. 116(a) (India) (prescribing a 90-day limitation period for appeals to the high court from original decrees, applicable where proceedings are governed by the CPC rather than the Family Courts Act), https://indiankanoon.org/doc/1317393/.

through the high court's supervisory and writ jurisdiction under Articles 226 and 227 of the Constitution.[123] High courts exercise this power sparingly, intervening only where the family court has exceeded its jurisdiction, committed a patent procedural error, violated principles of natural justice, caused manifest injustice, or imposed an order that results in undue hardship. This supervisory review is corrective rather than appellate in character and does not permit reappreciation of evidence as a matter of course.

Appeals from high court decisions lie to the Supreme Court of India primarily through special leave petitions under Article 136.[124] In family law matters, the Supreme Court has consistently emphasized restraint, declining to interfere with concurrent findings of fact unless intervention is compelled by overriding considerations of child welfare, a substantial error in the application of personal law, or the presence of significant constitutional or international dimensions. Particularly in cross-border custody disputes, the Court may exercise its discretionary jurisdiction to ensure uniformity, prevent irreparable harm to the child, or clarify the interaction between domestic family law and international legal principles.

2.2.9. Procedures, Generally

Procedural rules in family courts reflect a blend of statutory direction and judicial discretion. Although the system is designed to be simple, informal, and conciliatory, procedures often become complex because family disputes intersect with civil, criminal, and personal law frameworks.

A. Relaxed Procedural Rules

Section 10 of the Family Courts Act provides that family courts are not strictly bound by the CPC or the Indian Evidence Act and may adopt procedures guided primarily by principles of natural justice.[125] This flexibility allows courts to receive affidavit evidence, admit documents with fewer technical obstacles, rely on counselor reports, interact informally with parties, and hold hearings in camera when necessary.

B. Case Management and Conciliation

Section 9 imposes a mandatory duty on family courts to promote settlement. In practice, courts often conduct preliminary conciliation sessions, refer matters to mediation centers, involve counselors to assess emotional dynamics, and encourage early resolution of issues such as maintenance and visitation.[126]

123. India Const. arts. 226–227 (conferring writ and supervisory jurisdiction on high courts); Shyam v. Nath, AIR 2015 SC 3269 (India) (clarifying the scope of Article 227 as supervisory rather than appellate), https://indiankanoon.org/doc/34295630/.

124. India Const. art. 136 (Special Leave to Appeal); Chandran v. Union of India, Writ Petition (Crl.) No. 112 of 2007 (India) (reiterating restraint in interfering with concurrent factual findings in custody matters, subject to child welfare and international considerations), https://indiankanoon.org/doc/376248/.

125. Family Courts Act § 10.

126. *Id.* § 9.

Conciliation is frequently attempted even in cases involving allegations of cruelty or domestic violence, reflecting the conciliatory ethos embedded in the statute.[127]

C. Evidence-Taking, Cross-Examination, and Expert Input

Even with relaxed procedures, the principles of natural justice must be maintained. Witnesses are examined under oath, cross-examination is permitted, and documentary evidence must be properly proved.[128] Courts may also rely on expert testimony from psychologists, social workers, or medical professionals. In custody matters, judges frequently draw on home-study reports, child-interaction sessions, and school or medical records to evaluate the child's welfare.

The Supreme Court has clarified that while family courts may regulate their own procedure, findings cannot rest on untested material or deny parties a meaningful opportunity to contest adverse evidence. In *Gopalakrishnan v. Cochin Devaswom Board,* the Court reiterated that relaxation of procedural rules does not dilute the obligation to observe fairness and audi alteram partem.[129] Similarly, high courts have repeatedly held that custody determinations based on reports or statements not subjected to scrutiny, cross-examination, or judicial evaluation may vitiate the decision. The balance struck by Indian courts is therefore one of procedural flexibility without procedural arbitrariness.

In custody and guardianship matters, courts frequently rely on expert input to assist in evaluating the child's welfare. The Family Courts Act expressly authorizes courts to seek assistance from medical experts, psychologists, social workers, or welfare professionals, either formally or through court-directed reports.[130] Judges commonly consider home-study assessments, child-interaction sessions conducted in chambers, school records, and medical or psychological evaluations to gain insight into the child's emotional, educational, and developmental needs. While such reports are influential, they are not binding; courts retain ultimate responsibility for evaluating their probative value and must ensure that expert material is considered alongside, rather than in substitution for, tested evidence and judicial reasoning.

D. Interim Orders

Family courts routinely issue interim orders to address immediate needs arising during the pendency of proceedings, including interim maintenance, residence, temporary custody or visitation arrangements, and protective or restraining injunctions, such as orders restraining a parent from removing a child from

---

127. Discussed *supra.*

128. *Id.* § 10(1)–(3) (permitting family courts to evolve their own procedure while applying principles of natural justice and authorizing examination of witnesses); *see also* The Indian Evidence Act, 1872, § 3 (India) (general principles of proof, applied with flexibility in family courts), https://indiankanoon.org/doc/1953529/.

129. Gopalakrishnan v. Cochin Devaswom Board, AIR 2007 SC 3162, ¶¶ 24–26 (India), https://indiankanoon.org/doc/1306104/.

130. Family Courts Act § 12.

the court's jurisdiction.[131] These orders are grounded in the court's obligation to prevent hardship and safeguard welfare pending final adjudication. Interim custody and access orders, in particular, are expressly treated as provisional and revisable, and courts retain continuing authority to modify them upon a material change in circumstances or where the child's welfare so requires.[132] Indian courts have repeatedly emphasized that interim arrangements do not confer vested rights and must yield to the child's evolving needs and factual realities.

E. Recording of Reasons and Final Judgment

Final judgments of family courts must reflect reasoned decision-making, setting out the relevant facts, evaluating the evidence adduced, and explaining how the applicable personal law or statutory framework has been applied.[133] In custody and guardianship matters, courts are required to demonstrate, on the face of the judgment, that the welfare of the child has been treated as the paramount consideration, and that competing parental claims have been subordinated to that inquiry. Final decrees must comply with the formal requirements of the governing statute and procedural law and are subject to appellate scrutiny for errors of law, perversity in factual findings, procedural irregularities, or failure to consider material evidence. A reasoned judgment is particularly critical in custody cases, given the likelihood of appellate review and the long-term implications of custodial determinations.

F. Delays and Procedural Challenges

Notwithstanding the Family Courts Act's emphasis on speedy resolution and conciliation, delays remain a persistent feature of family litigation in India. Heavy caseloads, repeated mediation and counseling referrals, multiple interlocutory applications for interim relief, and the frequent coexistence of parallel criminal or quasi-criminal proceedings, such as maintenance, domestic violence, or criminal complaints, often prolong timelines substantially.[134] In cross-border disputes, additional delays may arise from service issues, foreign evidence, and jurisdictional objections. Foreign practitioners should therefore anticipate that Indian Family Court proceedings, particularly in contested custody matters, may extend significantly longer than comparable proceedings in U.S. family courts, despite statutory aspirations to expedition.

---

131. *Id.* §§ 7(1), 7(2) (conferring jurisdiction over interim and final reliefs relating to maintenance, custody, guardianship, and injunctions); Hindu Marriage Act §§ 24, 26 (interim maintenance and custody during pendency of proceedings).

132. *Sharma*, AIR 2015 SC 2232, ¶¶ 18–21 (holding that custody orders are always subject to modification based on the child's welfare); *Sahu*, AIR 2020 SC 577, ¶¶ 19–21 (recognizing continuing court oversight over custody and access arrangements).

133. CPC § 2(9), Order XX, Rule 4 (requirements of a reasoned judgment), applied to family courts subject to procedural flexibility under the Family Courts Act.

134. Family Courts Act § 9 (mandatory effort toward settlement); *Rajnesh*, AIR 2021 SC 569 (acknowledging systemic delays and multiplicity of proceedings in family disputes).

2.3. Divorce Law and Procedure

Divorce law in India operates within a pluralistic statutory framework shaped by the religious identity of the parties, the secular option under the Special Marriage Act, and layers of judicial interpretation that have evolved over seven decades of post-independence jurisprudence.[135] For U.S. practitioners advising clients in cross-border marriages, understanding the substantive grounds, filing requirements, evidentiary burdens, procedural timelines, and the role of family courts is indispensable. India does not have a uniform matrimonial code, and the divorce procedure applicable to a couple depends on whether the marriage was solemnized under Hindu, Muslim, Christian, Parsi, or secular law. These distinctions are not merely theoretical, they affect jurisdiction, grounds for divorce, waiting periods, the structure of pleadings, available defenses, the treatment of foreign decrees, and the likelihood of interim relief.

This section provides a comprehensive overview of divorce law and procedure in India, excluding financial issues, child support, spousal support, property division, enforcement of financial orders, custody, and issues relating to unmarried parents, all of which appear in later sections.

2.3.1. The Statutory Landscape Governing Divorce in India

As noted earlier, divorce law in India is statute-specific and turns primarily on the legal regime under which the marriage was solemnized. India does not recognize a single, uniform matrimonial code.[136] Instead, divorce rights and procedures flow from the applicable personal law statute or, where elected, the secular framework of the Special Marriage Act. These statutory distinctions are outcome-determinative: they shape jurisdiction, grounds for divorce, mandatory waiting periods, evidentiary thresholds, defenses, and the treatment of foreign proceedings.[137]

The principal enactments governing divorce (already discussed in the preceding sections) include the Hindu Marriage Act, 1955; the Special Marriage Act, 1954; the Indian Divorce Act, 1869 (as substantially amended); the Parsi Marriage and Divorce Act, 1936; and Muslim personal law as supplemented by the Dissolution of Muslim Marriages Act, 1939, and judicial precedent. Each statute reflects a distinct legislative philosophy and prescribes its own procedural and substantive architecture. As a result, similarly situated couples may encounter markedly different divorce pathways depending solely on the governing law.

A. Marriage Registration in India: Mandatory in Form, but Not Always Constitutive of Validity

Marriage registration is mandatory across India, but its legal consequences turn on the governing statute and the distinction Indian law draws between

135. Discussed *supra* 2.2.1. Historical Overview.
136. *Y. Narasimha Rao*, AIR Online 1991 SC 10, ¶ 9.
137. *Id.*

validity and registration. Following *Seema v. Kumar*, all states and union territories were directed to ensure compulsory registration of marriages irrespective of religion.[138]

For marriages governed by personal laws, *however*, registration is evidentiary rather than constitutive: a Hindu, Muslim, Christian, Sikh, or Parsi marriage is legally valid once it is solemnized in accordance with the prescribed religious rites, and failure to register generally does not render the marriage void, though it may attract statutory penalties.[139] This distinction is illustrated in the Hindu context, where courts have clarified that while a Hindu marriage does not become invalid merely because it is unregistered, it may nonetheless be void if the essential religious ceremonies were never performed. Referring to section 7 of the Hindu Marriage Act, 1955, the Supreme Court in *Rani v. Chanchal* has held:

> Where a Hindu marriage is not performed in accordance with the applicable rites or ceremonies such as *saptapadi* when included, the marriage will not be construed as a Hindu marriage. In other words, for a valid marriage under the Act, the requisite ceremonies have to be performed and there must be proof of performance of the said ceremony when an issue/controversy arise. Unless the parties have undergone such ceremony, there would be no Hindu marriage according to Section 7 of the Act and a mere issuance of a certificate by an entity in the absence of the requisite ceremonies having been performed, would neither confirm any marital status to the parties nor establish a marriage under Hindu law.[140]

By contrast, under the Special Marriage Act, 1954, registration is integral to the marriage itself, and no valid marriage comes into existence until it is registered before a marriage officer.[141]

The Special Marriage Act warrants particular attention in cross-border practice, as it establishes a fully secular matrimonial regime for interfaith and civil marriages and, upon divorce, (although it must be noted) that Indian courts frequently read its provisions in parallel with the Hindu Marriage Act where the statutory language is materially similar or where the Special Marriage Act is silent, particularly with respect to grounds for divorce and procedural safeguards.

For practitioners, the analysis therefore begins not with grounds, but with classification. Before assessing strategy or merits, counsel must identify the applicable statutory framework. In practice, this requires answering a small but critical set of threshold questions, including under which statute the marriage was solemnized; whether any subsequent registration occurred; which personal law governs the parties at the time of filing; where the parties currently reside; where they last resided together; and whether any foreign matrimonial

138. Seema v. Kumar, AIR 2006 SC 1158 (India), https://indiankanoon.org/doc/1037437/.

139. Hindu Marriage Act § 8(5).

140. Rani v. Chanchal, Transfer Petition (Civil) No. 2043 of 2023, at 7 (India), https://www.scobserver.in/wp-content/uploads/2024/05/Dolly-Rani-v-Manish-Kumar-Chanchal-Supreme-Court-Judgement.pdf.

141. Special Marriage Act §§ 13–14.

proceedings exist or are contemplated.[142] These determinations dictate the procedural trajectory of the case and frame every substantive issue that follows.

B. Types of Divorce: Contested and Mutual Consent

Indian divorce law broadly recognizes two procedural paths, mutual consent divorce and contested divorce, a classification that is sometimes loosely compared to no-fault and fault divorce in the United States, but with a critical difference: in India, a mutual consent divorce is not merely no-fault in character, it affirmatively requires the continuing consent of both spouses, and unilateral dissolution without fault is generally unavailable under central matrimonial statutes.[143]

Mutual consent divorce is provided for under the Hindu Marriage Act, 1955, the Special Marriage Act, 1954, and the Indian Divorce Act, 1869, and proceeds by way of a joint petition in which both spouses must establish statutory separation (typically one year), free and voluntary consent, and resolution of ancillary issues such as maintenance, property, and arrangements for children, subject always to the court's independent assessment of child welfare.[144]

Although the Hindu Marriage Act originally contemplated a mandatory six-month "cooling-off" period between the first and second motions, the Supreme Court clarified in *Singh v. Kaur* that this period is directory rather than mandatory and may be waived where the marriage has irretrievably broken down and all issues are settled; such waivers are now frequently granted, including in cases involving overseas or cross-border parties where prolonged timelines serve no practical purpose.[145] Similar principles have been applied under the Special Marriage Act, though courts often scrutinize such petitions more closely given the statute's secular and interfaith framework.[146]

By contrast, where mutual consent is absent (or where consent is withdrawn before the decree), divorce must proceed as a contested action based on one or more statutory grounds, such as cruelty, desertion, adultery, mental disorder, and so on (the ground of cruelty being the most contested one). Contested matrimonial litigation in India is typically pleading-intensive and evidence-driven, involving written statements, interim applications, documentary proof, witness examination, and final arguments, often over extended timelines. Throughout the proceedings, family courts simultaneously adjudicate interim relief relating to maintenance, custody, residence, and protective injunctions, a feature that can substantially lengthen and complicate contested cases as compared to mutual consent dissolutions.[147]

---

142. *Y. Narasimha Rao*, AIR Online 1991 SC 10, ¶ 13 (linking governing statute to jurisdiction, recognition, and procedural validity of divorce proceedings).

143. Hindu Marriage Act § 13B; Special Marriage Act § 28; Indian Divorce Act § 10A.

144. Hindu Marriage Act § 13B; Special Marriage Act § 28; Indian Divorce Act § 10A.

145. Singh v. Kaur, AIR 2017 SC 4417, ¶ 18 (India), https://indiankanoon.org/doc/79830357/.

146. Sureen v. Tirki, Civil Revision No. 31 of 2018, ¶ 7 (India) (noting that § 28 of the Special Marriage Act is *pari materia* with § 13B of the Hindu Marriage Act), https://indiankanoon.org/doc/61330837/.

147. Family Courts Act §§ 7–10.

C. Grounds for Divorce Under Major Statutes

Each Indian matrimonial law does not apply a uniform set of divorce grounds; instead, each governing statute defines its own grounds, with partial overlap but materially different evidentiary thresholds, waiting periods, and procedural consequences.

Under the *Hindu Marriage Act, 1955,* divorce may be granted on grounds including cruelty (physical or mental), desertion for a continuous period of at least two years, adultery, conversion to another religion, incurable unsoundness of mind or mental disorder, venereal disease in a communicable form, renunciation of the world, and presumption of death.[148] The act further permits divorce where there has been no resumption of cohabitation following a decree of judicial separation or RCR, reflecting the statute's structured, fault-based framework.[149]

The *Special Marriage Act, 1954,* largely mirrors these grounds but introduces important variations, including modified waiting periods, distinct procedural safeguards, and additional grounds such as the respondent's imprisonment for seven years or more; as a secular statute frequently invoked in interfaith and cross-border marriages, courts often interpret its provisions in parallel with the Hindu Marriage Act where the statutory language is materially similar.[150]

Under *Christian law,* governed by the Indian Divorce Act, 1869, divorce was historically fault-heavy and asymmetrical, but judicial interpretation and statutory amendments have significantly modernized the regime. Grounds now include adultery, cruelty, desertion, conversion, mental disorder, venereal disease, and noncompliance with decrees for RCR, with reforms aimed at ensuring gender-neutral access to relief.[151]

Muslim personal law follows a different structure: while Muslim husbands may dissolve marriage through talaq, the Supreme Court's decision in *Bano v. Union of India* invalidated instant triple talaq (*talaq-e-biddat*), reshaping the landscape of unilateral divorce.[152] Muslim wives may seek judicial divorce under the Dissolution of Muslim Marriages Act, 1939, on grounds including cruelty, non-maintenance, disappearance, impotence, or failure to perform marital obligations.[153] Although Muslim divorces often occur outside the civil court system, disputes relating to maintenance, custody, and dower routinely fall within the jurisdiction of family courts.

Finally, the *Parsi Marriage and Divorce Act, 1936,* provides a distinctive regime, recognizing grounds such as adultery, cruelty, desertion, unsoundness of mind, non-consummation, bigamy, and long-term imprisonment, and uniquely requires matrimonial causes to be adjudicated by a judge sitting with community delegates, reflecting the act's hybrid civil–communal character.[154]

148. Hindu Marriage Act § 13(1)(i)–(vii).
149. *Id.* § 13(1A).
150. Special Marriage Act § 27(1), (1A).
151. Indian Divorce Act §§ 10, 22, as amended by Act 51 of 2001 (India).
152. *Bano*, AIR 2017 SC 4609, ¶ 200.
153. Dissolution of Muslim Marriages Act § 2.
154. Parsi Marriage and Divorce Act §§ 30–32, 46.

D. Cruelty as a Ground for Divorce

"Cruelty" is a central ground for divorce under major Indian matrimonial statutes such as the Hindu Marriage Act, 1955, and the Special Marriage Act, 1954, yet it is deliberately left undefined in these civil laws.

Unlike criminal law, which provides a specific statutory definition of cruelty to women (now under the Bharatiya Nyaya Sanhita, previously Indian Penal Code section 498A), matrimonial courts apply an evolving, fact-sensitive civil standard that turns on the parties' social background, education, temperament, and the overall marital context.[155]

Indian courts distinguish between physical cruelty, which is often capable of objective proof, and mental cruelty, which the Supreme Court has described as conduct causing such acute mental pain and suffering that continued cohabitation becomes impossible. Specifically, the court made the following observations:

> Mental cruelty in Section 13(1)(i-a) can broadly be defined as that conduct which inflicts upon the other party such mental pain and suffering as would make it not possible for that party to live with the other. In other words, mental cruelty must be of such a nature that the parties cannot reasonably be expected to live together. The situation must be such that the wronged party cannot reasonably be asked to put up with such conduct and continue to live with the other party. It is not necessary to prove that the mental cruelty is such as to cause injury to the health of the petitioner. While arriving at such conclusion, regard must be had to the social status, educational level of the parties, the society they move in, the possibility or otherwise of the parties ever living together in case they are already living apart and all other relevant facts and circumstances which it is neither possible nor desirable to set out exhaustively. What is cruelty in one case may not amount to cruelty in another case. It is a matter to be Determined in each case having regard to the facts and circumstances of that case. If it is a case of accusations and allegations, regard must also be had to the context in which they were made.[156]

In *Ghosh v. Ghosh*, the Court emphasized that no uniform standard is possible and articulated a non-exhaustive set of illustrations of mental cruelty, including sustained humiliation, unilateral denial of marital intimacy without justification, repeated threats of suicide intended to terrorize the spouse, and conduct demonstrating a studied indifference that destroys the emotional foundation of marriage.[157]

In another case, the Supreme Court observed as follows:

> [C]ruelty may be mental or physical, intentional or unintentional. If it is physical the court will have no problem to determine it. It is a question of fact and degree. If it is mental the problem presents difficulty.

155. *See* Hindu Marriage Act § 13(1)(ia); Special Marriage Act § 27(1)(d).
156. Bhagat v. Bhagat, 1994 AIR 710, ¶ 16 (India), https://indiankanoon.org/doc/1848484/.
157. *Ghosh*, AIR Online 2007 SC 347, ¶¶ 98–101.

> First, the enquiry must begin as to the nature of the cruel treatment. Second, the impact of such treatment in the mind of the spouse. Whether it caused reasonable apprehension that it would be harmful or injurious to live with the other. Ultimately, it is a matter of inference to be drawn by taking into account the nature of the conduct and its effect on the complaining spouse. There may, however, be cases where the conduct complained of itself is bad enough and per se unlawful or illegal. Then the impact or the injurious effect on the other spouse need not be enquired into or considered. In such cases, the cruelty will be established if the conduct itself is proved or admitted.[158]

Subsequent decisions have consistently held that *"leveling disgusting accusations of unchastity"* amounts to grave mental cruelty,[159] that *"filing repeated false complaints and cases in the court against the spouse"* amounts to mental cruelty,[160] and that allegations that "have the propensity to irreparably damage the character and reputation" of the spouse amount to cruelty.[161] Courts have likewise recognized prolonged, unjustified denial of sexual relations, coercive isolation from parents or close family, and sustained psychological pressure through suicide threats as forms of mental cruelty when they render marital life intolerable.

Although cruelty is often pleaded alongside desertion or other grounds, Indian jurisprudence treats it as an independent and sufficient basis for divorce, distinct from and not to be conflated with the concept of cruelty as a criminal offense under penal law.

E. Desertion, Adultery, and Judicial Separation

Desertion requires proof that one spouse has abandoned the other without reasonable cause, without consent, and with the intention to permanently sever cohabitation for the prescribed statutory period, typically two continuous years under the Hindu Marriage Act and the Special Marriage Act.[162] Indian courts have consistently held that desertion has two essential elements: *factum deserendi* (the fact of separation) and *animus deserendi* (the intention to desert), both of which must coexist throughout the statutory period,[163] and the person seeking the divorce *"bears the burden of proving those elements."*[164] Temporary separations, failed reconciliation attempts, or brief resumptions of cohabitation do not automatically interrupt the desertion clock unless they reflect a genuine intent to restore marital life.[165] In cross-border marriages, physical separation caused by immigration barriers, employment transfers, or visa constraints complicates the

158. Rani v. Reddi, AIR 1988 SC 121, at 4 (India), https://indiankanoon.org/doc/1100461/.

159. Bhate v. Bhate, AIR 2003 SC 2462, ¶¶ 7–8 (India), https://indiankanoon.org/doc/1228342/; *Narendra*, AIR 2016 SC 4599, ¶ 12.

160. *Rao*, AIR 2013 SC 2176, ¶ 14 (emphasis added).

161. Majumdar v. Majumdar, AIR 2021 SC 1165, ¶ 13 (India), https://indiankanoon.org/doc/127845138/.

162. Hindu Marriage Act § 13(1)(ib); Special Marriage Act § 27(1)(b).

163. *Shah*, AIR 1957 SC 176.

164. *Pandey*, AIR 2002 SC 591.

165. *Id.*

analysis, and courts accordingly focus less on geographic distance and more on conduct evidencing intent to abandon the marital relationship.

Adultery, though no longer a criminal offense following *Shine v. Union of India*, remains a valid matrimonial ground across major statutes.[166] Modern courts do not require direct proof of sexual intercourse; instead, adultery may be established through compelling circumstantial evidence, including travel and hotel records, digital communications, sustained patterns of conduct, and corroborated witness testimony, provided the inference of an adulterous relationship is both reasonable and irresistible.

Judicial separation occupies a distinct remedial space, permitting spouses to live apart without dissolving the marriage. It may be sought on the same grounds as divorce and operates as a formal suspension of conjugal rights rather than a termination of marital status.[167] Where cohabitation does not resume within the statutory period following a decree of judicial separation, commonly one year, either spouse may seek divorce on the ground of non-resumption.[168] Judicial separation continues to have practical relevance for parties who, for religious, cultural, or financial reasons, wish to remain legally married while obtaining formal recognition of separation and relief from marital obligations.

F. Restitution of Conjugal Rights

RCR, though increasingly controversial, remains a statutory remedy under Indian matrimonial law, most notably under section 9 of the Hindu Marriage Act, 1955, and section 22 of the Special Marriage Act, 1954.

An RCR decree permits a court to direct a spouse who has withdrawn from the society of the other, without reasonable excuse, to resume cohabitation; enforcement is civil in nature (typically through attachment of property) and not through physical compulsion.[169] Persistent noncompliance with such a decree for the statutory period (commonly one year) may itself become a ground for divorce, reflecting the law's recognition that judicially compelled cohabitation has practical limits.[170] While the Supreme Court has upheld the constitutional validity of RCR on the ground that it serves a "social purpose" by affording spouses an opportunity for reconciliation,[171] the remedy has long attracted sustained constitutional and feminist critique. In *Sareetha v. Subbaiah*, the Andhra Pradesh High Court famously characterized section 9 as an "engine of oppression," holding that it violates the right to privacy, bodily autonomy, and reproductive choice under Article 21 of the Constitution;[172] this view, however, was

166. Shine v. Union of India, AIR 2018 SC 4898 (India), https://indiankanoon.org/doc/42184625/; Hindu Marriage Act § 13(1)(i).

167. Hindu Marriage Act §§ 10, 13; Special Marriage Act § 23.

168. Hindu Marriage Act § 13(1A)(i).

169. *Id.* § 9; Special Marriage Act § 22; CPC Order XXI, Rule 32.

170. Hindu Marriage Act § 13(1A)(ii); Special Marriage Act § 27(1A)(ii).

171. Rani v. Chadha, AIR 1984 SC 1562 (India), https://indiankanoon.org/doc/1382895/.

172. Sareetha v. Subbaiah, AIR 1983 AP 356, ¶ 38 (India), https://indiankanoon.org/doc/1987982/.

rejected by the Delhi High Court in *Kaur v. Choudhry* and later by the Supreme Court in *Rani v. Chadha*.[173]

In contemporary practice, particularly in *international and cross-border family law disputes*, RCR proceedings are frequently deployed as strategic tools rather than genuine attempts at reconciliation. As has been widely documented, a spouse remaining in India may file an RCR petition while simultaneously pursuing or contemplating divorce abroad, using the Indian proceeding to anchor jurisdiction, resist forum displacement, or blunt claims for spousal maintenance.

Courts have begun to scrutinize such misuse more closely. In *Madhapariya v. Madhapariya*, the Gujarat High Court set aside a family court order directing a wife to return from the United Kingdom to India to fulfill "marital obligations," holding that a spouse cannot, on the one hand, seek divorce and, on the other, demand RCR, and emphasizing that such orders ignore personal autonomy and practical realities of cross-border marriages.[174] The constitutional validity of RCR is currently under challenge before the Supreme Court, with petitions squarely raising questions of privacy, sexual autonomy, and gender equality in light of evolving Article 21 jurisprudence.[175]

As Indian family law increasingly intersects with international mobility and parallel proceedings, courts appear more alert to the risk that RCR, rooted in colonial-era notions of marital sanctity, may operate less as a reconciliatory remedy and more as a coercive litigation tactic.

G. Irretrievable Breakdown of Marriage

Although Indian matrimonial statutes continue to rely on enumerated fault-based grounds, the judiciary, led by the Supreme Court, has progressively recognized irretrievable breakdown of marriage as a compelling basis for dissolution in cases where the marital relationship has clearly ceased to exist, even though it is not a statutorily recognized ground for divorce in India.

In the absence of express statutory authority, the Supreme Court has invoked its plenary powers under Article 142 of the Constitution to dissolve marriages that are beyond salvage, repeatedly observing that where parties have lived apart for long periods, engaged in bitter or protracted litigation, and face no realistic prospect of reconciliation, insistence on strict proof of fault merely prolongs suffering and serves no legitimate purpose. In particular, the Supreme Court has urged the Indian central government "*to seriously consider*

173. Kaur v. Choudhry, AIR 1984 Del 66, ¶ 7 (India), https://indiankanoon.org/doc/191703/; *Rani*, AIR 1984 SC 1562.

174. Madhapariya v. Madhapariya, AIR Online 2021 Guj 31 (India), https://indiankanoon.org/doc/78922152/.

175. *See* Supreme Court of India, Writ Petitions (C) challenging Hindu Marriage Act § 9 and Special Marriage Act § 22 (notice issued 2019) (pending), Supreme Court Observer, *Challenge to Restitution of Conjugal Rights: Ojaswa Pathak v. Union of India* [Writ Petition (C) No. 250 of 2019], https://www.scobserver.in/cases/ojaswa-pathak-union-of-india-challenge-to-restitution-of-conjugal-rights-case-background/.

bringing an amendment in the Hindu Marriage Act, 1955 to incorporate irretrievable breakdown of marriage as a ground for the grant of divorce."[176]

This line of authority was definitively consolidated by a Constitution Bench in *Shailesh v. Shrinivasan*, which held that the Supreme Court may directly grant divorce on the ground of irretrievable breakdown under Article 142 in order to do "complete justice," even where one party opposes dissolution.[177]

At the same time, the Court has cautioned against the *unprincipled or inequitable deployment* of the doctrine. In *Prabhamani v. Lakshmeesha M.C.*, the Supreme Court emphatically held that irretrievable breakdown cannot be invoked to reward a spouse who is *"solely responsible"* for destroying the marriage and stands to benefit from the divorce.[178] Reversing a high court decree that had granted divorce on this ground, the Court criticized the use of the "bogey" of irretrievable breakdown to legitimize abandonment and neglect, particularly where the husband had deserted the wife and newborn child and resisted financial responsibility. Emphasizing fairness and accountability, the Court not only declined dissolution on that basis but also imposed substantial additional monetary compensation.

The doctrine has also been closely linked to the economic consequences of divorce, particularly permanent alimony. In *Jain v. Jain*, the Supreme Court granted divorce under Article 142 after noting that the parties had lived separately for more than two decades, and laid down detailed, though non-exhaustive, guidelines for determining permanent alimony once a marriage is dissolved on the ground of irretrievable breakdown.[179] The Court underscored that the objective is not to penalize the paying spouse, but to ensure that the financially dependent spouse is not left without means of support post-dissolution, directing courts to consider factors such as social and financial status, reasonable needs, standard of living during marriage, employment sacrifices, independent income, and litigation costs.

While high courts lack Article 142 powers, they frequently treat irretrievable breakdown as a persuasive and contextual factor, particularly when assessing cruelty or desertion in complex or long-separated marriages. The doctrine has assumed particular significance in cross-border marriages, where prolonged physical separation caused by immigration barriers, international employment, or residence in different jurisdictions is often compounded by parallel litigation abroad. In such cases, courts increasingly acknowledge that the factual reality of a dead marriage may outweigh formalistic resistance to divorce, even as they remain cautious not to allow the doctrine to become a shield for marital wrongdoing.

---

176. *Kohli*, AIR 2006 SC 1675; Sitole v. Ganga, AIR 2008 SC 3093 (India), https://indiankanoon.org/doc/1415536/.

177. *Sailesh*, Transfer Petition (Civil) No. 1118 of 2014.

178. Prabhamani v. Lakshmeesha M.C., Civil Appeal No. 8790 of 2024, ¶ 6 (India), https://api.sci.gov.in/supremecourt/2023/50872/50872_2023_4_38_54684_Order_12-Aug-2024.pdf.

179. Jain v. Jain, S.L.P. (Civil) Nos. 21710–21711 of 2024 (India), https://api.sci.gov.in/supremecourt/2024/41732/41732_2024_6_1502_57756_Judgement_10-Dec-2024.pdf.

H. Conversion, Renunciation, and Change of Religion

Conversion to another religion remains a recognized ground for divorce under several Indian personal law regimes, most notably the Hindu Marriage Act, 1955, and continues to attract careful judicial scrutiny. Indian courts draw a sharp distinction between a bona fide conversion, motivated by genuine religious conviction, and a strategic or opportunistic conversion undertaken to evade matrimonial obligations, defeat spousal rights, or manipulate jurisdiction.

Under the Hindu Marriage Act, conversion by one spouse to a religion other than Hinduism entitles the other spouse to seek divorce, but courts have repeatedly emphasized that the inquiry focuses not merely on formal conversion, but on its sincerity, permanence, and legal consequences.[180] Closely related, but conceptually distinct, is renunciation, which refers to a spouse's entry into a religious order and complete withdrawal from worldly and secular life; this ground is construed narrowly, and courts require clear, cogent evidence that the spouse has irrevocably abandoned ordinary social existence rather than merely adopting a heightened degree of religiosity.[181]

Although conversion and renunciation arise infrequently in contemporary matrimonial litigation, they retain important procedural and jurisdictional significance, particularly in cross-cultural and interfaith marriages. Conversion may alter the applicable personal law, affect the forum in which matrimonial relief is sought, or reshape the substantive rights available to the parties, including remedies relating to maintenance or succession. Courts have therefore remained vigilant against attempts to weaponize religious status to secure unfair advantage, especially where conversion is invoked mid-litigation or in parallel proceedings across jurisdictions.[182] In an era of increasing international mobility and plural marriages, these grounds continue to function less as routine bases for dissolution and more as sensitive fault lines where questions of faith, identity, and legal strategy intersect.

I. Mental Disorder and Unsoundness of Mind

Mental disorder or unsoundness of mind is a recognized ground for divorce under major Indian matrimonial statutes, including the Hindu Marriage Act, 1955, and the Special Marriage Act, 1954, but courts have consistently held that a mere medical diagnosis is insufficient. The statutory threshold requires proof that the mental condition is of such a nature and degree that the petitioner cannot reasonably be expected to live with the respondent.[183]

Indian courts therefore insist on a functional, impact-based inquiry, examining whether the disorder renders normal marital life impossible rather than

180. Hindu Marriage Act § 13(1)(ii); *see also Mudgal*, AIR 1995 SC 1531 (distinguishing genuine conversion from conversion undertaken to circumvent matrimonial law).

181. Hindu Marriage Act § 13(1)(vi); Das v. Ram, AIR 1954 SC 606, ¶¶ 9–11 (India) (discussing the legal meaning of renunciation and complete withdrawal from worldly life), https://indiankanoon.org/doc/150069/.

182. Thomas v. Union of India, (2000) 6 SCC 224 (India) (rejecting the use of religious conversion to defeat existing matrimonial obligations), https://indiankanoon.org/doc/1762508/.

183. Hindu Marriage Act § 13(1)(iii); Special Marriage Act § 27(1)(e).

whether the spouse suffers from a diagnosable illness. In *Gupta v. Gupta*, the Supreme Court made clear that mental illness must be shown to be continuous, incurable, or of such severity that cohabitation has become unreasonable, rejecting divorce claims based on episodic or manageable conditions.[184]

Similarly, the Court has cautioned that odd behavior, emotional volatility, or marital incompatibility cannot be equated with statutory mental disorder. Courts routinely rely on medical records, longitudinal treatment history, and expert psychiatric testimony, while remaining wary of allegations founded solely on self-serving narratives or marital discord.

In cross-border marriages, this ground presents heightened evidentiary and ethical challenges. Parties may reside in jurisdictions with differing mental health classifications, documentation practices, or privacy regimes, complicating proof and comparability. Indian courts have therefore emphasized the need for rigorous scrutiny to prevent misuse of this ground, particularly where the accusing spouse enjoys a strategic advantage due to geography, access to medical records, or control over treatment narratives.

In *Sekhar v. Latha*, the Supreme Court underscored that mental disorder cannot be used as a weapon in matrimonial litigation and must be established by clear, cogent, and contemporaneous medical evidence demonstrating a real breakdown of marital life.[185] The jurisprudence reflects a careful balance between compassion for mental illness and protection against its tactical invocation, especially in international or transnational marital disputes.

J. Muslim Divorces in India: Doctrine, Constitutional Limits, and Contemporary Position

1. Sources of Muslim Divorce Law in India

Muslim personal law in India derives from classical Islamic sources—Qur'an, Sunnat, ijma, and qiyas—subject to statutory recognition and constitutional limitation. The Muslim Personal Law (Shariat) Application Act, 1937, provides that in questions relating to marriage, dissolution of marriage, maintenance, and related matters, "the rule of decision" shall be Muslim personal law (Shariat) where the parties are Muslim.[186]

Although largely uncodified, Muslim divorce doctrine has been elaborated through judicial decisions, culminating most significantly in *Bano v. Union of India*,[187] where a Constitution Bench undertook a comprehensive examination of the forms of talaq and their constitutional status.

184. Gupta v. Gupta, AIR 1988 SC 2260, ¶¶ 13–15 (India), https://indiankanoon.org/doc/1329391/.

185. Sekhar v. Latha, AIR 2014 SC (Supp) 626, ¶ 21 (India), https://indiankanoon.org/doc/97362677/.

186. The Muslim Personal Law (Shariat) Application Act, 1937, § 2 (India).

187. *Bano*, AIR 2017 SC 4609.

2. Forms of Talaq Under Sunni Law

Under classical Sunni doctrine, divorce at the instance of the husband exists in three principal forms: *talaq-e-ahsan, talaq-e-hasan, and talaq-e-biddat.*

a. Talaq-e-Ahsan

The Supreme Court in *Bano* described talaq-e-ahsan as *"the most proper"* form of divorce. It consists of a single pronouncement of talaq followed by a waiting period (*iddat*), during which reconciliation remains possible. If cohabitation resumes during iddat, the divorce is revoked; if not, it becomes final upon expiry of the waiting period.

The Qur'anic framework emphasizes restraint and reconciliation. Surah II, verse 229 provides: *"A divorce is only permissible twice: after that, the parties should either hold together on equitable terms, or separate with kindness."* This structure reflects a normative preference for deliberation and reconciliation over instantaneous dissolution.

b. Talaq-e-Hasan

Talaq-e-hasan involves three pronouncements spaced over successive periods of purity (*tuhr*). The first two pronouncements are revocable; the third renders the divorce irrevocable. As the Court explained: "The distinction between 'talaq-e-ahsan' and 'talaq-e-hasan' is, that in the former there is a single pronouncement . . . whereas, in the latter there are three pronouncements . . . interspersed with abstinence."[188]

Both *ahsan* and *hasan* embed cooling-off intervals consistent with the Qur'anic ethic of reconciliation.

3. Constitutional Invalidation of Talaq-e-Biddat (Instantaneous Triple Talaq)

Talaq-e-biddat consists of either (1) one irrevocable pronouncement, or (2) three pronouncements made simultaneously (*"talaq, talaq, talaq"*). It operates instantaneously and irrevocably, without scope for reconsideration. Even classical jurists characterized this form as irregular. The Supreme Court noted that talaq-e-biddat was regarded as *"bad in theology, but good in law."* It was recognized primarily within the Hanafi school and was not grounded in the Qur'anic procedural model.

In *Bano v. Union of India*, a Constitution Bench by majority invalidated talaq-e-biddat. Justice Nariman (joined by Justice Lalit) held it violative of Article 14 as manifestly arbitrary. Justice Kurian Joseph held it invalid because it was contrary to the Qur'an and therefore not protected as an essential religious practice. Former Chief Justice of India Justice Kehar (joined by Justice Nazeer) dissented.

The operative result was clear: *instantaneous triple talaq ceased to have legal effect* as of August 22, 2017.

188. *Id.* ¶ 14 of the minority opinion penned by former Chief Justice of India Kehar.

4. Legislative Response: The 2019 Act

Parliament subsequently enacted the Muslim Women (Protection of Rights on Marriage) Act, 2019.[189] Section 3 declares that any pronouncement of talaq "*having the effect of instantaneous and irrevocable divorce*" is void and illegal. Section 4 criminalizes such pronouncement, prescribing imprisonment up to three years. The statute thus moved beyond civil invalidation to criminal sanction.

5. Retroactivity

Neither *Bano* nor the 2019 act expressly provides for retrospective invalidation of talaq-e-biddat pronounced prior to the judgment. Under settled constitutional doctrine, statutes and judicial invalidations are presumed prospective unless clearly stated otherwise. Accordingly, talaq-e-biddat divorces finalized prior to August 22, 2017, have generally been treated as legally effective when pronounced, absent independent grounds of challenge.

6. Nikah Halala

Where a divorce becomes irrevocable, Indian Muslim law prohibits remarriage between the same parties unless the wife marries another man and that marriage is consummated and dissolved.[190] This is known as *nikah halala*.

In *Ahmad v. Khatun*, the Privy Council enforced this doctrine strictly, holding that remarriage without fulfillment of the halala requirement was invalid and children born thereafter illegitimate under prevailing law.[191] The Supreme Court in *Bano* reiterated the doctrinal position that after an irrevocable third talaq, "the husband and wife cannot remarry, unless the wife first marries someone else, and only after her marriage with another person has been dissolved . . . can the couple remarry."

Nikah halala remains one of the most controversial aspects of classical Muslim divorce doctrine because it conditions remarriage between the same spouses, after an irrevocable divorce, upon the wife first marrying another man, the marriage being consummated, and thereafter dissolved by divorce or death. The rule derives from Qur'an 2:230, which provides that if a husband divorces his wife (after the prescribed number of pronouncements), "*he cannot, after that, re-marry her until after she has married another husband and he has divorced her.*"[192]

Historically, Indian courts enforced this bar strictly. In *Ahmad v. Khatun*, the Privy Council held that where an irrevocable talaq had taken place, remarriage between the same parties was invalid absent proof of an intervening marriage and its dissolution, and children born thereafter were treated as illegitimate under the prevailing doctrine.[193]

---

189. Muslim Women (Protection of Rights on Marriage) Act, 2019 (India), https://indiankanoon.org/doc/159392747/.

190. *Bano*, AIR 2017 SC 4609.

191. Ahmad v. Khatun, (1932) 59 IA 21 (PC) (India), https://indiankanoon.org/doc/655532/.

192. Qur'an 2:230 (as reproduced and discussed in *Bano v. Union of India*, AIR 2017 SC 4609, ¶ 7 of the majority opinion penned by Justice Kurian Joseph).

193. *Khatun*, (1932) 59 IA 21 (PC).

Halala has been criticized as facilitating coercive or transactional marriages undertaken solely to enable remarriage to the former husband, raising serious concerns under Articles 14, 15, and 21 of the Constitution. The constitutional validity of nikah halala is presently under consideration before the Supreme Court in public interest litigation, including *Begum v. Union of India*, which has been tagged with *Upadhyay v. Union of India*.[194] The matter remains pending, leaving unresolved whether the halala requirement can withstand contemporary constitutional scrutiny grounded in dignity, equality, and substantive due process.

7. Present Legal Position

The current position under Indian law may be summarized as follows:

1. Talaq-e-ahsan and talaq-e-hasan remain valid modes of divorce.
2. Talaq-e-biddat is void and illegal if pronounced after August 22, 2017.
3. The 2019 act criminalizes such pronouncement.
4. Retroactive invalidation of pre-2017 divorces is unlikely absent express legislative intent.
5. The halala doctrine continues to operate in cases of valid irrevocable divorce, subject to pending constitutional challenge.

K. Procedural Trajectory of a Contested Divorce Case

A contested divorce in India follows a broadly structured procedural sequence, though timelines and intensity vary significantly across jurisdictions and fact patterns. Proceedings commence with the filing of a detailed matrimonial petition setting out the statutory ground(s) for divorce and the supporting factual narrative, after which the family court issues summons to the respondent. Service may be effected through personal delivery, registered post, electronic means, or, where the respondent resides abroad, through consular channels or Hague Service Convention mechanisms, issues that assume particular significance in cross-border cases.[195] In practice, Indian family courts routinely dispense with strict service requirements where the respondent has actual notice or where insistence on formal service would defeat access to justice, particularly in cross-border matters.

Once the service is deemed complete, the respondent then files a written statement, contesting or contextualizing the allegations and, not infrequently, asserting counterclaims or alternative grounds for divorce. The litigation often expands

194. Begum v. Union of India, Writ Petition (C) No. 222 of 2018 (tagged with Upadhyay v. Union of India, Writ Petition (C) No. 699 of 2016) (pending before the Supreme Court of India).

195. Family Courts Act § 7; CPC Order V; Hague Convention on the Service Abroad of Judicial and Extrajudicial Documents in Civil or Commercial Matters, Nov. 15, 1965 (India), https://jusmundi.com/en/document/treaty/en-convention-on-the-service-abroad-of-judicial-and-extra judicial-documents-in-civil-or-commercial-matters-hague-convention-on-the-service-abroad-of-judicial-and-extrajudicial-documents-in-civil-or-commercial-matters-1965-monday-15th-november-1965.

substantially at the interim stage, where parties seek temporary relief relating to maintenance, custody, visitation, residence, travel restraints, or injunctions.[196]

In addition, parties frequently resort to an array of criminal complaints in parallel with the matrimonial proceedings. These commonly include allegations of cruelty and dowry harassment, criminal breach of trust in relation to stridhan, domestic violence proceedings seeking residence and protection orders, and, in some cases, accusations relating to cheating, intimidation, or misappropriation of property. Such criminal proceedings often run concurrently with divorce, custody, and maintenance actions before the family court, creating overlapping forums and strategic leverage. Indian courts have repeatedly acknowledged both the prevalence of this parallel litigation and the risk of its misuse, while also emphasizing that genuine criminal conduct arising from the marital relationship cannot be immunized merely because civil matrimonial remedies are pending.[197]

These interim proceedings frequently shape both the tempo and leverage dynamics of the case and can dominate the litigation for extended periods, especially in emotionally charged or international disputes. The matter then proceeds to the evidence stage, which typically involves affidavits-in-evidence, live cross-examination, and extensive documentary proof. Indian courts increasingly engage with digital evidence, such as WhatsApp messages, emails, call records, location data, and social media content, subject to compliance with statutory admissibility requirements for electronic records.[198] Where personal appearance is impractical, particularly for foreign-resident parties or witnesses, family courts routinely permit testimony via videoconferencing in furtherance of access to justice.

Throughout the proceedings, family courts remain statutorily obliged to make genuine efforts at conciliation and settlement, and judges may refer parties to mediation at multiple stages, even after evidence has commenced.[199] While this settlement-centric approach reflects the welfare-oriented philosophy of family law, it may also prolong proceedings where allegations are serious or reconciliation is objectively implausible. Ultimately, upon completion of evidence, the court hears final arguments, assesses credibility, applies the statutory grounds to the proved facts, and delivers a reasoned judgment either granting or refusing divorce. The resulting decree is appealable to the jurisdictional high court, with appellate review often focusing on factual appreciation, procedural fairness, and the correct application of matrimonial standards, issues discussed later in the chapter on appellate and transnational remedies (Section 2.2.8. Appeals).

---

196. Hindu Marriage Act §§ 24–26; Special Marriage Act §§ 36–38.

197. Bharatiya Nyaya Sanhita § 86 (replacing Indian Penal Code § 498A) (cruelty by husband or relatives); Bharatiya Nyaya Sanhita §§ 316–318 (criminal breach of trust, commonly invoked in stridhan disputes); Protection of Women from Domestic Violence Act §§ 12, 17–23.

198. Indian Evidence Act § 65B (now replaced by the Bharatiya Sakshya Adhiniyam, 2023 (India), https://indiankanoon.org/doc/70224818/).

199. Family Courts Act § 9.

L. Process of Mutual Consent Divorce

A mutual consent divorce proceeds significantly faster than contested litigation. The spouses jointly file a petition confirming that they have lived separately for the statutory period of at least one year under the Hindu Marriage Act, 1955, and the Special Marriage Act, 1954, and that their decision to dissolve the marriage is free, voluntary, and informed.[200] The court records their statements and verifies identity, consent, and jurisdiction.

Historically, a mandatory six-month "cooling-off" period separated the first and second motions, but the Supreme Court has clarified that this period is directory, not mandatory, and may be waived where the marriage has irretrievably broken down, all issues are settled, and prolonging the process would cause undue hardship.[201]

Courts now routinely grant waivers, a flexibility that is particularly valuable for NRI spouses who face travel constraints or immigration consequences from prolonged proceedings. During the second motion, the parties reaffirm their consent and seek a final decree; once the court is satisfied that consent continues and is genuine, divorce is granted immediately. Mutual consent divorces involving foreign-resident parties increasingly rely on remote appearances or sworn affidavits, though courts insist on strict procedural safeguards to guard against coercion or fraud.

M. Timelines and Delays

Despite statutory objectives favoring expeditious resolution, contested divorce proceedings in India frequently extend over several years. Chronic judicial backlogs, repeated interlocutory applications, mandatory or recurrent mediation referrals, difficulties in effecting service on foreign-resident parties, witness unavailability, and the parallel pursuit of criminal proceedings all contribute to protracted timelines. The Supreme Court has repeatedly taken judicial notice of matrimonial litigation dragging on for a decade or more, often accompanied by multiple rounds of proceedings before family courts, high courts, and the Supreme Court itself.

In *Kohli*, for instance, the parties had been embroiled in litigation for more than ten years, prompting the Court to remark that the marriage had become "virtually dead" and that continuation of the legal relationship served no purpose.[202] Similarly, in *Ghosh*, the Court acknowledged that prolonged separation and years of acrimonious litigation were themselves relevant to assessing the breakdown of the marital relationship.[203] In *Sitole*, the Court dissolved a marriage after noting that the parties had lived apart for more than 14 years, during which time multiple legal proceedings had failed to restore any semblance of marital life.[204]

200. Hindu Marriage Act § 13B(1); Special Marriage Act § 28(1).
201. *Singh*, AIR 2017 SC 4417.
202. *Kohli*, AIR 2006 SC 1675, ¶¶ 74–76.
203. *Ghosh*, AIR Online 2007 SC 347, ¶ 98.
204. *Sitole*, AIR 2008 SC 3093.

By contrast, mutual consent divorces can conclude within a matter of months, particularly where courts waive the statutory cooling-off period and ancillary issues are fully resolved. The growing judicial willingness to prioritize finality over formalism reflects an increasing recognition that delay itself can become a source of injustice in matrimonial disputes, especially for parties navigating immigration constraints or cross-border legal exposure.

2.3.2. Recognition of Foreign Divorce Decrees

Recognition of foreign divorce decrees turns on section 13 of the CPC, 1908.[205] India recognizes only those foreign judgments rendered by courts of competent jurisdiction, decided on the merits, consistent with Indian notions of natural justice, free of fraud, and not contrary to Indian law or public policy.[206] India does not recognize quick, or ex parte, foreign divorces when the parties are governed by a personal law that requires proof of fault or statutory grounds.[207] Recognition of foreign decrees is one of the most complex areas of U.S.–India family law and often determines whether parallel litigation in India is necessary.

A. Ex Parte Divorce Proceedings in India

When a respondent does not appear despite valid service, family courts may proceed ex parte.[208] The petitioner must still prove the statutory ground for divorce; dissolution is never automatic.[209] Ex parte decrees may be appealed or set aside if the respondent demonstrates lack of service, procedural irregularity, or sufficient cause for absence. These proceedings are common in cross-border marriages where one spouse refuses to participate or resides abroad; however, courts maintain strict procedural scrutiny in such cases.

B. Withdrawal, Reconciliation Attempts, and the Court's Conciliatory Mandate

Indian divorce proceedings unfold within a statutory framework that obligates courts to pursue reconciliation whenever it appears plausible.[210] Judges frequently halt hearings to send parties to conciliation or mediation, relying on counselors to explore whether the marital relationship can be salvaged. Although sincere efforts sometimes lead to resolution, the mandatory conciliatory approach can also prolong litigation in cases where one spouse has no genuine interest in reconciliation or where serious allegations make settlement unlikely. Courts must navigate the tension between statutory duties and practical realities, ensuring that conciliation does not become coercive or enable tactical delays.

205. CPC § 13.

206. *Id.*; *Y. Narasimha Rao*, AIR Online 1991 SC 10; *Satya*, AIR 1975 SC 105.

207. *Y. Narasimha Rao*, AIR Online 1991 SC 10; Saraph v. Saraph, AIR Online 1994 SC 381 (India), https://indiankanoon.org/doc/577389/.

208. Family Courts Act § 10; CPC Order IX, Rule 6(1)(a).

209. *Y. Narasimha Rao*, AIR Online 1991 SC 10 (recognition turns on merits/natural justice requirements); CPC § 13.

210. Family Courts Act § 9; Hindu Marriage Act § 23(2); Special Marriage Act § 34(2).

A party may withdraw a contested divorce petition at any stage, sometimes to pursue a more favorable jurisdiction, sometimes as part of settlement negotiations.[211] Withdrawal terminates the pending action without resolving the underlying matrimonial dispute. Courts typically permit withdrawal so long as it is not used to manipulate venue or "*prejudice the Defendant's*" substantive rights.[212] Where proceedings are withdrawn after significant evidence has been recorded, courts may impose conditions or clarify that withdrawal does not affect interim orders still in force.[213]

C. Procedural Integrity, Natural Justice, and Fairness Standards

Indian courts insist that matrimonial proceedings adhere to foundational principles of natural justice. Even though family courts enjoy procedural flexibility and are not strictly bound by the CPC or the Evidence Act, deviations cannot prejudice substantive fairness. Judges must provide each party a meaningful opportunity to present evidence, challenge adverse material, and participate fully in hearings. Ex parte proceedings are permitted only after valid service and with careful scrutiny of the petitioner's evidence. Procedural shortcuts that infringe upon fairness may render a judgment vulnerable on appeal.

Cross-border cases heighten concerns about natural justice, particularly when a foreign-resident spouse cannot appear easily in India. Courts increasingly accommodate such litigants by allowing remote testimony, accepting notarized affidavits, and granting adjournments to ensure due opportunity.[214] Nonetheless, when a party resists participation altogether, courts proceed cautiously, balancing fairness with the need for resolution.

D. Perjury, Fabrication, and Misuse of Process

Matrimonial litigation in India often involves sharply contested narratives. Allegations of cruelty, adultery, mental disorder, or abandonment may lead parties to inflate or, in some cases, even fabricate evidence. Courts remain alert to perjury, suppression of material facts, and strategic misuse of criminal complaints or protective statutes to gain leverage in the divorce process.[215] Although perjury prosecutions are rare, judges frequently comment on dishonest conduct and may draw adverse inferences, dismiss petitions, or deny discretionary relief when a party's conduct undermines the integrity of the proceedings.

Misuse of process also arises when litigants file multiple actions across jurisdictions to harass the opposing spouse or to create conflicting orders. High

---

211. CPC Order XXIII, Rule 1.

212. Bhoopathy v. Kokila, AIR 2000 SC 2132 (India) (discussing discretion/limits on withdrawal to prevent abuse under Order XXIII), https://indiankanoon.org/doc/823721/.

213. CPC Order XXIII, Rule 1.

214. State of Maharashtra v. Desai, AIR 2003 SC 2053, ¶ 25 (India) (recognizing/approving evidence by videoconferencing), https://indiankanoon.org/doc/560467/.

215. Indian Penal Code, 1860, §§ 191–193, 196–200 (India) (false evidence and related offenses), https://indiankanoon.org/doc/1569253/, recently reenacted as Bharatiya Nyaya Sanhita §§ 227–229, 232–236; CrPC § 340 (procedure for perjury-related complaints), recently reenacted as BNSS § 379.

courts retain broad supervisory powers to curb such abuse, consolidate overlapping cases, or quash proceedings that serve no legitimate purpose.[216]

E. Parallel Civil and Criminal Proceedings

A distinctive aspect of Indian matrimonial litigation is the interplay between civil divorce proceedings and related criminal or quasi-criminal actions. It is common for one spouse, often the wife, to initiate complaints under the Protection of Women from Domestic Violence Act, 2005, or under Indian Penal Code provisions relating to cruelty.[217] These proceedings may influence the divorce case, shape interim relief, or affect the credibility of witnesses. The pendency of criminal charges can also slow divorce litigation because courts must coordinate witness testimony and avoid inconsistent factual determinations.

Although civil and criminal cases proceed independently, judges often consider their cumulative effect. A criminal acquittal does not preclude findings of cruelty in a civil divorce, and findings of civil cruelty do not guarantee criminal conviction and that "criminal matters should be given precedence" over civil matters.[218] Nevertheless, parallel litigation complicates strategy for both sides and frequently extends the overall timeline.

F. International Dimensions of Indian Divorce Procedure

Indian divorce law intersects with international family law in complex ways, especially for couples living between India and the United States. Jurisdiction is flexible, enabling courts in India to entertain divorce petitions even when the couple last cohabited abroad or when the respondent resides overseas.[219] The petitioner's residence within India is often sufficient territorial nexus. This doctrine allows Indian litigation to proceed concurrently with foreign proceedings, creating significant strategic considerations.

Foreign spouses often encounter obstacles in participating fully in Indian proceedings due to geographical distance, visa constraints, and financial burdens. Courts increasingly rely on videoconferencing and affidavits to mitigate these challenges, but participation still requires careful planning. The recognition of foreign divorce decrees remains fraught; many U.S. no-fault decrees are unenforceable in India if they do not reflect grounds recognized under Indian law. Consequently, cross-border couples frequently find themselves in parallel litigation in both countries, each proceeding operating under distinct standards of jurisdiction, evidence, and public policy. This issue is discussed in detail in Chapter 3 (Section 3.2. Parallel Divorce and Child Custody Jurisdiction in India).

---

216. India Const. art. 227; CrPC § 482 (inherent powers of high court), recently reenacted as BNSS § 528.

217. Protection of Women from Domestic Violence Act; Indian Penal Code § 498A (cruelty by husband or relatives), now reenacted as Bharatiya Nyaya Sanhita §§ 85–86.

218. Sheriff v. State of Madras, AIR 1954 SC 397 (India) (also reflecting the general principle that civil and criminal proceedings operate independently and may proceed on different standards), https://indiankanoon.org/doc/500548/.

219. *See, e.g.*, Hindu Marriage Act § 19(iv) (jurisdiction/venue provisions); Special Marriage Act § 31(1).

G. International Service of Process

International service of process adds another layer of complexity. Where the Hague Service Convention applies, service must follow treaty procedures; where it does not, courts may rely on consular channels, registered courier to foreign addresses, or substituted service.[220] Challenges to service often become a tactical tool, particularly when a foreign-resident spouse seeks to delay or invalidate proceedings.[221] This issue is discussed in detail in Chapter 3 (Section 3.3. International Service of Process Under the Hague Service Convention).

H. Final Judgments and Decrees in Matrimonial Cases

A final judgment in a divorce case must articulate the facts, evaluate the evidence, interpret the statutory ground relied upon, and explain why dissolution is warranted.[222] Judges must address credibility issues, reconcile contradictory testimony, and ensure that findings comply with substantive personal law.[223] The decree that follows is the operative instrument dissolving the marriage; it must conform precisely to statutory requirements to avoid appellate complications.

The reasoning must be sufficiently detailed to enable meaningful appellate review.[224] Courts must also ensure that the decree does not inadvertently interfere with matters outside the scope of the current section, such as financial relief or custody, which require separate adjudication.[225]

2.3.3. Appeals and Post-Decree Challenges

In India, the appellate process for matrimonial decrees is governed by section 19 of the Family Courts Act, 1984, which provides for a first appeal to the high court. Unlike a second appeal under section 100 of the CPC, which is strictly "circumscribed by a substantial question of law," a first appeal allows the high court to act as a court of both fact and law, enabling a full re-evaluation of the evidence and the trial court's findings.

In this regard, the Supreme Court has observed:

> First appeal is a valuable right of the parties and unless restricted by law, the whole case is therein open for rehearing both on questions of fact and law. The judgment of the appellate Court must, therefore, reflect its conscious application of mind, and record findings supported by reasons, on all the issues arising along with the contentions put forth, and pressed by the parties for decision of the appellate Court.[226]

---

220. Convention on the Service Abroad of Judicial and Extrajudicial Documents in Civil or Commercial Matters art. 1, Nov. 15, 1965, 20 U.S.T. 361, 658 U.N.T.S. 163; CPC Order V, Rules 20, 25–26 (India) (substituted service; service where defendant resides outside India).

221. CPC Order V.

222. *Id.* Order XX, Rule 4.

223. Hindu Marriage Act § 23.

224. CPC Order XX, Rule 4.

225. Hindu Marriage Act §§ 24–26 (distinct relief relating to maintenance/expenses and children); CPC Order XX.

226. Hazari v. Tiwari, AIR 2001 SC 965, at 6 (India), https://indiankanoon.org/doc/1396621/.

In Indian practice, matrimonial litigants frequently exercise their right to a first appeal before the high court to seek a full de novo review of both facts and law, a process that contrasts sharply with the more restrictive appellate standards in New York or the United States, where appellate courts generally defer to the trial court's factual findings and focus primarily on identifying reversible legal errors or abuses of discretion.

As mentioned before, significant procedural complexity in cross-border cases is the conflict in limitation periods. While section 19(3) of the Family Courts Act prescribes a strict 30-day window for filing an appeal, section 28(4) of the Hindu Marriage Act, 1955 (and the Special Marriage Act), allows for a 90-day period. Although some high courts, such as the Bombay High Court and Rajasthan High Court, have held that the longer 90-day period should prevail to prevent frustrating a party's right to appeal, the Supreme Court has affirmed that the 30-day limit under the Family Courts Act is the operative rule.[227] In districts or jurisdictions where a family court has not been officially established, the 90-day limitation period under section 28(4) of the Hindu Marriage Act, 1955 (or section 39 of the Special Marriage Act, 1954), remains the operative rule for filing an appeal, as the shorter 30-day limit is specific to the procedural regime of the Family Courts Act, 1984.

Post-decree challenges also arise under provisions permitting the setting aside of ex parte decrees, review of judgments, or correction of clerical or arithmetical errors.[228] Courts exercise these powers sparingly, balancing the need for finality with the demands of fairness and natural justice.

The practical effects of divorce decrees extend beyond formal dissolution. Parties must update official records, immigration documents, and civil-status registrations. Foreign-resident spouses may need certified, apostilled, or otherwise authenticated decrees to effect changes in the United States. Because India lacks a centralized family law registry, verification often requires certified copies from the relevant family court. When parties remarry, courts or administrative authorities may require proof that the prior dissolution was legally valid, particularly where foreign or mutually inconsistent decrees exist.[229]

2.4. Financial Issues Arising from Divorce

Financial issues in Indian matrimonial law arise at the intersection of statutory personal law regimes, constitutional norms, and judicially developed equitable principles. Unlike the United States, where equitable distribution or community property statutes govern the division of marital assets, Indian family law is neither uniform nor codified in a consolidated framework. Instead, property division, spousal maintenance, and child support emerge from multiple statutes—the Hindu Marriage Act, the Special Marriage Act, the Indian Divorce

227. Singh v. Elton, Special Leave Petition (C) No. 10751 of 2021, ¶¶ 16–18 (India), https://api.sci.gov.in/supremecourt/2021/10410/10410_2021_39_10_28717_Judgement_23-Jul-2021.pdf.

228. CPC Order IX, Rule 13, Order XLVII, Rule 1, § 152.

229. *Y. Narasimha Rao*, AIR Online 1991 SC 10; *Saraph*, AIR Online 1994 SC 381.

Act, the Parsi Marriage and Divorce Act, the Guardians and Wards Act, and the CrPC—each interacting with judge-made law.

For U.S. practitioners advising clients in cross-border divorce disputes, it is essential to understand that India lacks the concept of "marital property" as defined in American law. Most assets legally titled in one spouse's name are treated as that spouse's separate property unless specific statutory grounds permit redistribution or monetary compensation. Financial relief therefore often occurs not through property division but through permanent alimony, lump-sum settlements, maintenance orders, and child support determinations, each governed by its own statutory and judicial standards.

Indian courts approach financial issues through a combination of statutory interpretation and equitable discretion. The Supreme Court has repeatedly emphasized that financial relief must be guided by principles of fairness, dignity, and the constitutional guarantees of equality and nondiscrimination, and that judicial delays should not be the norm.

In *Singh v. Meena*, the Court held that "delay in adjudication [of a spouse's maintenance rights] by the Family Court is not only against human rights but also against the basic embodiment of dignity of an individual."[230] Similarly, in *Rajnesh*, the Supreme Court established uniform guidelines for maintenance and financial disclosure, recognizing the need for consistency and transparency in a system previously characterized by fragmented approaches across states.[231] These precedents provide a foundation for courts to award monetary relief even in the absence of statutory authority to redistribute property. The court emphasized that maintenance is a tool for social justice and should ensure a dignified life rather than just a survival-level existence.[232]

In another matter the Supreme Court established that 25 percent of the net salary of the husband is generally considered a "just and proper" amount for alimony.[233] Very recently, in a broad sweep, the Supreme Court nearly tripled permanent alimony and introduced an automatic 5 percent biennial increase to account for inflation.[234]

Notwithstanding these important advances, structural limitations remain. Discovery and financial disclosure obligations in Indian matrimonial proceedings, while improved through judicial guidelines, are still far less rigorous than those mandated in jurisdictions such as New York, where sworn net-worth statements, compulsory document exchange, and meaningful sanctions for noncompliance are integral to the process. Indian law also continues to lack a comprehensive matrimonial-asset division regime; courts do not engage in equitable distribution of marital property as a matter of course, and financial outcomes depend heavily on discretionary maintenance and alimony awards

230. *Singh*, AIR 2014 SC 2875, at 2.

231. *Rajnesh*, AIR 2021 SC 569.

232. *Id.*

233. Chowdhury v. Chowdhury, AIR 2017 SC 2383, ¶ 16 (India), https://indiankanoon.org/doc/87785076/; Kumar v. Kumari, 1971 AIR 234 (India), https://indiankanoon.org/doc/1670667/.

234. Sadhukhan v. Sadhukhan, 2025 INSC 789 (India), https://www.casemine.com/judgement/in/68385ba795341e6a5135fefb.

rather than systematic asset allocation. As a result, even with progressive judicial interventions, Indian matrimonial finance law has not yet reached parity with the structured, disclosure-driven frameworks of New York and similar U.S. jurisdictions.

Unlike most U.S. states, India does not employ statutory child support or spousal support calculators, guidelines, or presumptive formulas to determine maintenance amounts. Indian courts exercise broad judicial discretion, assessing support on a case-by-case basis based on factors such as income, standard of living, needs of the claimant, and the paying spouse's capacity, without the aid of numerical benchmarks or income-shares models. While this flexibility allows courts to tailor relief to individual circumstances, it also results in wide variability, unpredictability, and forum-specific outcomes, particularly in cases involving comparable financial profiles. The absence of formula-based guidance stands in marked contrast to U.S. jurisdictions, where legislatively prescribed calculators promote consistency, transparency, and enforceability in both child support and spousal maintenance determinations.

This section presents an in-depth analysis of the three principal financial issues arising from divorce: the division of assets, spousal support, and child support. It draws from statutory provisions, leading Supreme Court and high court judgments, and comparative considerations relevant for foreign practitioners handling U.S.–India matrimonial disputes.

2.4.1. Governing Law: Financial Rights and Obligations of Divorcing Spouses

A. Absence of a Codified Marital-Property Regime

India does not follow the American concept of equitable distribution or community property. With narrow exceptions, property legally titled in one spouse's name remains that spouse's exclusive property after divorce. This principle is rooted in traditional personal laws and judicial interpretation.

While the Supreme Court of India has not explicitly issued a single ruling addressing the overarching absence of a "matrimonial property regime" in a consolidated manner, its consistent jurisprudence reinforces a separate property system by default. In several cases, the Court implicitly confirms this by clarifying that a wife's claim to the matrimonial home is a "right of residence" rooted in maintenance law, rather than a vested proprietary interest in the asset itself.[235] This position is further solidified by the Court's narrow interpretation of section 27 of the Hindu Marriage Act, which is seen not as a tool for equitable distribution of all marital assets, but as a specific provision limited to property jointly presented at the time of marriage.[236]

Because of this structure, financial relief in India often occurs through maintenance and permanent alimony rather than division of assets. Courts may infer beneficial ownership or constructive interests in property when evidence shows

235. Anand v. Reddy, AIR 2005 SC 986 (India), https://indiankanoon.org/doc/11266/.
236. Hindu Marriage Act § 27.

contribution by the non-titled spouse. The Supreme Court has acknowledged that courts may consider the economic imbalance created by one spouse holding all assets when awarding lump-sum alimony.[237]

For U.S. counsel, this means that a spouse returning to India after residing abroad cannot assume that marital assets accumulated internationally will be divided in India. Instead, the spouse must seek compensation through maintenance or a lump-sum award calibrated to their financial needs and the other spouse's ability to pay.

B. Hindu Law

The Hindu Marriage Act does not contain any provision authorizing courts to divide property on divorce. Relief must therefore come from section 25, which empowers courts to award permanent alimony, including lump-sum payments that may indirectly achieve a redistributive effect.[238] Courts may calibrate the lump-sum amount by considering the total value of marital assets, though without expressly awarding any percentage of property.

Additionally, Hindu wives may assert independent rights to stridhan (property of a Hindu female) recognized as their absolute property under section 14 of the Hindu Succession Act.[239] In *Rani v. Kumar*, the Supreme Court held that a husband has no ownership interest in his wife's stridhan and may be liable for "criminal breach of trust" for its misappropriation.[240] Such property, therefore, may play a critical role in financial recovery in divorce proceedings, particularly where the wife contributed substantial gifts, jewelry, or funds at marriage.

C. Special Marriage Act

The Special Marriage Act contains provisions for alimony but, like the Hindu Marriage Act, does not permit division of property. Section 27 allows suits regarding matrimonial property arising from the marriage,[241] but courts interpret this narrowly. In 2011, Madras High Court held that section 27 applies only to jointly owned property, not to unilateral claims to assets titled in one spouse's name. Thus, Special Marriage Act cases typically rely on alimony or negotiated settlements to resolve property claims.

D. Christian and Parsi Laws

Christian and Parsi marital statutes also lack redistribution mechanisms. The Indian Divorce Act authorizes permanent alimony under sections 36 and 37, and the Parsi Marriage and Divorce Act provides for alimony under sections 40

237. *Rao*, AIR 2013 SC 2176; Ahuja v. Ahuja, Civil Appeal No. 2483 of 2020 (India) (the Court was careful to distinguish the statutory protection of a "shared household" from any title or ownership rights, thereby maintaining the principle that property ownership remains tethered to individual title deeds rather than the marital union), https://taxguru.in/wp-content/uploads/2020/10/Satish-Chander-Ahuja-Vs-Sneha-Ahuja-Supreme-Court-of-India.pdf.

238. Hindu Marriage Act § 27.

239. Hindu Succession Act § 14 (property of a female Hindu to be her absolute property).

240. Rani v. Kumar, AIR 1985 SC 628 (India), https://indiankanoon.org/doc/1684706/.

241. Special Marriage Act § 27.

and 41. In both regimes, alimony is the primary vehicle through which courts address financial imbalance.

E. Muslim Personal Law and Property Claims

Muslim law does not provide for division of property upon divorce. Financial relief is structured through mahr (dower),[242] maintenance during the iddat period, and remedies under the Muslim Women (Protection of Rights on Divorce) Act, 1986.

Allahabad High Court defines "dower" as:

> A sum of money or other property promised by the husband to be paid or delivered to the wife in consideration of the marriage, and even where no dower is expressly fixed or mentioned at the marriage ceremony, the law confers the right of dower upon the wife as a necessary effect of marriage.[243]

Mahr functions as an enforceable contractual obligation, as affirmed in *Bano*,[244] and may provide significant financial compensation. In addition to mahr, courts may also order maintenance under secular laws, such as CrPC section 125, notwithstanding the 1986 act.[245]

In simple terms, iddat is a mandatory waiting period that a Muslim woman must observe after her marriage ends (either by divorce or the death of her husband) before she is legally allowed to marry someone else.[246]

In *Samad*, the Supreme Court reaffirmed that divorced Muslim women have a unilateral right to seek maintenance under the secular section 125 of the CrPC (now section 144 of the BNSS), which extends support beyond the traditional iddat period until they remarry. The Court clarified that the Muslim Women (Protection of Rights on Divorce) Act, 1986, serves as an additional remedy rather than a replacement for secular law, ensuring that religious personal laws do not undermine a woman's constitutional right to financial security and dignity. By treating maintenance as a matter of gender justice rather than charity, the Court ruled that this religion-neutral protection applies universally to all women, preventing destitution regardless of their faith.

F. Constructive Trusts and Judicial Innovation

Although Indian courts cannot divide property as in American law, they increasingly use equitable doctrines to prevent unjust enrichment. The Supreme Court has encouraged flexible interpretation of evidence to recognize women's contributions in traditionally male-dominated asset structures.[247]

---

242. Also spelled *mehr*.

243. Kadir v. Salima, (1886) ILR 8 All 149, ¶ 12 (India), https://indiankanoon.org/doc/119342/.

244. *Bano*, AIR 2017 SC 4609, ¶ 13 of the minority opinion penned by former Chief Justice of India Kehar.

245. Latifi v. Union of India, AIR 2001 SC 3958 (India), https://indiankanoon.org/doc/410660/; Samad v. State of Telangana, 2024 INSC 506 (India), https://indiankanoon.org/doc/7964121/.

246. Muslim Women (Protection of Rights on Divorce) Act § 2(b).

247. Devi v. Narayanan, AIR 1988 SC 1381 (India), https://indiankanoon.org/doc/70092/.

High courts have recognized beneficial interests in property where the non-titled spouse demonstrably contributed money or labor. Recently, the Madras High Court held that a wife is entitled to an equal share in assets purchased in the husband's name if they were acquired through joint contribution. Significantly, the court formally recognized the indirect contribution of a homemaker, stating that her 24-hour domestic labor facilitates the husband's ability to earn and save.[248] Such reasoning has been extended in several matrimonial cases, allowing courts to treat contributions toward mortgage payments, renovations, or business assets as grounds for compensatory relief through lump-sum awards, even if not characterized formally as ownership.

Despite these progressive judicial strides, the Indian framework remains fundamentally different from American community property or equitable distribution laws. In the United States, marital property is often legally defined as a shared pool, granting each spouse a vested right to roughly half of the assets acquired during the marriage.

G. Domestic Violence Proceedings and Property Relief

The Protection of Women from Domestic Violence Act, 2005, is a civil rights-protective statute intended to provide immediate remedial relief to women facing physical, emotional, sexual, or economic abuse within domestic relationships.[249] Importantly, a finding under the Protection of Women from Domestic Violence Act, 2005, does not enhance a woman's proprietary entitlements or result in redistribution of marital assets; relief under the act is protective and compensatory, not distributive.

The act's principal interface with marital property lies in its protection of residence and possession rather than ownership. Section 17 confers a statutory right to reside in the "shared household," irrespective of title, while section 19 authorizes residence orders restraining dispossession, regulating use, or directing alternate accommodation or rent in lieu thereof.[250] These remedies are designed to prevent economic abuse and homelessness during marital breakdown, not to alter property ownership or create matrimonial asset division.[251]

Monetary relief under the act similarly operates within defined limits. Orders under section 20 address loss of earnings, deprivation of financial resources, and maintenance arising from domestic violence, but they do not function as a proxy for equitable distribution or fault-based enhancement of financial claims. Domestic violence proceedings may therefore materially affect housing stability and short-term financial security, yet they do not recalibrate

---

248. Naidu v. Ammal, S.A. No. 59 of 2016, ¶¶ 45–46 (India), https://indiankanoon.org/doc/36080575/.

249. Protection of Women from Domestic Violence Act.

250. *Id.* §§ 17, 19.

251. Ahuja v. Ahuja, AIR Online 2020 SC 784 (India), https://indiankanoon.org/doc/62368827/.

proprietary rights or place Indian matrimonial law within a distributive framework comparable to that of New York or other U.S. jurisdictions.[252]

H. Cross-Border Property Issues

In international marriages, property may be located in multiple jurisdictions. Indian courts generally decline to adjudicate title to foreign immovable property but may consider the total financial context when awarding alimony. In *Rao v. Lakshmi* (*Y. Narasimha Rao*), the leading case on foreign divorce judgments, the Supreme Court emphasized that financial rights cannot be undermined by a foreign decree obtained without compliance with Indian public policy.[253]

For U.S. lawyers, this means that clients with assets abroad must prepare for the possibility that Indian courts will treat foreign holdings as part of the paying spouse's overall financial capacity even if Indian courts cannot seize or divide those assets.

2.4.2. Spousal Support (Maintenance)

Some of the definitions of the relevant terms in this section are discussed in Section 2.2.4.B of this chapter.

Spousal support in India arises from a network of overlapping statutes rather than from a unified family code. Although each personal law framework contains its own provisions governing interim and permanent maintenance, the underlying purpose, ensuring financial security for a dependent spouse, has been interpreted expansively by courts. Unlike in the United States, where long-term spousal support is often discretionary and may be limited by prenuptial agreements, Indian courts treat the duty of maintenance as a continuing moral and legal obligation that persists until the financially weaker spouse achieves reasonable economic stability. In *Singh*,[254] the Supreme Court declared that the objective of maintenance is to prevent a spouse from living in "destitution" or "vagrancy," emphasizing that financial support is not a gesture of charity but a "sacrosanct duty" rooted in statutory and constitutional protections.

A. Interim Spousal Support and Expenses of Proceedings

Interim maintenance plays a critical role in Indian matrimonial litigation, where cases often remain pending for several years. Each major marital statute authorizes temporary financial support while proceedings continue. Section 24 of the Hindu Marriage Act, section 36 of the Special Marriage Act, section 36 of the Indian Divorce Act, and section 39 of the Parsi Marriage and Divorce Act empower courts to award interim maintenance when a spouse lacks independent income sufficient for support.

Courts routinely state that the purpose of interim maintenance is to ensure a level playing field so that the financially disadvantaged spouse "*is not rendered*

---

252. *Compare* N.Y. Dom. Rel. Law § 236(B) (McKinney), *with* Protection of Women from Domestic Violence Act, 2005 (India).

253. *Y. Narsimha Rao*, AIR Online 1991 SC 10, ¶ 9.

254. *Singh*, AIR 2014 SC 2875.

destitute during the pendency of litigation."[255] In *Jain v. Jain,* the Supreme Court underscored that interim maintenance should be commensurate with the parties' social status and the paying spouse's capacity.[256] In *Rajnesh,* the Supreme Court mandated that interim maintenance must be decided within 60 days of service of notice to prevent the dependent spouse from suffering due to litigation delays.[257] High courts have repeatedly clarified that maintenance cannot be denied merely because the applicant is educated or capable of earning; the enquiry focuses on actual income, not theoretical employability. In *Shailja v. Khobbanna,* the Supreme Court reversed a family court decision reducing maintenance of the wife, while stating, *"Merely because the [wife] is capable of earning is not, in our opinion, sufficient reason to reduce the maintenance . . . ."*[258]

The applicant's bona fides are relevant, however. In *Jaiswal v. Jaiswal,* the Madhya Pradesh High Court dealt specifically with the following issue: *"Whether a spouse who has capacity of earning but chooses to remain idle, should be permitted to saddle other spouse with his or her expenditure."*[259] The court ultimately refused interim maintenance to the wife, who was deliberately avoiding employment in order to inflate her claim. Courts thus balance need and capacity, applying a fact-sensitive analysis that varies widely but is guided by the principle that neither party should suffer undue financial hardship during pending litigation. In addition, section 24 of the Hindu Marriage Act expressly states that court may order that the applicant be paid *"the expenses of the proceeding."* In cross-border cases, courts frequently adjust interim maintenance to account for currency exchange, cost of living abroad, and the expense of international travel, often permitting remote participation to reduce the financial burden on foreign-resident spouses.

New York law addresses interim spousal support through a more structured, formula-based regime, but with a closely aligned purpose. Temporary maintenance is governed by New York Domestic Relations Law section 236(B)(5)(a), which establishes presumptive guidelines designed to preserve the pre-divorce economic status quo and ensure that the less-monied spouse can participate meaningfully in the litigation.[260] Courts emphasize that interim support is not a final adjudication of rights but a provisional measure to prevent financial pressure from distorting the litigation process.[261] As in India, New York courts focus on actual income rather than speculative earning capacity at the temporary stage, while permitting income imputation where a spouse is deliberately

255. Qureshi v. Muzaffar, Crl. M.A. 3589/2025, ¶ 43 (India), https://indiankanoon.org/doc/107706650/.

256. Jain v. Jain, AIR 2017 SC 1640, ¶ 15 (India), https://indiankanoon.org/doc/185100634/.

257. *Rajnesh,* AIR 2021 SC 569; Hindu Marriage Act § 24.

258. Shailja v. Khobbanna, Criminal Appeal Nos. 125–126 of 2017, at 2 (India), https://indiankanoon.org/doc/176136151/.

259. Jaiswal v. Jaiswal, 2000 (3) MPLJ 100, ¶ 6 (India), https://indiankanoon.org/doc/1728023/.

260. N.Y. Dom. Rel. Law § 236(B)(5)(a) (McKinney).

261. Prichep v. Prichep, 858 N.Y.S.2d 667, 670–71 (N.Y. App. Div. 2008).

underemployed in bad faith.[262] Litigation expenses may also be awarded to promote parity between the parties during the pendency of the action.[263]

B. Permanent Alimony and Maintenance Under the Hindu Marriage Act

Permanent alimony under section 25 of the Hindu Marriage Act is one of the most flexible remedial tools available to Indian courts. The provision allows courts to order either periodic payments or a lump-sum award upon the granting of divorce. While the statute refers to "either spouse," courts acknowledge that women are the primary claimants due to structural economic disparities. Section 25 instructs courts to consider the parties' income, property, conduct, and other circumstances of the case, while ordering maintenance.

1. Determining the Maintenance Amount

In *Rajnesh*, the Supreme Court enlisted a (non-exhaustive) list of factors to be considered while determining maintenance:

> [T]he status of the parties; reasonable needs of the wife and dependant children; whether the applicant is educated and professionally qualified; whether the applicant has any independent source of income; whether the income is sufficient to enable her to maintain the same standard of living as she was accustomed to in her matrimonial home; whether the applicant was employed prior to her marriage; whether she was working during the subsistence of the marriage; whether the wife was required to sacrifice her employment opportunities for nurturing the family, child rearing, and looking after adult members of the family; [and] reasonable costs of litigation for a non-working wife.[264]

The Court then stressed the need for a "*careful and just balance*" between all relevant factors and stated that, while "*determining the maintenance amount*," courts should be mindful that such amount is "*reasonable and realistic*," in that it should be neither "*extravagant*" nor "*meagre*."[265]

2. Moral Conduct of the Parties

a. Conduct of the Wife

While certain provisions within Indian personal laws and criminal statutes link a wife's entitlement to maintenance with her moral conduct, Indian courts are progressively interpreting these provisions narrowly. However, there is no clear pattern still.

Statutory provisions under the Hindu Adoptions and Maintenance Act, the Hindu Marriage Act, and the CrPC condition maintenance on chastity or

262. Gaines v. Gaines, 969 N.Y.S.2d 190, 193 (N.Y. App. Div. 2013); Rosenberg v. Rosenberg, 981 N.Y.S.2d 260, 261 (N.Y. App. Div. 2014).

263. O'Shea v. O'Shea, 93 N.Y.2d 187, 190–91 (1999).

264. *Rajnesh*, AIR 2021 SC 569, at 29.

265. *Rajnesh*, AIR 2021 SC 569.

conduct.[266] The Chhattisgarh High Court recently held that a divorced wife living in adultery is disqualified from claiming maintenance under section 125(4) of the CrPC.[267] Similarly, Karnataka High Court denied maintenance to an "adulterous" wife under the provisions of the Protection of Women from Domestic Violence Act.[268] In another case for maintenance under section 125 of the CrPC, the Kerala High Court observed that the *"wife's right to claim maintenance is not absolute,"* and, that "a wife living in continuous adultery is not entitled to claim maintenance."[269]

However, on the other hand, the Indian Supreme Court held that a wife's refusal to live with her husband, by not complying with a decree for RCR under the Hindu Marriage Act, 1955, does not disqualify her from claiming maintenance where such refusal is supported by just cause.[270]

In simple terms, while allegations concerning a wife's "chastity" or "immorality" would have little to no relevance in a New York court's division of marital assets or determination of spousal support, they continue to find expression within the Indian family law framework.

b. Conduct of the Husband

Unlike the moral scrutiny historically directed at wives, Indian maintenance jurisprudence has consistently treated the husband's conduct, particularly neglect, refusal to maintain, and marital misconduct, as a relevant but non-determinative factor, with primary emphasis placed on his legal obligation to provide financial support. The statutory trigger for maintenance is not the husband's moral character but his failure or neglect to maintain a dependent wife who is unable to maintain herself.[271] The Supreme Court has emphasized that "*the obligation of the husband is on a higher pedestal when the question of maintenance*" arises.[272]

The courts have not been indifferent to serious misconduct on the part of the husband where such conduct bears on equity and good faith. In cases involving concealment of a subsisting marriage, abandonment, or deliberate evasion of responsibility, the Supreme Court has expressly declined to allow husbands

266. Hindu Adoptions and Maintenance Act § 18(3); Hindu Marriage Act § 25(3); CrPC § 125(4) (now section 144 of the BNSS); Singh v. Ramendri, AIR 2000 SC 1952 (India) (holding that forfeiture provisions must be strictly construed and do not extinguish the right to maintenance altogether), https://indiankanoon.org/doc/1728416/.

267. Dewangan v. Dewangan, 2025:CGHC:21793, ¶ 19 (India), https://indiankanoon.org/doc/155130906/.

268. Protection of Women from Domestic Violence Act § 12; Shanthakumari v. Thimmegowda, 2023:KHC:33789 (India), https://indiankanoon.org/doc/69121124/.

269. Jinesh v. Aswathy, R.P.(FC) No. 100/2023, ¶ 5 (India), https://indiankanoon.org/doc/178953137/.

270. Reena v. Dinesh, 2025 INSC 55, ¶ 38 (India), https://indiankanoon.org/doc/29987605/.

271. CrPC § 125(4) (now section 144 of the BNSS).

272. Farooqui v. Khan, AIR 2015 SC 2025, ¶ 18 (India), https://indiankanoon.org/doc/189967724/.

to rely on technical defenses to defeat maintenance claims.[273] In interim maintenance proceedings especially, allegations relating to the husband's conduct are assessed primarily to the extent they demonstrate neglect, financial control, or imbalance in access to resources, rather than as a moral inquiry. This asymmetry, where the husband's misconduct strengthens the case for maintenance, while the wife's alleged misconduct may still be pleaded as a statutory disqualification, highlights the uneven manner in which "conduct" continues to operate within Indian maintenance law.

In another case highlighting the gender-based morality check, the Kerala High Court struck down discriminatory portions of section 10 of the Indian Divorce Act, 1869, which applied only to Christians. The court held that the act violated Articles 14, 15, and 21 of the Constitution because it required Christian wives to prove adultery in addition to cruelty or desertion to obtain a divorce, whereas husbands only had to prove adultery.[274]

By contrast, New York's maintenance framework is formally gender-neutral and does not condition spousal support on the moral conduct of either party. Maintenance is determined by statute based on economic factors such as income, earning capacity, duration of the marriage, and standard of living, without reference to sexual behavior or notions of chastity.[275] Fault is expressly excluded from consideration in fixing maintenance, except in rare cases of egregious misconduct not rising to ordinary marital fault.[276] As a result, allegations of "immorality" or personal conduct have little to no bearing on a New York court's maintenance determination, underscoring a sharp doctrinal departure from conduct-based maintenance regimes.

3. Financial Disclosure Requirements

Financial awards in maintenance proceedings are, in principle, tied to the paying spouse's financial capacity. Indian courts routinely direct parties to disclose an "asset profile" comprising income, employment or business interests, movable and immovable property, investments, liabilities, tax returns, and lifestyle indicators. Courts are not confined to declared income alone and may draw inferences from expenditure patterns, travel history, property ownership, and overall financial behavior, as recognized by the Bombay High Court in *Gada v. Gada*, where the court increased the wife's monthly maintenance amount by seven times upon finding that the husband had lied about his income under oath.[277]

---

273. Badshah v. Godse, AIR 2014 SC 869, ¶ 16 (India), https://indiankanoon.org/doc/15901386/.

274. Indira G. v. Sundaram, AIR 1995 Ker 252, ¶¶ 1, 43–50 (India), https://indiankanoon.org/doc/1591531/.

275. N.Y. Dom. Rel. Law § 236(B)(6)(a).

276. Howard S. v. Lillian S., 14 N.Y.S.3d 490, 492 (N.Y. App. Div. 2015); O'Brien v. O'Brien, 66 N.Y.2d 576, 585 (1985).

277. Gada v. Gada, 2025:BHC-AS:47605-DB, ¶¶ 62–72 (India), https://indiankanoon.org/doc/162475718/.

The Supreme Court's decision in *Rajnesh* sought to institutionalize this approach by mandating standardized affidavits of disclosure in all maintenance proceedings, expressly acknowledging that concealment and suppression of financial information had become systemic.[278]

Recently, the Delhi High Court in *Makhija v. Makhija* held, "*Financial disclosures . . . must be adjudicated on the basis of the material on record and assessed in the background of social realities.*"[279]

On paper, therefore, Indian maintenance law reflects a strong commitment to transparency and informed adjudication, and courts have increasingly emphasized stricter compliance, as reflected in recent case law. In practice, however, these measures continue to fall short of the disclosure obligations, and the meaningful penal consequences for willful nondisclosure, found in most developed legal systems.

For instance, Indian family law does not contain an explicit statutory provision imposing an affirmative obligation on spouses to proactively disclose their income and assets to each other or to the court. Unlike jurisdictions such as California, there is no express "affirmative and continuing duty" of financial disclosure embedded in Indian matrimonial statutes; disclosure is typically driven by court directions or procedural rules rather than a self-executing obligation.[280] By contrast, California law imposes a mandatory, ongoing duty of disclosure that operates independent of discovery requests. In *In re Marriage of Feldman*, the California Court of Appeal clarified that a spouse must not only fully respond to requests for financial information, but that the disclosure obligation exists regardless of whether the other spouse has sought such information, eliminating the need for an initiating request altogether.[281]

Recognizing this institutional gap, the Delhi High Court, in a detailed judgment addressing financial discovery in maintenance proceedings, observed as follows: "This Court is of the view that the mandatory filing of the affidavit of assets, income and expenditure by the parties in a detailed prescribed form should be incorporated in the statutes, as in the developed countries."[282]

Statutorily, Indian courts derive their authority to compel disclosure from general procedural law rather than a dedicated matrimonial discovery regime. The CPC, 1908, lays down the court's power to order discovery (section 30), and permits discovery and inspection of documents (Order XI), admissions (Order XII), summoning of witnesses and documents (Order XVI), and examination and cross-examination of parties (Order XVIII).[283] Family courts, while

278. *Rajnesh*, AIR 2021 SC 569.

279. Makhija v. Makhija, Crl. Rev. P. 723/2024, ¶ 30 (India), https://indiankanoon.org/doc/191072775/.

280. *See generally* CPC, 1908; Family Courts Act (containing no provision imposing an affirmative, continuing duty of financial disclosure between spouses in matrimonial proceedings).

281. *In re* Marriage of Feldman, 153 Cal. App. 4th 1470, 1485–88 (Cal. Ct. App. 2007).

282. Sharma v. Sharma, AIR 2015 Del 53, ¶ 91 (India), https://indiankanoon.org/doc/174517725/.

283. CPC § 30 (Power to Order Discovery), Order XI (Discovery and Inspection), Order XII (Admissions), Order XVI (Summoning and Attendance of Witnesses), Order XVIII (Examination of Witnesses) (India).

not strictly bound by the CPC, are empowered under section 10 of the Family Courts Act, 1984, to lay down their own procedure, guided by principles of natural justice.[284] In addition, where a party fails to comply with discovery directions, Order XI, Rule 21 of the CPC authorizes courts to strike out pleadings or dismiss claims or defenses.[285] Where false statements are made under oath, courts may also initiate proceedings for perjury under section 340 of the CrPC read with sections 191 and 193 of the Indian Penal Code.[286] These provisions, taken together, theoretically provide courts with meaningful tools to respond to dishonest disclosure.

In practice, however, these statutory consequences are rarely invoked in routine maintenance litigation. Maintenance proceedings, particularly under section 125 of the CrPC and interim applications under personal laws, are treated as summary and time-sensitive, and courts are often reluctant to engage the full machinery of civil discovery or initiate collateral proceedings for perjury. Pleadings are seldom struck out under Order XI, Rule 21, and prosecutions for false evidence remain exceptional rather than normative. As a result, parties frequently circumvent disclosure obligations by underreporting income, routing earnings through family-controlled entities, claiming cash-based livelihoods, withholding foreign assets, or producing selective or incomplete tax documentation. While courts may draw adverse inferences in appropriate cases,[287] such inferences are discretionary, unevenly applied, and often insufficient to neutralize deliberate concealment. The evidentiary burden of exposing dishonesty therefore falls disproportionately on the economically weaker spouse, despite the formal availability of sanctions.

By contrast, New York's maintenance regime operates within a tightly enforced discovery framework. Parties are required to file sworn statements of net worth and are subject to full civil discovery under the Civil Practice Law and Rules. Nondisclosure, misrepresentation, or concealment of assets may result in adverse inferences, imputation of income, monetary sanctions, attorney's fees, reopening of judgments, and findings of contempt or fraud.[288] New York courts have repeatedly emphasized that truthful financial disclosure is foundational to equitable relief and that dishonesty in disclosure undermines the integrity of the matrimonial process itself.[289]

The comparative distinction is structural rather than doctrinal: while Indian case law now formally provides for disclosure and sanctions, weak discovery norms and restrained enforcement permit strategic noncompliance, a result far less likely under New York's disclosure-driven matrimonial system.

284. Family Courts Act § 10.

285. CPC Order XI, Rule 21.

286. CrPC § 340, now reenacted as BNSS § 379; Indian Penal Code §§ 191, 193, now reenacted as Bharatiya Nyaya Sanhita §§ 227, 228.

287. *Sharma*, AIR 2015 Del 53, ¶¶ 74–84.

288. N.Y. Dom. Rel. Law § 236(B); N.Y. C.P.L.R. § 3126.

289. Mahoney-Buntzman v. Buntzman, 12 N.Y.3d 415, 422–23 (2009).

C. Alimony and Maintenance Under the Special Marriage Act and Other Personal Laws

Spousal support under the Special Marriage Act, particularly section 37, broadly parallels section 25 of the Hindu Marriage Act but applies to civil and interfaith marriages. Courts emphasize the secular character of the statute and parity between spouses, interpreting the Special Marriage Act liberally to ensure financial protection comparable to that available under religious personal laws.[290] Given that Special Marriage Act marriages frequently involve interfaith couples, NRIs, or spouses with transnational assets, courts often adopt a pragmatic approach, taking into account foreign income, differing costs of living, and cross-border enforcement realities.

Maintenance under Christian and Parsi personal laws follows a similar framework. The Indian Divorce Act provides for maintenance pendente lite and permanent alimony, and judicial intervention has eliminated earlier gender-based distinctions within the statute. Under the Parsi Marriage and Divorce Act, courts may award maintenance after considering the parties' property and conduct, with the presence of community delegates affecting procedure but not the underlying financial principles.

Spousal support under Muslim personal law reflects a combination of classical doctrine, statutory reform, and constitutional adjudication. A Muslim wife is entitled to mehr (dower), recognized as a debt owed by the husband.[291] Following divorce, maintenance is statutorily addressed by the Muslim Women (Protection of Rights on Divorce) Act, 1986, which requires the husband to make a "reasonable and fair provision." In *Latifi*, the Supreme Court held that this obligation extends beyond the iddat period through a lump-sum provision, harmonizing the statute with constitutional guarantees of dignity and equality.[292] Subsequent decisions have clarified that divorced Muslim women may still invoke the general maintenance remedy where such provision has not, in fact, been made.

2.4.3. Child Support

Child support in India is governed by a combination of statutory obligations, equitable principles, and constitutional protections. While the United States relies on formula-driven guidelines and structured enforcement tools across states, India's approach remains judicially determined and fact-specific. Courts evaluate the standard of living enjoyed by the child, the financial resources of both parents, and the best interests and welfare of the child, a principle repeatedly affirmed by the Supreme Court as paramount in all family law proceedings.

---

290. *Indira G.*, AIR 1995 Ker 252.
291. Bibi v. Bibi, AIR 1916 PC 46 (India), https://indiankanoon.org/doc/962828/.
292. *Latifi*, AIR 2001 SC 3958.

The Delhi High Court has recently agreed to consider framing guidelines on child custody, visitation rights, and parenting plans.[293] However, the actual formulation and implementation of such guidelines could still take many years.

A. Who Is Responsible to Pay Child Support?

Indian law impose a non-derogable duty on *both parents* to provide for the financial, educational, medical, and overall developmental needs of their children In *Nagpal*, the Supreme Court reiterated that the welfare of the child transcends parental disputes and imposes a sustained responsibility on both parents, regardless of marital conflict or geographical separation. Therefore, even if one parent is awarded physical custody, the noncustodial parent's financial obligation remains intact.[294]

In 2025, in *Makhija*, the Delhi High Court held:

> [A] Court of law cannot burden, nor does the law mandate, that the working mother should be forced to exhaust herself physically, emotionally, and financially, and allow the father to take refuge behind selective, misleading disclosures about his income and technical pleas. . . .
>
> The law of maintenance, while being applied by a Court of law, cannot be treated as a mere contest between two parties as to who earns less on paper, but requires an overall and holistic assessment as to who is bearing the real burden of upbringing, daily sustenance, and needs of growing children, as compared to one who is prima facie and evidently shirking his responsibilities by misleading the Court.[295]

Thus, Indian courts interpret child support as an absolute legal and moral obligation that neither parent may avoid. This duty flows not only from personal law statutes but also from constitutional commitments to dignity and nondiscrimination, particularly:

- **Article 14: Right to Equality**. This article ensures that children are treated as a special class requiring equal protection of the laws to prevent exploitation of their dignity.
- **Article 15(3): Special Provisions**. This article expressly allows the state to make "special provisions" for children, which courts use to justify protective discrimination in maintenance laws.
- **Article 39(f): Directive Principles**. This article mandates that the state provide children with opportunities and facilities to develop in a healthy manner and be protected against abandonment or exploitation.

---

293. Ayushman Initiative for Child Rights v. High Court of Delhi, Writ Petion (C) 1565/2026 & C.M. Appl. 7595/2026 (India), https://delhihighcourt.nic.in/app/showlogo/1770283525_fa2f7510f6cad3af_683_15652026.pdf/2026.

294. *Nagpal*, AIR 2009 SC 557, ¶ 46.

295. *Makhija*, Crl. Rev. P. 723/2024, ¶¶ 28–29.

Collectively, these articles reinforce the state's and society's obligation to protect children's welfare.[296] Section 125 of the CrPC (now section 144 of the BNSS) mandates maintenance for children regardless of their legitimacy.

B. Statutory Basis for Child Support Under Personal Laws

Although there is no legislated mathematical formula or calculator, most Indian matrimonial statutes incorporate specific provisions enabling courts to award maintenance for children. Section 26 of the Hindu Marriage Act authorizes courts to issue orders regarding the maintenance and education of minor children during and after matrimonial litigation.[297] The Special Marriage Act similarly empowers courts to make financial arrangements for children's welfare, and Christian and Parsi marital statutes also provide mechanisms for child support.[298] These statutory frameworks operate alongside the secular remedy provided in section 125 of the CrPC, which is available to all children irrespective of religion, legitimacy, or custodial status.

Indian courts have consistently interpreted maintenance provisions with a strong focus on the immediate needs of children. For instance, although section 24 of the Hindu Marriage Act formally provides for *interim maintenance to a spouse*, courts have construed the provision broadly to include expenses relating to minor children residing with the applicant parent, recognizing that a child's subsistence cannot realistically be separated from that of the caregiving parent.[299] In *Sehgal v. District Judge Dehradun*, the Supreme Court held:

> Section 24 of the Act no doubt talks of maintenance of wife during the pendency of the proceedings but this section, in our view, cannot be read in isolation and cannot be given restricted meaning to hold that it is maintenance of the wife alone and no one else. Since wife is maintaining the eldest unmarried daughter, her right to claim maintenance would include her own maintenance and that of her daughter. This fact has to be kept in view while fixing the maintenance pendente lite for the wife. We are aware of the provisions of Section 26 of the Act providing for custody of minor children, their maintenance and education but that section operates in its own field.[300]

Interim maintenance orders are intended to provide swift and effective relief and are therefore insulated from routine appellate challenge, ensuring that financial support to children is not delayed by prolonged litigation.[301] This child-centric approach was reinforced by the Supreme Court in *Rajnesh v. Neha*, which directed that interim maintenance, inclusive of child support, be decided

296. India Const. arts. 14, 15(3), 39(f).

297. Hindu Marriage Act § 26.

298. Special Marriage Act § 38; Indian Divorce Act § 41; Parsi Marriage and Divorce Act § 49.

299. Hindu Marriage Act § 24; Sumathi v. Sharavanakumar, CRP (PD) No. 486 of 2013, ¶ 13 (India), https://indiankanoon.org/doc/26407098/.

300. Sehgal v. District Judge Dehradun, AIR 1997 SC 3397, at 3 (India), https://indiankanoon.org/doc/796258/.

301. *Id.*

expeditiously, emphasizing that a child's education and development cannot be placed on hold pending final adjudication.[302]

C. Child Support Under Section 125 of the Code of Criminal Procedure

Section 125 of the CrPC is one of the most powerful child support mechanisms in Indian law.[303] The provision applies uniformly across all religious communities and imposes liability on any parent with sufficient means who neglects or refuses to maintain their minor child. The jurisdiction is summary, intended to prevent destitution and ensure immediate relief. The Supreme Court has stated that CrPC section 125 *"is a measure of social justice intended to protect women and children."*[304]

In *Rajnesh,* the Supreme Court established comprehensive guidelines for child support determinations under section 125. The Court mandated standardized disclosure affidavits, detailed examination of educational and healthcare expenditures, and consideration of the lifestyle the child would have enjoyed had the marriage remained intact.[305] The *Rajnesh* judgment has transformed child support litigation by introducing uniformity into a previously fragmented jurisprudence. Courts must now consider the child's school fees, extracurricular needs, medical insurance, transportation, and other developmental requirements, making section 125 an expansive and modern tool for securing meaningful financial support.

D. Standards for Determining Amounts of Child Support

Indian courts do not apply mathematical formulas. Instead, they examine financial disclosures, comparative lifestyles, developmental needs, and the earning potential of both parents. The overarching principle is that the child should not suffer a diminished life merely because the parents' marriage has dissolved. In several cases, the Indian courts have reiterated that a child is entitled to a standard of living commensurate with the paying parent's means, not merely survival-level maintenance.

Courts increasingly consider private-school fees, international education costs, digital-learning expenses, childcare arrangements, extracurricular activities, and medical insurance as legitimate components of child support. The Supreme Court emphasized that both parents must contribute proportionately to a child's true needs rather than engage in minimal compliance. High Courts have extended this principle to include laptops, online education subscriptions, special-needs therapy, and long-term educational planning.

When one parent dramatically outearns the other, courts may require the wealthier parent to shoulder a significantly greater share. Indian courts have held that a child of affluent parents should not be forced into a frugal lifestyle inconsistent with the family's pre-divorce environment. The judgment reflects a growing judicial acknowledgment that child support must reflect socio-economic context.

302. *Rajnesh,* AIR 2021 SC 569.

303. CrPC § 125 (now section 144 of the BNSS).

304. Vimal v. Veeraswamy, 1991 S.C.R. (1) 904, 905 (India), https://indiankanoon.org/doc/861619/.

305. *Rajnesh,* AIR 2021 SC 569.

E. Discussion on Rajnesh v. Neha

In 2020, In *Rajnesh v. Neha*, the Supreme Court delivered what has rightly come to be regarded as a landmark decision in Indian maintenance jurisprudence, not because it altered substantive rights, but because it fundamentally restructured the procedural framework governing financial disclosure and adjudication.[306] Confronted with the reality that maintenance applications were routinely delayed and inconsistently decided, the Court noted that *"in practice . . . in a vast majority of cases, the applications are not disposed of within the time frame prescribed."* It therefore considered it necessary *"to frame guidelines to ensure that there is uniformity and consistency in deciding the same."*[307] This institutional self-awareness, combined with the issuance of binding national guidelines, elevated the judgment beyond the resolution of an individual dispute.

The Court located maintenance law within its constitutional and social-justice foundations, reiterating that such provisions are *"a measure of social justice and specially enacted to protect women and children,"* falling within the sweep of Articles 15(3) and 39.[308] At the same time, it emphasized that maintenance must be calibrated to secure a standard of living *"neither luxurious nor penurious, but . . . modestly consistent with the status of the family."*[309] These twin principles, protection against destitution and proportional fairness, framed the Court's intervention in the mechanics of financial disclosure.

What renders *Rajnesh* particularly significant is its recognition that adjudication of maintenance had been undermined by incomplete and strategic financial disclosures. Maintenance is to be determined on the basis of the respondent's *"financial capacity . . . and other relevant factors,"* yet courts were often compelled to proceed without standardized information.[310] To address this structural deficiency, the Court mandated the filing of detailed affidavits of disclosure of assets and liabilities in a prescribed format. By institutionalizing comprehensive disclosure of income, expenditures, assets, liabilities, and dependent obligations, the Court shifted maintenance adjudication from conjecture to evidentiary discipline. This reform applies across statutes and forums, thereby introducing national uniformity where fragmentation previously prevailed.

Equally transformative was the Court's attempt to harmonize overlapping jurisdictions. Acknowledging that maintenance may be claimed under multiple enactments, it held that while remedies are independent, duplication without transparency would be inequitable. It therefore directed that in subsequent proceedings, prior maintenance orders must be disclosed so that the court may grant an adjustment or set-off of the said amount. In doing so, the Court preserved statutory autonomy while preventing multiplicity from degenerating into inconsistency.

306. *Id.*
307. *Id.* Part A(iii) (emphasis added).
308. *Id.* Part B (emphasis added).
309. *Id.*
310. *Id.*

The judgment's landmark stature thus lies in its systemic vision. It did not merely affirm interim maintenance in an individual case; it imposed a structured regime of financial transparency, cross-forum disclosure, and time-bound adjudication. By aligning procedural reform with constitutional purpose, *Rajnesh v. Neha* recalibrated maintenance law toward greater consistency, accountability, and institutional credibility.

F. General Guidelines and Directions in Rajnesh v. Neha

Having articulated the need for uniformity and transparency, the Court issued operative directions of general application.

On the problem of parallel (domestic) proceedings, the Court held that it is necessary to disclose the previous proceedings and the orders issued in such proceedings, in the subsequent proceedings, so that there is no conflicting order issued by different courts.[311] It further directed that the court "*would consider an adjustment or set-off of the amount awarded in the previous proceeding(s), while determining whether any further amount is to be awarded in the subsequent proceeding.*"[312] This direction was intended to prevent duplication, inconsistent awards, and strategic forum use.

With respect to financial disclosure, the Court mandated that the "*Affidavit of Disclosure of Assets and Liabilities annexed as Enclosures I, II and III of this judgment . . . shall be filed by both parties in all maintenance proceedings.*"[313] The filing of the affidavit was not left to judicial discretion; it was framed as a uniform procedural requirement across forums.

Where disputes arise regarding disclosure, "*the aggrieved party may seek permission of the Court to serve interrogatories, and seek production of relevant documents from the opposite party under Order XI of the CPC.*"[314] The Court also clarified that "*the income of one party is often not within the knowledge of the other spouse,*" and that courts may invoke section 106 of the Evidence Act,[315] since the income, assets and liabilities of a party "*are within the personal knowledge of the party concerned.*"[316]

To preserve flexibility over time, the Court directed that if "*there is a change in the financial status of any party, or there is a change of any relevant circumstances, or if some new information comes to light, the party may submit an amended/supplementary affidavit,*" which would be considered at final determination.[317] It cautioned that maintenance pleadings "*should be responsible pleadings,*" and that

311. *Id.* Part B, Section VI(a)(ii).

312. *Id.* Part B, Section VI(a)(i) (emphasis added).

313. *Id.* Part B, Section VI(b) (emphasis added).

314. *Id.* Part B, Section II(xi)(f) (emphasis added).

315. Indian Evidence Act § 106 ("Burden of proving fact especially within knowledge: When any fact is especially within the knowledge of any person, the burden of proving that fact is upon him. Illustrations (a) When a person does an act with some intention other than that which the character and circumstances of the act suggest, the burden of proving that intention is upon him. (b) A is charged with travelling in a railway without a ticket. The burden of proving that he had a ticket is on him.").

316. *Rajnesh*, AIR 2021 SC 569, Section II(xi)(f) (emphasis added).

317. *Id.* Section II(xi)(g) (emphasis added).

if *"false statements and misrepresentations are made, the Court may consider initiation of proceeding u/S. 340 Cr.P.C., and for contempt of Court."*[318] At the same time, it carved out a narrow exemption, holding that where parties belong to the economically weaker sections, live below the poverty line, or are casual laborers, *"the requirement of filing the Affidavit would be dispensed with."*[319]

Finally, addressing delay in interim relief, the Court directed that the *"Family Court/District Court/Magistrate's Court must make an endeavour to decide the I.A. for Interim Maintenance by a reasoned order, within a period of four to six months at the latest, after the Affidavits of Disclosure have been filed."*[320]

Read together, these directions operationalize the broader principles articulated in the discussion section: transparency, coordination across forums, and time-bound adjudication. They represent not incremental clarification, but a deliberate attempt to standardize maintenance procedure at a national level.

2.4.4. Enforcement: Mechanisms and Challenges

While noting the issues with the enforcement of maintenance orders, the Supreme Court has noted:

> Enforcement of the order of maintenance is the most challenging issue, which is encountered by the applicants. If maintenance is not paid in a timely manner, it defeats the very object of the social welfare legislation. Execution petitions usually remain pending for months, if not years, which completely nullifies the object of the law.[321]

An order of maintenance in India may be enforced through different statutory mechanisms depending on the forum and the source of the order. Maintenance awarded under the Hindu Marriage Act may be executed before the family court through the civil execution framework, while maintenance granted under the Protection of Women from Domestic Violence Act is enforceable before the judicial magistrate. Maintenance orders issued under the general criminal-law remedy are executed before the magistrate's court. Family court orders are expressly made executable through the procedural codes governing civil and criminal enforcement. Where a party willfully fails to comply with a maintenance order, the court may recover arrears in the manner prescribed for *fines* and, in appropriate cases, impose *short-term imprisonment* to compel compliance.[322]

The Supreme Court held that if a spouse fails to pay interim maintenance, the court has the power to *"strike off their defense"* in the main litigation.[323] This means the faulting party (usually the husband) is barred from contesting the divorce or custody case until the arrears are cleared. The Court emphasized

318. *Id.* Section II(xi)(h) (emphasis added).

319. *Id.* Section II(xi)(i) (emphasis added).

320. *Id.* Section II(xi)(j) (emphasis added).

321. *Id.* at 37.

322. *Rajnesh*, AIR 2021 SC 569; Hindu Marriage Act § 28A, read with § 24; Family Courts Act § 18; CPC, Order XXI, Rule 94; Protection of Women from Domestic Violence Act § 20(6); CrPC §§ 125(3), 128.

323. *Rajnesh*, AIR 2021 SC 569.

that maintenance is a social-justice measure that cannot be defeated by dilatory tactics. As a corollary, where interim maintenance remains unpaid, courts have recognized that the defaulting spouse may be *disentitled from being heard* in related proceedings, including appeals, until compliance is secured.

Cautious Approach: Although, in *Rajnesh*, the Supreme Court has also cautioned that *the power to strike off a defaulting spouse's defense must be exercised with care*, several high courts have emphasized that this power is not universal and cannot be invoked mechanically.[324] Courts have held that where the statute itself provides a specific mechanism for recovery of interim maintenance, such as attachment, recovery as arrears of fine, or imprisonment, the proper course is to pursue those remedies rather than to strike off the defense. In proceedings under section 125 of the CrPC in particular, high courts have clarified that neither the CrPC nor the Family Courts Act expressly or impliedly confers a power to strike off the defense, and that such a power cannot be assumed as inherent.[325] Striking off the defense in these circumstances has been viewed as procedurally erroneous and, in some cases, counterproductive, as it may prolong rather than expedite enforcement of maintenance orders.

Thus, while noting the difficulty with respect to enforcement of maintenance orders, and laying down the possible options, the Supreme Court has also noted:

> Striking off the defence of the respondent is an order which ought to be passed in *the last resort*, if the Courts find default to be wilful and contumacious, particularly to a dependant unemployed wife, and minor children.
>
> *Contempt proceedings* for wilful disobedience may be initiated before the appropriate Court.[326]

Enforcement mechanisms include attachment of wages, garnishment of bank accounts, seizure of property, and, in extreme cases, civil imprisonment. Nonpayment is treated seriously; in *Shantha v. Shivananjappa*, the Karnataka High Court held that deliberate nonpayment of child support constitutes both contempt and criminal neglect under CrPC section 125. Courts may also suspend passports, restrict international travel, or issue look-out circulars to prevent evasion by NRI parents.[327]

Cross-border enforcement remains discretionary and varies by jurisdiction. U.S. states applying the Uniform Interstate Family Support Act may recognize Indian child support orders when procedural protections were adequate. Indian courts have begun encouraging cross-border cooperation, although gaps remain due to the absence of treaty-based enforcement.

324. Singh v. Murti, 1991 Cri LJ 2353 (India), https://indiankanoon.org/doc/1832291/.

325. Dwivedi v. Dwivedi, Cr. R. No. 757/2016 (India), https://indiankanoon.org/doc/97368179/.

326. *Rajnesh*, AIR 2021 SC 569, at 41 (emphasis added).

327. Shantha v. Shivananjappa, 2004 AIR Kant H.C.R. 1550 (India), https://indiankanoon.org/doc/163238/.

2.5. Child Custody Law and Procedure

2.5.1. Overview and Theoretical Foundations

Child custody law in India rests on the overarching doctrine that the welfare of the child is paramount. This principle cuts across statutory enactments, personal laws, and constitutional jurisprudence, and has been repeatedly reaffirmed by the Supreme Court of India as the controlling standard in all custody and guardianship disputes. Unlike American family law systems, which are largely governed by codified state statutes articulating multi-factor "best interests of the child" tests, Indian custody law derives from a hybrid framework combining the 19th-century Guardians and Wards Act, 1890, religion-specific personal laws, and expansive judge-made law grounded in equity and constitutional values.

The Supreme Court has consistently clarified that custody proceedings in India are not adversarial determinations of parental entitlement but exercises of parens patriae jurisdiction, under which courts act as guardians of the child's welfare rather than arbiters of parental rights. In *Nagpal*, the Court emphasized that "the child's welfare is of paramount consideration and not the rights of the parents under a statute."[328] This reasoning mirrors, in functional terms, the American "best interests" doctrine, but Indian courts apply it with even greater flexibility, unconstrained by statutory checklists or presumptions.

Indian jurisprudence rejects any notion of custody as proprietary. In *Jacob*, the Supreme Court held that custody orders are inherently temporary and subject to continuous revision due to *"changed conditions and circumstances, including the passage of time."*[329] This position contrasts with many U.S. jurisdictions, where custody orders acquire quasi-finality absent a showing of a substantial change in circumstances. Indian courts, by contrast, maintain continuing supervisory jurisdiction, reflecting the view that child welfare is a dynamic inquiry.

2.5.2. Statutory Framework Governing Child Custody

A. Guardians and Wards Act, 1890

The Guardians and Wards Act, 1890, is the principal secular statute governing custody and guardianship in India. Sections 7 and 17 of the act empower courts to appoint guardians of the person or property of a minor whenever such appointment is necessary for the welfare of the child. Section 17 directs courts to consider the age, sex, and religion of the minor; the character and capacity of the proposed guardian; the wishes of the deceased parents; and, where appropriate, the child's own preference.

Despite its colonial origins, the act remains the procedural backbone of custody litigation. Indian courts have interpreted its provisions expansively to accommodate contemporary views on child psychology, emotional security, and social development. In *Hussain v. Ahmed*, the Supreme Court reiterated that

328. *Nagpal*, AIR 2009 SC 557, ¶ 35.
329. *Jacob*, AIR 1973 SC 2090.

statutory factors listed in section 17 are illustrative, not exhaustive, and must yield to the overarching inquiry into welfare.[330]

American family law statutes similarly direct courts to examine multiple contextual factors, but the key difference lies in formalization. U.S. statutes codify factors such as parental fitness, stability, and continuity of care, whereas Indian courts derive these considerations from judicial interpretation rather than legislative mandate.

B. Personal Laws and Custody

Indian personal laws supplement the Guardians and Wards Act but do not override its welfare standard. For instance, under Hindu law, section 6 of the Hindu Minority and Guardianship Act, 1956, recognizes the father as the natural guardian of a legitimate minor child, with the mother occupying that role after him.[331] However, judicial interpretation has substantially diluted the statutory preference.[332]

1. Custody Under Muslim Law

Muslim personal law draws a distinction between guardianship (wilayat) and custody or physical care (hizanat), with custody of young children traditionally vesting in the mother.[333] At the same time, Indian courts have consistently emphasized that such personal law principles are subordinate to the overarching consideration of the child's welfare. In *Hussain v. State of Uttar Pradesh*, the Supreme Court declined to apply rigid personal law rules where their enforcement would be detrimental to the child's interests.[334]

Under Muslim personal law, the father is recognized as the natural guardian of the child. However, the rules governing custody differ between schools of law. Under *Shia* law, a mother is entitled to the custody of a minor son until the age of two years and of a minor daughter until the age of seven years. Under *Sunni* law, a mother is entitled to custody of a minor son until he attains the age of seven years and of a minor daughter until she reaches puberty. In *Zarabibi v. Rezzak*, it was held that the mother's right to custody of minor children for the prescribed period continues to operate even after divorce.[335]

Notwithstanding these doctrinal positions, courts have repeatedly reaffirmed that the best interests of the child must prevail over formal personal law entitlements. Thus, where the father asserted custody rights as the natural guardian under Muslim personal law, the Allahabad High Court held that although the father may have a prima facie right to custody, such a claim can

330. Hussain v. Ahmed, AIR 2010 SC 1417, ¶¶ 31–33 (India), https://indiankanoon.org/doc/1655422/.

331. Hindu Minority and Guardianship Act § 6.

332. Discussed *infra* Section 2.5.3. Typical Issues in Indian Custody Matters.

333. Begum v. Hussain, AIR 1986 MP 221 (India), https://indiankanoon.org/doc/956599/.

334. Hussain v. State of Uttar Pradesh, AIR 1964 SC 1625 (India), https://indiankanoon.org/doc/211970/.

335. Zarabibi v. Rezzak, (1910) 12 Bom LR 891 (India), https://www.courtkutchehry.com/judgements/791144/zarabibi-vs-abdul-rezzak-nakshbandi/.

be displaced where the welfare of the child lies in remaining with the mother.[336] The court underscored that children cannot be treated as chattel or property and that custody determinations must be guided by humanitarian considerations and the child's overall welfare.

More recently, in *Hussain v. Ahmed,* the Supreme Court addressed a situation in which the children were residing with their maternal grandparents following the mother's death and the father sought custody. While acknowledging that the father is the natural guardian under Muslim law, the Court held that it could not ignore the preferences of the minor children or their best interests. On the facts of the case, the Court concluded that it would not be in the children's interest to disturb the existing custodial arrangement and accordingly directed that custody remain unchanged, while granting the father visitation rights.[337]

2. Custody Under Christian Law

Sections 41 to 43 of the Indian Divorce Act, 1869, govern matters relating to the custody of children of Christian parents. Even in proceedings under the Indian Divorce Act, the controlling consideration in custody determinations remains the welfare of the minor child.

In *Jacob,* the Court observed that children are not mere playthings for their parents, and emphasized that the absolute rights of parents over the lives and destinies of their children have, under modern conditions, yielded to the consideration of the child's welfare as a human being.[338] This articulation reflects the broader shift away from parental entitlement toward a child-centric approach in custody adjudication.

3. Custody Under Parsi Law

Section 49 of the Parsi Marriage and Divorce Act, 1936, empowers the court to make appropriate orders concerning the custody, maintenance, and education of children below the age of 18 years. In *Dolikuka v. Dolikuka,* the high court declined to grant custody of a minor daughter to the mother on the ground that she was a working woman.[339] The mother alleged that the father had alienated the child against her. On appeal, the Supreme Court held that a parent's employment cannot be treated as a decisive or disqualifying factor in custody determinations, and found that the high court had erred in denying custody to the mother on that basis.[340] Custody was accordingly granted to the mother, with visitation rights awarded to the father.

More broadly, courts have consistently prioritized the presumed welfare of the child over strict adherence to personal law provisions. This approach reflects a sustained judicial effort to apply custody laws through a uniform, child-centric lens, ensuring that the welfare of the child remains paramount irrespective of religious affiliation. The absence of significant resistance from

336. Khalid v. Parveen, AIR 1988 All 252 (India), https://indiankanoon.org/doc/1124048/.
337. *Hussain,* AIR 2010 SC 1417, ¶¶ 50–53.
338. *Jacob,* AIR 1973 SC 2090.
339. Dolikuka v. Dolikuka, Bom. H.C. Appeal No. 102 of 1981 (India).
340. Dolikuka v. Dolikuka, AIR 1982 SC 1276 (India), https://indiankanoon.org/doc/1304490/.

faith-based groups has facilitated greater harmonization across personal laws, contributing to substantive equality in the treatment of children from different religious backgrounds and reinforcing the recognition of the mother's role as a primary caregiver.

2.5.3. Typical Issues in Indian Custody Matters

Jurisdiction in child custody proceedings is primarily territorial and is governed by section 9 of the Guardians and Wards Act, which vests jurisdiction in the court where the minor "ordinarily resides." Indian courts interpret "ordinary residence" as the place of settled habitation, not temporary or strategically created presence. In *Majoo v. Majoo*, the Supreme Court held that ordinary residence must reflect a degree of continuity and intention to reside, rejecting attempts at forum shopping through recent relocation.[341]

This approach parallels, but is not identical to, the American concept of "home state" jurisdiction under the UCCJEA. While both frameworks seek to deter forum shopping, Indian courts retain significantly greater flexibility and may assume jurisdiction based on immediate and overriding welfare considerations, even where a child's residence history is fragmented or unsettled. Unlike the UCCJEA, Indian custody law does not impose a fixed residential or durational requirement as a precondition to jurisdiction.

A. Nature of Custody Proceedings and Judicial Discretion

Custody proceedings in India are inquisitorial rather than strictly adversarial. Judges play an active role in interacting with the child, reviewing social welfare inputs, and assessing parental conduct beyond the pleadings. At the threshold, the court must bear in mind that in matters concerning the custody and care of a minor, it acts in its capacity as parens patriae, with the welfare of the child constituting the controlling and paramount consideration. The Supreme Court has stated the following in this regard:

> The word "welfare" . . . has to be construed literally and must be taken in its widest sense. The moral and ethical welfare of the child must also weigh with the Court as well as its physical well-being. Though the provisions of the special statutes which govern the rights of the parents or guardians may be taken into consideration, there is nothing which can stand in the way of the Court exercising its parens patriae jurisdiction arising in such cases.[342]

In *Kundu*, the Supreme Court underscored that technical rules of evidence must yield where necessary to determine the child's true welfare.[343]

Courts frequently conduct in-camera interviews with children, commission home-study reports, and rely on counselor or psychologist assessments. While similar practices exist in American custody litigation, Indian courts exercise

341. *Majoo*, AIR 2011 SC 1952.
342. *Nagpal*, AIR 2009 SC 557, ¶ 43.
343. *Kundu*, Civil Appeal No. 4960 of 2008, ¶ 56.

broader discretion and are less constrained by formal evidentiary rules. This flexibility allows courts to respond sensitively to individual circumstances but also introduces significant variability in outcomes across jurisdictions.

B. *Parens Patriae* Jurisdiction and the Overriding Standard of the Best Interest/Welfare of the Child

The Supreme Court has clearly articulated the scope of Indian courts' parens patriae jurisdiction as follows:

> A child, as has been ubiquitously articulated in different legal forums, is not a chattel or a ball to be shuttled or shunted from one parent to the other. The Court exercises paren patrae jurisdiction in custody or guardianship wrangles; it steps in to secure the welfare of the hapless child of two adults whose personal differences and animosity has taken precedence over the future of their child. . . .
>
> Upon a guardianship petition being laid before the Court, the concerned child ceases to be in the exclusive custody of the parents; thereafter, until the attainment of majority, the child continues in curial curatorship.[344]

Thus, it is a well-settled principle of law that, while exercising parens patriae jurisdiction, courts are guided by the sole and paramount consideration of what would best serve the welfare and interests of the minor child, to which all other considerations must yield.[345] Accordingly, whenever a question relating to the custody of a minor arises, the matter is to be determined not on the basis of the legal rights of the parties, but on the dominant and overriding criterion of the child's best interests, which remains the controlling consideration throughout.[346]

While the "best interest of the child" is the paramount consideration in custody disputes, it is largely a judicially evolved doctrine rather than a defined term in specific custody statutes like the Guardians and Wards Act, 1890. The Juvenile Justice (Care and Protection of Children) Act, 2015, provides the only formal statutory definition in India of the "best interest of child" under section 2(9) as "*the basis for any decision taken regarding the child, to ensure fulfilment of his basic rights and needs, identity, social well-being and physical, emotional and intellectual development.*"[347]

The governing factors in child custody disputes are derived through precedent-based law. There is no exhaustive list of such factors. Very recently, while ordering the return of children removed from Qatar to India, the Supreme Court stated:

344. ABC v. State, AIR 2015 SC 2569, ¶¶ 1, 20 (India), https://indiankanoon.org/doc/162566950/.

345. Kansagra v. Kansagra, AIR Online 2020 SC 875, ¶ 11.1 (India), http://indiankanoon.org/doc/181712544/.

346. *Chandran*, Writ Petition (Crl.) No. 112 of 2007, ¶ 18.

347. Juvenile Justice Act § 2(9).

> There is no dispute with the proposition that in matters of custody, the paramount consideration is the welfare of the children but nonetheless there are a host of other factors which weigh before the court while passing the final order of custody. These host of factors may include the conduct of the parties, their financial capacity, their standard of living, as well as the comfort and education of the children.[348]

The Supreme Court in *Sakhamuri* stated:

> The crucial factors which have to be kept in mind by the Courts for gauging the welfare of the children equally for the parent's can be inter alia, delineated, such as (1) maturity and judgment; (2) mental stability; (3) ability to provide access to schools; (4) moral character; (5) ability to provide continuing involvement in the community; (6) financial sufficiency and last but not the least the factors involving relationship with the child, as opposed to characteristics of the parent as an individual.[349]

No single factor is dispositive of the outcome.

1. Child's Preference

In Indian child custody jurisprudence, a child's preference is recognized as a significant and relevant factor, but it is neither conclusive nor binding. Courts have consistently held that the "paramount consideration" in all custody determinations is the welfare and best interests of the child, which prevails over all other considerations. Accordingly, a child's stated preference is assessed as one element within a broader, holistic inquiry, rather than treated as determinative.

a. Statutory Basis for Considering the Child's Opinion

The Guardians and Wards Act, 1890, expressly permits courts to take into account the wishes of a minor in appropriate cases. Section 17(3) of the act empowers the court to consider the preference of a minor who is of an age and capacity sufficient to form an "intelligent preference" when appointing or declaring a guardian. Further, section 17(5) of the act provides that the court shall not appoint or declare a guardian against the will of the minor. In addition to the Guardians and Wards Act, section 26 of the Hindu Marriage Act, 1955, authorizes courts to pass custody, maintenance, and education orders with respect to minor children "consistently with their wishes, wherever possible," thereby reinforcing the relevance of the child's perspective within custody adjudication.

b. At What Age Is a Child's Preference Considered?

Indian custody law does not prescribe a rigid or uniform age at which a child's preference must be considered. Instead, courts have adopted a flexible, fact-specific approach, placing greater weight on the wishes of children who are sufficiently mature to express a clear and reasoned preference. As a general

---

348. Malik v. Aftab, Arising out of S.L.P. (C) No. 28934 of 2025, ¶ 22 (India), https://indiankanoon.org/doc/28712247/.

349. *Sakhamuri*, AIR 2019 SC 2881, ¶ 49.

practice, courts tend to accord greater significance to the views of children aged nine or ten years and above, provided the preference appears voluntary and informed. The Law Commission of India has recommended that the wishes of a child aged 14 years or older must be considered by the court.[350] At the same time, courts have, in appropriate cases,[351] interacted with younger children, sometimes as young as seven years old, often in chambers, to understand their feelings and inclinations, while remaining cautious of the greater susceptibility of younger children to parental influence or coaching.

c. Landmark and Recent Case Law

Judicial precedent has repeatedly affirmed the relevance of a child's preference, subject to the overriding consideration of welfare. The Supreme Court has emphasized that where a child is old enough to form an intelligent preference, such preference must be taken into account, as contemplated under section 17(3) of the Guardians and Wards Act, as illustrated in *Kansagra v. Kansagra*.[352] In *Vohra v. Bhalla*, both the trial court and the Supreme Court interacted with a seven-year-old child in chambers in order to ascertain his wishes.[353] More recently, in *Wadhwa v. Wadhwa*, the Supreme Court personally interacted with a child above five years of age and upheld the child's preference to reside with the father, placing weight on the child's emotional comfort and the presence of grandparents in the household.[354] In *Singh v. Singh*, the Court took note of "parental alienation syndrome," observing that the child had been subtly and systematically influenced to favor one parent over the other, resulting in significant emotional distress.[355]

d. Limitations

At the same time, the Supreme Court has consistently reiterated that a child's preference, while important, cannot eclipse the paramount consideration of the child's welfare. In *Ganguli v. Ganguli*, the Court made it clear that the expressed wishes of the child must be evaluated in the context of overall welfare (in this case the child's wish to stay with his father aligned with the overall welfare analysis).[356] Similarly, in *Gowda v. State of Karnataka*, the Court prioritized the holistic best interests of the child over the child's stated wishes and ordered the

350. Law Commission of India, *Report No. 257: Reforms in Guardianship and Custody Laws in India* 57 (May 2015), https://highcourtchd.gov.in/sub_pages/left_menu/publish/year_books/Report%20No.257%20Custody%20Laws.pdf.

351. *Aftab*, Arising out of S.L.P. (C) No. 28934 of 2025, ¶ 30.

352. Kansagra v. Kansagra, AIR Online 2021 SC 860, ¶ 11.3 (India), https://indiankanoon.org/doc/114691445/.

353. Vohra v. Bhalla, AIR 2010 SC 1675, ¶¶ 13–14 (India), https://indiankanoon.org/doc/1064641/.

354. Wadhwa v. Wadhwa, Arising out of S.L.P. (Crl.) No. 12458/2024, ¶¶ 5, 15 (India), https://indiankanoon.org/doc/165891087/.

355. Singh v. Singh, AIR 2017 SC 929 (India), https://indiankanoon.org/doc/48721287/.

356. Ganguli v. Ganguli, AIR 2008 SC 2262, ¶ 17 (India), https://indiankanoon.org/doc/858575/.

child's return to the United States after considering all relevant circumstances affecting welfare.[357]

In *Kundu,* the Supreme Court stated specifically that, "[i]f the minor is old enough to form an intelligent preference or judgment, the Court must consider such preference as well, though the final decision should rest with the Court as to what is conducive to the welfare of the minor."[358]

Courts exercise considerable caution in acting upon a child's stated preference and do not follow it mechanically. The emphasis remains on whether the preference reflects an "intelligent preference" formed independently, rather than one shaped by undue influence, pressure, or parental alienation. Where there is evidence suggesting that a child's views may have been manipulated or coached, courts are reluctant to rely on such preferences. In assessing custody, courts also examine a range of other factors bearing on the child's welfare, including emotional stability, educational continuity, financial security, the moral character and conduct of each parent, and the child's health, safety, and long-term development.

2. Financial Soundness

While financial stability is a relevant factor, its contours are neither fixed nor uniform and must be assessed in the context of the particular circumstances. A parent's limited financial means does not, by itself, operate as a disqualification for the grant of child custody. Indian courts have consistently held that material prosperity cannot be treated as the sole or determinative factor in custody adjudication. Rather, the paramount consideration remains the child's overall and holistic welfare, of which financial capacity is only one component.

Courts place greater emphasis on emotional stability, continuity of care, and the quality of the child's relationship with each parent than on relative financial superiority. A parent's inability to offer a higher standard of living does not, in itself, render that parent unfit to have custody.

Where one parent, often the mother, faces financial disadvantage following separation, courts routinely address this imbalance by directing the financially stronger parent to provide maintenance or child support to meet the child's needs, including education, healthcare, and day-to-day upbringing. Custodial rights are thus not made contingent upon economic strength.

While a parent's financial capacity is relevant to ensuring that the child's basic needs, such as health, education, and safety, are adequately met, it is assessed alongside a range of other considerations, including parental conduct, emotional availability, the stability of the caregiving environment, the child's expressed preferences where appropriate, and the child's overall emotional and psychological well-being.

---

357. Gowda v. State of Karnataka, Civil Appeal Nos. 4987 of 2022, ¶ 8 (India), https://indiankanoon.org/doc/174872729/.

358. *Kundu,* Civil Appeal No. 4960 of 2008, ¶ 56.

a. Landmark and Recent Case Law

In *Ganguli*, the Supreme Court held, "*Better financial resources of either of the parents or their love for the child may be one of the relevant considerations but cannot be the sole determining factor for the custody of the child.*"[359] Custody was granted to the father not just because of his stability, but because the child expressed a strong preference for the environment in which he was already settled.[360] Similarly, in *Kundu*, the Court emphasized that custody is a "human problem" requiring a "human touch." It ruled that better financial resources might be relevant but are *not determinative*.[361] In *Majumdar v. Datta*, the court specifically held:

> It is settled beyond doubt that in matters relating to custody of child, its not the legal right of the claimant which is decisive, but it is the welfare of the child which is the primary and paramount test and no one can recover custody of a child merely by, *brandishing his legal right or financial affluence*.[362]

In *Kansagra*, the Court noted that holistic growth, including emotional bonds and educational needs, outweighs mere financial stability.[363] Yet, very recently, in *Aftab*, the Court emphasized the parties' "financial capacity" and "*their standard of living*" as relevant factors, against the overarching backdrop of a child's welfare.[364]

C. Gender-Based Preferential Rights of Custody and the Evolution of Joint Parenting

Both Indian and American family law systems profess adherence to the "best interests of the child," but the operational frameworks differ significantly. In the United States, custody determinations are guided by statutory schemes that emphasize joint custody, shared parenting, and parental equality in the absence of abuse or neglect. Indian law, by contrast, does not presume joint custody, though this trend has slightly begun to shift.

1. Father's Right to Custody

Although certain provisions of the Indian family law have been understood to accord a preferential position to the father, that position appears to have been shifting over the decades.

With respect to the Guardians and Wards Act, for instance, the Supreme Court, in a landmark judgment, clarified that such preference is neither absolute nor indefeasible. The Court held that a father's claim to custody must yield to the paramount consideration of the welfare of the minor. In particular, it stated:

359. *Ganguli*, AIR 2008 SC 2262, ¶ 14.
360. *Id.* ¶ 17.
361. *Kundu*, Civil Appeal No. 4960 of 2008, ¶ 56.
362. Majumdar v. Datta, AIR 1991 Cal 76, ¶ 1 (India) (emphasis added), https://indiankanoon.org/doc/943936/.
363. *Kansagra*, AIR Online 2021 SC 860, ¶ 11.3.
364. *Aftab*, Arising out of S.L.P. (C) No. 28934 of 2025, ¶ 22.

> If the custody of the father cannot promote their welfare equally or better than the custody of the mother, then, he *cannot claim indefeasible right* to their custody under S.25 merely because there is no defect in his personal character and he has attachment for his children which every normal parent has.[365]

In yet another case, the Supreme Court observed, in the context of a father's preferential custodial rights vis-à-vis the overarching welfare of the child:

> It is, no doubt, true that father is presumed by the statutes to be better suited to look after the welfare of the child, being normally the working member and head of the family, yet in each case the Court has to see primarily to the welfare of the child in determining the question of his or her custody.[366]

In *Majumdar*, the Court went ahead to note:

> A legal guardian [in this case the father] cannot claim [a custody] order *merely by dangling his legal right*, unless he can demonstrate that his custody would be conducive to the better or greater welfare of the child than what it is having and is expected to have in the existing custody of the person, even though without a legal right to such custody.[367]

Similarly, under section 6(a) of the Hindu Minority and Guardianship Act, 1956, the mother's right was historically restricted by the "tender years doctrine." Section 6(a) of the act provides, inter alia, that the father is the natural guardian of a minor and, *after him*, the mother. Section 6(a) also provides that the custody of a child who has not reached the age of five years shall ordinarily be with the mother.

However, in *Hariharan v. Reserve Bank of India*, the Supreme Court historically observed that the expression "*after*" need not be understood as connoting "*after the death of the father.*"[368] In the context in which it is used, it signifies "*in the absence of*," with the term "*absence*" referring to the father's absence from the care of the minor child or depiction of "*total apathy of the father towards the child.*"

In *Kundu*, the Supreme Court expressly curtailed the father's preferential right by prioritizing his criminal and moral conduct over his statutory status.[369] Thus, even though the father was the natural guardian and had no proven defect in character beyond pending allegations, the Court denied him custody because his past behavior (alleged involvement in the mother's death) created an environment unsuitable for the child.[370]

---

365. *Jacob*, AIR 1973 SC 2090, at 13–14 (emphasis added).

366. *Ganguli*, AIR 2008 SC 2262, ¶ 14.

367. *Majumdar*, AIR 1991 Cal 76, ¶ 6 (emphasis added).

368. Hariharan v. Reserve Bank of India, AIR 1999 SC 1149 (India), https://indiankanoon.org/doc/1241462/.

369. *Kundu*, Civil Appeal No. 4960 of 2008.

370. *Id.*

In a recent judgment, the Supreme Court utilized its *review jurisdiction* to reverse a decision that had shifted custody from the mother to the father.[371] The Court relied heavily on a clinical psychologist's report showing the 11-year-old child suffered from severe separation anxiety at the prospect of leaving his primary caregiver (the mother).[372] It held that hyper-technical legal approaches must be abandoned in favor of the parens patriae doctrine to prevent irreversible psychological harm to the child.[373]

2. Judicial Evolution

In 2015, the Law Commission of India undertook a review of the existing legal framework governing custody and guardianship, focusing on the Guardians and Wards Act, 1890, and the Hindu Minority and Guardianship Act, 1956. The Commission recommended legislative amendments aimed to "*[p]rovide for equal legal status of both parents with respect to guardianship and custody.*"[374]

Thus, Indian courts have begun engaging more proactively with shared or joint custody models. In *Singh*, the Supreme Court endorsed the concept of shared parenting and emphasized the importance of "[i]nvolvement of both parents."[375]

A relatively rare illustration of the Indian legal system's engagement with the concept of joint parenting arises in the context of an international parental abduction matter from 2019 involving the removal of children from the United States to India. In directing the return of the abducted children to the United States, the Supreme Court emphasized joint parenting (although seemingly in a non-divorce context) as a factor relevant to the children's best interests:

> In the present case, there is every possibility that the parties may reconcile and start over their relationship afresh, at least for the sake of happiness of their own offspring if for no other reason. The parties are indeed mature and sensible enough to understand that the ordinary wear and tear of married life has to be put up in within the larger interests of their own happiness and of the healthy, normal growth and development of their offspring, whom destiny has entrusted to their joint parental care. Spouses must come over the temperamental disharmony which usually exists in every marriage, rather than magnifying it with impulsive desires and passions. Parents are not only caretakers, but they are instrumental in the development of their child's social, emotional, cognitive and physical wellbeing and work harmoniously to give their children a happy home to which they are justly entitled to. We hope and trust that the parties will forget and forgive their differences and join hands

371. Baby Mathew v. Kumar, 2025 INSC 853, ¶ 35 (India), https://indiankanoon.org/doc/109558386/.

372. *Id.* ¶ 34.

373. *Id.* ¶ 16.

374. Law Commission of India, *supra* note 350, at 2 (emphasis added).

375. *Singh*, AIR 2017 SC 929.

together in providing the congenial atmosphere which may be good not for themselves but also for the development of their minor children. . . .

In our view, the best interest of the children being of paramount importance will be served if they return to US and enjoy their natural environment with love, care and attention of their parents. . . .[376]

In *Seetharam v. Rathnam*, the court accorded significant weight to the child's expressed desire for joint parenting, noting his wish to maintain meaningful relationships both with his paternal grandparents and with his younger siblings. Observing the maturity and willingness of each parent to support the child's relationship with the other, the court concluded that an arrangement of shared parenting best served the child's interests.[377]

This development brings Indian jurisprudence closer to American norms, though implementation remains uneven (not only in domestic but also in international child custody context), because there have been several cases since 2019 where the courts did not order the return of a child who was brought to India without the consent of the other parent.

D. Sole Custody and Primary Caregiving Considerations: The Norm

Sole custody remains the dominant custodial arrangement in India, particularly where one parent has historically served as the primary caregiver. Courts placed significant weight on continuity of care, stability, and minimizing disruption to the child's daily life. The Supreme Court in *Kundu* held that handing custody to a parent who has not been significantly involved in daily caregiving may be detrimental, even if that parent possesses superior financial resources.[378]

Indian courts routinely reiterate that financial capacity alone cannot determine custody. Emotional availability, consistency, and the child's sense of security are treated as central factors. This principle aligns with American jurisprudence rejecting economic advantage as a decisive custody determinant, though U.S. courts may place greater institutional emphasis on facilitating joint parental involvement even when caregiving roles were previously unequal.

Gender presumptions have substantially eroded. While younger children were once almost automatically placed with mothers, courts now explicitly state that there is no legal presumption favoring either parent. In *Sharma*, the Supreme Court clarified that maternal preference for young children cannot be mechanical and must yield to a fact-based welfare inquiry.[379] That said, mothers continue to receive custody in many cases due to prevailing caregiving patterns rather than formal legal preference.

---

376. *Sakhamuri*, AIR 2019 SC 2881, ¶¶ 55–56 (emphasis added).

377. Seetharam v. Rathnam, AIR Online 2020 Kar 1865, ¶ 2 (India), https://indiankanoon.org/doc/62005291/.

378. *Kundu*, Civil Appeal No. 4960 of 2008.

379. *Sharma*, AIR 2015 SC 2232.

E. Visitation, Access, and Parenting Time

Visitation rights in India are recognized as integral to a child's welfare rather than as derivative parental privileges. Courts consistently stress that a child has a right to maintain contact with both parents. In *Nagpal*, the Supreme Court observed that denial of access to one parent may cause emotional harm and undermine the child's holistic development.[380]

Visitation schedules vary widely depending on geography, distance, parental conflict, and the child's age. Courts increasingly permit liberal visitation, including overnight stays, holiday sharing, and electronic communication. In *Chandran*, the Supreme Court recognized that modern communication technology must be leveraged to maintain parent–child relationships, particularly in transnational families.[381]

Indian visitation arrangements remain more judicially managed than their American counterparts. U.S. courts often rely on parenting plans negotiated by the parties, with detailed calendars and enforcement mechanisms. Indian courts, by contrast, frequently retain active supervision, modifying access orders in response to compliance or conflict. Repeated denial of visitation may result in adverse custody consequences, as courts increasingly view parental alienation as harmful to child welfare, although the doctrine itself remains underdeveloped in Indian jurisprudence.

F. Impact of Domestic Violence and Abuse Allegations

Allegations of domestic violence have a significant, but carefully calibrated, impact on custody determinations in India. Courts distinguish between spousal conflict and behavior that directly endangers or traumatizes the child. While Indian courts do not apply statutory presumptions analogous to those found in many U.S. jurisdictions, where proven domestic violence may trigger rebuttable presumptions against custody, Indian judges exercise strong discretion to protect children from exposure to violent environments.

In *Sharma*, the Supreme Court held that allegations of violence must be examined in the context of the child's safety and emotional health, not merely as part of the marital dispute. The Court emphasized that even when violence is directed primarily at a spouse, prolonged exposure may adversely affect the child's development.[382]

Courts may order supervised visitation, restrict overnight access, or temporarily limit contact while investigations or criminal proceedings are pending. In *Ghosh*, although the case primarily involved cruelty, the Supreme Court recognized that hostile domestic environments can have far-reaching consequences for children, thereby justifying cautious custodial arrangements.[383]

Comparatively, U.S. family courts often rely on statutory domestic violence findings, child protective services involvement, and structured risk assessments.

---

380. *Nagpal*, AIR 2009 SC 557.
381. *Chandran*, Writ Petition (Crl.) No. 112 of 2007.
382. *Sharma*, AIR 2015 SC 2232.
383. *Ghosh*, AIR Online 2007 SC 347.

Indian courts, lacking such institutionalized systems, rely more heavily on judicial evaluation, interim protection orders under the Protection of Women from Domestic Violence Act, 2005, and counsel reports to assess risk.

G. Parental Alienation and Access Interference

Indian courts increasingly recognize that interference with the child's relationship with the other parent is antithetical to child welfare, though the doctrine of parental alienation has not been fully formalized. The Supreme Court in *Singh* acknowledged that systematic obstruction of access arrangements can deeply harm a child's emotional health and undermine the court's custody framework.[384]

High courts have begun treating persistent denial of visitation as a serious custodial violation rather than a mere procedural infraction. In *Raghavan*, the Supreme Court observed that a parent's unwillingness to facilitate access may reflect an inability to place the child's interests above personal grievances. Although the Court declined to adopt a rigid alienation doctrine, it recognized relational harm as a welfare concern.

This approach corresponds with American jurisprudence, where intentional alienation and denial of parenting time may justify custody modification. However, Indian courts exercise greater caution, emphasizing remediation and counseling before imposing drastic custodial changes.

H. Enforcement of Custody and Access Orders

Enforcement of custody and visitation orders remains one of the most challenging aspects of Indian family law. Courts possess broad powers, including contempt proceedings, police assistance orders, and modification of custody arrangements, but practical enforcement often depends on parental compliance and judicial persistence.

In *Chandran*, the Supreme Court recognized that enforcement mechanisms must be responsive to the realities of family conflict and geographic mobility. Courts may issue directions to facilitate access, impose time-bound compliance requirements, or warn of adverse inferences where a parent repeatedly frustrates contact.[385]

Indian courts also rely on their continuing jurisdiction to recalibrate custody when enforcement difficulties persist. Unlike many U.S. systems where enforcement and modification proceedings are distinct, Indian courts treat persistent noncompliance as inherently relevant to the welfare analysis.

I. Modification of Custody Orders

Custody orders in India are inherently revisable. Courts routinely emphasize that custody arrangements must evolve with the child's age, educational needs, health considerations, and changing family dynamics. In *Jacob*, the Supreme

384. *Singh*, AIR 2017 SC 929.

385. *Chandran*, Writ Petition (Crl.) No. 112 of 2007.

Court underscored that custody determinations are never final and remain subject to continuing judicial oversight.[386]

Subsequent decisions reaffirm that relocation, remarriage, significant changes in parental circumstances, or demonstrated harm may justify modification. This approach closely parallels American modification standards but operates with greater judicial flexibility and less emphasis on formal thresholds such as *substantial change in circumstances.*

J. Relocation of Children Within India

Relocation disputes within India arise most commonly when the custodial parent seeks to move to another city or state for employment, remarriage, family support, or educational opportunities for the child. Indian courts treat relocation not as a matter of parental convenience but as a question of child welfare. Unlike many American jurisdictions that apply formal relocation statutes requiring advance notice and enumerating specific factors, Indian courts resolve relocation disputes through a discretionary welfare analysis grounded in precedent.

In *Ganguli,* the Supreme Court upheld the mother's right to relocate with the child, emphasizing continuity of caregiving and the absence of any demonstrable harm caused by relocation. The Court rejected the notion that a noncustodial parent's convenience could override a custodial environment that promoted stability and emotional security. At the same time, the Court affirmed the importance of preserving access, directing structured visitation to mitigate the impact of distance.[387]

Indian courts do not impose a formal burden of proof on the relocating parent comparable to the heightened scrutiny applied in some American states. Instead, the relocating parent must demonstrate that the move is bona fide and consistent with the child's welfare, while the objecting parent bears the burden of establishing detriment. Courts frequently balance factors such as educational continuity, quality of life, emotional dependence, and feasibility of continued access.

2.5.4. Role of State Institutions and Child Welfare Committees

Child Welfare Committees established under the Juvenile Justice (Care and Protection of Children) Act, 2015, occasionally intersect with custody disputes, particularly where abuse, neglect, or abandonment allegations arise. While these bodies do not supplant family courts in matrimonial custody disputes, their findings may influence custody outcomes.

Courts examine Committee reports cautiously, recognizing their protective mandate but reaffirming that custody between parents remains a judicial function. This coordination resembles American child protective services involvement in custody litigation, though Indian oversight mechanisms remain less institutionalized.

386. *Jacob,* AIR 1973 SC 2090.
387. *Ganguli,* AIR 2008 SC 2262.

A. Long-Term Supervision and Continuing Jurisdiction

Indian courts maintain *continuing jurisdiction* over custody matters even after final orders are passed. This supervisory role enables courts to revisit access schedules, schooling disputes, or relocation issues as circumstances evolve. In *Jacob*, the Supreme Court emphasized that custody orders are inherently temporary expressions of welfare assessment and must remain open to revision.[388]

Unlike American systems that often require formal modification motions and heightened thresholds, Indian courts permit relatively fluid re-examination, reflecting a paternalistic but child-focused judicial philosophy.

B. Comparative Reflections on Predictability and Discretion

From a comparative perspective, Indian custody law prioritizes equitable discretion over predictability. American family law emphasizes statutory clarity, procedural safeguards, and standardized evaluative tools. Indian law emphasizes individualized justice responsive to social complexity and relational nuance.

Neither approach is inherently superior. Indian discretion allows courts to address extreme circumstances with sensitivity, particularly in cross-border disputes. However, variability creates uncertainty for litigants and foreign practitioners accustomed to codified standards.

C. Enforcement of Custody and Access Orders Across Jurisdictions

The enforcement of custody and visitation orders presents persistent challenges in the Indian legal system, particularly where parties reside in different jurisdictions or where one parent is resistant to compliance. Although family courts possess authority to issue and modify custody orders, enforcement frequently requires supervisory intervention by high courts exercising writ jurisdiction or contempt powers. Indian courts treat refusal to comply with custody or access orders not merely as a procedural violation but as conduct potentially adverse to the child's welfare.

From time to time, courts have expressed concern over repeated obstruction of visitation and emphasized that access orders must be enforced meaningfully, not reduced to symbolic gestures. Courts routinely warn that persistent noncompliance may justify modification of custody arrangements, including transfer of primary custody in extreme cases. This approach mirrors American doctrines under which denial of parenting time may constitute a substantial change in circumstances supporting modification.

However, Indian courts exercise enforcement power cautiously. Contempt proceedings are generally employed as a last resort, given courts' reluctance to expose children to further conflict or parental incarceration. Instead, courts often combine enforcement directives with counseling obligations, structured visitation schedules, and clear warnings of adverse consequences for continued noncompliance.

388. *Jacob*, AIR 1973 SC 2090.

D. Contempt Jurisdiction and Coercive Remedies

Indian courts possess constitutional contempt powers that extend to enforcement of custody and visitation orders. High courts and the Supreme Court may impose fines, issue coercive directions, or, in rare cases, order detention for willful disobedience. In *Chandran*, the Supreme Court emphasized that contempt jurisdiction exists to uphold judicial authority and protect the child's welfare, not to punish spouses.[389]

Despite the theoretical availability of coercive remedies, courts generally prioritize corrective intervention. Repeated defiance of access orders may result in directions seeking police assistance or mandatory production of the child before the court. These measures resemble American enforcement mechanisms such as supervised exchanges or law enforcement assistance clauses, though Indian courts retain a greater degree of direct oversight.

E. Long-Distance and Virtual Parenting Arrangements

As geographic separation between parents becomes increasingly common, Indian courts have begun formalizing long-distance parenting arrangements. Courts routinely incorporate provisions for videoconferencing, telephonic communication, and digital interaction to preserve parent–child bonds. In *Chandran*, the Supreme Court acknowledged that physical distance cannot extinguish parental relationships and encouraged use of technology to facilitate continuous contact.[390]

This judicial recognition aligns with American practice, where virtual visitation has gained statutory recognition in several states. Indian courts, however, implement virtual access through discretionary orders rather than codified parenting-time frameworks. Judges may tailor frequency and duration based on the child's age, schooling schedule, and emotional response to digital interaction.

F. Relocation After Custody Determination

Post-decree relocation requests are evaluated under a welfare standard similar to that applied at the initial custody stage. Courts examine whether relocation significantly disrupts the child's stability, education, or access to the non-relocating parent. In *Rao*, while primarily addressing matrimonial cruelty, the Supreme Court acknowledged that unilateral parental decisions affecting children may warrant judicial scrutiny even after final orders.[391]

Courts frequently impose safeguards such as extended holiday access, allocation of travel expenses, and conditions prohibiting relocation without court permission. This approach parallels American relocation jurisprudence but lacks formal statutory notice or objection procedures, instead relying on judicial discretion and equitable balancing.

389. *Chandran*, Writ Petition (Crl.) No. 112 of 2007.
390. *Id.*
391. *Rao*, AIR 2013 SC 2176.

G. Role of Family Courts in Ongoing Supervision

Family courts in India serve not only as adjudicators but as continuing supervisory bodies overseeing compliance, adjustment, and long-term implementation. Courts frequently schedule review hearings to monitor access compliance, schooling issues, or behavioral concerns reported by parents or counselors. This supervisory approach reflects the court's parens patriae role and differs from American systems where post-decree judicial involvement is typically more limited absent formal modification petitions.

While intensive supervision enhances child protection, it also contributes to docket congestion and prolonged litigation. Nevertheless, courts view oversight as necessary when parental cooperation remains fragile.

2.6. Unmarried Partners and Parents

2.6.1. Introduction

The legal treatment of unmarried partners and parents presents one of the most dynamic and contested areas of family law in India. As social norms evolve and increasing numbers of couples choose to cohabit without marriage, courts have been compelled to reconcile traditional family law frameworks with contemporary lived realities. This section examines how Indian law conceptualizes and regulates unmarried partnerships, the rights and obligations arising from such relationships, and the status of children born outside formal marriage.

2.6.2. Historical Reluctance and Social Context in India

Indian family law historically derived legitimacy, rights, and obligations almost exclusively from marriage. Classical Hindu law, Muslim personal law, and colonial-era statutes alike presumed marriage as the gateway to familial recognition. Unmarried cohabitation was socially stigmatized and legally invisible. This normative preference for marriage persisted well into the post-independence era, with courts often reluctant to acknowledge nonmarital relationships except in exceptional circumstances.

In *Gokalchand v. Kumari*, the Supreme Court held that while long and continuous cohabitation may give rise to a presumption of marriage, such a presumption is "rebuttable."[392] The Court observed that continuous cohabitation over a number of years could justify an inference of lawful marriage, particularly where the parties were treated by society as husband and wife and there was no material suggesting otherwise. However, the Court was careful to emphasize that this presumption operates only in the absence of contrary evidence. Where circumstances exist that weaken or displace the inference of marriage, the presumption must yield. The decision thus reflects a historically cautious judicial approach, in which cohabitation was not independently favored or legitimized, but was tolerated only to the extent that it could be assimilated into the legal framework of marriage, and even then, subject to rebuttal.

---

392. Gokalchand v. Kumari, 1952 AIR 231 (India), https://indiankanoon.org/doc/1388066/.

Although contemporary Indian jurisprudence has begun to address live-in relationships more openly, judicial acceptance remains uneven and periodically reverts to moral and social conservatism. This tension is evident in recent high court decisions that continue to view such relationships with suspicion rather than neutrality. For instance, in *Ujjawal v. State of Haryana*, the Punjab and Haryana High Court declined to grant protection to a live-in couple, observing that such arrangements could uproot the "social fabric of society."[393] Similarly, in *Khandal v. State of Rajasthan*, the Rajasthan High Court reiterated that a live-in relationship involving a married person does not merit legal protection.[394]

Yet, in the broader social context, economic mobility, urbanization, and globalization have challenged these traditional assumptions, compelling Indian courts to engage with the legal implications of live-in relationships.

2.6.3. Emergence of Legal Recognition of Live-In Relationships

The first significant shift in Indian jurisprudence came through constitutional and criminal-law adjudication rather than family statutes. In *Prasad v. Dy. Director of Consolidation*, the Supreme Court recognized a long-term live-in relationship as giving rise to a *"strong presumption"* of marriage, emphasizing social stability and legitimacy rather than formal ceremony.[395] Subsequent decisions expanded this reasoning, though not without inconsistency.

In *Singh v. State of U.P.*, the Supreme Court held that live-in relationships between consenting adults do not constitute an offense and an adult woman is free to *"live with anyone she likes."*[396] While the case arose in a criminal context, its broader significance lay in the Court's affirmation that nonmarital cohabitation is not per se illegal or immoral.

However, courts have remained *markedly reluctant* to extend legal protection to live-in relationships *where one party has a subsisting marriage*. In *Sarma v. Sarma*, the Supreme Court drew a clear distinction between relationships resembling marriage and those that undermine an existing marital bond, holding that a live-in relationship involving a married person does not warrant the same legal recognition or protection:

> All live-in- relationships are not relationships in the nature of marriage. Appellant's and the respondent's relationship is, therefore, not a "relationship in the nature of marriage" because it has no inherent or essential characteristic of a marriage, but a relationship other than "in the nature of marriage" and the appellant's status is lower than the status of a wife and that relationship would not fall within the definition of

393. Ujjawal v. State of Haryana, Writ Petition (Cr.) 4268/2021 (O&M) (India), https://images.assettype.com/barandbench/2021-05/39bea1ba-ae7e-4b8d-8774-33fe2d71316a/Ujjawal_v__State_of_Haryana.pdf.

394. Khandal v. State of Rajasthan, S.B. Crl. Misc. (Petition) No. 3023/2021, https://images.assettype.com/barandbench-hindi/2021-06/d7b95a24-3fb7-474b-9c8d-888e9cef02ec/Rashika_Khandal_v__State_of_Rajasthan.pdf.

395. Prasad v. Dy. Director of Consolidation, AIR 1978 SC 1557 (India), https://indiankanoon.org/doc/215649/.

396. Singh v. State of U.P., AIR 2006 SC 2522 (India), https://indiankanoon.org/doc/1364215/.

> "domestic relationship" under Section 2(f) of the DV Act. If we hold that the relationship between the appellant and the respondent is a relationship in the nature of a marriage, we will be doing an injustice to the legally wedded wife and children who opposed that relationship.[397]

2.6.4. Statutory Interface: What Defines Relationships "in the Nature of Marriage"

The most explicit statutory recognition of unmarried partnerships in India appears in the Protection of Women from Domestic Violence Act, 2005. Section 2(f) defines a "domestic relationship" to include not only marriage but also a "*relationship in the nature of marriage.*"[398]

Put simply, what comes closest in law to a live-in relationship is a "*relationship in the nature of marriage,*" and because the term "live-in relationship" has not been given independent statutory recognition, courts continue to rely on this formulation.[399] At the same time, courts remain cautious not to equate casual cohabitation, concubinage, or a "keep-like" arrangement with a "relationship in the nature of marriage."[400] Nevertheless, this phrase has generated extensive litigation and judicial interpretation.

In *Velusamy*, the Supreme Court attempted to define the term "in the nature of marriage." The Court articulated the criteria as follows:

> In our opinion a "relationship in the nature of marriage" is akin to a common law marriage. Common law marriages require that although not being formally married: (a) The couple must hold themselves out to society as being akin to spouses; (b) They must be of legal age to marry; (c) They must be otherwise qualified to enter into a legal marriage, including being unmarried; (d) They must have voluntarily cohabited and held themselves out to the world as being akin to spouses for a significant period of time. . . .
>
> In our opinion a "relationship in the nature of marriage" under the 2005 Act must also fulfill the above requirements, and in addition the parties must have lived together in a "shared household" as defined in Section 2(s) of the Act. Merely spending weekends together or a one night stand would not make it a "domestic relationship".[401]

2.6.5. Rights and Remedies of Unmarried Partners in India

Despite incremental recognition, Indian law does not confer upon unmarried partners the full spectrum of rights available to married spouses. There is no

397. Sarma v. Sarma, 2013 AIR SCW 6783, ¶ 65 (India), https://indiankanoon.org/doc/192421140/.

398. Protection of Women from Domestic Violence Act § 2(f).

399. Velusamy v. Patchaiammal, AIR 2011 SC 479, at ¶¶ 20, 35 (India), https://indiankanoon.org/doc/1521881/.

400. *Id.* ¶ 34.

401. *Id.* ¶ 33.

statutory framework governing property division, maintenance, or inheritance between cohabiting partners as such. Maintenance claims are typically routed through section 125 of the CrPC, 1973, which provides relief to a "wife." Judicial interpretation has occasionally extended this provision to women in relationships akin to marriage, though outcomes remain fact-specific and uncertain.

For instance, In *Bhatiya v. State of Gujarat*, the Supreme Court held that only a woman who is a legally wedded wife is entitled to maintenance under section 125 of the CrPC:

> However, desirable it may be, as contended by learned counsel for the appellant to take note of the plight of the unfortunate woman, the legislative intent being clearly reflected in Section 125 of the Code, there is no scope for enlarging its scope by introducing any artificial definition to include woman not lawfully married in the expression "wife".[402]

However, in *Chanmuniya v. Kushwaha*, a single Bench of the Supreme Court considered whether long-term cohabitation could give rise to a presumption of a valid marriage entitling a woman to maintenance under section 125 of the CrPC; whether strict proof of marriage is required for such a claim, particularly in light of the Protection of Women from Domestic Violence Act, 2005; and whether a marriage performed under customary rites, though not strictly compliant with section 7(1) of the Hindu Marriage Act, 1955, or other personal laws, could nonetheless support a claim for maintenance under CrPC section 125.[403] While referring the broader questions to a larger Bench, the Court expressed the following view:

> We are of the opinion that a broad and expansive interpretation should be given to the term "wife" to include even those cases where a man and woman have been living together as husband and wife for a reasonably long period of time, and strict proof of marriage should not be a pre-condition for maintenance under Section 125 of the Cr.P.C, so as to fulfil the true spirit and essence of the beneficial provision of maintenance under Section 125.[404]

This reasoning was subsequently followed and affirmed in *Badshah*, where the Supreme Court reiterated that a purposive interpretation of CrPC section 125 is necessary to prevent injustice to women in long-term relationships resembling marriage.[405]

However, short-term relationships, such as one-night stands or weekend affairs, as well as adulterous relationships are subjected to closer judicial scrutiny and, more often than not, fail to meet the criteria of a "relationship in the nature of marriage."

---

402. Bhatiya v. State of Gujarat, AIR 2005 SC 1809 (India), https://indiankanoon.org/doc/1590152/.

403. Chanmuniya v, Kushwaha, AIR 2010 SC (Supp) 29, ¶ 45 (India), https://indiankanoon.org/doc/1949767/.

404. *Id.* ¶ 46.

405. *Badshah*, AIR 2014 SC 869, ¶¶ 21–22.

2.6.6. Children Born to Unmarried Parents: Indian Law

Indian law has been more progressive in addressing the status of children born outside marriage. Section 16 of the Hindu Marriage Act, 1955, legitimizes children of void and voidable marriages for certain purposes, though it restricts inheritance rights to parental property. Judicial interpretation has gradually expanded protections for children born from live-in relationships, emphasizing constitutional values of equality and dignity.

In the 2011 case *Revanasiddappa v. Mallikarjun*, the Supreme Court held that children born from long-term live-in relationships should not suffer legal or social disabilities and may inherit property from their parents.[406] The Court's reasoning was anchored in Articles 14 and 21 of the Constitution, rejecting moralistic distinctions that penalize children for parental choices.

It is important to note that because of the significance of the *Revanasiddappa* case, the matter was referred to a larger *three-judge bench* to settle the conflict regarding *ancestral property*. Accordingly, in 2023, the Supreme Court delivered a definitive and expansive ruling that substantially strengthened, among other things, the rights of children born to unmarried partners. Moving beyond earlier uncertainty that confined such rights largely to self-acquired property, the Court clarified that these children are also entitled to a share in joint Hindu family (ancestral) property.[407] At the same time, the Court drew a clear boundary on the scope of this entitlement, holding that under the legal fiction created by section 16(3) of the Hindu Marriage Act, 1955, the child's claim is limited to the share that would have fallen to the parent in a notional partition, and does not extend to the shares of other coparceners.[408] Anchoring its reasoning in constitutional values, the Court reaffirmed that a child's right to property is an aspect of dignity protected under Article 21, and cannot be defeated by the parents' failure to enter into a legally valid marriage.

Similarly, the Court in *Tulsa v. Durghatiya* reiterated that long cohabitation gives rise to a presumption of marriage, thereby conferring legitimacy upon children born of such unions.[409] In another case, the Supreme Court reaffirmed that if a man and woman live together for a long time as husband and wife, a *presumption of marriage* arises, and consequently, the children are entitled to a share in the *family property*.[410] With respect to the burden of proof, the Court remarked:

> It is well settled that if a man and a woman live together for long years as husband and wife, there would be a presumption in favour of wedlock. Such a presumption could be drawn under Section 114 of the

406. Revanasiddappa v. Mallikarjun, AIR 2011 SC (Supp) 155, ¶ 35 (India), https://indiankanoon.org/doc/138849/.

407. Revanasiddappa v. Mallikarjun, 2023 INSC 783, ¶¶ 41–43, 45, 54(ix) (India), https://indiankanoon.org/doc/30241407/.

408. *Id.* ¶ 45.

409. Tulsa v. Durghatiya, AIR 2008 SC 1193, ¶ 13 (India), https://indiankanoon.org/doc/988131/.

410. Krishnan v. Valsan, Civil Appeal No. 64066407/2010, ¶ 27 (India), https://indiankanoon.org/doc/80285666/.

Evidence Act. Although, the presumption is rebuttable, *a heavy burden* lies on him who seek to deprive the relationship of legal origin to prove that no marriage took place.[411]

These decisions underscore a child-centric approach that prioritizes welfare and equality over formal marital status.

2.6.7. Custody and Child Support: Children of Unmarried Parents in India

Custody disputes involving unmarried parents in India are governed primarily by the Guardians and Wards Act, 1890. The statute adopts a welfare-of-the-child standard, allowing courts to appoint guardians irrespective of parental marital status. Indian courts have increasingly recognized the custodial rights of unwed mothers, particularly in early childhood.

A. Mother's Preferential Rights to Custody

In *ABC*, the Supreme Court held that an unwed mother may be appointed the sole guardian of her child without requiring disclosure or consent of the biological father, where such disclosure is not in the child's best interests. The Court went on to state that it was *"abundantly clear that the predominant legal thought in . . . India is to bestow guardianship and related rights to the mother of a child born outside of wedlock."*[412] This decision marked a significant departure from patriarchal assumptions embedded in earlier guardianship jurisprudence.

B. Father's Rights

While the ruling favored the mother's privacy, it explicitly noted that a putative father who has not shown interest in the child does not have an automatic equal standing. However, the Court also clarified that a father who *does* wish to be involved is not precluded from later approaching the court to establish paternity and claim custody or visitation based on the child's best interests.[413]

C. Child Support

In India, a child born to unmarried parents has an enforceable right to maintenance from the biological father, irrespective of the parents' marital status or religion. This right is most commonly enforced under criminal law through section 125 of the CrPC (now replaced by section 144 of the BNSS), which applies uniformly across religions and expressly obligates a father with sufficient means to maintain his illegitimate minor child, whether a son or daughter, until the child attains majority. Support/maintenance may extend beyond the age of 18 only where the child suffers from a physical or mental disability that prevents self-support. Under Hindu personal law, additional protections exist: section 20

411. *Id.* ¶ 15 (emphasis added).
412. *ABC*, AIR 2015 SC 2569, ¶ 15.
413. *Id.* ¶ 11.

of the Hindu Adoption and Maintenance Act, 1956, places a clear duty on a Hindu father to maintain both legitimate and illegitimate children.

D. Determining Paternity

In Indian law, paternity has traditionally been governed by a strong legal presumption under section 112 of the Indian Evidence Act, 1872, which treats a child born during the subsistence of a valid marriage as the legitimate child of the husband, rebuttable only by proof of non-access and not by medical or scientific evidence.[414] This presumption, intended to protect the status of the child and the institution of marriage, long operated even where biological paternity was doubtful. A significant doctrinal shift occurred in *Roy v. Roy*, where the Supreme Court held that when a conclusive legal presumption comes into direct conflict with scientifically accurate DNA evidence, the latter must prevail.[415] At the same time, the Court adopted a calibrated approach, clarifying that if DNA testing "can be avoided, it should be avoided."[416] While a court cannot physically compel a party to undergo DNA testing, refusal to comply with such a direction permits the drawing of an adverse inference under section 114 of the Evidence Act.[417] Although *Roy* arose in the context of a marital relationship, its reasoning has broader relevance for cases involving unmarried partners, where paternity is established not through marital presumptions but through evidence-based inquiry, including DNA testing where justified, thereby ensuring that biological fathers cannot evade maintenance obligations on technical grounds while also protecting individuals from being wrongly burdened with paternity absent proof.[418]

E. Noncompliance

Noncompliance with a maintenance order can result in coercive enforcement, including attachment of property and, in appropriate cases, short-term imprisonment for continued default.[419] Maintenance orders can also be enforced as money decrees of a civil court under CrPC section 128 (BNSS section 147), allowing for the *attachment of salary*, bank accounts, or immovable property.

2.6.8. Live-In Relationships, Morality, and Constitutional Values

Indian jurisprudence on unmarried relationships frequently reflects tension between social morality and constitutional morality. While early decisions occasionally invoked cultural norms to limit relief, more recent Supreme Court judgments emphasize individual autonomy, privacy, and dignity as core constitutional commitments.

414. Indian Evidence Act § 112.

415. Roy v. Roy, AIR 2015 SC 418, ¶ 17 (India), https://indiankanoon.org/doc/159613381/.

416. *Id.* ¶ 10.

417. *Id.* ¶ 9(22), (23).

418. *See generally* Badwaik v. Badwaik, AIR 2014 SC 932 (India) (recognizing primacy of DNA evidence in determining paternity), https://indiankanoon.org/doc/139951018/.

419. CrPC § 125(3) (now section 144(3) of the BNSS).

In *Johar v. Union of India*, although not directly addressing live-in relationships, the Court articulated a powerful vision of constitutional morality that has influenced subsequent family law decisions.[420] This framework has allowed courts to reframe nonmarital cohabitation as a matter of personal liberty rather than social deviance, reinforcing the legitimacy of judicial protection for unmarried partners and parents.

2.6.9. Cross-Border Dimensions, Judicial Evolution, and the Need for Reform

The legal position of unmarried partners and parents in India acquires particular significance in cross-border family disputes, especially in India–U.S. matters involving custody, relocation, child support, and parentage, where relationships recognized in one jurisdiction may lack equivalent legal status in another. Indian courts are increasingly called upon to assess foreign custody orders, parenting arrangements, and support claims arising from nonmarital relationships, while U.S. courts must often navigate Indian legal constraints when determining parental rights, best interests, or enforceability. In both systems, there is a discernible shift toward functional, child-centered approaches that prioritize welfare over formal marital status; yet in India, the absence of comprehensive statutory recognition continues to complicate enforcement, comity, and predictability, particularly in international relocation and Hague-adjacent disputes.

Judicial intervention has played a central role in this evolution. Through constitutional interpretation and purposive construction of criminal and civil statutes, Indian courts have incrementally expanded protections relating to maintenance, domestic violence, legitimacy, custody, and inheritance for children born outside marriage. At the same time, significant doctrinal gaps remain in areas such as financial security, property division, and succession for unmarried partners, resulting in a jurisprudence that is both progressive and fragmented. A comparative view of American family law highlights alternative models grounded in clear parentage regimes, equitable remedies, and routine application of best interest standards to unmarried parents without moral judgment. As nonmarital family forms become increasingly visible, mobile, and transnational, the future coherence of Indian family law will likely depend on whether legislative reform can consolidate these judicial advances, reduce uncertainty, and align statutory frameworks with constitutional values of autonomy, equality, dignity, and the paramount welfare of children.

2.7. Prenuptial and Postnuptial Agreements

Indian family law has historically resisted the characterization of marriage as a purely contractual relationship. While marriage in India may involve contractual elements, it is doctrinally treated as a social and legal institution governed

420. Johar v. Union of India, AIR 2018 SC 4321 (India), https://indiankanoon.org/doc/168671544/.

by personal law statutes and welfare-based judicial oversight. This foundational premise has shaped the Indian courts' cautious, and often skeptical, approach to nuptial agreements, particularly those executed prior to marriage.

Unlike jurisdictions that expressly recognize premarital and postmarital agreements by statute, India has no dedicated legislative framework governing such contracts. Neither the Hindu Marriage Act, 1955, the Special Marriage Act, 1954, nor the codified Muslim personal law regimes provide for the direct enforcement of financial settlements entered into before marriage or upon its dissolution. As a result, Indian courts assess these agreements only indirectly, through general principles of contract law, public policy considerations, and the non-waivable rights conferred by matrimonial statutes.

The Supreme Court of India has repeatedly emphasized that marriage under Indian law is a status rather than a bargain. This doctrinal position has informed judicial reluctance to enforce agreements that appear to predetermine the consequences of marital breakdown or restrict statutory entitlements arising from marital status. Courts have viewed such agreements as potentially undermining the protective objectives of matrimonial legislation, particularly those relating to maintenance, residence, and child welfare.

At the same time, Indian courts have not adopted a blanket rejection of all nuptial arrangements. Instead, they draw a clear distinction between agreements executed before marriage and those entered into after marriage, particularly once marital discord has arisen. Prenuptial agreements are frequently viewed as speculative arrangements that anticipate marital breakdown and are therefore treated with suspicion on public policy grounds. By contrast, postnuptial or separation agreements are more likely to be assessed as pragmatic settlements addressing existing disputes rather than as impermissible restraints on marital rights. This distinction has become central to the modern judicial approach and underpins much of the case law discussed in the sections that follow.

The Indian Contract Act, 1872, provides the formal analytical entry point for nuptial agreements. Parties invoking such agreements must establish free consent, lawful consideration, and an object not opposed to public policy. Indian courts, however, have consistently held that agreements that restrain legal proceedings, oust jurisdiction of matrimonial courts, or attempt to contract out of statutory protections may be void under sections 23 and 28 of the Contract Act. Nuptial agreements often collide with these provisions because they intersect directly with rights created by family law statutes.

Public policy has been the principal doctrinal tool through which Indian courts have limited the enforceability of nuptial agreements. Agreements that appear to incentivize separation, facilitate divorce, or preempt judicial discretion in matrimonial matters have been treated as suspect. This is particularly true in cases involving maintenance waivers or predetermined financial settlements, where courts have underscored that statutory maintenance obligations arise from status and cannot be privately extinguished in advance.

The absence of a statutory regime has also resulted in inconsistent judicial treatment across jurisdictions. While some high courts have acknowledged the evidentiary or persuasive value of nuptial agreements in resolving financial disputes, others have rejected them outright as contrary to the ethos of Indian family law. The lack of uniformity reflects the tension between evolving social practices, particularly among transnational families, and the protective orientation of Indian matrimonial jurisprudence.

The conceptual framework governing nuptial agreements in India is therefore one of conditional tolerance rather than outright prohibition or acceptance. Agreements are not enforceable merely because they satisfy contractual formalities. They must also survive scrutiny under matrimonial statutes, welfare principles, and public policy doctrine. This framework places Indian law in marked contrast with jurisdictions such as the United States, where nuptial agreements are presumptively valid and subject primarily to procedural safeguards.

Understanding this conceptual posture is essential before examining the specific treatment of prenuptial and postnuptial agreements under Indian law. The sections that follow build on this framework to analyze how Indian courts have addressed such agreements in practice, where they have drawn enforceability lines, and how these domestic principles interact with cross-border matrimonial arrangements.

2.7.1. Prenuptial Agreements Under Indian Law

India's judicial reluctance to validate prenuptial agreements can be traced to the early 20th century, most notably the Calcutta High Court's 1901 decision in *Jemadai v. Singh*. Decided in a period when marriage was understood as a matter of social status rather than private contract, the case articulated a public policy objection to agreements executed in contemplation of marriage, characterizing them as speculative arrangements that anticipate marital failure.[421] This early articulation of judicial policy laid the foundation for a doctrinal divide that continues to shape Indian family law: prenuptial agreements are treated with deep skepticism, while postnuptial and separation agreements, entered into after disputes have arisen, are more readily assessed as pragmatic settlements.

Not long after, in *Aiyar v. Balammal*, the Madras High Court struck down the validity of a prenup while stating:

> The parties are *Hindus and Brahmans*. The law to be applied in determining their marital obligations is the Hindu Law. . . . It may be doubted whether under that law any agreement between husband and wife to live apart from each other is valid. It may well be deemed to be *forbidden by the Hindu Law*. . . . Even apart from the Hindu Law the agreement, we think, must be regarded *as opposed to public policy* and therefore not enforceable.[422]

Similarly, in *Fatma v. Aiyab*, the Bombay High Court ruled that an agreement providing for a wife's maintenance in the event of a future separation

421. Jemadai v. Singh, (1901) ILR 28 Cal 751, ¶¶ 37–44 (India), https://indiankanoon.org/doc/1567532/.

422. Aiyar v. Balammal, (1911) ILR 34 Mad 398, ¶ 2 (India) (emphasis added), https://indiankanoon.org/doc/42103/.

was *"void,"* and *"against public policy"* because it "encourages, future separation between the spouses."[423]

A. Foundational Objection to Prenuptial Agreements

The foundational objection to prenuptial agreements in India stems from the doctrinal understanding that marriage creates a legal status governed by statute, not merely a consensual arrangement between private parties. Courts have repeatedly held that rights and obligations flowing from marriage, particularly those *relating to maintenance, support, and residence, are statutory incidents that cannot be prospectively waived by contract.*[424] This reasoning has led courts to treat prenuptial agreements with suspicion, especially where they appear to predetermine outcomes upon divorce or separation. Indian courts have also expressed concern that prenuptial agreements *may offend public policy*[425] *by encouraging separation or contemplating marital breakdown* as a foreseeable outcome. Judicial reasoning in this area reflects a normative judgment that marriage should not be entered into with contractual exit terms that undermine its stability or statutory safeguards.

While this foundational hostility has never been formally repudiated, more recent decisions suggest a subtle, if cautious, shift in judicial posture. In a rare modern example, *Deshprabhu v. Deshprabhu*, the Bombay High Court considered a prenuptial agreement as evidence of the parties' intent to maintain separation of assets, even as it stopped short of expressly ruling on the broader enforceability or validity of such agreements.[426] This limited acknowledgment reflects an emerging willingness to consider prenuptial arrangements as contextual evidence, rather than as binding contracts, within the continuing constraints of Indian public policy.

B. Marital Settlement Agreements

In contrast to the historical suspicion directed at prenuptial agreements, often criticized as arrangements that anticipate or even encourage marital breakdown, Indian courts have not subjected marital settlement agreements (often confused with "postnuptial" agreements in India) executed after the breakdown of a marriage to comparable scrutiny. Where the relationship has irretrievably failed, courts have generally approached postnuptial or separation agreements as pragmatic instruments designed to bring finality and reduce further litigation. In Singh v. Kaur, the Supreme Court emphasized that where there is no real possibility of reconciliation, courts should facilitate constructive outcomes for the parties, including by giving effect to mutually agreed settlements, especially where the parties have "arrived at genuine settlement which takes care of alimony, custody of child or any other pending issues between the parties."[427]

---

423. Fatma v. Aiyab, (1912) 14 Bom LR 1178 (India), https://indiankanoon.org/doc/123010/.

424. The Indian Contract Act, 1872, § 28 (India), https://indiankanoon.org/doc/171398/.

425. *Id.* § 23.

426. Deshprabhu v. Deshprabhu, Writ Petion No. 934/2015 (India), https://www.casemine.com/judgement/in/5b684b424a932645d86ee095.

427. *Singh*, AIR 2017 SC 4417, ¶ 13 (emphasis added).

More recently, in *Sailesh v. Sreenivasan*, the Court reaffirmed its power under Article 142 of the Constitution to dissolve marriages and uphold negotiated settlements while observing that *"[p]ublic policy underlying the legislations dealing with family and matrimonial matters is to encourage mutual settlement,"* and that courts must *"ensure that the settlement between the parties is achieved without pressure, force, coercion, fraud, misrepresentation, or undue influence."*[428]

Together, these decisions underscore a consistent judicial distinction: while prenuptial agreements remain doctrinally suspect, settlements arising from an acknowledged marital breakdown are viewed as legitimate mechanisms for orderly dispute resolution rather than as impermissible incentives to marital failure. The enforceability of such agreements remains contingent upon judicial approval, statutory compatibility, and welfare considerations.

C. Absence of Authoritative Supreme Court Endorsement of Prenuptial Agreements

This absence of authoritative endorsement has further entrenched uncertainty. While high courts have addressed prenuptial arrangements sporadically, there is no binding precedent affirming their enforceability as contracts governing divorce or financial relief. This judicial silence has effectively preserved the status quo, under which prenuptial agreements remain legally precarious and strategically unreliable within India.

In practical terms, prenuptial agreements under Indian law function more as planning instruments than enforceable contracts. They may influence negotiations, inform settlement discussions, or carry weight in foreign jurisdictions, but within India they do not displace statutory rights or judicial discretion. Practitioners advising clients must therefore treat such agreements as limited-value documents whose legal effect is subordinate to matrimonial statutes and welfare principles.

This judicial posture distinguishes Indian law sharply from jurisdictions that recognize prenuptial agreements as presumptively valid. The contrast becomes particularly salient in cross-border marriages, where parties may assume that an agreement valid abroad will carry similar force in India.

2.7.2. Statutory Touchpoints Affecting Indian Nuptial Agreements

Although Indian law does not contain a consolidated statutory framework governing prenuptial or postnuptial agreements, several statutes operate as decisive touchpoints that shape their validity, scope, and practical utility. Indian courts do not assess nuptial agreements in isolation. Instead, they examine such agreements through the cumulative effect of general contract law, matrimonial statutes, and procedural rules that preserve judicial oversight in family matters. These statutory intersections explain why nuptial agreements, even when voluntarily executed, remain subordinate to legislative policy.

The Indian Contract Act, 1872, is the initial analytical gateway through which nuptial agreements are examined. Courts assess whether the agreement

428. *Sailesh*, Transfer Petition (Civil) No. 1118 of 2014, ¶¶ 22, 38.

satisfies the requirements of free consent, lawful consideration, and lawful object. However, section 23 has played a particularly restrictive role in nuptial agreement jurisprudence. Courts have repeatedly held that agreements whose object defeats the provisions of matrimonial statutes, restricts access to legal remedies, or undermines statutory welfare protections are opposed to public policy and therefore void. Nuptial agreements frequently encounter this barrier because they attempt to regulate rights that the legislature has chosen to protect through mandatory norms.

In *Pillai v. Vijayalakshmi*, the Kerala High Court, ruled that an agreement that restricts a party from enforcing their statutory rights in a matrimonial dispute is hit by various provisions of the Indian Contract Act, while holding:

> It is a basic principle of law that an agreement which is opposed to public policy cannot be enforced in a court of law. Section 23 of the Contract Act renders such an agreement void if its consideration or object is unlawful. If the object or consideration of an agreement would defeat the provisions of any law, and if it is opposed to public policy, the agreement will be treated as unlawful, and consequently void. In that view of the matter, a clause in an agreement that the wife shall not be entitled to claim maintenance from the husband cannot be used as a defence in proceedings [u]nder Section 125 of the Code.[429]

Section 28 of the Contract Act has also influenced judicial treatment of nuptial agreements. Indian courts have been wary of agreements that directly or indirectly restrain legal proceedings in matrimonial matters. Clauses that seek to preclude divorce proceedings, limit access to maintenance claims, or impose penalties for invoking statutory remedies have been viewed as impermissible restraints. Courts have consistently held that private agreements cannot oust the jurisdiction of family courts or civil courts in matters governed by statute.

A. Matrimonial Statutes Versus Contractual Autonomy

1. The Hindu Marriage Act, 1955

This act establishes a comprehensive framework governing divorce, maintenance, and ancillary relief. While the act encourages settlement and compromise in appropriate cases, it does not permit parties to contractually predetermine outcomes that the statute reserves for judicial discretion. Courts have therefore treated nuptial agreements addressing maintenance or financial relief as subject to review under statutory standards of fairness and adequacy, regardless of prior consent.

2. The Special Marriage Act, 1954

The Special Marriage Act, often invoked in interfaith or civil marriages, similarly does not recognize binding nuptial agreements governing divorce consequences. Although the act provides greater formal equality between spouses,

---

429. Pillai v. Vijayalakshmi, 1987 Cri LJ 765, ¶ 6 (India), https://indiankanoon.org/doc/795933/.

it preserves judicial control over maintenance and financial relief. Agreements executed under this regime have been scrutinized no less rigorously than those under personal law statutes, reinforcing the principle that statutory entitlements cannot be waived in advance.

3. Muslim Law

In contrast to the sacramental conception of marriage under several other Indian personal laws, Muslim law treats marriage (nikah) as a civil contract, thereby providing a comparatively more receptive doctrinal foundation for pre-marital stipulations. As early as 1886, Justice Syed Mahmood of Allahabad High Court famously observed that *"marriage among Muhammadans is not a sacrament, but purely a civil contract."*[430] The court ruled that the rights and obligations of the spouses arise immediately upon the completion of this contract by proposal (*Ijab*) and acceptance (*Qubul*).[431]

However, in the decades that followed, several Indian courts have emphasized the "sacramental" dimensions of Muslim marriage as well, declining to treat nikah as a purely contractual arrangement. The Kerala High Court in *Amina v. Koye* observed:

> Juristically, it may be a contract as opposed to a sacrament. But it cannot be considered as a contract pure and simple to be governed exclusively by the provisions of the Contract Act. Rules to be applied for interpreting a [M]uslim marriage are not exclusively confined and cabined within the four walls of the general statutes—Contract Act and allied Acts. It is always to be understood and interpreted in the light of the personal laws of the parties and the ethic content and ethos of the institution of marriage, as popularly understood by the Muslims in the country[.][432]

Central to the contractual framework of a Muslim marriage is the *nikahnama*, which permits parties to incorporate agreed conditions concerning mahr (dower), maintenance, residence, and even the delegation of the husband's right of divorce (*talaq-e-tafweez*). Indian courts have historically upheld such stipulations so long as they do not contravene Islamic principles or broader public policy. As early as 1910, the Privy Council affirmed that a husband's promise to pay a fixed monthly allowance, commonly referred to as *kharcha-i-pandan* (often described in older English authorities as "betel-box expenses" or "pin money"), constituted an enforceable condition of a marriage settlement.[433]

Similarly, in *Itwari v. Asghari*, the Supreme Court observed that although Muslim law recognizes a husband's right to polygamy, a contractual stipulation granting the first wife the right to reside separately or seek dissolution if the husband contracts a second marriage is valid and not per se opposed to public policy.[434]

---

430. *Kadir*, (1886) ILR 8 All 149, ¶ 8 (emphasis added).
431. *Id.*
432. Amina v. Koye, 1985 Cri LJ 1996, ¶ 16 (India), https://indiankanoon.org/doc/1787607/.
433. Khan v. Begam, (1910) 12 Bom LR 638 (India), https://indiankanoon.org/doc/1020411/.
434. Itwari v. Asghari, AIR 1960 All 684, ¶ 10 (India), https://indiankanoon.org/doc/1456722/.

However, such agreements remain subject to the overarching constraint of section 23 of the Indian Contract Act, 1872. While Muslim law allows greater contractual flexibility, any term deemed "opposed to public policy" or designed to defeat statutory protections may be invalidated. Clauses that amount to a complete waiver of maintenance rights or that effectively undermine the essence of the marital relationship may not withstand scrutiny. For example, in *Fatma*, the Bombay High Court held void an agreement providing for maintenance upon a contemplated future separation, reasoning that it tended to encourage marital rupture.[435] In *Samad v. State of Telangana*, the Supreme Court reiterated that a Muslim woman's entitlement to maintenance under section 125 of the CrPC (now codified as section 144 of the BNSS) operates independently of personal law norms and cannot be curtailed by private contractual arrangements, and is a statutory right of all divorced women irrespective of the faith they follow.[436]

Thus, even within the contractual architecture of Muslim marriage, courts balance party autonomy against the state's interest in preserving marital stability and safeguarding statutory welfare protections. This approach stands in marked contrast to the historical judicial hostility toward prenuptial agreements under Hindu law, where marriage has traditionally been viewed as a sacrament rather than a negotiable legal arrangement. While Hindu prenuptial agreements have often been treated as inherently suspect for anticipating marital failure, Muslim nikahnama stipulations are analyzed within a recognized contractual framework and evaluated primarily for consistency with public policy and statutory mandates, reflecting a fundamentally different doctrinal starting point.

4. Christian Law

Christian marriage law in India offers a more limited but explicit statutory acknowledgment of nuptial agreements. Governed primarily by the Indian Christian Marriage Act, 1872, and the Divorce Act, 1869, this framework departs from the sacramental finality often associated with other personal laws by expressly recognizing the relevance of premarital and postmarital settlements. Section 40 of the Divorce Act, 1869, empowers courts, upon granting a decree of dissolution or nullity, to inquire into the existence of any "ante-nuptial or post-nuptial settlements" made in favor of either spouse or their children, and to pass appropriate orders regarding the application of property so settled.[437] Such agreements, however, do not operate as self-executing contracts. Rather, they serve as inputs into judicial discretion and remain subject to the public-policy limitations embodied in section 23 of the Indian Contract Act, 1872. Courts have therefore declined to enforce clauses that waive statutory maintenance rights or seek to exclude the court's jurisdiction altogether.

A notable exception to the broader Indian skepticism toward prenuptial agreements exists in Goa, where premarital contracting is embedded within

435. *Fatma*, (1912) 14 Bom LR 1178.
436. *Samad*, 2024 INSC 506.
437. Indian Divorce Act § 40.

the region's civil-law tradition under the Portuguese Civil Code, 1867. In the absence of a prenuptial agreement, spouses in Goa are governed by the default *regime of communion of assets*, under which all property, whether acquired before or during the marriage, is jointly owned and divided equally upon dissolution.[438] Couples wishing to depart from this default must execute a prenuptial contract before a civil registrar or notary public selecting an alternative matrimonial property regime, such as separation of property. Preserved through the Goa, Daman and Diu (Administration) Act, 1962, this framework makes Goa the only Indian jurisdiction in which the financial consequences of marriage and divorce can be deliberately structured through a binding contract executed prior to solemnization.[439]

5. Procedural Law

The CPC, 1908, becomes relevant where parties seek to enforce nuptial agreements through civil suits or to rely on them defensively in matrimonial proceedings. Courts have distinguished between enforcing an agreement as a contract and considering it as part of a compromise under Order XXIII, Rule 3. Where nuptial agreements are incorporated into consent decrees, courts have emphasized that judicial approval transforms the agreement into an order of the court, subject to modification where circumstances or welfare considerations demand.

As discussed previously, maintenance statutes operate as particularly strong statutory overrides. Rights under section 125 of the CrPC have been treated as social welfare obligations that cannot be contracted away. Courts have consistently held that agreements purporting to waive or limit section 125 relief do not bind criminal courts, regardless of the parties' consent. This position has significantly curtailed the enforceability of nuptial agreements that attempt comprehensive financial finality.

Child-related provisions in nuptial agreements encounter the strongest statutory resistance. Under both personal law statutes and the Guardians and Wards Act, 1890, custody and visitation determinations are governed exclusively by the welfare of the child. Courts have repeatedly held that any agreement between parents relating to custody or access is subject to judicial review and may be disregarded entirely if inconsistent with welfare. Nuptial agreements attempting to fix child-related outcomes in advance have therefore been treated as nonbinding expressions of intent at best.

The cumulative effect of these statutory touchpoints is a legal environment in which nuptial agreements are tolerated but tightly circumscribed. Indian law permits spouses to record financial understandings, intentions, and settlements, but it does not allow private ordering to displace statutory protections or judicial discretion.

Understanding these statutory constraints is essential before examining how courts have applied them in concrete cases.

---

438. Portuguese Civil Code, 1867, https://www.indiacode.nic.in/bitstream/123456789/8312/1/ocrportuguesecivilcode.pdf.

439. The Goa, Daman and Diu (Administration) Act, 1962, §§ 5, 9(1) (India), https://indiankanoon.org/doc/113241309/.

2.7.3. Financial Arrangements and Property Division

Financial arrangements constitute the most litigated and most constrained aspect of nuptial agreements under Indian law. Indian courts have consistently held that while spouses may record understandings regarding finances, such arrangements do not operate as binding determinants of financial relief upon separation or divorce. The legal framework governing property and maintenance reflects a deliberate legislative choice to prioritize statutory protection and judicial discretion over private ordering.

Indian matrimonial law does not recognize a concept of marital or community property. Property rights are determined primarily by title, contribution, and applicable statutory provisions, rather than by marital status alone. As a result, nuptial agreements purporting to allocate ownership of present or future assets upon divorce encounter immediate doctrinal resistance. Courts have emphasized that property division is not an automatic consequence of marriage in India and cannot be contractually engineered in advance through premarital or postmarital arrangements.

Agreements that seek to characterize assets as joint or separate have been treated cautiously. Where such agreements merely record existing ownership or financial contributions, courts have occasionally referred to them as evidentiary material. However, where agreements attempt to reallocate proprietary rights prospectively or upon dissolution of marriage, courts have declined to enforce them, holding that such redistribution lacks statutory foundation. Indian courts have reiterated that proprietary rights in immovable property, in particular, cannot be altered by private agreement without compliance with property and registration laws.

Maintenance-related clauses within nuptial agreements have been subjected to even stricter scrutiny. Courts have consistently held that maintenance obligations arise from statute and public policy, not from contract. Agreements purporting to waive maintenance entirely, cap future claims, or predetermine lump-sum settlements have been treated as nonbinding. Judicial reasoning in this area emphasizes that maintenance serves a social welfare function and is intended to protect economically vulnerable spouses from destitution, irrespective of prior contractual consent.

As discussed previously, the Supreme Court has repeatedly affirmed that statutory maintenance rights cannot be extinguished by private agreement, particularly where circumstances change over time. Even where a nuptial agreement records a mutually agreed financial settlement, courts have reserved the power to reassess adequacy at the time relief is sought. This approach reflects recognition that financial vulnerability may emerge long after the execution of an agreement, rendering prior consent an unreliable indicator of present welfare.

Postmarital settlement agreements addressing financial arrangements have received comparatively greater judicial engagement, particularly where they arise in the context of separation or pending litigation. Courts have been willing to consider agreed maintenance amounts or one-time settlements as reflective of the parties' intentions, but only after examining fairness, voluntariness, and compliance with statutory standards. Such agreements are treated as persuasive rather than dispositive, and courts have declined to enforce them mechanically where they appear unconscionable or inadequate.

Property-related clauses in postnuptial agreements have similarly been assessed through a lens of practicality rather than contractual finality. Courts have considered agreements that facilitate sale of jointly owned property, division of proceeds, or temporary financial arrangements pending litigation. However, agreements that purport to permanently bar claims or conclusively resolve property disputes without judicial scrutiny have been viewed with skepticism.

Indian courts have also rejected attempts to use nuptial agreements to shield assets from statutory claims. Clauses designed to insulate one spouse's property from maintenance enforcement or to preclude execution against assets have been held ineffective. Courts have emphasized that enforcement mechanisms under matrimonial and criminal statutes cannot be circumvented through private agreement.

Another recurring issue is the treatment of foreign assets referenced in nuptial agreements. Indian courts have been reluctant to give effect to clauses allocating foreign property or applying foreign marital property regimes, particularly where such clauses conflict with Indian public policy or statutory protections. While courts may acknowledge the existence of foreign arrangements, they have consistently maintained that relief granted in India must conform to domestic law.

In practice, financial arrangements within nuptial agreements function as negotiating tools rather than enforceable outcomes. They may shape expectations, influence settlement discussions, or provide a framework for consent orders, but they do not override statutory entitlements or judicial discretion. Practitioners advising clients must therefore caution against assuming that financial clauses will be upheld simply because they were voluntarily agreed upon.

The judicial approach to financial arrangements and property division reinforces a central theme of Indian nuptial agreement jurisprudence: autonomy yields to protection. While parties may attempt to structure their financial relationship through agreement, Indian law preserves the court's authority to intervene where necessary to secure fairness and welfare.

2.7.4. Drafting Considerations for Indian Nuptial Agreements

Drafting nuptial agreements within the Indian legal framework requires a calibrated approach that acknowledges the limits of enforceability while maximizing practical utility. Indian courts have repeatedly signaled that the value of such agreements lies not in their contractual finality, but in their ability to inform judicial discretion, facilitate settlement, and reduce factual uncertainty. Effective drafting therefore demands realism about what Indian law permits and precision in how agreements are framed.

The first and most critical consideration is *purpose*. Nuptial agreements in India should not be drafted as instruments intended to conclusively determine future matrimonial relief. Courts have consistently rejected attempts to use agreements to preempt statutory rights or bind judicial outcomes. Drafting that openly acknowledges judicial oversight and statutory supremacy is more likely to be treated as credible and persuasive than drafting that purports to create finality. Agreements that present themselves as records of understanding rather than as dispositive contracts align more closely with Indian judicial sensibilities.

Voluntariness and informed consent must be demonstrable on the face of the document. Courts scrutinize nuptial agreements closely for indicators of coercion, undue influence, or imbalance in bargaining power. This scrutiny is particularly intense where agreements are executed in proximity to marriage or during periods of emotional vulnerability. Clear recitals regarding independent advice, disclosure of assets, and absence of pressure can enhance the agreement's evidentiary value, even if they do not guarantee enforcement.

Timing plays a decisive role in how agreements are received. Postnuptial agreements executed after disputes have arisen or during separation are more likely to be treated as legitimate attempts at resolution rather than as speculative arrangements. Drafting should therefore reflect the context in which the agreement is executed, avoiding language that suggests premeditation of marital breakdown. Courts have been more receptive to agreements that respond to existing circumstances than to those that anticipate future contingencies.

Financial clauses require particular care. Drafting that attempts to waive statutory maintenance or conclusively fix financial relief is unlikely to survive judicial scrutiny. Agreements are more effective when they record interim arrangements, acknowledge voluntary support, or outline intentions subject to statutory review. Language that recognizes the court's power to reassess adequacy reinforces credibility and avoids the appearance of attempting to contract out of statutory protections.

Property-related provisions should be drafted conservatively. Agreements that merely record existing ownership, contributions, or management arrangements are more likely to be treated as reliable factual records. By contrast, clauses that purport to reallocate ownership or create future proprietary rights risk being disregarded entirely. Drafting should avoid language suggestive of a community property regime or automatic division upon divorce, concepts not recognized under Indian law.

Registration and execution formalities must also be approached thoughtfully. While registration does not confer enforceability on nuptial agreements per se, properly executed and, where appropriate, registered documents carry greater evidentiary weight. Courts have been more inclined to consider agreements that reflect procedural seriousness than informal or ambiguous instruments. However, practitioners must avoid overstating the legal effect of registration, which does not cure substantive infirmities.

Cross-border implications require special attention. Many nuptial agreements involving Indian parties are drafted with foreign enforceability in mind. While such agreements may be valid and enforceable abroad, drafting must anticipate that Indian courts will assess them independently. Including severability clauses, governing law provisions, and acknowledgments of statutory override can mitigate risk without creating false expectations.

Finally, practitioners must manage client expectations with candor. Indian law does not reward over-lawyering in this area. Drafting that is modest, transparent, and aligned with statutory realities is more likely to assist clients than aggressive contractual language that courts will disregard. The objective is not to eliminate judicial discretion, but to guide it responsibly.

In sum, effective drafting of Indian nuptial agreements requires acceptance of constraint. Agreements succeed not by asserting authority, but by respecting the contours of Indian family law. When drafted with restraint and clarity, they can serve as valuable tools for documentation, negotiation, and cross-border planning, even within a legal system that resists contractual finality in matrimonial matters.

CHAPTER 3

International Issues

3.1. Scope of the Chapter

This chapter examines how India structures divorce and child-custody jurisdiction in cross-border disputes, and why jurisdictional conflict in Indian family law is rarely a technical skirmish and almost always outcome-determinative. It explains how marriages solemnized under personal law statutes, particularly the Hindu Marriage Act (HMA) and the Special Marriage Act, retain their statutory character even after migration, permanent residence, or foreign citizenship, and how section 13 of the Code of Civil Procedure (CPC) functions as a strict gatekeeper to recognition of foreign decrees.

It analyzes the Supreme Court's insistence that foreign divorces must rest on jurisdictional foundations recognized under Indian law and on grounds available under the governing statute, and why the absence of *"irretrievable breakdown"* in the HMA continues to produce limping legal status for non-resident Indians (NRIs) divorced abroad but still married in India. It also addresses domicile doctrine with precision: the presumption against change of domicile, the demand for *"strong proof"* of abandonment of domicile of origin, and the courts' refusal to allow unilateral migration to displace the protective reach of Indian matrimonial statutes.

The chapter situates these doctrinal rules within lived realities. It explains the legislative and judicial recalibration that followed decades of NRI marriages in which wives were left stranded abroad or rendered remediless at home, including the 2003 amendment to section 19 of the HMA permitting wives to file where they reside. It does not romanticize this pro-wife orientation; it contextualizes it. Indian courts' reluctance to accept easy claims of foreign domicile and their skepticism toward quick foreign divorces are not abstract formalism but a historically informed response to structural vulnerability. At the same time, the chapter acknowledges the evolving demographic of financially independent, globally mobile spouses creating tension between legacy protectionism and contemporary equality.

It then turns to the most destabilizing feature of cross-border Indian matrimonial litigation: parallel proceedings. Anti-suit injunctions, forum non conveniens, and welfare-based jurisdiction are treated not as isolated doctrines but as strategic levers in a race-to-the-courthouse environment. The Supreme Court's framework in *Modi Entertainment* and its caution in *Thakur* are examined alongside decisions where Indian courts have restrained foreign proceedings, particularly where the foreign ground of divorce is not statutorily recognized in India.

The chapter draws out the nuanced pattern: Indian courts are not reflexively interventionist, but they are willing to intervene when foreign litigation threatens to produce non-recognizable decrees, strategic oppression, or procedural unfairness. It also highlights a practice-driven reality that American lawyers routinely underestimate: Indian courts sometimes grant urgent anti-suit relief even while Hague service abroad remains pending, effectively freezing U.S. proceedings and shifting leverage before treaty-compliant service is completed.

Service of process is treated as a jurisdictional fault line rather than a clerical step. The chapter explains India's accession to the Hague Service Convention, its formal objection to Article 10 methods, and the mandatory use of the Central Authority. It confronts the practical truth that Hague service into India is slow, often many months, and that defects in treaty compliance resurface at enforcement or recognition stages, particularly under CPC section 13. It analyzes Indian case law emphasizing that actual notice does not cure treaty noncompliance and that substituted service is a post-failure remedy, not a shortcut. For U.S. practitioners accustomed to flexible service doctrines, the message is blunt: missteps in Hague service can derail recognition years later.

The criminal dimension is addressed with equal candor. Section 498A (now section 85 of the *Bharatiya Nyaya Sanhita*) is examined as both shield and sword in transnational matrimonial disputes. The chapter explains cognizable status, non-compoundability, non-bailability, extraterritorial reach under section 4 of the Indian Penal Code (IPC) and section 188 of the Code of Criminal Procedure, 1973 (CrPC), and the Supreme Court's safeguards in *Kumar* and related jurisprudence. It also acknowledges the lived litigation reality: first information reports (FIRs) filed in India can trigger lookout circulars, arrest risk upon entry, and immigration consequences abroad, often reshaping civil negotiations overnight. The analysis is careful not to caricature the statute as either inherently abusive or infallibly protective; instead, it situates 498A within a broader ecosystem where criminal process frequently intersects with civil leverage in cross-border breakdowns.

Finally, the chapter frames forum non conveniens within India's welfare-centric family jurisprudence. It explains why, in custody matters, the Supreme Court has insisted that there is *"no forum convenience in wardship jurisdiction"* when the child's welfare is paramount, and how this principle operates as a counterweight to convenience-based abstention. It contrasts Indian courts' readiness to retain jurisdiction in cases involving vulnerable spouses with their willingness, in appropriate circumstances, to defer to a more natural forum. The comparative discussion underscores that U.S. courts approach anti-suit relief with far greater restraint, relying instead on abstention and statutory custody frameworks, whereas Indian courts, though formally cautious, have shown greater readiness to restrain foreign proceedings in order to prevent manifest injustice or the creation of unenforceable decrees.

In sum, this chapter equips American lawyers with structural literacy about India's jurisdictional architecture in divorce and custody disputes. It explains how personal law pluralism, domicile doctrine, recognition rules, Hague service compliance, anti-suit injunction practice, criminal prosecution, and welfare-based reasoning interact in real cases. The central observation running through the chapter is this: in India–U.S. family disputes, jurisdiction is rarely neutral. It is a strategic terrain shaped by history, statutory design, constitutional values, and pragmatic judicial responses to transnational inequality. Understanding that terrain is indispensable before advising a client to file first, concede service, ignore a foreign summons, or assume that a foreign decree will quietly travel across borders.

3.2. Parallel Divorce and Child Custody Jurisdiction in India

The phenomenon of competing jurisdiction lies at the heart of international family law disputes. Unlike purely domestic cases, cross-border family litigation frequently involves multiple sovereign legal systems that may each assert authority over the same marriage, children, or financial consequences arising from family breakdown. The resulting jurisdictional overlap creates not only procedural complexity but also significant strategic and ethical challenges for litigants and their counsel.

In international family law, jurisdiction is not merely a technical gateway; it is often outcome-determinative. The choice of forum can dictate the substantive law applied, the availability and quantum of financial relief, the speed of proceedings, the enforceability of orders, and, most critically in child-related cases, the future life trajectory of a child. Courts across jurisdictions have therefore grappled with the tension between sovereign authority, party autonomy, judicial comity, and the need to prevent abusive or opportunistic litigation conduct.

3.2.1. Exclusive and Continuing Divorce Jurisdiction in India

At a conceptual level, jurisdiction refers to the legal authority or power of a court to adjudicate a dispute and bind the parties before it. In cross-border family law, jurisdiction typically arises from a combination of factors such as birth, domicile, habitual residence, nationality, or physical presence. However, unlike commercial disputes, family law jurisdiction is deeply intertwined with personal status, public policy, and the welfare of children, rendering purely territorial or consent-based models inadequate.

Indian courts have historically exercised jurisdiction over matrimonial causes through statutory frameworks tied to personal laws, supplemented by procedural rules under the CPC, 1908. The emphasis on nationality and personal law affiliation, particularly in HMA and Special Marriage Act cases, distinguishes Indian jurisdictional doctrine from that of many common-law jurisdictions, including the United States, where domicile and residence play a more decisive role.[1]

1. *See* CPC, 1908, § 20 (India); The HMA, 1955, § 19 (India).

Competing jurisdiction typically arises where one party invokes the jurisdiction of an Indian court based on prior matrimonial ties to India, while the other initiates proceedings in a foreign forum grounded in residence or domicile. In such cases, both courts may validly assert jurisdiction under their respective legal systems, even though simultaneous proceedings create the risk of inconsistent outcomes.

Under Indian law, a marriage solemnized in India under the *HMA, 1955*, continues to be governed by that statute notwithstanding the parties' subsequent migration abroad or acquisition of foreign citizenship. The governing matrimonial law is ordinarily fixed by the statute under which the marriage was solemnized, and personal law does not dissolve merely because the matrimonial home shifts to another jurisdiction. Section 1(2) of the HMA expressly extends the act to Hindus domiciled in India who are outside the territory of India, reflecting a legislative intent that the statute travel with the individual rather than remain territorially confined.[2]

Indian courts have consistently treated an HMA marriage as dissoluble only in accordance with the grounds and procedures prescribed by that act, unless a foreign decree satisfies the strict recognition standards embodied in section 13 of the CPC.[3] The Supreme Court's decision in *Rao v. Lakshmi* (*Y. Narasimha Rao*) clarified that a foreign divorce decree is conclusive in India only if the foreign court exercised jurisdiction recognized under Indian matrimonial law and granted relief on a ground available under the HMA.[4] A decree founded solely on grounds such as "irretrievable breakdown of marriage," a basis frequently invoked in foreign jurisdictions but not codified under the HMA, will ordinarily not be recognized in India unless it reflects the voluntary and informed submission of both parties to that jurisdiction and ground.[5]

3.2.2. Domicile, Citizenship, or Permanent Resident Status

Importantly, the initiation of permanent residence process abroad (and in some cases even acquiring foreign citizenship) does not automatically extinguish the continued application of the HMA to a marriage solemnized under it. Indian courts have rejected the proposition that a unilateral change of nationality or domicile can displace the statutory framework governing the marriage at its inception.[6] While discussing the *concept of domicile* in the context of an international divorce concerning Australia and India, the Supreme Court observed that the HMA *"will apply to Hindu outside the territory of India only if such a Hindu is domiciled in the territory of India."*[7] While distinguishing the *"domicile of choice"* from the *"domicile of origin,"* the Court further observed that a change of domi-

2. HMA § 1(2).
3. CPC § 13.
4. Rao v. Lakshmi (*Y. Narasimha Rao*), AIR Online 1991 SC 10, ¶¶ 6, 12, 13 (India).
5. *Id.*; *see also* Satya v. Singh, AIR 1975 SC 105, ¶¶ 19, 20, 41 (India), https://indiankanoon.org/doc/1774034/.
6. *Y. Narasimha Rao*, AIR Online 1991 SC 10, ¶ 12.
7. Gopal v. Rajini, AIR 2013 SC 2678, at 8 (India) (emphasis added), https://indiankanoon.org/doc/140502088/.

cile can be established by *"residing in the country of choice with intention of continuing to reside there indefinitely."*[8] The Court also clarified that, unless proven otherwise, *"there is presumption against the change of domicile. Therefore, the person who alleges it has to prove that."*[9] Ultimately, the Court held that a short-term residential tenancy agreement, the enrollment of the parties' child in a local school in Warrawee, Australia, and the initiation of permanent residence procedures for the entire family in Australia were, in and of themselves, insufficient to establish that the husband had acquired an Australian domicile.[10] The court also noted that the husband had not shown enough evidence to establish that he had in fact abandoned the Indian domicile of origin. In *Goel v. Goel*, the Supreme Court further solidified its stance on domicile by holding, *"It is well-settled that strong proof would be required to establish that a person has abandoned the domicile of origin and has acquired a new domicile."*[11]

The court in *Goel* went on to state:

> [Where] the parties were married in [India] and . . . the marriage was solemnized under the Hindu law, the divorce proceedings must also be initiated under the Hindu Marriage Act. The . . . husband cannot raise an objection to the . . . wife initiating proceedings of divorce in India under the provisions of the Act only because he is a US citizen and domiciled in USA.[12]

In addressing whether both spouses must be domiciled in India for Indian courts to assume jurisdiction, the courts have held that the existence of an Indian domicile in even one spouse is sufficient to found jurisdiction:

> If we accept the contention of the appellant/husband that both the parties must be domiciled in India for a petition to be maintainable in India, it would lead to an absurd and untenable inference that after the marriage, if a wife is abandoned in a foreign land on being deserted by the husband, she will be left with no remedy other than to institute/contest the case in a foreign land where she may have no financial means, wherewithal or support for the same.[13]

Thus, parties to an HMA marriage who obtain a divorce abroad without satisfying the recognition requirements of Indian law may find that they remain married in India, with continuing implications for status, remarriage, succession, and criminal liability under bigamy provisions.[14]

---

8. *Id.* at 10 (emphasis added).
9. *Id.* (emphasis added).
10. *Id.*
11. Goel v. Goel, AIR Online 2020 Del 1364, ¶ 31 (India) (emphasis added), https://indiankanoon.org/doc/54184917/.
12. *Id.* ¶ 33.
13. *Id.* ¶ 35.
14. *See* IPC § 494 (India) (bigamy) (now reflected in the Bharatiya Nyaya Sanhita § 82).

3.2.3. Legal Grey Area for Non-Resident Indians

The interaction between the HMA and contemporary judicial practice has produced a persistent legal grey area for NRIs. For instance, section 13 of the HMA sets out an exhaustive list of statutory grounds for divorce and, despite repeated Law Commission recommendations, continues to exclude "irretrievable breakdown of marriage."[15]

At the same time, the Supreme Court of India has, over the years, invoked its extraordinary constitutional power under Article 142 to dissolve marriages precisely on the ground that they have irretrievably broken down. The Supreme Court has accurately acknowledged that compelling parties to remain bound to a marriage that is beyond repair serves no social or legal purpose and may itself amount to *cruelty*,[16] while urging the Indian government "*to seriously consider bringing an amendment in the Hindu Marriage Act, 1955 to incorporate irretrievable breakdown of marriage as a ground for the grant of divorce*."[17]

However, *Article 142 empowers the Supreme Court alone* to transcend statutory limitations in order to "*do complete justice*" between the parties in exceptional cases, where the marriage is "*totally unworkable, emotionally dead and beyond salvation*."[18] In *Sailesh*, the Court reaffirmed that it may dissolve a marriage on the ground of irretrievable breakdown, while simultaneously emphasizing that this power is discretionary, case-specific, and does not create a substantive right in favor of litigants:

> [W]e wish to clearly state that grant of divorce on the ground of irretrievable breakdown of marriage by this Court is not a matter of right, but a discretion which is to be exercised with great care and caution, keeping in mind several factors ensuring that "complete justice" is done to both parties.[19]

Thus, in practice and for most of the cases, trial courts and high courts, while dealing with foreign divorce judgments, remain strictly bound by the text of the HMA and lack any authority to introduce irretrievable breakdown of marriage as an independent ground for divorce, and therefore treat it as inconclusive under section 13 of the CPC.

The practical consequence is deeply unsettling for NRI couples. A divorce lawfully obtained abroad on the basis of irretrievable breakdown of marriage may be treated as legally ineffective in India, even though the Supreme Court of

15. HMA § 13; *see also* Law Commission of India, *Seventy-first Report on The Hindu Marriage Act, 1955—Irretrievable Breakdown of Marriage as a Ground of Divorce* (Apr. 1978), https://cdnbbsr.s3waas.gov.in/s3ca0daec69b5adc880fb464895726dbdf/uploads/2022/08/2022080518.pdf; Law Commission of India, *217th Report on Irretrievable Breakdown of Marriage—Another Ground for Divorce* (Mar. 2009), https://indiankanoon.org/doc/117804397/.

16. A statutorily recognized ground of divorce under the HMA.

17. Kohli v. Kohli, AIR 2006 SC 1675 (India) (emphasis added), https://indiankanoon.org/doc/1643829/.

18. Sailesh v. Sreenivasan, Transfer Petition (Civil) No. 1118 of 2014 (India) (emphasis added), https://indiankanoon.org/doc/37623680/.

19. *Id.* ¶ 33.

India itself relies on the same concept to terminate dead marriages. This leaves parties in a state of "limping legal status," divorced for all practical purposes in one jurisdiction but continuing to be married under Indian law, with serious implications for remarriage, succession, and personal status.

3.2.4. Pro-Wife Provisions in India

Indian courts have historically adopted a stringent approach when assessing claims that a spouse has abandoned an Indian domicile, particularly in the context of marriages involving NRIs. More broadly, Indian matrimonial law contains several gender-specific provisions intended to protect wives. This strictness is not accidental; it is rooted in a conscious legislative and judicial response to a recurring pattern of vulnerability faced by Indian wives in cross-border marriages. This section includes a few examples of how the Indian courts and legislature have developed jurisprudence that would essentially favor a wife of Indian origin who was stranded abroad after her marriage to an NRI.

Traditionally, a significant number of such marriages were *"arranged"* in India, often with little or no premarital courtship. Following the marriage, the wife would relocate abroad as a "tag-along" spouse, dependent on the husband for immigration status, financial support, and social integration. In many cases, she was unable to work due to visa restrictions or the nontransferability of her professional qualifications, lacked a support network, and experienced profound cultural and social isolation. The husband, by contrast, was typically professionally settled, financially independent, and socially integrated in the foreign jurisdiction, giving him every incentive to remain abroad even as the marriage deteriorated. When such marriages broke down, the imbalance became legally consequential.

For instance, upon returning to India, many wives found themselves unable to initiate divorce proceedings because the jurisdictional rules under the unamended section 19 of the HMA tied jurisdiction to the place of marriage, the last matrimonial residence, or the husband's place of residence, criteria that were often impossible to satisfy once the husband remained overseas or asserted residence elsewhere. Compounding this disadvantage, husbands frequently obtained quick no-fault divorces abroad, fully aware that the wife lacked the means or ability to contest proceedings in a foreign country. These decrees, while effective abroad, often left the wife without maintenance, property relief, or meaningful remedies.

It was against this backdrop that Parliament amended section 19 of the HMA in 2003 to introduce clause (iiia), permitting a wife to institute divorce proceedings at the place where she resides at the time of filing.[20] The amendment reflected a clear policy choice: to counteract the systemic disadvantage faced by Indian wives in transnational marriages and to prevent husbands from escaping Indian matrimonial law through unilateral relocation or jurisdictional engineering.

20. HMA § 19(iiia).

Similarly, this history directly informs the courts' reluctance to lightly accept claims that an Indian domicile has been abandoned. Assertions of a "domicile of choice" acquired abroad are scrutinized closely because, if accepted too readily, they would allow a spouse, most often the husband, to place himself outside the protective framework of the HMA altogether. Indian courts therefore require clear and compelling evidence of both physical residence abroad and a settled intention to permanently abandon Indian domicile. Temporary employment, short-term housing, children's school enrollment, or even the initiation of permanent residence processes are typically regarded as equivocal indicators, insufficient on their own to demonstrate a decisive break from Indian domicile. This judicial caution reflects a broader concern: that loosening the threshold for abandoning Indian domicile would undermine the very safeguards that Indian law was designed to provide.

While contemporary cases increasingly involve wives who are financially independent, informed, and assertive of their rights, the legal framework continues to be shaped by the historical realities that prompted legislative intervention. As a result, Indian courts remain vigilant against attempts to invoke foreign residence or nascent immigration ties as a means of avoiding Indian matrimonial jurisdiction, ensuring that domicile is not transformed into a convenient legal fiction to the detriment of fairness and access to justice.

3.2.5. The Dreaded Section 498A and Non-Resident Indians

Section 498A of the IPC has had a disproportionate and often destabilizing impact on marriages involving NRIs. In cross-border relationships, marital breakdown frequently unfolds across multiple legal systems, but criminal proceedings under section 498A are typically initiated in India, often at a stage when the husband resides abroad and has limited practical ability to respond. The provision's broad framing, coupled with the relative ease of registering an FIR naming not only the husband but also his parents and extended family, has meant that matrimonial disputes involving NRIs can escalate rapidly into criminal litigation with transnational consequences. In practice, the filing of an FIR is frequently used as a coercive device, to compel the husband's physical appearance in India, to expose him to the risk of arrest upon entry, or to create immediate procedural jeopardy capable of paralyzing parallel civil and foreign proceedings.

For Indian husbands residing overseas, section 498A proceedings can be uniquely disruptive, triggering arrest warrants, lookout circulars, passport complications, and significant immigration consequences, even before any meaningful adjudication occurs. These risks are often poorly understood by foreign family law counsel advising on divorce, custody, or relocation, who may mistakenly treat the Indian criminal case as peripheral or negotiable. In practice, section 498A frequently becomes the central pressure point in cross-border strategy, shaping settlement dynamics, travel feasibility, and parallel proceedings in foreign courts. Although the Supreme Court of India has, over time, taken measured steps to curb misuse of the provision, including directing that arrests not be made mechanically and requiring police to ordinarily proceed by issuing a notice of appearance under section 41A of the CrPC in offences punishable with up to seven years' imprisonment, the lived reality of cross-border enforcement continues to diverge sharply from doctrinal safeguards, leaving substantial scope for coercion and abuse.

Section 498A of the IPC, now referred to as section 85 of the Bharatiya Nyaya Sanhita, 2023, is discussed in this chapter by its IPC designation for ease of reference and continuity with the existing jurisprudence. Similarly, references to the CrPC, 1973, are retained for ease of reference, notwithstanding its replacement by the Bharatiya Nagarik Suraksha Sanhita, 2023.

A. Commencement of Proceedings Under IPC Section 498A

An offense under section 498A of the IPC is cognizable and criminal in nature. Proceedings are ordinarily commenced in one of two ways: first, by providing information at the appropriate police station, upon which the police may register an FIR and initiate investigation; and second, by filing a private complaint before a magistrate under section 200 of the CrPC. Where the police refuse to register an FIR despite disclosure of a cognizable offense, the complainant may approach a superior police officer under CrPC section 154(3). If that remedy is ineffective, the complainant may seek a judicial direction under CrPC section 156(3), pursuant to which the magistrate may order registration of the FIR and investigation upon being satisfied that a cognizable offense is disclosed.

The constitutional framework governing registration of FIRs was clarified by a Constitution Bench of the Supreme Court in *Kumari v. State of Uttar Pradesh*, which held that registration of an FIR is mandatory where information discloses commission of a cognizable offense. The Court, however, recognized matrimonial disputes, including cases under section 498A, as a limited category in which a brief preliminary inquiry may precede registration to determine whether a cognizable offense is made out.[21] In addition, certain high courts, including the Delhi High Court in *Chandrabhan v. State*, have emphasized the need for caution in matrimonial matters and issued administrative directions discouraging routine registration of FIRs and mechanical arrests, and encouraging supervisory oversight and efforts at reconciliation.[22] While such directions reflect judicial concern regarding misuse of section 498A, they do not displace the statutory scheme or the binding constitutional principles governing cognizable offenses.

B. Territorial Jurisdiction and Venue in Section 498A Proceedings

As a general rule, territorial jurisdiction in criminal matters is governed by section 177 of the CrPC, which provides that every offense shall ordinarily be inquired into and tried by a court within whose local jurisdiction it was committed.[23] Historically, this meant that a complaint under IPC section 498A could be filed only at the place where the alleged acts of cruelty occurred, typically

21. Kumari v. State of Uttar Pradesh, AIR 2014 SC 187 (Constitution Bench) (India), https://indiankanoon.org/doc/10239019/.

22. Chandrabhan v. State, Bail Application No. 1627/2008 (Delhi High Court) (India), https://www.498a.org/contents/judgements/HC_Delhi_Bail_Anticipatory_2008_1627_2008.pdf.

23. Bharatiya Nyaya Suraksha Sanhita § 197.

the matrimonial home. That position was expanded by the Supreme Court in *Devi v. State of Uttar Pradesh*, where the Court held that courts at the place where the wife takes shelter after leaving or being driven away from the matrimonial home on account of alleged cruelty may also, depending on the facts, exercise jurisdiction over an offense under section 498A.[24] As a result, a complainant may now initiate proceedings not only where the alleged cruelty occurred, but also at the place where she is residing or has taken shelter following separation.

C. Persons Who May Be Charged Under IPC Section 498A: Meaning of "Relative"

Section 498A of the IPC permits criminal proceedings to be instituted against the husband and his "relative(s)." The statute itself does not define the term "relative." In *Suvetha v. State by Inspector of Police*, the Supreme Court held that, in the absence of a statutory definition, the term must be given its commonly understood meaning and construed strictly, given the penal nature of the provision.[25] The Court explained that the expression "relative" would ordinarily include persons related by blood, marriage, or adoption, and cautioned against an expansive interpretation that would extend criminal liability beyond the legislative intent. This construction was reaffirmed in *Gajra v. State of NCT of Delhi* and *State of Punjab v. Singh*, where the Supreme Court reiterated that only those having a direct relationship by blood, marriage, or adoption with the husband fall within the scope of section 498A.[26] As a result, persons with no legally cognizable familial relationship cannot be prosecuted under the provision merely on the basis of association or proximity.

D. Effect of the Accused's Residence on Jurisdiction and Transfer

The residence of the accused does not, by itself, defeat jurisdiction in a prosecution under IPC section 498A. Although section 177 of the CrPC provides that every offense shall ordinarily be tried by a court within whose local jurisdiction it was committed, the Supreme Court in *Devi* held that courts at the place where the wife takes shelter after leaving or being driven away from the matrimonial home may also, depending on the facts, exercise jurisdiction over a complaint under section 498A.[27] Accordingly, proceedings may be initiated in India even where the accused resides in another state or outside India.

The accused may seek transfer of the proceedings. Applications for transfer may be made under CrPC section 408 before the sessions court, under CrPC section 407 before the high court, or under CrPC section 406 before the Supreme

24. Devi v. State of Uttar Pradesh, Criminal Appeal No. 71 of 2019 (India), http://indiankanoon.org/doc/83560110/.

25. Suvetha v. State by Inspector of Police, AIR 2009 SC (Supp) 1451 (India), https://indiankanoon.org/doc/953117/.

26. Gajra v. State of NCT of Delhi, AIR 2010 SC 2712 (India), https://indiankanoon.org/doc/194281998/; State of Punjab v. Singh, AIR 1996 SC 1393 (India), https://indiankanoon.org/doc/1046545.

27. *Devi*, Criminal Appeal No. 71 of 2019.

Court, depending on the forum in which the case is pending. Transfer is discretionary and will be ordered only where it is expedient in the interests of justice.

Where the accused resides abroad, initiation of proceedings may give rise to extradition requests, subject to the existence of an applicable treaty and satisfaction of the principle of dual criminality. In practice, extradition based solely on section 498A may encounter difficulty in jurisdictions lacking an equivalent offense, and authorities may therefore rely on the underlying criminal conduct to meet treaty requirements. Extradition remains governed by treaty law and the domestic law of the requested state and is not automatic upon registration of a 498A case.

E. Extraterritorial Application of IPC Section 498A

IPC section 498A may apply to acts alleged to have occurred outside India, subject to statutory limitations. Under section 4 of the IPC, offenses committed by an Indian citizen outside India are deemed triable under Indian law. Procedurally, section 188 of the CrPC governs such cases and provides that where an offense is committed outside India by an Indian citizen, the accused may be dealt with as if the offense had been committed in India, subject to the requirement of prior sanction of the Central Government.

The scope and operation of CrPC section 188 in the context of section 498A were clarified by a three-judge bench of the Supreme Court in *Venkateshwarlu v. State of Andhra Pradesh*.[28] In that case, the alleged acts of cruelty and dowry-related offenses occurred in Botswana after the parties had relocated abroad, yet criminal proceedings were initiated in India. The Supreme Court held that while the magistrate was competent to take cognizance of the offense and issue process without prior sanction, the trial could not commence unless and until sanction of the Central Government under CrPC section 188 was obtained. It is therefore settled that an offense under IPC section 498A is triable in India even if the alleged acts occurred outside Indian territory, but commencement of trial is contingent upon statutory sanction.

F. Investigative Steps Following Registration of a Section 498A Case

If conciliation efforts by the police fail, the complaint proceeds to investigation. In matrimonial disputes, the Supreme Court has recognized that the police may conduct a preliminary inquiry before registering an FIR in order to determine whether a cognizable offense is disclosed.[29] Once the inquiry is completed and the FIR is registered under section 154 of the CrPC, the investigation formally begins.

Registration of an FIR does not automatically result in arrest. Arrest is governed by CrPC sections 41 and 41A and the principles laid down by the Supreme Court, which require that arrest not be made mechanically and that notice of appearance ordinarily be issued in offenses punishable with imprisonment up to seven years, including IPC section 498A. If the accused resides

28. Venkateshwarlu v. State of Andhra Pradesh, AIR 2011 SC 2900 (India), https://indiankanoon.org/doc/833591/.

29. *Kumari*, AIR 2014 SC 187.

outside India, the FIR may nonetheless be registered in India and investigation may proceed, with appropriate legal steps taken to secure the accused's participation in accordance with law.

During investigation, the police record statements of witnesses under CrPC section 161 and collect documentary and other evidence. Statements or confessions may also be recorded by a magistrate under CrPC section 164. Recording under section 164 is discretionary and not mandatory in prosecutions under section 498A, though it may be resorted to where considered necessary for evidentiary purposes. Upon completion of investigation, the police submit a final report under CrPC section 173 before the competent magistrate. If insufficient evidence is found, a closure report is filed. If sufficient material exists, a charge sheet is filed setting out the evidence and the offenses alleged, upon which the magistrate proceeds in accordance with law.

G. Citizenship, Overseas Status, and Liability for Acts Committed Outside India

Indian citizenship is not an absolute prerequisite for prosecution under IPC section 498A in respect of acts alleged to have occurred outside India. Indian citizens are amenable to prosecution for extraterritorial offenses by virtue of section 4 of the IPC, read with section 188 of the CrPC, subject to the requirement of prior sanction of the Central Government before commencement of trial. Overseas citizens of India, though not Indian citizens, have likewise been treated as amenable to Indian criminal jurisdiction in appropriate cases, with trials proceeding subject to compliance with CrPC section 188.

Foreign nationals married to Indian women may also, in certain circumstances, be prosecuted under section 498A for acts committed outside India. Section 3 of the IPC provides that any person who is liable under Indian law to be tried for an offense committed beyond India shall be dealt with as if the offense had been committed within India. Indian courts have relied on this provision to sustain jurisdiction over foreign spouses where the statutory and procedural requirements are otherwise satisfied. Practical enforcement, however, remains constrained by issues of extradition, which ultimately depend on the existence and scope of an applicable extradition treaty and satisfaction of the principle of dual criminality.

Judicial directions in individual cases illustrate these enforcement challenges. In *Marlapudi v. Marlapudi*, the Andhra Pradesh High Court addressed issues arising from the accused's departure from India during the pendency of proceedings under section 498A and issued directions to ensure cooperation with the trial process.[30] The decision underscores that while Indian courts may assert jurisdiction, securing the physical presence of an accused residing abroad remains contingent on treaty mechanisms and cooperation of foreign authorities.

30. Marlapudi v. Marlapudi, 2003 (5) ALD 307 (India), https://indiankanoon.org/doc/5294238/.

H. Arrest, Custody, and the Legal Significance of "Cognizable," "Non-Compoundable," and "Non-Bailable" Offenses

An accused in a prosecution under IPC section 498A cannot be arrested mechanically or automatically upon registration of an FIR. Although section 498A is a cognizable offense, arrest is governed by sections 41 and 41A of the CrPC and the principles laid down by the Supreme Court. The police are required to assess whether arrest is necessary on the facts of the case and, in offenses punishable with imprisonment up to seven years, ordinarily issue a notice of appearance instead of making an immediate arrest.[31] If an arrest is made, the accused must be produced before a magistrate within 24 hours.[32]

A "cognizable offense" is defined under CrPC section 2(c) as an offense for which a police officer may arrest without a warrant, as specified in the First Schedule or under any other law in force.[33] The significance of a cognizable classification is that the police may register an FIR and initiate investigation without prior judicial approval. This does not, however, dispense with statutory and constitutional safeguards governing arrest. By contrast, in non-cognizable offenses, the police may not arrest without a warrant and cannot investigate without judicial authorization.

Section 498A is also classified as a non-compoundable offense, meaning that it cannot be compromised or withdrawn by the parties as of right under CrPC section 320. Once the court has taken cognizance, the proceedings ordinarily continue to their conclusion. That said, the Supreme Court has recognized that high courts may, in appropriate cases, exercise inherent jurisdiction to quash proceedings arising from matrimonial disputes where the parties have settled and continuation of the prosecution would amount to abuse of process.[34]

Finally, section 498A is a non-bailable offense, which means that bail cannot be granted as a matter of right by the police and must be sought from a judicial authority.[35] Grant of bail remains subject to judicial discretion, and courts routinely consider factors such as the nature of allegations, necessity of custody, and compliance with statutory safeguards.

I. Arrest of Non-Resident Indians upon Entry into India: Lookout Circulars and Proclaimed Offender Proceedings

An NRI accused in a section 498A prosecution is not automatically arrested upon arrival in India. If the accused has cooperated with the investigation, responded to notices under section 41A of the CrPC, or obtained anticipatory bail under section 438 of the CrPC, courts may find no justification for coercive

31. CrPC §§ 41, 41A; Kumar v. State of Bihar, AIR 2014 SC 2756 (India), https://indiankanoon.org/doc/2982624/.

32. CrPC § 57.

33. *Id.* § 2(c).

34. Singh v. State of Punjab, AIR 2012 SC (Cri) 1796 (India), https://indiankanoon.org/doc/69949024/; Singh v. State of Punjab, Criminal Appeal No. 686/2014 (India), https://api.sci.gov.in/jonew/judis/41348.pdf.

35. CrPC § 2(a); CrPC First Schedule.

measures such as issuance of a lookout circular. Arrest, even in cognizable offenses, remains subject to statutory safeguards and judicial scrutiny.

In *Social Action Forum for Manav Adhikar v. Union of India*, the Supreme Court reaffirmed that arrests in section 498A cases must conform to the safeguards laid down in *Kumar v. State of Bihar* and that courts should ensure that coercive processes are not issued mechanically.[36] Where an accused is cooperating with the investigation, the issuance of coercive measures may be unwarranted.

However, if the accused fails to respond to summons, evades investigation, or does not comply with court directions, the court may initiate proceedings under CrPC sections 82 and 83 for proclamation and attachment, and the accused may be declared a proclaimed offender in accordance with law. In appropriate cases, investigating agencies may also seek issuance of a lookout circular to prevent departure from or facilitate detention upon arrival in India. Interpol Red Corner Notices are governed by international mechanisms and are not automatically issued upon registration of a section 498A case; they typically arise in the context of extradition proceedings and require separate procedural compliance. Where lawful coercive measures are in place, an accused may be detained upon entry into India and produced before the appropriate court.

J. Defensive Measures Available to Accused Persons in Section 498A Proceedings

The defensive options available to an accused under IPC section 498A are broadly similar whether the accused is located in India or abroad, though the timing and manner of their invocation may differ. Importantly, arrest is not automatic upon registration of an FIR, regardless of the accused's location, and is governed by statutory safeguards and judicial precedent. An accused who is within India may be required to cooperate with the investigation upon registration of the FIR, while an accused residing abroad is ordinarily notified and called upon to participate in the investigation in accordance with law.

1. Anticipatory Bail

One of the primary safeguards available to an accused is anticipatory bail under section 438 of the CrPC. Anticipatory bail may be sought by any person who apprehends arrest in connection with a non-bailable offense, including section 498A. If granted, the order operates to ensure that in the event of arrest, the accused is released on bail subject to conditions imposed by the court, which commonly include cooperation with the investigation, appearance before authorities when required, and restrictions on foreign travel without prior permission.

An accused residing outside India may also seek anticipatory bail by filing an application before the appropriate Indian court, including through an authorized representative acting under a power of attorney. Grant of anticipatory bail in such cases can significantly reduce the risk of arrest upon entry into India, provided the accused complies with the conditions imposed by the court.

---

36. Social Action Forum for Manav Adhikar v. Union of India, AIR 2018 SC 4273 (India), https://indiankanoon.org/doc/81618143/.

In practice, where arrest is not considered necessary, the police are required to issue a notice of appearance under CrPC section 41A, directing the accused to cooperate with the investigation without taking him into custody.

2. Other Defensive Measures

In addition to bail-related relief, an accused may take steps to preserve documentary and electronic evidence relevant to the matrimonial relationship, particularly where allegations of cruelty or dowry harassment are disputed. Where appropriate, an accused may initiate independent criminal proceedings if legally sustainable, though such steps must be approached with caution and on the basis of credible material.

The accused may also seek quashing of the FIR or criminal proceedings by invoking the inherent jurisdiction of the high court under CrPC section 482, where the allegations, even if taken at face value, do not disclose the commission of an offense or where continuation of the proceedings would amount to abuse of process. Finally, where an accused is acquitted after trial, the law permits initiation of separate proceedings, including for defamation, subject to satisfaction of the statutory requirements and evidentiary thresholds applicable to such claims.

K. Judicial and Procedural Safeguards Against Abuse of Section 498A

Indian courts have repeatedly acknowledged concerns regarding the misuse of IPC section 498A and have introduced procedural safeguards to curb arbitrary arrests and coercive practices. In *Kumar*, the Supreme Court observed that the provision, though intended as a shield to protect women, had often been deployed as a weapon in matrimonial disputes, necessitating stricter control over arrest and investigation.[37]

One such safeguard relates to the registration of FIRs in matrimonial disputes. While registration of an FIR is generally mandatory where a cognizable offense is disclosed, the Supreme Court in *Kumari* recognized matrimonial disputes as a limited category in which the police may conduct a preliminary inquiry before registration, in order to assess whether a cognizable offense is made out.[38] This has been supplemented in practice by efforts at reconciliation through police or women's cells, though such efforts are not a statutory precondition to registration.

Arrest in section 498A cases is also subject to strict limitations. In *Kumar v. State of Uttar Pradesh*, the Supreme Court held that arrest should not be made routinely or mechanically and must be justified by necessity, emphasizing that deprivation of liberty is a serious matter.[39] These principles were reaffirmed and operationalized in *Kumar v. State of Bihar*, where the Court directed that arrests should be made only in accordance with the parameters set out in CrPC section 41 and that, in appropriate cases, a notice of appearance under CrPC section 41A should be issued instead of effecting arrest. The Court further mandated

37. *Kumar*, AIR 2014 SC 2756.

38. *Kumari*, AIR 2014 SC 187.

39. Kumar v. State of Uttar Pradesh, AIR 1994 SC 1349 (India), https://indiankanoon.org/doc/768175/.

supervisory oversight, documentation of reasons for arrest or non-arrest, and active judicial scrutiny before authorizing detention.

Additional safeguards were reiterated in *Social Action Forum for Manav Adhikar*, where the Supreme Court clarified that while section 498A remains non-compoundable, high courts may exercise inherent jurisdiction under CrPC section 482 to quash proceedings arising from matrimonial disputes where the parties have settled and continuation of the prosecution would amount to abuse of process.[40] The Court also emphasized that coercive measures, such as impounding passports or seeking Red Corner Notices against persons ordinarily residing outside India, should not be undertaken routinely and must be justified on the facts of each case.

3.3. International Service of Process Under the Hague Service Convention

In India–U.S. litigation, service of process is often underestimated as a technical formality rather than appreciated as a jurisdictional fault line. A recurring source of confusion is the mistaken assumption that because India has not signed the Hague Abduction Convention, it is somehow outside the Hague framework altogether. In reality, while India is not a party to the Hague Convention on the Civil Aspects of International Child Abduction, it is a signatory to the Hague Service Convention, and strict compliance with that treaty is mandatory when serving process in India.

Compounding this misunderstanding is a frequent failure to account for how extraordinarily slow Hague service in India can be, delays that are rarely factored into litigation strategy or case timelines at the outset. As a result, practitioners may proceed informally or rely on assumptions about actual notice, only to face last-minute challenges by the India-based respondent, or even sua sponte concerns raised by the court, questioning whether service was properly effected under the Convention. In cross-border cases, actual notice does not substitute for treaty compliance, and missteps in service, particularly when coupled with significant delay, can destabilize proceedings at even the most advanced stages of litigation.

3.3.1. India's Accession to the Hague Service Convention

India acceded to the Hague Convention on the Service Abroad of Judicial and Extrajudicial Documents in Civil or Commercial Matters on November 23, 2006, and the Convention entered into force for India on August 1, 2007. As a result, service of U.S. judicial documents on parties located in India is governed exclusively by the Convention when it applies, and domestic service rules or informal methods are displaced by the treaty framework.[41]

40. *Social Action Forum for Manav Adhikar*, AIR 2018 SC 4273.

41. Hague Convention on the Service Abroad of Judicial and Extrajudicial Documents in Civil or Commercial Matters, Nov. 15, 1965, 20 U.S.T. 361.

Critically, India has made a formal declaration objecting to all of the alternative service methods permitted under Article 10 of the Convention. This includes objections to service by postal channels, service through judicial officers or other competent persons, and service through private agents.[42] Consequently, service through mail, courier, email, WhatsApp, or process servers is categorically impermissible for service in India under the Convention.

For U.S. litigants, this means that service must proceed exclusively through India's designated Central Authority, the Ministry of Law and Justice (Department of Legal Affairs), New Delhi. Any deviation from this prescribed channel exposes the service to challenge and renders resulting proceedings vulnerable to dismissal, vacatur of orders, or nonrecognition abroad.

3.3.2. The Hague Service Process for Serving a Party in India

To initiate service under the Hague Service Convention from the United States to India, the request must be signed by an attorney or a clerk of court.[43] The requesting party must complete the official Hague request form (commonly referred to as Form USM-94) in duplicate and submit it, together with two sets of the documents to be served and any required translations, directly to India's Central Authority.[44]

India does not require translation of documents into a local language where the documents are in English, as English is an official language of the Indian judiciary. However, documents must be complete, legible, and procedurally proper under the law of the requesting state. The Central Authority does not correct defects or omissions in the request and will return incomplete applications unexecuted.

Once received, the Ministry of Law and Justice forwards the request to the appropriate district court or local judicial authority having territorial jurisdiction over the respondent's address. Service is then effected in accordance with Indian procedural law, typically through court process servers or local police authorities. Upon completion, the executing court transmits proof of service back through the Central Authority, which then issues a formal Certificate of Service under Article 6 of the Convention, and sends it back to the official who initiated the request.

3.3.3. Timeframes and Practical Realities

In practice, Hague service in India is *notoriously slow*. While the Convention itself contemplates expeditious transmission, service commonly takes *six to 12 months*, and in some cases significantly longer. Delays are attributable to several systemic factors, including chronic understaffing at the Central Authority,

---

42. Hague Conference on Private International Law, Declarations and Reservations: India (Art. 10 Objections) (2006).

43. U.S. State Department, *India Judicial Assistance Information*, https://travel.state.gov/content/travel/en/legal/Judicial-Assistance-Country-Information/India.html.

44. *Id.*

administrative bottlenecks at the district court level, and the absence of enforceable timelines within the Indian service machinery.[45]

Additional practical challenges routinely arise:

- **Backlogs and administrative delay**. Requests often remain pending for months before being transmitted to the local court, with little visibility or ability to expedite.
- **Address sensitivity**. Minor discrepancies in addresses, such as missing landmarks or outdated locality names, frequently result in failed service and restarting the process.
- **No tolerance for informal substitutes**. India does not recognize "substantial compliance" or good-faith attempts at service outside the Convention framework. Any attempt to bypass the Central Authority, even where the respondent has actual notice, risks invalidation.
- **Judicial scrutiny**. Indian courts have vacated ex parte orders and declined to recognize foreign proceedings where service did not strictly comply with Convention requirements.[46]

3.3.4. Indian Judicial Treatment of Hague Service Compliance

Having outlined India's treaty position and the mechanics of Hague service previously, Indian case law becomes relevant at the point where service fails, is bypassed, or is improvised, and litigants seek to rely on "actual notice," substituted service, or ex parte orders to keep proceedings alive. Indian courts have approached these situations with a pronounced emphasis on treaty fidelity, particularly when service defects surface at enforcement or recognition stages.

A. Actual Notice Does Not Cure Treaty Noncompliance

Indian courts previously rejected the argument that actual or informal notice cures noncompliance with the Hague Service Convention where it applies. While domestic courts have increasingly permitted electronic or substituted service for defendants located within India, that flexibility has not been extended to cross-border service governed by treaty obligations.

In cases involving overseas respondents, courts have emphasized that Hague service is not merely about notice in fact, but about notice delivered through a channel accepted by the receiving state.[47] Accordingly, informal service, whether by email, messaging applications, or courier, has been held insufficient where treaty-mandated procedures were bypassed, even if the respondent was demonstrably aware of the proceedings.

B. Substituted Service as a Post-Hague Remedy, Not a Shortcut

More recent decisions reflect a limited doctrinal refinement. Indian courts have clarified that substituted service may be considered only *after* a bona fide

45. *See* Practical Handbook on the Operation of the Hague Service Convention (HCCH).
46. *See* Indian high court decisions vacating ex parte relief for defective foreign service.
47. Mollykutty v. Jacob, RFA No. 92/2022 (India), https://indiankanoon.org/doc/94791253/.

attempt at Hague service has been made and has failed, particularly where there is evidence that the respondent is deliberately evading service.[48]

This distinction matters. Substituted service is treated not as an alternative to the Hague framework, but as a contingent remedy available once treaty-compliant service proves impossible due to obstruction. Courts have cautioned against allowing substituted service to become a parallel track that undermines treaty obligations.

C. Consequences for Recognition and Enforcement of Foreign Judgments

The strictest scrutiny of service compliance is likely to appear in proceedings seeking recognition or enforcement of foreign judgments in India. Indian courts are likely to examine whether defendants were served in accordance with the Hague Convention before foreign courts proceeded ex parte. Where service was effected through impermissible means, courts may treat the resulting judgments as vulnerable under section 13(d) of the CPC, on the ground that the proceedings violated principles of natural justice.

This approach has been particularly pronounced in matrimonial disputes, where foreign divorce decrees and custody orders are frequently challenged in India on service-related grounds. In such cases, defects in Hague service might be sufficient to defeat recognition, regardless of whether the respondent had informal knowledge of the proceedings.

D. Treaty Compliance Within India's Dualist Framework

Indian courts have also situated Hague service within India's broader constitutional approach to international law. This has produced a calibrated judicial position: while service through the Central Authority under the Convention remains the preferred and safest route where India is the receiving state, domestic procedural provisions may operate alongside the Convention where the receiving state has not objected to alternative methods.[49] Where India's own objections apply, however, courts have made clear that domestic flexibility must yield to treaty commitments.

E. Judicial Trajectory

Taken together, Indian case law reflects a movement from early formalism toward cautious procedural pragmatism, without abandoning the core principle that Hague-compliant service is mandatory where applicable. Courts have resisted allowing efficiency or convenience to override treaty fidelity, while preserving limited discretion in cases of demonstrated evasion.

For international family law practitioners, the lesson is clear: service defects under the Hague Convention are not technicalities in Indian courts. They are jurisdictional vulnerabilities that can resurface years later, particularly at enforcement, recognition, or modification stages.

48. Sundaran v. Sivadasan, RFA No. 210/2019 (India), https://indiankanoon.org/doc/190436035/.

49. *Id.*

3.3.5. Service Delays as a Catalyst for Anti-Suit Injunctions

The prolonged and rigid nature of Hague service in India frequently creates a strategic opening for the India-based respondent to seek an *anti-suit injunction* from an Indian court. Where a respondent learns, often informally, that U.S. proceedings are underway without valid Hague service, they may characterize the foreign litigation as oppressive, vexatious, or violative of principles of natural justice.

Indian courts have demonstrated a willingness to entertain such applications, particularly where the foreign plaintiff has proceeded ex parte, sought interim relief, or obtained coercive orders without first effecting valid Convention service. In these circumstances, defects in service are not treated as mere technicalities but as jurisdictional and fairness concerns. An anti-suit injunction, once granted, places the U.S. litigant in an untenable position: continuing the U.S. action risks contempt proceedings in India, while halting the U.S. case may result in loss of momentum or adverse procedural consequences.

Thus, *service under the Hague Service Convention is not merely a procedural formality* in India–U.S. litigation. It is often the first battleground, and missteps at this stage frequently precipitate the very anti-suit injunctions that complicate and derail cross-border disputes. This dynamic is examined in greater detail in the following section.

3.4. Anti-Suit Injunctions

Anti-suit injunctions occupy a uniquely sensitive position in Indian–international family law. They represent one of the few judicial tools by which a domestic Indian court directly restrains a party from pursuing proceedings before a foreign sovereign court. For this reason, such injunctions implicate not only private rights between litigants but also principles of international comity, judicial restraint, and respect for foreign legal systems. In family law disputes, where issues of personal status, child welfare, and financial security intersect, courts have been especially cautious in exercising this extraordinary power.

3.4.1. Nature and Scope of Anti-Suit Injunctions in Indian Matrimonial Disputes

An anti-suit injunction is an order directed at a litigant, not at a foreign court, restraining that party from instituting or continuing proceedings in another jurisdiction. Indian courts have repeatedly emphasized this distinction to justify the exercise of such power without formally infringing upon the sovereignty of foreign courts.[50] In *Modi Entertainment*, the Supreme Court of India articulated the governing principles to be considered when a court is asked to grant an anti-suit injunction. The Court held that the following factors must guide the exercise of discretion: (1) the defendant against whom the injunction is sought

50. Modi Entertainment Network v. W.S.G. Cricket Pte. Ltd., AIR 2003 SC 1177 (India), https://indiankanoon.org/doc/1857811/.

must be amenable to the personal jurisdiction of the court; (2) the refusal of the injunction must result in injustice or defeat the ends of justice; and (3) the court must remain mindful of the principle of comity, that is, respect for the foreign court in which the commencement or continuation of proceedings is sought to be restrained.[51]

Although *Modi Entertainment* did not arise in the matrimonial context, the Supreme Court's articulation of anti-suit injunction principles has been applied across subject areas. The Court emphasized that the grant of an anti-suit injunction is an equitable remedy, grounded in the court's in personam jurisdiction over the party sought to be restrained. Indian courts therefore possess the power to issue such injunctions against a party amenable to their personal jurisdiction in an appropriate case. However, because the remedy is discretionary and equitable in nature, it *must be exercised sparingly* and with circumspection.[52] An anti-suit injunction should be granted only where the refusal to do so would *defeat the ends of justice* and result in the perpetuation of injustice.

In matrimonial and custody disputes, anti-suit injunctions are most commonly sought where parallel proceedings threaten to result in conflicting decrees, oppressive litigation, or strategic abuse of process. Indian courts have recognized that family law disputes are particularly susceptible to such abuse, given disparities in economic power, immigration status, and geographic mobility between spouses.

The Supreme Court while dealing with a U.S.–India matrimonial dispute in *Thakur v. Thakur* observed:

> (9) Anti-Suit Injunctions are meant to restrain a party to a suit/proceeding from instituting or prosecuting a case in another court, including a foreign court. Simply put, an anti-suit injunction is a judicial order restraining one party from prosecuting a case in another court outside its jurisdiction. The principles governing grant of injunction are common to that of granting anti-suit injunction. The cases of injunction are basically governed by the doctrine of equity.
>
> (10) It is a well-settled law that the courts in India have power to issue anti-suit injunction to a party over whom it has personal jurisdiction, in an appropriate case. However, before passing the order of anti-suit injunction, courts should be very cautious and careful, and it should be granted sparingly and not as a matter of routine as such orders involve a court impinging on the jurisdiction of another court, which is not entertained very easily specially when . . . it restrains the parties from instituting or continuing a case in a foreign court.[53]

51. *Id.*
52. *Id.*
53. Thakur v. Thakur, AIR 2018 SC 2094, ¶¶ 9–10 (India), https://indiankanoon.org/doc/25279730/.

A. Statutory and Jurisprudential Basis in Indian Law

Indian courts derive the power to grant anti-suit injunctions primarily from their inherent jurisdiction under section 151 of the CPC.[54] Although no statute expressly codifies anti-suit injunctions in the family law context, the Supreme Court of India has confirmed that civil courts possess inherent authority to restrain vexatious or oppressive proceedings where the ends of justice so require.

The leading articulation of the governing principles appears in *Modi Entertainment*, where the Supreme Court set out a structured framework for determining when anti-suit injunctions may be granted.[55] While *Modi Entertainment* arose from a commercial dispute, its principles have since been applied, albeit cautiously, in matrimonial and family law cases. Courts have consistently stressed that the power must be exercised sparingly and only in exceptional circumstances.

B. Declining to Issue an Anti-Suit Injunction

The Court in *Thakur* declined to grant an anti-suit injunction after carefully applying the "grave injustice" and "ends of justice" tests to the facts before it.[56] At the outset, it noted that "*there is no dispute to the fact that both the parties are permanent citizens of U.S.*" and that "*undisputedly, the Circuit Court, Florida, USA is also having the concurrent jurisdiction in the given case.*"[57] Against that backdrop, the husband's assertion that he would suffer grave injustice if the Florida proceedings were allowed to continue was found to be unsupported.

The Court emphasized that the appellant-husband had himself "*been residing [in the U.S.] after 2007*" and had nevertheless chosen to initiate the anti-suit injunction proceedings in India "*through another person by empowering him through a power of attorney.*"[58] On these facts, the Court held that "*there is nothing brought on record to show how the appellant-husband would suffer grave injustice if the injunction restraining the respondent-wife from pursuing the divorce petition in Florida is not granted.*"[59] It further concluded that "*even if the injunction is declined, it cannot be said that the ends of justice will be defeated and injustice will be perpetuated,*" thereby failing the core equitable threshold for such relief.[60]

The Court also rejected the husband's argument that the Florida proceedings should be restrained because the wife had sought divorce on the ground of irretrievable breakdown, a ground not available to her under the Hindu Marriage Act. Significantly, the Court noted that the husband had already raised this contention before the Florida court, where "*both the parties will produce evidence with regard to the question whether their marriage is governed by the Act or any other law.*"[61] In this context, the Court underscored the importance of comity, observing that a "*foreign court cannot be presumed to be exercising its jurisdiction*

54. CPC § 151.
55. *Modi Entertainment*, AIR 2003 SC 1177.
56. *Thakur*, AIR 2018 SC 2094, ¶ 18 (emphasis added).
57. *Id.* (emphasis added).
58. *Id.* (emphasis added).
59. *Id.* (emphasis added).
60. *Id.* (emphasis added).
61. *Id.* ¶ 19 (emphasis added).

wrongly" even if the husband were ultimately able to establish that the parties continued to be governed by Hindu law in respect of their matrimonial dispute.[62] On this reasoning, the Court declined to interfere with the foreign proceedings by way of an anti-suit injunction.[63]

C. Granting an Anti-Suit Injunction

Nonetheless, there have been cases in which Indian courts have gone a different way and granted anti-suit relief even in the face of parallel foreign proceedings. In *Sankaranarayanan v. Shashidar,* the Madras High Court was confronted with competing proceedings in Chennai and Washington, alongside Hague Convention litigation concerning the child in the United States.[64] The court began by reaffirming that the power of Indian courts to grant anti-suit injunctions "is no longer *res integra,*" relying on *Modi Entertainment,* and reiterating that such relief operates in personam and must be exercised with due regard to comity.[65] It also rejected the argument that a family court lacks jurisdiction to grant such relief, holding that explanation (d) to section 7 of the Family Courts Act—empowering it to grant "an order or injunction in circumstances arising out of a marital relationship"—is wide enough to encompass anti-suit injunctions.[66]

On facts, the court distinguished *Thakur,* noting that the special features that weighed against injunction there were absent here. In *Thakur,* both parties were U.S. citizens and the husband was residing in the United States; here, the husband was "an Indian citizen and is a resident of Singapore," had initiated proceedings in Chennai on September 4, 2024, and had entered only a limited appearance in Washington to question jurisdiction.[67] The wife, though an American citizen, was residing in Singapore when she invoked the jurisdiction of the Washington court. Significantly, the court recorded that *"nowhere during the course of the arguments or in the lengthy counter affidavit, has the respondent pleaded that she would not get justice in the Courts in India."*[68] Interestingly, whereas in *Thakur* the Supreme Court emphasized concurrent jurisdiction and absence of grave injustice, the Madras High Court here focused on sequencing (India being first seized), residence, and demonstrable prejudice.

The court further underscored that *"most of the evidences and witnesses are situated in Singapore and in India,"* and that compelling the husband to contest proceedings in Washington would cause *"serious prejudice,"* both financially and practically. The marriage had been solemnized in India, and under section 31 of the Special Marriage Act, the Chennai Family Court possessed jurisdiction to entertain the petition.[69]

---

62. *Id.* (emphasis added).
63. *Id.* ¶¶ 18–20 (emphasis added).
64. Sankaranarayanan v. Shashidar, C.R.P. (PD) No. 4521 of 2024, ¶¶ 37–38 (India), https://indiankanoon.org/doc/59382303/.
65. *Id.* ¶ 34; *see also Modi Entertainment,* AIR 2003 SC 1177.
66. *Sankaranarayanan,* C.R.P. (PD) No. 4521 of 2024, ¶¶ 45–46.
67. *Id.* ¶¶ 59–60.
68. *Id.* ¶ 62 (emphasis added).
69. *Id.* ¶ 78 (emphasis added).

Of particular importance was the ground invoked in Washington, "*irretrievably broken down*," which is not a ground available under section 27 of the Special Marriage Act.[70] The court reasoned that any decree granted solely on that ground "*will not be recognized in India*," and that there was a "distinct possibility" of such a decree resulting in an "empty decree or a brutum fulmen."[71] The non-recognizability of a prospective foreign decree was expressly treated as a relevant factor while considering anti-suit relief.

Finally, while acknowledging the principle of comity, the court held that the parties had never agreed to submit to the jurisdiction of the American courts and that the family court at Chennai, "*having seized the jurisdiction earlier*," was entitled to proceed with the dispute.[72] It therefore restrained the wife from proceeding further with the divorce action in the United States, subject to detailed conditions including enhanced maintenance and litigation expenses.

The decision thus illustrates that, notwithstanding *Thakur*, Indian courts will grant anti-suit injunctions where the natural forum is India, the foreign ground of divorce is not statutorily recognized, and concrete prejudice, rather than speculative injustice, is demonstrated.

D. Court's Direction Not to "Precipitate the Matter"

In practice, particularly during the proverbial "race to the courthouse," Indian courts have often adopted an intermediate, pragmatic approach before issuing an anti-suit injunction. Rather than immediately restraining the respondent from proceeding with the foreign proceedings, courts may first seek an assurance from the respondent that, while parallel matters remain pending, the respondent will not "precipitate the matter" by pressing ahead in the foreign forum so as to create a fait accompli. Where such an assurance is forthcoming, courts have sometimes deferred coercive relief in favor of orderly adjudication. Conversely, where the respondent "*was unable to take a firm stand*," or where conduct suggests a strategic attempt to advance the foreign proceedings notwithstanding, the Indian courts have proceeded to examine the anti-suit injunction on merits and, if warranted, granted relief to prevent abuse of process and frustration of justice.[73]

E. Emergency Anti-Suit Relief and the Practical Erosion of Hague Service

In practice, and notwithstanding the formal service requirements under the Hague Service Convention, Indian courts have occasionally proceeded with urgent anti-suit applications in transnational family disputes on a pragmatic footing. Where a proceeding has already been instituted in a U.S. forum—such as New York—and the respondent thereafter approaches an Indian court seeking anti-suit relief, courts have, in some instances, entertained and granted interim restraint orders even while Hague service remains pending or incomplete. This dynamic can

70. *Id.* ¶ 54 (emphasis added).

71. *Id.* ¶¶ 73, 75 (emphasis added).

72. *Id.* ¶ 70.

73. Bhatnagar v. Lall, Arising out of S.L.P. (Civ.) No. 14948/2020 (India), https://indiankanoon.org/doc/28245647/.

materially prejudice the party who filed first in the United States: despite having invoked a court of competent jurisdiction and while actively attempting to comply with international service requirements, that party may find its foreign proceedings effectively frozen by an Indian interim order obtained without full service. This appears to reflect a practice-driven emphasis on preventing a perceived risk of the foreign matter being "precipitated," rather than a doctrinal relaxation of service norms, with questions of formal service often deferred—leaving the U.S.-based litigant to bear the immediate procedural disadvantage.

Whether the refusal of an anti-suit injunction represents the norm depends heavily on the factual matrix of each case. Indian courts have not adopted a rigid presumption either in favor of or against restraining foreign proceedings. Rather, the jurisprudence reflects a calibrated, fact-sensitive approach in which the equities of the parties, the degree of connection to the competing fora, the stage and conduct of the foreign proceedings, and considerations of international comity are weighed together. While courts have declined to grant anti-suit injunctions in cases involving strong foreign ties and concurrent jurisdiction, they have also intervened where foreign proceedings were found to be oppressive, strategically abusive, or procedurally unfair. As such, the grant or refusal of an anti-suit injunction cannot be characterized as a categorical norm, but instead turns on whether, in the totality of circumstances, equitable restraint is necessary to prevent injustice.

F. Comparative Perspective: U.S. Law on Anti-Suit Injunctions

U.S. courts approach anti-suit injunctions with greater restraint than Indian courts, particularly in family law matters. While federal courts possess the power to issue anti-suit injunctions under principles of equity, such relief is considered exceptional and is typically reserved for cases involving clear threats to jurisdiction or important public policies.[74]

Although such injunctions formally operate only against the litigating party and not directly against the foreign court, U.S. courts recognize that they effectively constrain the jurisdiction of a court of another sovereign.[75] For that reason, principles of international comity assume a central role in the analysis.[76] American courts have therefore cautioned that anti-foreign-suit injunctions should be used "sparingly" and granted "only with care and great restraint," emphasizing the diplomatic and jurisdictional sensitivities that accompany interference with parallel proceedings abroad.[77]

In the family law context, U.S. courts are generally reluctant to restrain foreign matrimonial or custody proceedings, preferring instead to rely on doctrines such as forum non conveniens, abstention, or statutory frameworks like

74. China Trade & Dev. Corp. v. M.V. Choong Yong, 837 F.2d 33 (2d Cir. 1987).

75. United States v. Davis, 767 F.2d 1025, 1038 (2d Cir. 1985).

76. Peck v. Jenness, 48 U.S. (7 How.) 612, 625 (1849).

77. *Davis*, 767 F.2d at 1038; Canadian Filters (Harwich) Ltd. v. Lear-Siegler, Inc., 412 F.2d 577, 578 (1st Cir. 1969); *see also* Laker Airways Ltd. v. Sabena, Belgian World Airlines, 731 F.2d 909, 927 (D.C. Cir. 1984); Compagnie des Bauxites de Guinée v. Ins. Co. of N. Am., 651 F.2d 877, 887 (3d Cir. 1981).

the Uniform Child Custody Jurisdiction and Enforcement Act (UCCJEA) in child custody cases. Anti-suit injunctions are more commonly encountered in commercial or intellectual property disputes than in family law.

Recent U.S. decisions illustrate both the availability of anti-suit injunctions in family matters and the relatively high threshold that governs their issuance. In *Salkhi v. Behroyan*, the California Court of Appeal upheld an anti-suit injunction requiring the husband to dismiss divorce proceedings he had initiated in Iran after the parties had already entered into a marital settlement agreement in California.[78] The Iranian filing was viewed as an attempt to circumvent financial and custodial obligations previously resolved in the California judgment. While acknowledging that anti-suit injunctions should be "ordered sparingly" out of respect for international comity, the court found exceptional circumstances: the foreign proceeding threatened the integrity of a valid California judgment and undermined the parties' negotiated settlement. The injunction was therefore justified to preserve the court's authority and prevent evasion of its orders.

By contrast, in *Niemeyer v. Niemeyer*, involving parallel proceedings in Turkey, a Florida court declined to issue anti-suit relief.[79] The court reiterated the high bar applicable in U.S. jurisprudence and found insufficient evidence, at that stage, that the Turkish proceedings would "prevent Florida's jurisdiction" or threaten a "vital Florida policy." The mere existence of parallel litigation abroad did not, without more, justify injunctive interference. Taken together, these cases demonstrate that U.S. courts will intervene where a foreign action is demonstrably evasive or undermines an existing domestic judgment, but will refrain from doing so absent a clear showing of jurisdictional impairment or policy harm.

Thus, where U.S. courts have considered anti-suit relief in family cases, they have emphasized the need to avoid direct interference with foreign sovereign adjudication and have required a strong showing that the foreign proceedings would undermine fundamental domestic policies or due process rights. This contrasts with the Indian approach, where courts have shown greater willingness, though still cautious, to intervene in order to prevent manifest injustice.

3.5. Forum Non Conveniens (Inconvenient Forum)

While anti-suit injunctions represent a direct judicial response to competing jurisdiction, the doctrine of forum non conveniens offers a more restrained, indirect mechanism for regulating parallel proceedings. Rather than restraining a party from pursuing foreign litigation, the doctrine permits a court to decline or stay its own jurisdiction where another forum is demonstrably more appropriate for adjudication. In international family law, this doctrine has assumed

78. Salkhi v. Behroyan (*In re* Marriage of Salkhi & Behroyan), No. A165484, 2023 WL ___ (Cal. Ct. App. Dec. 5, 2023), https://www.casemine.com/judgement/us/65714ab27eb9195f0af3c398.

79. Niemeyer v. Niemeyer, No. 3D24-1692 (Fla. Dist. Ct. App. Apr. 23, 2025), https://caselaw.findlaw.com/court/fl-district-court-of-appeal/117193864.html.

increasing significance as courts seek to balance access to justice with fairness, efficiency, and international comity.

3.5.1. Evolution of the Doctrine in Indian Jurisprudence

In India, the doctrine is often invoked inversely via an anti-suit injunction. Rather than the Indian court declining its own jurisdiction, it is asked to restrain a party from proceeding in a foreign court that is deemed non conveniens.

In *Modi Entertainment*, the Supreme Court explained that, "*in a case where more forums than one are available,*" the court considering an anti-suit injunction "*will examine as to which is the appropriate forum (forum conveniens) having regard to the convenience of the parties,*" and may grant restraint where the foreign proceedings are "*oppressive or vexatious or in a forum non-conveniens.*"[80] The Court framed this discretion within three controlling considerations: (1) the defendant must be "*amenable to the personal jurisdiction of the court*"; (2) if injunction is declined, "*the ends of justice will be defeated and injustice will be perpetuated*"; and (3) "*the principle of comity—respect for the court in which the commencement or continuance of action/proceeding is sought to be restrained—must be borne in mind.*"[81]

At the same time, *Modi Entertainment* cautioned that where parties have agreed, under a jurisdiction clause, to submit to a foreign court as a "*neutral foreign forum,*" proceedings in the court of choice "*cannot per se be treated as vexatious or oppressive nor can the court be said to be forum non-conveniens,*" and "*ordinarily no anti-suit injunction will be granted*" in such a "*forum conveniens and favoured forum.*" The Court added that "*the burden of establishing that the forum of the choice is a forum non-conveniens or the proceedings therein are oppressive or vexatious would be on the party so contending,*" and that typical convenience objections (including "*hardship and incurring of heavy expenditure on taking the witnesses to the English Court*") are deemed to have been foreseen when parties agreed to the foreign forum and "*cannot be valid grounds to interdict prosecution*" there.[82]

A. Welfare-Anchored Jurisdiction

The doctrine of *forum non conveniens* is rooted in the equitable discretion of Indian courts to prevent abuse of jurisdiction. It is, by its nature, intensely fact-dependent and capable of being argued in either direction. On one hand, the doctrine reflects the recognition that jurisdictional competence does not necessarily imply jurisdictional suitability. On the other, the Supreme Court has cautioned that "*there is no forum convenience in wardship jurisdiction,*" emphasizing that the adjudicative mandate is peremptorily governed by the paramount consideration of the child's unreserved welfare.[83]

Indian family law jurisprudence reveals a second, converse strand of reasoning, one that may be described as the *functional opposite* of forum non

80. *Modi Entertainment*, AIR 2003 SC 1177 (emphasis added).
81. *Id.* (emphasis added).
82. *Id.* (emphasis added).
83. Gupta v. Gupta, AIR 2018 SC (Supp) 674, ¶ 34 (India), https://indiankanoon.org/doc/69261674/.

conveniens. In certain circumstances, particularly where a child is physically present within India, courts have exercised jurisdiction even where traditional connecting factors might otherwise point elsewhere. In Indian family law, the opposite of forum non conveniens thus performs a critical function. Matrimonial and custody disputes typically implicate deeply personal facts, ongoing relationships, and long-term consequences, all of which call for proximity to evidence, witnesses, and, most importantly, the child. Indian courts have therefore acknowledged that rigid adherence to jurisdictional entitlement may, in appropriate cases, undermine rather than advance substantive justice.

This protective orientation is particularly evident in cases involving transnational marriages and power asymmetries. For instance, although the Supreme Court in *Saraph* did not engage with forum non conveniens as a doctrinal construct, its reasoning reflects a position fundamentally opposed to convenience-based jurisdictional displacement in matrimonial disputes. The Court framed the issue through the lens of gendered vulnerability, expressly characterizing the phenomenon of NRI-initiated foreign matrimonial proceedings as a "*new social evil,*" and situating it within the broader "*plight of women*" deserted through foreign decrees.[84] Rather than treating foreign courts as neutral or equivalent fora, the Court emphasized that Indian wives are often left without meaningful access to justice abroad, describing the typical victim as a "*helpless, poor, educated girl,*" whose marriage breakdown results in the loss of "*status, service, dignity and peace.*"[85] This articulation leaves little doctrinal space for an argument that forum convenience or procedural efficiency should justify jurisdictional deference.

More significantly, the Court rejected the premise that the mere availability of a foreign forum could warrant Indian judicial restraint. Instead, it underscored the affirmative responsibility of Indian courts to prevent jurisdictional maneuvers that operate oppressively rather than equitably. This approach culminated in the Court's recommendation for legislative intervention, including that "*no marriage between a NRI and an Indian woman which has taken place in India may be annulled by a foreign court,*" and that provision be made for "*adequate alimony to the wife in the property of the husband both in India and abroad.*"[86] These observations reveal a clear normative preference for jurisdictional retention in matrimonial disputes, grounded in access to justice and substantive protection rather than forum convenience. Read doctrinally, *Saraph* thus functions as an implicit repudiation of forum non conveniens reasoning in Indian family law, particularly where its application would exacerbate inequality or undermine the legal agency of the deserted spouse.

B. Indian Courts Historically Approached Forum Non Conveniens with Caution

This is particularly so in matrimonial matters governed by personal statutes. Unlike commercial disputes, where the doctrine was readily invoked, family

84. *Saraph,* AIR Online 1994 SC 381 (emphasis added).
85. *Id.* ¶¶ 2–3 (emphasis added).
86. *Id.* ¶ 4 (emphasis added).

law cases raised concerns about statutory intent and legislative silence. Over time, however, the Supreme Court of India has clarified that discretionary doctrines may coexist with statutory jurisdiction, provided they are exercised judiciously. The modern Indian articulation of forum non conveniens draws heavily from common-law principles, adapted to local realities. Courts have emphasized that the doctrine does not negate jurisdiction but regulates its exercise.[87] This distinction has allowed courts to remain faithful to statutory frameworks while acknowledging the practical burdens imposed by transnational litigation.

Indian courts have on limited occasions addressed pleas of forum non conveniens primarily in the context of anti-suit injunctions, with a strong emphasis on comity and a party's own procedural elections. In *Singh v. Bhatia*, the Delhi High Court examined a suit seeking to restrain the wife from pursuing divorce proceedings in Singapore on the assertion that Indian courts constituted the "proper and convenient Forum" and that Singapore was a "Forum of inconvenience."[88] The court noted that, notwithstanding this plea, the husband had himself approached the Singapore court seeking a stay of the divorce proceedings "by taking shelter under the principle of forum non-conveniens," thereby inviting the foreign court to determine whether it was the appropriate forum.[89] Significantly, the appellant did not challenge the Singapore court's jurisdiction on grounds such as domicile, but confined his application to a request for stay under the rule permitting a defendant to contend that "Singapore is not the proper forum for the dispute."[90]

Against this backdrop, the Division Bench held that, having submitted to the jurisdiction of the Singapore court and elected to argue forum non conveniens there, the appellant was bound to "await decision of his application filed in the Court of Singapore."[91] The Court expressly reiterated that the appellant's case before the Indian court was "premised on the principle of Forum non-convenience" and not on any foundational lack of jurisdiction of the foreign court.[92] Indian courts, therefore, declined to conduct a parallel assessment of convenience once the litigant had chosen to raise that very issue before the foreign forum. The decision illustrates that while forum non conveniens is a recognized ground in Indian anti-suit injunction jurisprudence, its invocation is tightly circumscribed where a party has already submitted to the foreign court and sought a determination there as to the "proper Forum."[93]

3.5.2. Factors Considered by Indian Courts

Indian courts have developed a non-exhaustive list of factors relevant to forum non conveniens determinations. These include the place of marriage, last matrimonial home, residence of parties, location of children, availability of evidence,

87. *Modi Entertainment*, AIR 2003 SC 1177.
88. Singh v. Bhatia, RFA (OS) 12/2014 (India), https://indiankanoon.org/doc/115942637/.
89. *Id.* ¶ 16.
90. *Id.* ¶¶ 9–11.
91. *Id.* ¶ 13.
92. *Id.* ¶ 12.
93. *Id.* ¶¶ 15–16.

enforceability of relief, and relative hardship. Courts have repeatedly cautioned against rigid weighting, emphasizing that the inquiry is inherently fact-specific.

Importantly, courts have also considered the stage of proceedings. Where substantial progress has been made in one forum, courts are reluctant to disturb the status quo absent compelling reasons. This temporal sensitivity underscores the importance of early jurisdictional strategy in cross-border family litigation.

A. Forum with the Closest Concern

In *Sandhu v. Sandhu*, the Supreme Court articulated what has since become a foundational factor in Indian forum analysis in family law: the forum having the "*most intimate contact with the issues arising in the case*."[94] Rejecting jurisdictional claims based on the child's physical presence alone, the Court held that jurisdiction "*is not attracted by the operation or creation of fortuitous circumstances such as the circumstance as to where the child . . . is brought or for the time being lodged*," warning that such an approach would merely "*encourag[e] forum-shopping*."[95] Instead, the Court emphasized that jurisdiction must follow "*functional lines*," such that "*in matters relating to matrimony and custody, the law of that place must govern which has the closest concern with the well-being of the spouses and the welfare of the offsprings of marriage*."[96] Applying this principle, the Court attached decisive weight to the fact that the spouses had "*made England their home*," that the child was born there, and that obligations relating to marriage and parenthood were incurred in that forum, rendering it "*reasonable and just*" for English courts to assume jurisdiction.[97] Significantly, the Court framed this analysis not merely as a jurisdictional preference, but as a protective imperative, observing that it was the Court's "*duty and function to protect the wife against the burden of litigating in an inconvenient forum*" created through unilateral and wrongful removal of the child.[98]

B. Relative Hardship and the Wife's Residence

In *Nagam v. Nigam*, the Supreme Court reaffirmed that matrimonial jurisdiction cannot be exercised in disregard of the practical hardship faced by the spouse defending the proceedings. The petition arose from a wife's request to transfer matrimonial proceedings instituted by the husband at Jabalpur, on the ground that she would face "*acute hardship*" in contesting the matter there while residing in Hyderabad and caring for her minor daughter.[99] Although section 19 of the HMA permits filing at multiple locations, the Court acknowledged that "*having regard to the convenience of the wife transfer is normally allowed*."[100] Recog-

---

94. Sandhu v. Sandhu, AIR 1984 SC 1224 (India) (emphasis added), https://indiankanoon.org/doc/768055/.

95. *Id.* (emphasis added).

96. *Id.* (emphasis added).

97. *Id.* (emphasis added).

98. *Id.* (emphasis added).

99. Nagam v. Nigam, AIR 2017 SC 1345 (India) (emphasis added), https://indiankanoon.org/doc/43287493/.

100. *Id.* ¶ 5 (emphasis added).

nizing that the Court was *"flooded with petitions of this nature,"* the Bench emphasized the systemic burden caused by forum choices that necessitate repeated transfer petitions and observed that matrimonial matters *"required to be dealt with expeditiously are delayed."*[101] The Court therefore explored structural solutions to reduce hardship, including requiring the husband to deposit litigation expenses where proceedings are instituted away from the wife's place of residence. *Nagam* underscores that in matrimonial disputes, relative hardship, caregiving responsibilities, and practical access to justice are legitimate and weighty considerations in determining the appropriate forum.

C. Limits on Forum Non Conveniens at the Threshold Stage

In *Sinha v. Sinha*, the Delhi High Court clarified the limits of applying forum non conveniens in matrimonial proceedings, particularly at the threshold stage.[102] The family court had returned the husband's petition despite acknowledging that it possessed territorial jurisdiction under section 19 of the HMA, on the ground that the family court at Gurugram would be a *"more convenient jurisdiction"* for the parties.[103] Reversing this approach, the high court held that *"the principle of forum non conveniens is not a principle which can be applied by a Family Court to non-suit a petitioner,"* especially where the court itself records that it has jurisdiction to entertain the petition.[104] The court emphasized that once jurisdiction is established, concerns regarding inconvenience to the respondent must be addressed through procedural safeguards, such as directing deposit or payment of litigation expenses, rather than by declining jurisdiction altogether.[105] Significantly, the court underscored that forum non conveniens cannot be used to preemptively deny access to a competent forum, particularly before issuance of summons, and reaffirmed that questions of inconvenience or transfer must follow, not precede, the assumption of jurisdiction.[106] *Navin Sinha*, thus, reinforces that in Indian family law, forum non conveniens operates as a *post-jurisdictional, discretionary consideration*, and not as a threshold bar to the exercise of statutorily conferred matrimonial jurisdiction.

D. Anti-Forum Shopping and Comity-Driven Restraint

The limits of Indian courts' willingness to entertain parallel proceedings are illustrated in *Varghese v. Tower Vision Ltd.*, where the Delhi High Court applied forum restraint principles with particular rigor in a commercial dispute.[107] The court condemned the initiation of parallel proceedings after adverse outcomes abroad as a *"classic case of forum shopping,"* describing it as a *"pernicious practice"*

---

101. *Id.* (emphasis added).

102. Sinha v. Sinha, Mat. App. (F.C.) 136/2023 (India) (emphasis added), https://indiankanoon.org/doc/183513915/.

103. *Id.* ¶ 1 (emphasis added).

104. *Id.* ¶ 5 (emphasis added).

105. *Id.* ¶ 6.

106. *Id.* ¶¶ 5–7.

107. Varghese v. Tower Vision Ltd., RFA (OS) 136/2012 (India), https://indiankanoon.org/doc/191981526/.

that *"leads not only to the multiplicity of proceedings but also to the abuse of the process of the court."*[108] Emphasizing judicial discipline and international comity, the court held that permitting re-litigation in India after a consensual foreign settlement would be *"impinging upon the well-established principle of comity"*[109] and amount to *"re-litigation which is an abuse of process."*[110] The court further underscored that CPC section 151 empowers courts to act *"to prevent the abuse of the process of the court and to secure the ends of justice,"* particularly where a party approaches Indian courts *"after being unlucky in the first round abroad."*[111] Significantly, the court's strict application of forum restraint was grounded in the commercial nature of the dispute, the existence of a global settlement, and the absence of any welfare-based or protective considerations, factors that sharply distinguish such cases from transnational matrimonial and custody disputes, where Indian courts have been more reluctant to prioritize comity or convenience over access to justice and substantive protection.

E. Real and Substantial Connection

In *Mayar v. M.V. Fortune Express,* the Supreme Court reaffirmed that forum non conveniens operates most stringently where the invocation of Indian jurisdiction amounts to an abuse of process or deliberate forum shopping.[112] While acknowledging that Indian courts may possess jurisdiction, the Court emphasized that *"the issue is not one of possession of jurisdiction but of its exercise,"* particularly where parties have contractually chosen a foreign forum.[113] The Court cautioned that allowing proceedings to continue merely because arrest or security could be obtained in India would be *"putting the cart before the horse,"* as it would encourage litigants to ignore *"solemnly agreed clauses of forum selection"* and rush to Indian courts for tactical advantage. Drawing upon *Spiliada Maritime Corp. v. Cansulex Ltd.,*[114] the Court reiterated that the burden lies on the defendant to show that another forum is *"clearly or distinctly more appropriate,"* assessed by reference to factors such as *"real and substantial connection,"* convenience, expense, availability of witnesses, and the governing law.[115] At the same time, the Court underscored that a stay may be refused where the alternative forum would deprive the plaintiff of a *"legitimate personal or juridical advantage,"* or where the plea of convenience masks an attempt to defeat substantive justice.[116] Read doctrinally, *Mayar* situates forum non conveniens as a *disciplinary tool,* aimed at curbing opportunistic litigation and enforcing procedural good faith, rather than as a welfare-balancing doctrine, thereby underscoring why

108. *Id.* ¶ 16 (emphasis added).
109. *Id.* (emphasis added).
110. *Id.* ¶ 49 (emphasis added).
111. *Id.* ¶ 16 (emphasis added).
112. Mayar v. M.V. Fortune Express, AIR 2006 SC 1828 (India), https://indiankanoon.org/doc/1903089/.
113. *Id.* (emphasis added).
114. Spiliada Maritime Corp. v. Cansulex Ltd., AIR 2003 Bom 163 (India), https://indiankanoon.org/doc/361618/.
115. *Mayar,* AIR 2006 SC 1828 (emphasis added).
116. *Id.* (emphasis added).

Indian courts have been reluctant to transpose its logic wholesale into matrimonial and custody disputes.

3.6. Recognition and Enforcement of Foreign Decrees

3.6.1. Statutory Framework Under the Code of Civil Procedure

Recognition of foreign matrimonial decrees in India is governed principally by sections 13 and 14 of the CPC.[117] Section 13 establishes six circumstances under which a foreign judgment is not "conclusive" between the parties, including lack of jurisdiction, decisions not made on the merits, judgments founded on incorrect views of international law, decrees obtained by fraud, judgments violating Indian law, and violations of natural justice. Indian courts apply these exceptions rigorously in family cases, particularly in divorces obtained abroad by Indian citizens or persons governed by Indian personal law. Section 14 creates a rebuttable presumption of validity for foreign judgments, but this presumption rarely survives judicial scrutiny in matrimonial matters because Indian courts treat divorce and child-related issues as matters of significant public policy.

The statutory framework reflects India's long-standing commitment to preserving the integrity of personal laws and ensuring that foreign courts do not indirectly override substantive matrimonial rights. Thus, unlike commercial judgments, where enforcement tends to be more mechanical, foreign matrimonial decrees undergo a substantive examination to determine conformity with Indian law.

3.6.2. Domicile, Jurisdiction, and the Foreign Divorce Problem: *Satya v. Singh*

The conceptual foundation of India's approach to foreign divorce decrees lies in the Supreme Court's decision in *Satya v. Singh*.[118] Decided nearly two decades before *Y. Narasimha Rao* (the landmark judgment concerning recognition of foreign divorce decrees), *Satya* framed the jurisdictional inquiry not merely as a question of procedural competence under foreign law, but as one of *substantive legitimacy under Indian matrimonial policy.*

In *Satya*, the Supreme Court refused to recognize an ex parte divorce decree obtained from Nevada after the husband temporarily relocated to that state for the sole purpose of invoking its liberal divorce regime. The Court held that such a maneuver amounted to a *fraud on jurisdiction*, bringing the case squarely within the exception contained in section 13(e) of the CPC. In a forceful articulation of public policy limits on comity, the Court observed: "*No country is bound by comity to give effect in its courts to divorce laws of another country which are repugnant to its own laws and public policy.*"[119]

117. CPC §§ 13–14.
118. *Satya*, AIR 1975 SC 105.
119. *Id.* (emphasis added).

A close reading of Satya reveals an implicit but powerful doctrinal move: *Indian courts would not assess jurisdiction in foreign matrimonial matters solely by asking whether the foreign court had jurisdiction under its own law*. Instead, they would inquire whether the assumption of jurisdiction was consistent with *Indian conceptions of domicile and matrimonial authority*.

This approach brings into sharp relief a recurring and deeply confusing asymmetry. In *domestic Indian divorce proceedings*, courts rarely engage in any meaningful analysis of domicile, and Indian matrimonial statutes do not even prescribe a clearly defined minimum residency threshold comparable to those found in U.S. state statutes. Yet, when the divorce decree is *foreign*, Indian courts routinely elevate domicile into a decisive (and often dispositive) jurisdictional requirement.

The resulting tension is best illustrated by a common hypothetical encountered in India–U.S. family law practice.

Hypothetical Scenario: Husband (H) and Wife (W) marry in India under the HMA. Shortly thereafter, they relocate to a U.S. state (say, California or New Jersey) and live there continuously for several years. They work, pay taxes, rent or purchase a home, have children, and clearly satisfy the state's statutory residency requirement for divorce (typically six months to one year). H files for divorce in that U.S. state, and the court unquestionably has jurisdiction under local law.

From the perspective of the U.S. court, the jurisdictional inquiry is complete.

From the perspective of an Indian court, however, the analysis may only be beginning. Despite years of residence abroad, the Indian court may still question whether either spouse ever *abandoned their Indian domicile* or acquired a domicile of choice in the foreign state. If domicile is found lacking (or inadequately established), the foreign court may be deemed not to be a "court of competent jurisdiction" within the meaning of CPC section 13(a), even though its jurisdiction was unimpeachable under U.S. law.

This disconnect lies at the heart of much of the confusion surrounding foreign divorce recognition in India. Section 13(a) of the CPC conditions the conclusiveness of a foreign judgment on it having been pronounced by a court of competent jurisdiction, and Indian courts have consistently interpreted "competence" in matrimonial matters through the lens of *Indian statutory and policy considerations*, not foreign procedural sufficiency.

Satya thus planted the seed of a doctrine that privileged domicile over residency and public policy over comity, without fully articulating how these principles should operate across different personal laws and foreign legal systems.

3.6.3. The Supreme Court Takes Charge: *Y. Narasimha Rao*

It was almost 20 years later that the Supreme Court decisively systematized this area of law in *Y. Narasimha Rao*.[120] In doing so, the Court transformed the domicile-centric, fraud-based reasoning of *Satya* into a comprehensive

120. *Y. Narasimha Rao*, AIR Online 1991 SC 10.

statutory framework grounded in sections 13 and 14 of the CPC and Indian matrimonial law.[121]

In *Y. Narasimha Rao*, the Court articulated three cumulative conditions for recognition of a foreign divorce decree:

1. The foreign court must have assumed jurisdiction on a basis recognized by Indian matrimonial law.
2. The decree must have been granted on a ground available under the personal law governing the parties in India.
3. The judgment must be one where both spouses voluntarily, consciously, and unambiguously submitted to the jurisdiction of the foreign court.

Applying these principles, the Supreme Court refused to recognize an ex parte divorce decree obtained by the husband from an Indiana court. The Court held that jurisdiction founded solely on the husband's residence in Indiana did not satisfy the jurisdictional requirements under the HMA. Equally important, the ground on which the divorce had been granted was not one recognized under Indian matrimonial law.

In paragraphs 12–16 of the judgment, the Court explicitly reconciled *Satya* with the statutory scheme of the CPC, emphasizing that foreign matrimonial judgments cannot be evaluated in isolation from Indian personal law.[122]

The Court made clear that CPC sections 13 and 14 do not merely create procedural presumptions, but mandate a substantive examination of jurisdiction, grounds, and fairness.

While *Y. Narasimha Rao* remains the governing landmark judgment, its application has proven challenging in practice. The decision entrenches a doctrinal framework that is internally coherent within Indian law, yet fundamentally misaligned with residency-based jurisdictional regimes prevalent in countries such as the United States. As a result, foreign divorce decrees that are routine, valid, and enforceable abroad may nonetheless fail at the threshold in India, often to the surprise of litigants who believed their marital ties had been conclusively dissolved.

3.6.4. Irretrievable Breakdown of Marriage and the *Y. Narasimha Rao* Paradox

The doctrinal clarity promised by *Y. Narasimha Rao* becomes significantly more complex when viewed through the lens of *irretrievable breakdown of marriage* (also commonly described as irreconcilable differences). Notably, irretrievable breakdown is not a statutory ground for divorce under Indian matrimonial laws, including the HMA. Yet, paradoxically, the Supreme Court of India has, over the years, repeatedly granted divorces on this very basis by invoking its extraordinary powers under Article 142 of the Constitution, treating

121. CPC §§ 13–14.

122. *Y. Narasimha Rao*, AIR Online 1991 SC 10, ¶¶ 12–16.

irretrievable breakdown as a permissive, though not legislatively codified, ground for dissolution.[123]

This creates a structural inconsistency in the application of *Y. Narasimha Rao*. On the one hand, the judgment insists that a foreign divorce decree can be recognized only if it is granted on a ground available under Indian personal law. On the other hand, Indian courts themselves have acknowledged that certain marriages are beyond repair and have dissolved them on grounds not expressly enumerated in statute. The result is a doctrinal asymmetry: an Indian court may itself dissolve a marriage on the basis of irretrievable breakdown, yet refuse to recognize a foreign divorce decree granted on an analogous ground, such as "irreconcilable differences," on the ground that no such statutory ground exists in Indian law. High courts have repeatedly followed this rule.

This tension is particularly pronounced in India–U.S. cases. U.S. courts routinely grant divorces on no-fault grounds premised on irreconcilable differences, often after minimal residency requirements are satisfied. While such decrees may reflect a factual marital breakdown identical to that which would persuade the Indian Supreme Court to exercise its Article 142 powers, *Y. Narasimha Rao* prevents recognition of the foreign decree because the ground does not formally exist within Indian matrimonial statutes. Consequently, the same factual matrix may yield diametrically opposite outcomes depending on whether the divorce is sought domestically or abroad.

The *Y. Narasimha Rao* framework thus exposes a deeper unresolved conflict between statutory rigidity and equitable judicial practice. Until irretrievable breakdown is formally incorporated into Indian matrimonial legislation, or the recognition doctrine is recalibrated to account for the Supreme Court's own jurisprudence, foreign divorces granted on no-fault grounds will continue to occupy an uncertain and often contradictory legal space within Indian law.

3.6.5. Continuing Judicial Rigidity

Despite the Supreme Court's repeated acknowledgment of irretrievable breakdown of marriage as a permissible basis for divorce through its extraordinary powers, Indian high courts have, in recent years, continued to refuse recognition to foreign divorce decrees granted on analogous no-fault grounds.

A recent illustration is provided by a decision of the Gujarat High Court, where the court declined to recognize a divorce decree passed by the Federal Circuit Court of Australia, notwithstanding the parties' long residence abroad and acquisition of foreign citizenship.[124] The marriage had been solemnized in India under Hindu law, after which the parties relocated to Australia and later became Australian citizens. The husband initiated divorce proceedings in Australia, which were granted and upheld on review. The wife, however,

123. *See, e.g.*, *Kohli*, AIR 2006 SC 1675; *Ghosh*, AIR Online 2007 SC 347; Kumar v. Shametha, AIR 2019 SC 4914 (India) (recognizing irretrievable breakdown as a basis for dissolution through Article 142), https://indiankanoon.org/doc/37507130/.

124. Shah v. Shah, RFA No. 2426/2023 (India), https://indiankanoon.org/doc/101333859/.

challenged the foreign decree in India and sought restitution of conjugal rights, contending that the Australian court lacked jurisdiction under Indian law.

Allowing the wife's appeal, the Gujarat High Court relied squarely on *Y. Narasimha Rao* to hold that matrimonial disputes arising from marriages solemnized in India must be governed by the law under which the marriage was performed, and that the application of foreign matrimonial law in such circumstances was impermissible. The Court emphasized that although the parties had acquired foreign citizenship, both had voluntarily retained their domicile of birth, as evidenced by their Overseas Citizenship of India status.[125] Consequently, the husband could not invoke a foreign forum merely to take advantage of more favorable divorce laws.

Significantly, the court rejected the argument that the existence of a foreign divorce decree ousted the jurisdiction of Indian family courts. It held that where the validity of a foreign decree is itself in question, section 7 of the Family Courts Act, 1984, expressly empowers Indian family courts to adjudicate upon matrimonial status.[126] The matter was accordingly remitted for adjudication on the wife's claim for restitution of conjugal rights and declaration that the foreign divorce decree was null and void.

This decision underscores the continuing rigidity with which Indian courts apply *Y. Narasimha Rao*, even in the face of evolving Supreme Court jurisprudence on irretrievable breakdown. The result is a persistent doctrinal disconnect: while Indian courts may themselves dissolve marriages on equitable grounds not found in statute, foreign decrees founded on equivalent no-fault principles remain vulnerable to nonrecognition.

3.6.6. Voluntary Submission to Foreign Jurisdiction: Divorce and Child Custody

Indian courts attach importance to whether parties have voluntarily and meaningfully submitted to the jurisdiction of a foreign court, but the significance of such submission differs markedly between foreign divorce decrees and foreign child custody determinations. While participation may substantially influence recognition in matrimonial matters, it operates within a more limited and contingent framework in custody disputes, where the welfare of the child remains paramount.

A. Foreign Divorce Decrees: True Meaning of "Participation" and the Surrounding Conflict

In cases concerning foreign divorce decrees, Indian courts have shown greater willingness to accord recognition where both spouses appeared voluntarily before the foreign court, they participated in the proceedings on the merits, and the decree was granted on a ground recognized under Indian matrimonial law. In such circumstances, objections based on lack of jurisdiction are often weakened by the conduct of the parties themselves.

125. *Id.* ¶ 51.
126. *Id.* ¶ 63.

The Delhi High Court's decision in *Malik v. Malik* illustrates this approach. There, the court recognized a divorce decree issued by a New Jersey court after finding that both spouses had participated meaningfully in the New Jersey proceedings, had submitted lengthy evidence, and that the decree was founded on "cruelty," a ground expressly available under Indian law.[127]

The court further emphasized that, under sections 13 and 14 of the CPC, a foreign judgment must be presumed to be final and rendered by a court of competent jurisdiction on its face, and cannot be disregarded or treated as inconsequential unless and until the aggrieved party affirmatively seeks and obtains a declaration from a competent Indian court establishing that one of the statutory exceptions to recognition applies.[128]

In fact, the court went on to state: "Participation before the Court is not a ground for setting aside its judgment. The grounds for setting aside a foreign judgment are given in Section 13 CPC and this is not one of the grounds."[129]

Nonetheless, Indian courts have consistently refused recognition where participation was merely formal or where a spouse was unable to meaningfully contest the proceedings due to financial, logistical, or immigration-related constraints. Mere service of process or technical appearance has not been treated as sufficient to establish genuine submission to jurisdiction.

This approach is grounded in the Supreme Court's understanding of natural justice in the context of foreign matrimonial proceedings, particularly under section 13(d) of the CPC. In *Y. Narasimha Rao*, the Court articulated why, in family law matters, a foreign judgment cannot be tested solely by reference to procedural regularity, and why a deeper inquiry into the fairness of the proceedings is required. In particular, the Court stated:

> [Section 13(d) of the CPC], which makes a foreign judgment unenforceable on th[e] ground that the proceedings in which it is obtained are opposed to natural justice, states no more than an elementary principle on which any civilized system of justice rests.
>
> However, in matters concerning the family law such as the matrimonial disputes, this principle has to be extended to mean something more than mere compliance with the technical rules of procedure.
>
> If the rule of *audi alteram partem* has any meaning with reference to the proceedings in a foreign court, for the purposes of the rule it should *not be deemed sufficient* that the respondent has been duly served with the process of the court. It is necessary to ascertain whether the respondent was in a position to present or represent himself/herself and contest effectively the said proceedings.
>
> This requirement should apply equally to the appellate proceedings if and when they are file[d] by either party. If the foreign court has not ascertained and ensured such effective contest by requiring the *petitioner*

127. Malik v. Malik, Crl. Rev. P. No. 253/2010, ¶¶ 26–29 (India), https://indiankanoon.org/doc/168325158/.

128. *Id.* ¶ 24.

129. *Id.* ¶ 25.

> *to make all necessary provisions for the respondent to defend including the costs of travel, residence and litigation* where necessary, it should be held that the proceedings are in breach of the principles of natural justice.[130]

Similarly, in *Kalia v. Kalia*, the Delhi High Court refused to recognize the Canadian decree, holding that the wife could not be expected to travel to Canada to contest the proceedings due to her lack of financial means.[131] The court held that if a spouse is financially incapable of defending themselves in a foreign forum, any decree passed by that court is a *violation of natural justice*.[132]

B. Foreign Child Custody Orders: Effect of Voluntary Participation by Both Parties

In child custody matters, voluntary participation in foreign proceedings assumes an even more nuanced and limited role. Where both parents have engaged fully in foreign custody proceedings, particularly where detailed or consent-based orders have been passed, Indian courts have, in a rather limited number of cases, refrained from conducting a parallel, de novo custody inquiry.

The general rule though (as clarified by the Supreme Court and high courts on several occasions) is that foreign custody decrees are one factor in a holistic analysis and may be disregarded if compliance would jeopardize the child's welfare. In other words, even where a foreign court held jurisdiction consistent with international expectations, Indian courts independently assess whether return or relocation is appropriate. Thus, recognition of foreign custody decrees involves a case-specific assessment driven by child welfare rather than strict enforcement criteria.

In *Chandran*, the Supreme Court ordered the return of a child to the United States after noting that both parents had participated extensively in U.S. custody proceedings and that multiple orders regulating custody and parenting arrangements had already been passed by the foreign court.[133] The Court held that, in such circumstances, the foreign court was better positioned to undertake a comprehensive custody determination.

Indian courts have also, in several cases, taken note of which parent first invoked the jurisdiction of the foreign court, particularly where that parent later acted inconsistently with the foreign court's orders. In *Sahu*, the Supreme Court treated it as a relevant consideration that the mother had approached the U.S. court, entered into a consent arrangement, and subsequently acted in breach of that order.[134]

---

130. *Y. Narasimha Rao*, AIR Online 1991 SC 10, ¶ 12 (emphasis added).

131. Kalia v. Kalia, AIR 1996 Del 54, ¶ 4 (India), http://indiankanoon.org/doc/914650/.

132. *Id.* ¶ 11.

133. Chandran v. Union of India, Writ Petition (Crl.) No. 112 of 2007, ¶ 21 (India), https://indiankanoon.org/doc/376248/.

134. Sahu v. State of Rajasthan, AIR 2020 SC 577, ¶ 31 (India), https://indiankanoon.org/doc/144083733/.

Similar reasoning informed the Court's analysis in *Sakhamuri*, where the mother initiated custody proceedings in the United States and later advanced inconsistent positions before Indian and U.S. courts.[135]

1. Limits of the Initiation Factor: *Nathan v. State of Haryana*

At the same time, Indian courts have made it clear that initiation of foreign proceedings is not determinative, and that its weight may diminish depending on subsequent conduct and procedural developments in India. This limitation is evident in *Nathan v. State of Haryana*, where the Punjab and Haryana High Court declined to order the return of a child notwithstanding the fact that the mother had earlier initiated custody proceedings in the state of New York.[136]

In *Nathan v. State of Haryana*, the high court placed greater emphasis on the fact that, after the child's arrival in India, the mother promptly initiated divorce and custody proceedings before an Indian family court, well before the father invoked writ jurisdiction in India. Although a New York court had subsequently passed a custody order in favor of the father, the high court declined to attach decisive weight to that order and directed the parties to pursue their remedies before the Indian family court. The court's approach underscores that prior initiation of foreign proceedings, while relevant, does not override the Indian court's assessment of forum appropriateness and the child's welfare.

2. Paramountcy of Welfare over Comity

Across these decisions, Indian courts have consistently reiterated that principles such as comity of courts, the first-in-time doctrine, and the notion of "intimate contact" must ultimately yield to the paramount consideration of the child's welfare.[137]

Unlike foreign divorce decrees, where voluntary submission may significantly influence recognition, foreign custody orders are evaluated within a fact-sensitive, welfare-driven framework, resistant to rigid jurisdictional rules or automatic deference.

3.6.7. Fraud and Misrepresentation in Foreign Proceedings: Mail Order Divorce, Suppressing Material Facts

Section 13(e) of the CPC renders foreign judgments unenforceable if obtained through fraud. Fraud on jurisdiction, such as misrepresentation of domicile, residence, or personal law status, is a common ground for refusal of recognition. In *Patel v. Maniben*, the Gujarat High Court held that the husband had misled the Mexican court regarding his *domicile and residence* to fulfill local jurisdictional requirements. Because the husband falsely represented jurisdictional facts, the

135. Sakhamuri v. Kodali, AIR 2019 SC 2881, ¶ 48 (India), https://indiankanoon.org/doc/75878380/.

136. Nathan v. State of Haryana, CRWP No. 1671 of 2023 (O&M) (Punjab & Haryana H.C. Aug. 21, 2023) (India), https://indiankanoon.org/doc/171491290/.

137. Vadanan v. State of Tamil Nadu, AIR 2015 SC 2243, ¶¶ 53, 56 (India), https://indiankanoon.org/doc/85436368/; Raghavan v. State of NCT of Delhi, Criminal Appeal No. 972 of 2017, ¶ 40 (India), https://indiankanoon.org/doc/53310178/.

court ruled the decree was *obtained by fraud* and was therefore null and void in India.[138] The court was particularly cautious of placing any reliance on a *"mail order divorce."*[139]

Courts may also consider it fraudulent when a spouse suppresses ongoing Indian proceedings while obtaining a foreign divorce. In *Sarkar v. Sarkar*, the Calcutta High Court held that a foreign divorce obtained through the *"intentional, purposeful and motivational suppression"* of the fact, such as a pending divorce suit in India, is invalid and does not bar the maintenance of the Indian suit.[140]

3.6.8. Enforcement Mechanisms and Limitations

Foreign decrees deemed conclusive under section 13 may be executed in India under CPC section 44A, but this applies only when the decree originates from a "reciprocating territory" notified by the government of India.[141]

The United States is not a reciprocating territory.[142] Accordingly, under section 14 of the CPC, upon production of a certified copy of a foreign judgment, the court *shall presume* it was pronounced by a court of competent jurisdiction. This is a *"rebuttable presumption"*;[143] *"the burden is upon the defendant who resists execution."*[144]

Even for reciprocating territories such as the United Kingdom or Singapore, execution may still be denied if the decree violates statutory grounds, natural justice, or Indian public policy; *"[b]y virtue of Sub-section (3) the Court shall refuse execution if it is shown to the satisfaction of the Court that the Decree falls within any of the Exceptions in clauses (a) to (f) of Section 13."*[145] Section 44A thus does not override section 13, it merely provides a procedural mechanism for execution once conclusiveness has been judicially determined.

Enforcement complications often arise when a foreign decree dissolves the marriage but fails to address ancillary relief. Because Indian courts treat marriage as continuing unless the foreign decree is recognized, uncertainty may persist regarding marital status, remarriage rights, inheritance, and domestic maintenance claims.[146]

138. Patel v. Maniben, AIR 1985 Guj 187, ¶ 18 (India), https://indiankanoon.org/doc/707330/.

139. *Id.* ¶ 17 (emphasis added).

140. Sarkar v. Sarkar, C.O. 3680 of 2004, ¶ 12 (India) (emphasis added), https://www.casemine.com/judgement/in/56ea882f607dba36fd0b8536.

141. CPC § 44A.

142. *See* Ministry of Law and Justice, Government of India, Notifications issued under CPC § 44A (no notification designating the United States as a reciprocating territory).

143. Alcon Electronics Pvt. Ltd. v. Celem S.A., AIR 2017 SC 1 (India), https://indiankanoon.org/doc/28356393/.

144. International Woolen Mills v. Standard Wool (U.K.) Ltd., AIR 2001 SC 2134, ¶¶ 24–26 (India) (emphasis added), https://indiankanoon.org/doc/1728792/.

145. *Id.* (emphasis added).

146. *Saraph*, AIR Online 1994 SC 381 (emphasizes safeguarding the interests of women stranded in foreign marriages); *Y. Narasimha Rao*, AIR Online 1991 SC 10, ¶¶ 12–16; *Satya*, AIR 1975 SC 105.

3.6.9. Parallel Proceedings and Conflicting Decrees

Indian courts frequently confront situations where parties initiate proceedings simultaneously in India and abroad.[147] Foreign proceedings do not automatically bar Indian courts from exercising jurisdiction, and high courts routinely hold that Indian courts may proceed with matrimonial or custody matters despite pending litigation abroad, even when the foreign case is more advanced.[148] Conflicts may arise where foreign decrees or interim orders contradict proceedings in India; in such cases, Indian courts prioritize compliance with *Indian personal law requirements, statutory protections, and domestic jurisdictional principles* over deference to foreign outcomes.[149]

The Supreme Court in *Y. Narasimha Rao* explicitly recognized that a foreign decree that does not satisfy Indian statutory requirements leaves the marriage intact in India, regardless of its validity abroad. This can produce complex outcomes for parties remarrying abroad or relying on foreign decrees for immigration or taxation purposes. American practitioners must therefore analyze recognition risk at the outset of representation.[150]

3.6.10. Practical Consequences for Indian and Foreign Practitioners

The recognition regime produces significant practical implications. A spouse who is divorced abroad may still be legally married in India. A financial order based on foreign income assessments may be unenforceable unless the foreign court's jurisdiction and procedural fairness meet Indian standards.

The doctrine ultimately reinforces India's commitment to statutory personal laws, due process, and child welfare. For U.S. and international practitioners, the key insight is that Indian courts do not mechanically enforce foreign matrimonial decrees but instead apply a layered statutory and constitutional analysis. Success in cross-border litigation therefore requires careful alignment of foreign strategy with Indian recognition principles.

3.7. International Child Custody Issues Concerning India

Child custody disputes in India are no longer confined to the territorial, cultural, and procedural assumptions that once underpinned family law adjudication. Increasing global mobility, transnational marriages, and the scale of the Indian diaspora have ensured that a significant and growing subset of custody disputes now arise across borders. These cases do not merely raise questions of parental

147. *Vadanan*, AIR 2015 SC 2243, ¶ 56 (recognizing the reality of parallel proceedings in India and abroad in family law disputes).

148. *Raghavan*, Criminal Appeal No. 972 of 2017, ¶¶ 38–40 (holding that that the first strike rule is not an absolute bar); Bandi v. Rao, AIR 2014 SC 918, ¶ 17 (India), https://indiankanoon.org/doc/132346468/.

149. *See* Majoo v. Majoo, AIR 2011 SC 1952, ¶¶ 69–71 (India) (holding that foreign custody orders do not automatically oust Indian jurisdiction and must yield to Indian statutory and welfare considerations), https://indiankanoon.org/doc/637664.

150. *Y. Narasimha Rao*, AIR Online 1991 SC 10.

fitness or welfare in the abstract; they implicate competing jurisdictions, parallel proceedings, conflicting legal systems, and the limits of judicial authority in an interconnected world. Indian courts have been required to respond to this reality despite the absence of a treaty-based international child return mechanism.

Indian child custody jurisprudence can, therefore, be broadly understood as operating across two distinct, though occasionally intersecting, planes. The first consists of *purely domestic custody disputes*, governed by statutory frameworks, personal laws, and the settled welfare-based jurisprudence that applies where the child, parents, and relevant events are all situated within India. That body of law, and the principles that animate it, have been addressed in the preceding chapter.

The second plane, which is the focus of this chapter, concerns *international child custody disputes*, cases involving the cross-border removal or retention of children, typically following the breakdown of an international marriage or relationship. In these cases, Indian courts are called upon to adjudicate not only questions of welfare, but also questions of jurisdictional propriety, comity, timing, and remedial scope. Crucially, this body of law has developed not through legislation or treaty implementation, but through the *constitutional writ jurisdiction* of Indian courts.

Unlike many jurisdictions that address international parental child abduction through the Hague Convention on the Civil Aspects of International Child Abduction, India has consciously chosen not to accede to that Convention. As a result, Indian courts do not operate within a treaty-mandated return framework. Yet, international child removal disputes involving India have not remained unregulated or rare. Instead, Indian courts, particularly the high courts and the Supreme Court, have incrementally developed a *judge-made framework* through the exercise of habeas corpus jurisdiction under Articles 32 and 226 of the Constitution. This framework has come to function, in practice, as India's principal response to international child custody disputes. Indian courts have justified this intervention by anchoring international child custody disputes in their parens patriae jurisdiction, treating the child's physical presence within India as sufficient to trigger the state's constitutional duty to safeguard the child's welfare, even in the face of competing foreign proceedings.

This chapter proceeds from the premise that *writ jurisdiction is not incidental or exceptional* in international child custody matters involving India. On the contrary, it has become the dominant procedural pathway through which such disputes are addressed. In the absence of a Hague mechanism, left-behind parents almost invariably approach Indian constitutional courts seeking the return of a child who has been brought into India without consent or retained there in breach of foreign custody arrangements. Correspondingly, taking parents invoke the same jurisdiction to resist return and to seek judicial endorsement of the child's continued presence in India.

The prominence of writ jurisdiction in this context is not accidental. It is a direct response to structural realities. India has one of the largest emigrant populations in the world, with millions of Indian citizens and persons of Indian origin residing abroad as students, professionals, dependents, and permanent residents. A substantial number of international marriages involving Indian nationals are formed and dissolved outside India, particularly in jurisdictions such as the United States, the United Kingdom, Canada, Australia, parts of Europe, and the Middle East. Where such relationships break down, questions of child custody frequently acquire a transnational dimension. The invocation of Indian writ jurisdiction in these cases is, therefore, not a reflection of forum shopping alone, but a predictable outcome of demographic scale and global mobility.

Indian courts have repeatedly emphasized that matters concerning children engage their parens patriae jurisdiction. When a child is physically present within India, constitutional courts have asserted the authority, and, at times, the obligation, to examine whether that child's presence is lawful and whether the child's welfare requires judicial intervention. This assertion of authority has allowed Indian courts to entertain international custody disputes even where foreign courts have already exercised jurisdiction or issued custody orders. At the same time, Indian courts have consistently cautioned that writ jurisdiction is an extraordinary remedy, to be exercised sparingly and with sensitivity to the facts of each case.

What has emerged over time is a distinctive jurisprudence that does not neatly replicate either domestic custody adjudication or Hague-style summary return proceedings. Indian courts, while declining to be bound by foreign custody orders or treaty obligations, have nevertheless developed a *structured set of considerations* to guide the exercise of writ jurisdiction in international cases. These include the child's habitual or ordinary residence, the length of time spent in India, the degree of settlement and acclimatization, the conduct of the parents, the existence and nature of foreign proceedings, allegations of harm, and, where appropriate, the views of the child. Depending on the facts, courts may undertake a *summary inquiry* focused on the propriety of return, or may decline writ relief altogether and direct the parties to pursue a full-fledged custody determination before the appropriate domestic forum.

This duality, between summary constitutional intervention and deferential restraint, has become a defining feature of India's international child custody jurisprudence. Unlike domestic custody proceedings, which are designed to culminate in a comprehensive welfare determination, writ proceedings in international cases often function as *gatekeeping mechanisms*. The writ court determines whether the dispute should be remitted to the child's home jurisdiction, absorbed into the Indian domestic custody system, or left to unfold through parallel proceedings. In doing so, Indian courts have sought to balance child welfare with judicial comity, without formally subordinating one to the other.

It is also important to note that Indian writ jurisdiction in international custody matters is at times, mistakenly, analogized to the concept of temporary emergency jurisdiction under the UCCJEA in the United States. While both doctrines are triggered by the child's physical presence and are described as extraordinary, their scope and consequences differ materially. Indian writ jurisdiction is much broader, constitutionally grounded, discretionary, and capable of resulting either in immediate return or in prolonged domestic adjudication. This breadth has contributed to its centrality in international disputes involving India, while also generating criticism regarding uncertainty and unpredictability.

The judicial development of this writ-based framework has taken place against the backdrop of India's refusal to accede to the Hague Convention. That refusal, and the policy concerns that motivated it, have profoundly shaped the trajectory of Indian jurisprudence in this area. At the same time, the case law reveals that Indian courts have not operated in isolation from international norms. Without adopting treaty obligations, courts have often engaged, implicitly and explicitly, with concepts that closely resemble Hague principles, adapting them to Indian constitutional and welfare-based reasoning.

This chapter does not proceed on the assumption that India's writ jurisprudence is either an adequate substitute for the Hague Convention or an inherently deficient alternative. Rather, it seeks to examine how this body of law has evolved, the standards that govern it, and the consequences it produces for parents and children caught in cross-border disputes. The discussion begins, in the next section, with an examination of *India's reluctance to sign the Hague Convention*, tracing the historical, institutional, and policy considerations that led to that decision. Against that background, the chapter then turns to a detailed analysis of writ jurisdiction as the principal doctrinal mechanism through which Indian courts address international child custody disputes today.

3.7.1. India's Reluctance to Accede to the Hague Convention

A. Historical Engagement with the Hague Abduction Convention

The Hague Convention on the Civil Aspects of International Child Abduction was concluded on October 25, 1980, with the objective of securing the prompt return of children wrongfully removed to or retained in a contracting state and of ensuring that rights of custody and access under the law of one contracting state are effectively respected in other contracting states.[151] The Convention was designed as a procedural instrument, not a custody-determination mechanism, premised on the understanding that questions of long-term custody should ordinarily be decided by the courts of the child's habitual residence.

India has been aware of the Convention for several decades and has periodically engaged with the question of accession. The issue has arisen in response to a growing number of international parental child removal cases involving Indian nationals, particularly in jurisdictions such as the United States, the United Kingdom, Canada, and Australia.[152] These cases brought sustained attention to the absence of a structured international return mechanism under Indian law and highlighted the increasing intersection between Indian family law and transnational custody disputes.

Formal consideration of the Hague Convention within India began at least as early as the late 2000s, when the Law Commission of India was tasked with

151. Convention on the Civil Aspects of International Child Abduction, Oct. 25, 1980, T.I.A.S. No. 11,670, 1343 U.N.T.S. 89, https://assets.hcch.net/docs/e86d9f72-dc8d-46f3-b3bf-e102911c8532.pdf.

152. *See* Stutee Nag, *International Child Custody Disputes Between India and the United States: No Hague, So Vague!*, 36 Journal of the American Academy of Matrimonial Lawyers 445, 446–48 (2024), https://www.aaml.org/wp-content/uploads/02_MAT_36_2_Article-8_Child-Custody.pdf.

examining whether accession would be appropriate in the Indian legal and social context.[153] This engagement reflected a recognition that existing domestic legal remedies, principally under the Guardians and Wards Act, 1890, and the constitutional writ jurisdiction of high courts, were being pressed into service to resolve disputes that were fundamentally international in character.

India's engagement with the Convention has also been shaped by its participation in broader international legal discourse. While India is not a signatory to the Hague Abduction Convention, it is a member of the Hague Conference on Private International Law and has acceded to other Hague instruments.[154] The question of accession to the 1980 Convention has therefore never been one of isolation from international law, but rather of selective participation based on perceived compatibility with domestic legal principles and policy priorities.

Despite repeated consideration, India has not moved toward accession. Instead, successive governmental and expert bodies have expressed reservations grounded primarily in child welfare concerns, the perceived rigidity of the Convention's return mechanism, and apprehensions regarding its operation in cases involving allegations of domestic violence.[155] These concerns, while evolving in articulation over time, have remained central to India's engagement with the Convention and ultimately culminated in the government's decision not to accede.

As a result, India occupies a distinctive position in the global landscape of international child abduction law: a jurisdiction that has long been aware of, and has actively studied, the Hague framework, yet has consciously opted to address international child custody disputes through domestic constitutional and statutory mechanisms rather than through treaty-based obligations. The implications of this choice, and the reasons underlying it, are examined in the sections that follow.

B. The Law Commission's Consideration of Accession

India's first formal and structured engagement with the Hague Convention on the Civil Aspects of International Child Abduction occurred through the *218th Report of the Law Commission of India* (March 2009), titled *Need to Accede to the Hague Convention on the Civil Aspects of International Child Abduction (1980)*.[156] The report situates the problem within the broader effects of globalization, observing that "*the number of divorce cases and custody disputes has increased ever since the*

153. Law Commission of India, *218th Report on the Need to Accede to the Hague Convention on the Civil Aspects of International Child Abduction* (Mar. 2009), https://cdnbbsr.s3waas.gov.in/s3ca0daec69b5adc880fb464895726dbdf/uploads/2022/08/2022081042.pdf.

154. Hague Conference on Private International Law, *Status Table* (listing India as a member state and party to select Hague Conventions), https://www.hcch.net/en/instruments/conventions/status-table.

155. *See Report of Justice Rajesh Bindal Committee to Examine the Civil Aspects of International Child Abduction Bill, 2016, and the Protection of Children (Inter-Country Removal and Retention) Bill, 2016* (2018) [hereinafter *Report of Justice Rajesh Bindal Committee*], https://images.assettype.com/barandbench/import/2018/05/Justice-Rajesh-Bindal-Committe-Report-on-Civil-Aspects-of-International-Child-Abduction-Bill1.pdf.

156. Law Commission of India, *supra* note 153.

advent of globalization and technological development," and that *"international parental child abduction/child removal finds its root here."*[157]

The Commission defined international parental child abduction as *"the removal of a child by one parent from one country to another without the approval of the other parent,"* explaining that such removal *"encompasses an interference with the parental rights or right to contact with the removed child"* and has created *"considerable amount of confusion specifically in the area of competence of courts with regard to jurisdictional aspects."*[158]

In outlining the structure of the Hague Convention, the Commission emphasized that the Convention *"seeks to protect children from harmful effects of abduction and retention across international boundaries by providing a procedure to bring about their prompt return."*[159] Importantly, the report recognized that the Convention is designed as a return mechanism rather than a custody determination regime.

The Commission expressly addressed the consequences of India's non-signatory status. It warned that *"the fact of India not being a signatory to the Hague Convention . . . may have a negative influence on a foreign judge who is deciding on the custody of a child."* Without the reciprocal guarantee *"that the child will be swiftly returned to the country of origin,"* a foreign court *"may be reluctant to give permission for the child to travel to India."*[160] The Commission therefore reasoned that accession would *"bring the prospect of achieving the return to India of children who have their homes in India."*[161]

In clear terms, the Commission noted: *"The time has come for some international perspective in this regard,"* and that *"India should keep pace and change according to the changing needs of the society."*[162] It ultimately recommended that *"the Government may consider that India should become a signatory to the Hague Convention."*[163]

While acknowledging Supreme Court decisions addressing international custody disputes in the absence of the Convention, the 218th report did not regard judicial discretion alone as sufficient to address the structural difficulties arising from cross-border child removal. Instead, it framed accession as a necessary step to introduce reciprocity, procedural clarity, and international confidence in India's handling of such disputes.

The 2009 report thus reflects a moment of institutional endorsement of accession, grounded not in abandonment of the welfare principle, but in recognition of the practical limitations of a purely domestic response to an increasingly transnational problem.

C. The Bindal Committee (2018) and the Proposed Domestic Framework

Following renewed debate on India's accession to the Hague Convention, the Ministry of Women and Child Development constituted a *High-Level Committee*

157. *Id.* at 6 (emphasis added).
158. *Id.* (emphasis added).
159. *Id.* at 11 (emphasis added).
160. *Id.* at 20 (emphasis added).
161. *Id.* at 7 (emphasis added).
162. *Id.* (emphasis added).
163. *Id.* (emphasis added).

under the chairmanship of Justice Rajesh Bindal in May 2017 to examine the Civil Aspects of International Child Abduction Bill, 2016, and to recommend an appropriate legal framework.[164] The Committee's mandate extended beyond the narrow question of accession and included an examination of *"the legal issues involved by taking all viewpoints into account,"* with particular emphasis on the experiences of parents and children affected by inter-country removal.[165]

At the outset, the Committee situated the problem within the social reality of transnational Indian families, observing that *"large number of women married to Indians abroad, are compelled to come to India with their children when they undergo violence in their marriages,"* and that the breakdown of such marriages has a profound impact on children.[166] This concern informed the Committee's overall approach and framed its skepticism toward a return mechanism perceived as overly rigid.

One of the Committee's most consequential observations was its insistence that international child removal cases cannot be resolved through a *"mechanical exercise."* In a passage that captures the core of its reasoning, the Committee stated: "Rights of children cannot be decided by a mechanical exercise, rather, proper application of mind should be there at every stage. Speed should not compromise with quality. Hurry should not bury justice to the future of the society."

This formulation reflects the Committee's central anxiety: that the summary return model under the Hague Convention may prioritize expedition at the expense of a nuanced welfare assessment, particularly in cases involving allegations of domestic violence. The Committee repeatedly emphasized that while the Hague Convention proclaims that *"the best interest of children is of paramount importance in matters relating to their custody,"*[167] its operational structure deliberately excludes a merits-based custody inquiry and limits the role of the requested state's courts. The Committee viewed this feature with caution in the Indian context, especially where returning parents, most often mothers, alleged abuse, coercion, or vulnerability upon return to the foreign jurisdiction.

After surveying international studies, stakeholder submissions, and comparative materials, the Committee concluded that India should not accede to the Hague Convention in its existing form. Instead, it recommended the development of a *domestic statutory framework* tailored to Indian conditions, capable of addressing inter-country parental child removal while preserving judicial discretion to examine welfare concerns.[168] The Committee's report ultimately culminated in the drafting of the *Protection of Children (Inter-Country Removal and Retention) Bill, 2016*, reflecting a deliberate preference for a standalone legislative solution over treaty accession.

The Bindal Committee thus marked a decisive shift in India's engagement with the Hague Convention. Whereas the 2009 Law Commission report had emphasized reciprocity and international confidence, the Bindal Committee

164. *Report of Justice Rajesh Bindal Committee, supra* note 155.
165. *Id.* at 4–5 (Terms of Reference) (emphasis added).
166. *Id.* Foreword (i) (emphasis added).
167. *Id.* at 8 (summarizing objectives of the Hague Convention) (emphasis added).
168. *Id.* Chapter 10 (Recommendations) & Chapter 11 (Draft Bill).

foregrounded welfare, domestic violence, and the perceived risks of summary return. This recalibration of priorities would directly inform the government's decision not to accede to the Convention and would shape the judicial and legislative landscape that followed.

D. The Absence of Implemented Alternatives

Following the Bindal Committee's recommendation against accession to the Hague Convention, the government of India did not proceed with treaty ratification. At the same time, the alternative domestic framework proposed by the Committee has not yet been brought into force. The Protection of Children (Inter-Country Removal and Retention) Bill, 2016, appended to the Committee's report as a draft legislative response, remains un-enacted. No statutory central authority has been established under domestic law, and no codified procedural structure currently governs international child removal cases in India.

In practical terms, this means that India today operates without either a Hague Convention return mechanism or a legislatively enacted substitute framework. International child abduction disputes involving India therefore continue to be addressed through existing judicial powers, most notably constitutional writ jurisdiction, rather than through a specialized statutory regime.

The implications of this position are visible in the India–U.S. context. The *U.S. Department of State's 2025 Annual Report on International Child Abduction* identifies India as demonstrating a "*pattern of noncompliance*" in cases involving U.S. children wrongfully removed to or retained in India.[169] Because India is not a Convention partner with the United States, the Hague return mechanism is unavailable, and cases proceed through domestic litigation and diplomatic engagement rather than treaty-based procedures.[170]

The report explains that where the Hague Convention "*is not an option,*" the available avenues may include "*mediation, litigation in foreign courts, or assistance from law enforcement to pursue criminal charges.*"[171] These mechanisms, while legally available, do not provide the centralized institutional coordination or standardized timelines that characterize Convention partnerships.

At the same time, the report reiterates the United States' broader diplomatic position that accession to the Convention remains "*the best means of ensuring that countries establish procedures to address abduction cases.*"[172] In this respect, India occupies a distinctive position: it has formally examined accession, declined to

169. U.S. Department of State, *Annual Report on International Child Abduction 2025*, at 49 (Apr. 2025) (listing India among countries demonstrating a pattern of noncompliance), https://ar.usembassy.gov/wp-content/uploads/sites/111/2025/05/2025-Annual-Report-on-International-Child-Abduction.pdf.

170. *Id.* at 18–19 (describing the Department's role in non-Convention cases and the absence of treaty-based remedies).

171. *Id.* at 18 (emphasis added).

172. *Id.* at 9 (emphasis added) ("We also actively encourage countries to become a party to the Convention, which is the best means of ensuring that countries establish procedures to address abduction cases.").

proceed, and proposed an alternative legislative model, yet that model has not been operationalized.

The result is a legal landscape in which international parental child removal cases are resolved through general judicial doctrine rather than through a treaty or dedicated statutory scheme. The burden of balancing comity, welfare, urgency, and procedural fairness therefore rests squarely on the constitutional courts. It is within this doctrinal space that India's writ jurisprudence on international child custody has evolved.

3.7.2. Writ Jurisdiction in International Child Custody: Governing Standards and Judicial Filters

A. Writ Jurisdiction as the Threshold Gatekeeper

In international child custody disputes, Indian constitutional courts are not called upon to exercise ordinary custody jurisdiction at the threshold. The invocation of writ jurisdiction, most commonly through a petition for habeas corpus, serves a *gatekeeping function*, enabling the court to examine whether the child's presence in India warrants immediate constitutional scrutiny or whether the dispute should be resolved through ordinary custody proceedings.

The writ court's inquiry at this stage is limited. The existence of alternative statutory remedies does not, by itself, bar the exercise of writ jurisdiction, particularly where a minor child is alleged to be unlawfully removed to or retained within India. Physical presence of the child within the territorial jurisdiction of the court has consistently been treated as sufficient to invoke constitutional oversight, without predetermining the forum ultimately suited to decide long-term custody.

At the threshold, the writ court does not assume the role of a custody court. Instead, it determines whether the facts justify continued constitutional intervention, a summary return inquiry, or a deferral to guardianship proceedings. This preliminary filtering function, rather than adjudication of parental rights, defines the distinctive role of writ jurisdiction in international child custody matters.

1. Paramountcy of Welfare: The Controlling Standard in Writ Proceedings

The contemporary position of Indian law on international child custody disputes under writ jurisdiction was authoritatively restated by the Supreme Court in *Raghavan*.[173] The Court made it clear that in habeas corpus proceedings concerning a minor child, *the welfare of the child is the paramount and overriding consideration*, and that neither the principle of comity of courts nor the existence of a foreign custody or wardship order can be given primacy over that consideration.[174] The Court cautioned that the writ of habeas corpus cannot be employed *"for mere enforcement of the directions given by the foreign court"* or to convert the Indian court into *"an executing court"* of a foreign order, emphasizing that such orders *"must yield to the welfare of the child."*[175] Rejecting any notion

173. *Raghavan*, Criminal Appeal No. 972 of 2017.
174. *Id.* ¶ 40.
175. *Id.* (emphasis added).

of a presumptive or automatic return, the Court held that even in a summary inquiry, it is open to the writ court to *decline return* of the child, "*irrespective of a pre-existing order of return of the child by a foreign Court,*" if the child's welfare so demands.[176] In either a summary or an elaborate inquiry, the decisive question, the Court reiterated, is not the legality of removal, the citizenship of the child, or the forum first approached, but the determination of welfare "*bearing in mind the totality of facts and circumstances of each case independently.*"[177]

2. Difference Between Summary and Elaborate Inquiry

The Supreme Court in *Joshi v. Unde* supplied the *structural framework* for how Indian courts should exercise jurisdiction in international custody disputes.[178] The Court clarified, "*The crucial question as to whether the court (in the country to which the child is removed) would exercise the summary or elaborate procedure is to be determined according to the child's welfare.*"[179]

While distinguishing summary inquiry from an elaborate inquiry, the Court explained that summary return may be appropriate where the court is approached "*promptly and quickly*" and the child has not yet "*developed roots*" in India, whereas an elaborate inquiry is warranted where substantial time has "*lapsed*" or the child has settled into a stable environment, in which case the fact of removal, however unauthorized, "*would not come in the way*" of an independent welfare determination.[180] This distinction, expressly grounded in the welfare principle rather than comity or treaty obligation, has since become the doctrinal spine of India's writ jurisprudence in international child custody matters.

3. Application of Summary Return

Proceeding expressly on the footing that the Court was exercising *summary jurisdiction*, the Court in *Chandran* emphasized that such an approach is warranted where the child's "*natural habitat*" lies abroad, the foreign court has the "*closest and most intimate contact*" with the custody dispute, and no material is placed before the Court to indicate that return would be harmful to the child.[181] While reiterating that welfare remains the paramount consideration, the Court clarified that in a summary inquiry the writ court may legitimately refrain from undertaking a full merits analysis and instead leave "*all aspects relating to the welfare of the child to be investigated by the court in his own native country,*" where that course itself accords with the child's best interests.[182] On the facts before it, the Court found that the child had not developed roots in India, that the petition had been pursued without delay, and that there was "*nothing on record*"

176. *Id.* ¶ 26 (emphasis added).
177. *Id.* (emphasis added).
178. Joshi v. Unde, AIR Online 1997 SC 558 (India), https://indiankanoon.org/doc/672255/.
179. *Id.*
180. *Id.* (emphasis added).
181. *Chandran,* Writ Petition (Crl.) No. 112 of 2007, ¶ 20 (emphasis added).
182. *Id.* (emphasis added).

to suggest that return would cause harm, thereby justifying restoration of the child to the foreign jurisdiction for further adjudication.[183]

4. Limits on Summary Return

This summary return jurisdiction, however, remains strictly discretionary; as clarified in *Raghavan*, there is no presumption in favor of repatriation, and welfare remains controlling even at the threshold.

5. Ordinary Residence and the Child's "Natural Environment"

In *Sakhamuri*, the Supreme Court reaffirmed that in international custody disputes, the welfare inquiry is closely tied to the child's *ordinary residence* and established environment, rather than formal or incidental connecting factors.[184] Affirming the high court's view under section 9 of the Guardians and Wards Act, the Court held that the family court at Hyderabad lacked territorial jurisdiction because the children were *"not the ordinary residents"* within its jurisdiction, and that *"merely because their marriage was solemnized in Hyderabad would not confer"* custody jurisdiction.[185] In examining the writ proceedings, the Court accepted that the foreign jurisdiction had the *"closest concern"* with the children's welfare and described the United States as their *"natural environment."*[186]

At the same time, *Sakhamuri* does not establish a presumption of repatriation based on ordinary residence. Rather, it illustrates that residence and habitat are *welfare factors*, not determinative rules. Consistent with *Raghavan*, ordinary residence informs the welfare inquiry but does not override it.

6. Some of the Important Factors That Courts Consider

In fact, in *Sakhamuri*, the Court noted:

> The crucial factors which have to be kept in mind by the Courts for gauging the welfare of the children equally for the parent's can be inter alia, delineated, such as (1) maturity and judgment; (2) mental stability; (3) ability to provide access to schools; (4) moral character; (5) ability to provide continuing involvement in the community; (6) financial sufficiency and last but not the least the factors involving relationship with the child, as opposed to characteristics of the parent as an individual.[187]

7. Maintainability of Habeas Corpus in Child Custody Matters

In *Gaud v. Tewari*, the Supreme Court clarified that the writ of habeas corpus remains maintainable in child custody disputes where the minor is in the custody of a person not legally entitled to retain the child.[188] The Court reiterated that *"[t]he detention of a minor by a person who is not entitled to his legal custody is treated*

183. *Id.* ¶ 23 (emphasis added).
184. *Sakhamuri*, AIR 2019 SC 2881.
185. *Id.* ¶ 27 (emphasis added).
186. *Id.* ¶ 56 (emphasis added).
187. *Id.* ¶ 49.
188. Gaud v. Tewari, AIR 2019 SC 2318 (India), https://indiankanoon.org/doc/184268381/.

as equivalent to illegal detention for the purpose of granting writ, directing custody of the minor child," and that the availability of remedies under the Guardians and Wards Act does not bar recourse to the constitutional remedy.[189] At the same time, the Court emphasized that habeas corpus proceedings are summary in nature, and where a detailed inquiry is warranted, the writ court may decline to exercise extraordinary jurisdiction and *"direct the parties to approach the civil court."*[190]

8. Contact and Visitation as an Integral Component of Welfare

In *Sahu*, the Supreme Court expanded the welfare inquiry beyond questions of custody and return, emphasizing that a child's well-being necessarily includes meaningful and continuing contact with both parents. The Court observed that a child *"requires the love, affection, company, [and] protection of both parents,"* characterizing such contact not merely as a parental privilege but as a basic human right of the child.[191] Recognizing the realities of transnational families, the Court underscored that even where custody is vested in one parent or the child resides in another country, courts must ensure that the noncustodial parent is not excluded from the child's life. To that end, the Court issued detailed directions mandating regular visitation and *"contact rights"* or *"visitation rights"* including daily video calls of specified duration, noting that modern technology enables sustained parental bonds across borders.[192] The Court further articulated the concept of *"two happy homes,"* clarifying that where a single household with both parents is not possible, judicial orders must strive to preserve the child's emotional and psychological connection with both parents through structured and enforceable contact arrangements.[193]

Conduct and "Wrongful Removal" as Subordinate to Welfare: In *Sethi v. Bhaskar*, the Supreme Court reaffirmed that in international child custody proceedings under writ jurisdiction, allegations of wrongful removal, parental misconduct, or competing parental rights do not operate as independent or determinative considerations.[194] The Court examined a situation in which one parent relied heavily on the asserted illegality of the child's removal from a foreign jurisdiction and the existence of foreign proceedings, and expressly rejected the proposition that such circumstances could operate as a determinative or threshold rule. Instead, the Court reaffirmed that the legality or illegality of the child's removal is relevant *only insofar as it bears upon the welfare of the child*, and does not give rise to any independent presumption in favor of repatriation.

Significantly, the Court treated parental conduct, delay, and competing foreign proceedings as contextual facts rather than controlling factors, emphasizing that the writ court's task is not to adjudicate fault between parents but to assess the child's present and future well-being on the totality of circumstances.

189. *Id.* ¶ 14 (emphasis added).
190. *Id.* ¶ 19 (emphasis added).
191. *Sahu*, AIR 2020 SC 577, ¶ 19 (emphasis added).
192. *Id.* ¶ 22 (emphasis added).
193. *Id.*
194. Sethi v. Bhaskar, Criminal Appeal No. 82/2022 (India), https://indiankanoon.org/doc/107349125/.

3.7.3. Judicially Identified Factors Under the Welfare Inquiry

A. Consent, Acquiescence, and Shared Parenting History

Indian courts have treated *consent and subsequent acquiescence* as material considerations within the welfare inquiry in international child custody disputes, particularly where such conduct undermines the claim that the child's presence in India constitutes illegal detention warranting repatriation. Where a parent has expressly consented to the child's continued stay in India, or where post-removal conduct reflects acceptance of the child's relocation and integration, courts have declined to direct return, holding that repatriation in such circumstances may not advance the child's welfare.

The Supreme Court's decision in *Majoo* constitutes the clearest articulation of this principle. In that case, the father had *expressly consented in writing* to the mother remaining in India with the minor child and to the child's admission in a school in Delhi. The Court relied on the father's letter stating, "*As you wish to stay in India with Kush . . . I give my whole-hearted support and request you to put Kush in an Indo-American school or equivalent at Delhi this year,*" and on subsequent email correspondence evidencing continued support for the arrangement.[195]

The father later sought to retract this consent by alleging coercion and duress. The Supreme Court rejected that contention, noting that the allegation of coercion remained *unproved*, and that the father's subsequent conduct was inconsistent with any claim that the arrangement was involuntary. The Court held that a *unilateral reversal of a jointly taken parental decision* could not alter the factual position regarding the child's residence, observing that "*the unilateral reversal of a decision by one of the two parents could not change the fact situation as to the minor being an ordinary resident of Delhi, when the decision was taken jointly by both the parents.*"[196]

Similarly, in *Pandey v. State of U.P.*, where the Allahabad High Court declined to order the return of two minor children to the United States,[197] the court relied on documentary evidence demonstrating that the mother had *expressly consented* to the children's admission to school in India. The court noted that the petitioner-mother had herself emailed copies of her passport and Aadhaar card, stating: "*I am only providing you for using it in school admission for kids.*"[198] The court accepted that both children were admitted to school in India "*with the consent of the mother,*" and held that, in light of such conduct, "*it is not a case of any illegal detention but the children are living and studying with their father with the consent of her mother.*"[199] On this basis, the court concluded that a writ of habeas corpus was not maintainable and declined to interfere with the children's continued residence in India.[200]

195. *Majoo*, AIR 2011 SC 1952 (emphasis added).

196. *Id.* (emphasis added).

197. Pandey v. State of U.P., Habeas Corpus Writ Petition No. 67/2023 (India), https://indiankanoon.org/doc/25337918/.

198. *Id.* ¶ 15 (emphasis added).

199. *Id.* ¶ 16 (emphasis added).

200. *Id.* ¶¶ 28–29.

B. Passage of Time and the Child's Degree of Settlement

Indian courts have repeatedly treated the *passage of time between the child's removal and the invocation of writ jurisdiction*, and the child's consequent degree of settlement in India, as substantive welfare considerations in international child custody disputes. Delay is not approached as a procedural default alone; rather, it is assessed for its impact on the child's stability, continuity, and lived reality at the time judicial intervention is sought.

Across jurisdictions, courts have declined to direct repatriation where a parent has approached the writ court *after a significant lapse of time*, during which the child has developed educational routines, social relationships, and emotional anchors in India. In such cases, the courts have been reluctant to unsettle an environment that has already crystallized, particularly where the child's daily life in India has become the only stable frame of reference.

This approach is evident in cases involving *prolonged delay*, where the writ petition was instituted several years after the child's removal. In *Kandavelou v. Commissioner of Police*, the Madras High Court noted that although the child was only about two and a half years old at the time of removal, more than four years had elapsed by the time the habeas corpus petition was heard.[201] The court treated the child's extended residence, schooling, and integration in India as a strong factor militating against return, notwithstanding the existence of foreign custody orders. Similarly, in *Viswanathan v. State of Karnataka*, the Karnataka High Court declined to entertain a writ petition filed nearly five years after the child was brought to India, observing that the child had been residing in India for a substantial period and that interim custody orders had already been issued by the Indian family court.[202] The court emphasized that such delayed invocation of habeas corpus could not be used to dislodge a settled custodial arrangement or to characterize continued custody as unlawful.

Courts have adopted a comparable approach even where the delay is *less pronounced*, typically in the range of one and a half to two years. In *Khaitan v. State of West Bengal*, the Calcutta High Court declined to direct the return of a minor child to the United States where the writ petition was filed nearly two years after the child's arrival in India.[203] The court noted that the child had lived in India for a longer period than in the foreign jurisdiction and treated this comparative residence as a relevant welfare consideration. In *Sasidharan v. Superintendent of Police*, the Kerala High Court similarly refused repatriation where the father approached the writ court after a delay of approximately two years, emphasizing that the child's life and routine were now centered in India and that writ jurisdiction was ill-suited to disturb such settled circumstances.[204]

201. Kandavelou v. Commissioner of Police, H.C.P. No. 1631/2015 (India), https://indiankanoon.org/doc/190514221/.

202. Viswanathan v. State of Karnataka, Criminal Appeal No. 1482/2017 (India), https://indiankanoon.org/doc/34514160/.

203. Khaitan v. State of West Bengal, W.P.A. 6937/2020 (India), https://indiankanoon.org/doc/74920641/.

204. Sasidharan v. Superintendent of Police, Writ Petition (Crl.) No. 18/2020 (India), https://indiankanoon.org/doc/99476077/.

Notably, Indian courts have also declined return in cases involving *even shorter delays*, where the child's age and rapid integration amplified the welfare impact of disruption. In *Mahuwala v. State of Gujarat*, the Gujarat High Court considered a delay of approximately one and a half years to be a relevant factor, observing that during this period the child had settled into a new environment in India and that repatriation would risk physical and psychological harm.[205] Likewise, in *Shukla v. State of U.P.*, the Allahabad High Court refused to order the return of a child who had been brought to India at a very young age and had spent the formative years of early childhood in India by the time the writ petition was adjudicated, treating the child's integration and continuity of care as decisive.[206]

Taken together, these decisions demonstrate that *Indian courts do not apply a rigid temporal threshold* in assessing delay. Instead, they evaluate the *qualitative consequences of time*, the child's settlement, schooling, emotional security, and sense of normalcy. As the period of residence in India lengthens and the child's life becomes increasingly anchored there, courts have shown growing reluctance to characterize continued custody as unlawful or to direct repatriation through writ proceedings, even where the initial removal lacked consent or where foreign custody orders exist.

C. Delay Attributable to Concealment or Obstruction

Indian courts have drawn a principled distinction between delay attributable to inaction by the left-behind parent and delay *caused by concealment or obstruction* on the part of the taking parent. Where the lapse of time is the product of evasive conduct, such as withholding the child's whereabouts, repeatedly changing locations, or frustrating service, courts have declined to treat the passage of time as a factor weighing against writ relief.

This distinction was articulated with particular clarity by the Supreme Court in *Chandran*. Although nearly two years had elapsed between the child's removal to India and the adjudication of the habeas corpus petition, the Court refused to apply the usual delay-and-settlement logic. The record showed that the taking parent had concealed the child's whereabouts for an extended period, necessitating the involvement of investigative authorities to trace the child. In these circumstances, the Court observed that there had been "*no occasion for the child developing roots in this country*," noting that the child and the taking parent had been "*moving from one State to another*" and had remained untraceable for a substantial period.[207]

Crucially, the Court treated concealment as *interrupting the welfare inference ordinarily drawn from the passage of time*. The delay in adjudication was not attributed to acquiescence or inertia on the part of the left-behind parent, but to active obstruction by the taking parent. The Court therefore declined to allow

205. Mahuwala v. State of Gujarat, AIR 2020 Guj 100 (India), https://indiankanoon.org/doc/67858782/.

206. Shukla v. State of U.P., Habeas Corpus Writ Petition No. 43/2020 (India), https://indiankanoon.org/doc/141740158/.

207. *Chandran*, Writ Petition (Crl.) No. 112 of 2007, ¶¶ 21–22 (emphasis added).

the taking parent to rely on the very instability she had created to resist return, holding that delay caused by concealment cannot be invoked to defeat writ relief or to manufacture a claim of settlement.[208]

Chandran thus operates as a *limiting principle* within the broader delay jurisprudence. While Indian courts have shown increasing reluctance to order repatriation where children have settled in India over time, that reluctance does not extend to situations where settlement is illusory or engineered through concealment. In such cases, the welfare inquiry remains focused on the absence of stability, continuity, and lawful access, rather than on the mere passage of time.

D. Untoward Conduct of the Taking Parent

1. Stealth and Surreptitious Removal

Indian courts have treated *stealth at the point of removal*, where a parent removes a child under false pretenses or without disclosing an intention to relocate permanently, as conduct that undermines both jurisdictional integrity and the welfare inquiry. The concern is not the passage of time that follows, but the *manufacture of jurisdiction through deception*.

In *Gahun v. Gahun*, the Delhi High Court found that the mother travelled from Canada to India with the minor child on return tickets for what was represented as a short visit, while concealing her intention to settle permanently in India. The court held that it was "*never disclosed to the petitioner that the respondent was permanently coming back to India with the child*," and that the circumstances clearly established a deliberate attempt to remove the child from the jurisdiction of the Canadian courts.[209] The court cautioned that jurisdiction under the Guardians and Wards Act cannot be allowed to rest on residence created through such stratagems, observing that residence procured through stealth cannot be equated with ordinary residence.

Stealth, in this sense, is treated as *antecedent conduct* that distorts the welfare inquiry by depriving courts of the opportunity to supervise custody at the point of transition. Indian courts have therefore declined to allow a parent to derive advantage from a relocation achieved through misrepresentation, even where subsequent factors might otherwise favor stability.

2. Inconsistent Statements and Suppression of Material Facts

Distinct from stealth is the taking parent's *conduct before courts*, including inconsistent pleadings, selective disclosure, or suppression of parallel proceedings. Indian courts have treated lack of candor as directly relevant to the welfare inquiry because custody adjudication depends upon a truthful presentation of the child's legal and factual context.

In *Chandran*, the Supreme Court emphasized that habeas corpus jurisdiction in child custody matters presupposes a clear determination of whether custody is lawful. The Court underscored that inconsistent positions and suppression

---

208. *Id.* ¶¶ 20–23.

209. Gahun v. Gahun, 130 (2006) DLT 524, ¶ 17 (India) (emphasis added), https://indiankanoon.org/doc/330740/.

of material facts frustrate that inquiry and cannot be used to reshape the welfare narrative in the taking parent's favor.[210] While the Court ultimately ordered return on the facts of that case, it made clear that *credibility and candor are integral to the court's ability to assess welfare,* particularly in transnational custody disputes.

3. Defiance of Court Orders and Procedural Abuse

Indian courts have treated *defiance of court orders and procedural abuse* by the taking parent as conduct that directly undermines the welfare inquiry, particularly where such conduct distorts the factual record before the court or frustrates effective judicial supervision of custody. While welfare remains the controlling consideration, courts have emphasized that welfare cannot be assessed in a vacuum created by deliberate noncompliance, suppression, or manipulation of the judicial process.

In *Bandi v. Rao,* the Supreme Court was confronted with a pattern of conduct in which the mother had removed the minor child to India in violation of subsisting orders of a U.S. court restraining international travel, and thereafter repeatedly failed to comply with directions issued by the Andhra Pradesh High Court. The record revealed that the appellant had given assurances to the high court regarding compliance while simultaneously preparing to challenge its orders before the Supreme Court, and had failed to produce the child or disclose material documents despite specific judicial directions.[211] The Supreme Court noted that the appellant had shown *"scant regard for the orders passed"* by both the foreign court and the Indian high court, and held that she could not be permitted to take advantage of her own defiance or lack of candor in resisting return. Upholding the high court's direction requiring the mother to submit to the jurisdiction of the U.S. court, subject to protective safeguards, the Supreme Court underscored that respect for court orders and procedural integrity is not antithetical to welfare, but a necessary precondition for its meaningful assessment.

Accordingly, Indian courts have drawn a clear distinction between competing factual narratives and *conduct that actively impedes judicial scrutiny.* Where a taking parent has approbated and reprobated across jurisdictions, or failed to disclose material proceedings or orders, such conduct has weighed against that parent in the overall welfare analysis.

E. Untoward Conduct of the Left-Behind Parent

1. Invocation of Criminal Process as a Strategic Lever

Indian courts have cautioned that the *initiation and continuation of criminal proceedings as a pressure tactic* in an international child custody dispute may itself undermine the welfare inquiry. While the availability of criminal remedies is not denied, courts have been careful to ensure that criminal process is not

210. *Chandran,* Writ Petition (Crl.) No. 112 of 2007, ¶¶ 20–23.

211. *Bandi,* AIR 2014 SC 918.

deployed to secure a coercive advantage in what is, at its core, a custody dispute requiring a welfare-centric resolution.

This concern was directly addressed by the Supreme Court in *Chandran.* In that case, the father had initiated criminal proceedings in India against the mother following the child's removal. While directing the return of the child on the facts before it, the Supreme Court expressly took note of the pendency of criminal complaints and observed that their continuation would operate as a coercive impediment to compliance with the Court's directions. The Court therefore directed that the criminal proceedings be withdrawn, recording that the father had undertaken to do so. The Court observed that the continuation of such proceedings would be inconsistent with a resolution focused on the child's welfare and the orderly restoration of custody arrangements.[212]

Significantly, the Court did not treat the criminal complaints as irrelevant background noise, but as *conduct capable of distorting the welfare inquiry.* By requiring their withdrawal as a condition accompanying return, the Court made clear that criminal process should not be used to *compel submission, punish relocation, or create leverage* in international custody disputes. The decision thus reflects a calibrated judicial response: while the left-behind parent's grievances were not dismissed, the strategic use of criminal law was curtailed to prevent escalation and to ensure that custody determination remained anchored in the child's best interests rather than inter-parental coercion.

2. Allegations of Sexual Abuse and the Risk-Sensitive Approach of Writ Courts

Indian writ courts have demonstrated marked caution where allegations of sexual misconduct or abuse are raised against the left-behind parent, even when such allegations remain contested or unadjudicated. At the habeas corpus stage, where the inquiry is summary in nature, courts have treated such allegations as relevant to the threshold welfare assessment, particularly in determining whether summary return is appropriate.

This sensitivity is evident in *Nathan v. State of Haryana,* where the Punjab and Haryana High Court declined to direct the return of the minor child to the United States despite the existence of foreign custody orders in favor of the father.[213] The court recorded detailed submissions regarding allegations of *"sexual perversion, inappropriate behaviour and physical/mental harm"* attributed to the petitioner-father, as well as references to therapeutic interventions and complaints made to authorities abroad.[214] While the court *did not conduct a full evidentiary trial into the veracity of these allegations,* it observed that serious disputed questions of fact relating to the child's welfare required adjudication by the competent family court rather than summary determination in writ jurisdiction.

Importantly, the high court emphasized that in habeas corpus proceedings, the court must consider the *"totality of the facts and circumstances whilst ensuring the best interest of the minor child,"*[215] and that where the family court is already

212. *Chandran,* Writ Petition (Crl.) No. 112 of 2007, ¶¶ 31–33.

213. *Nathan,* CRWP 1671 of 2023.

214. *Id.* ¶ 7 (emphasis added).

215. *Id.* ¶ 21 (emphasis added).

seized of the matter, the writ court should be *"slow in interfering."*[216] The existence of serious allegations bearing upon the child's safety was treated as one of the factors justifying refusal of summary repatriation.

Nathan thus illustrates a critical doctrinal reality: *even unproven allegations of sexual misconduct may be determinative at the threshold stage,* not because they are accepted as established fact, but because writ courts are unwilling to order immediate return where credible concerns relating to the child's safety are raised and require detailed evidentiary scrutiny. In such circumstances, the left-behind parent's position may be weakened, not by a finding of guilt, but by the court's institutional reluctance to summarily override risk-based objections without a plenary inquiry.

3. Substance Abuse and Violent Conduct of the Left-Behind Parent

Indian courts have treated *substance abuse and associated violent behavior of the left-behind parent* as a serious welfare concern capable of decisively undermining a claim for return, particularly at the writ stage. Where credible material demonstrates that the left-behind parent suffers from alcohol dependency or has exhibited violent conduct, courts have declined to prioritize foreign custody orders over the child's immediate safety and well-being.

This approach is most clearly articulated by the Supreme Court in *Sharma v. Sharma.*[217] In that case, while setting aside the high court's direction to return the children to the father in the United States, the Court placed significant reliance on the factual record of the divorce proceedings abroad, which disclosed that the respondent-father *"was alcoholic and had used violence against Sarita."* The Court expressly noted that although the children held American citizenship and may have access to better educational opportunities in the United States, it was *"doubtful if the respondent will be in a position to take proper care of the children when they are so young,"* given his alcoholism and personal circumstances.[218]

The Supreme Court treated the father's substance abuse not as a peripheral allegation, but as a *central welfare determinant,* observing that the children were of tender age, that one child was a young girl, and that continuity of care with the mother, who had not been found wanting in caregiving, was preferable in the circumstances. Significantly, the Court reached this conclusion despite the existence of a U.S. divorce decree granting custody to the father, reiterating that such foreign orders *"cannot override the consideration of welfare of the minor children."*[219]

Sharma thus illustrates that *conduct of the left-behind parent bearing upon safety, sobriety, and caregiving capacity may outweigh jurisdictional and comity-based considerations.* Where credible evidence of alcohol abuse or violence exists, Indian courts have been unwilling to expose children to potential risk through summary repatriation, instead favoring a fuller inquiry or continued custody with the taking parent in India.

---

216. *Id.* ¶ 24 (emphasis added).
217. Sharma v. Sharma, AIR 2000 SC 1019 (India), https://indiankanoon.org/doc/59950409/.
218. *Id.* ¶ 6 (emphasis added).
219. *Id.* (emphasis added).

F. Conduct That Strengthened the Taking Parent's Position

1. Initiating Plenary Custody Proceedings in India

Although unilateral relocation may invite scrutiny, Indian courts have treated the *prompt initiation of substantive custody proceedings before a competent Indian court* as conduct that strengthens the taking parent's position in the welfare inquiry. The filing of a plenary petition under the Guardians and Wards Act or section 26 of the HMA reflects submission to judicial supervision and willingness to have custody determined through a structured evidentiary process.

This approach is illustrated in *Nathan,* where the Punjab and Haryana High Court declined to entertain a writ of habeas corpus filed by the left-behind parent after the mother had already instituted substantive proceedings before the family court at Gurugram and obtained an interim protective order. The high court noted that the respondent-mother had "*already approached the Family Court at Gurugram*" and that an interim order had been passed restraining interference in the life of the child and preventing removal from jurisdiction without court permission.[220] The court emphasized that the petitioner was fully aware of these proceedings but had failed to disclose them while invoking writ jurisdiction.[221]

Crucially, the high court held that once a competent family court was "*already [seized] of the matter,*" the writ court ought to be slow in exercising extraordinary jurisdiction, particularly where disputed questions of fact relating to custody required a detailed inquiry.[222] The availability of a substantive remedy, coupled with the pendency of custody proceedings, weighed against summary interference.

The decision reflects a broader judicial theme: *submission to plenary adjudication in India, even after cross-border removal, is treated as conduct consistent with institutional accountability rather than unilateral defiance.* By invoking the jurisdiction of the family court and seeking interim protection through lawful process, the taking parent positions the custody dispute within a structured forum equipped to undertake a comprehensive welfare assessment. In such circumstances, courts have regarded the existence of ongoing Indian proceedings as reinforcing stability rather than as evidence of forum shopping.

2. Presence of a Wholesome Joint Family and Supportive Care Environment

Indian courts have repeatedly recognized that the *existence of a stable, supportive family environment in India,* particularly involving grandparents and extended family, may weigh in favor of the taking parent when assessing the child's welfare post-removal. This consideration is not rooted in cultural preference but in the court's assessment of continuity of care, emotional security, and practical support structures available to the child.

In *Gupta v. Gupta,* while ultimately directing return of the child to the mother, the Supreme Court expressly acknowledged the father's submission that the child, after being brought to India, had "*been admitted to a reputed school and had*

---

220. *Nathan,* CRWP 1671 of 2023 (emphasis added).

221. *Id.* ¶ 5.

222. *Id.* ¶ 17 (emphasis added).

accustomed himself to a congenial family environment, informed with love and affection, amongst others of his grand-parents."[223] Although this factor did not prevail on the peculiar facts of that case, the Court treated the presence of grandparents and a stable household as a *relevant welfare consideration*, not as an extraneous or impermissible factor.

The Supreme Court's reasoning in *Raghavan* further reinforces this approach. There, the Court placed weight on the fact that the child, upon return to India, was living with her maternal grandparents and extended family, in contrast to a more isolated nuclear setting abroad.[224] The Court observed that such an environment contributed to the child's sense of security and emotional well-being, and could not be disregarded merely because it arose after relocation.

These decisions reflect a consistent judicial position: *where the taking parent demonstrates that the child is embedded in a nurturing, multi-generational support system*, Indian courts have treated this as a factor strengthening resistance to summary repatriation. The inquiry remains child-centric, focused on lived caregiving realities rather than abstract jurisdictional expectations.

3. Facilitating Contact Between the Child and the Left-Behind Parent

Indian courts have consistently treated the taking parent's willingness to *facilitate contact and visitation* with the left-behind parent as conduct that materially strengthens the taking parent's position in the welfare inquiry. Preservation of the child's relationship with both parents has been viewed not as a concession, but as an indicator of bona fides and child-centric parenting.

In *Raghavan*, while declining to order repatriation, the Supreme Court was careful to emphasize that refusal of return did not imply severance of the father-child relationship. The Court expressly directed that the father be afforded access, observing that the child was entitled to *"meaningful contact"* with the noncustodial parent and that arrangements must be made to ensure continued interaction, including through electronic modes.[225] The Court's insistence on maintaining access reflected its view that a taking parent who does not obstruct contact acts consistently with the child's welfare, even where custody is retained in India.

A similar factual sensitivity is visible in *Gowda v. State of Karnataka*, where the record showed that the father was able to promptly establish communication with the maternal family after the child was brought to India. The Supreme Court noted that upon learning the whereabouts of the child and being able to interact with family members, the father withdrew the criminal complaint that had been lodged.[226] The absence of obstruction in communication, and the immediate availability of contact, were relevant to the Court's assessment of whether custody in India could be characterized as illegal in the strict sense.

---

223. *Gupta*, AIR 2018 SC (Supp) 674, ¶¶ 16, 35 (emphasis added).

224. *Raghavan*, Criminal Appeal No. 972 of 2017, ¶¶ 23, 46–47.

225. *Id.* ¶¶ 68–70.

226. Gowda v. State of Karnataka, Civil Appeal Nos. 4987 of 2022 (India), https://indiankanoon.org/doc/174872729/.

In *Sakhamuri*, the Supreme Court went further in expressly linking *visitation and contact* to the child's welfare. While reiterating that the best interests of the child were paramount, the Court emphasized that the noncustodial parent must be afforded *"reasonable visitation"* and that the child should not be deprived of interaction with either parent.[227] The Court accordingly molded relief to ensure continued access, underscoring that facilitation of visitation is a relevant indicator of cooperative parenting rather than adversarial retention.

Taken together, these decisions demonstrate that Indian courts attach significance to *post-removal conduct that preserves parental bonds*. A taking parent who enables communication, does not obstruct visitation, and supports structured contact with the left-behind parent is less likely to be viewed as acting in bad faith. Such conduct has been treated as reinforcing the legitimacy of continued custody in India under a welfare-centric analysis.

G. Conduct That Strengthened the Left-Behind Parent's Position

1. Prompt Invocation of Jurisdiction and Timely Assertion of Custodial Rights

Indian courts have repeatedly treated the *prompt invocation of judicial remedies* by the left-behind parent as conduct that strengthens the case for repatriation or, at a minimum, for serious consideration of restoring jurisdiction to the court of habitual residence. Timeliness functions as a proxy for continuing parental concern and militates against inferences of acquiescence, abandonment, or tactical delay.

In *Chandran*, the Supreme Court placed decisive weight on the fact that the father had *"approached the court promptly"* after the child's removal. The Court expressly rejected the argument that the passage of time should be held against him, noting that there was nothing to suggest that return would be harmful and that delay in adjudication could not be attributed to parental inaction.[228] The Court's emphasis on promptness underscored that where a parent acts with urgency, courts are less inclined to allow a unilateral removal to crystallize into a settled custodial reality.

This emphasis on expedition was further sharpened in *Vadanan v. State of Tamil Nadu*, where the Supreme Court articulated what has often been described as the *"first strike"* principle. The Court held that where a court of competent jurisdiction abroad has passed substantive interim orders prior in time, *"due respect and weight ought to be given"* to such orders, particularly where that court has the *"closest concern"* with the child.[229] The Court noted that the father *"did not waste any time"* in approaching the foreign court, and cautioned that, absent special reasons, domestic courts should refrain from undertaking an elaborate inquiry that would undermine the primacy of the first-seized forum.[230]

Taken together, these decisions establish that *prompt invocation of jurisdiction operates as conduct that strengthens the left-behind parent's position*. Expedition

227. *Sakhamuri*, AIR 2019 SC 2881, ¶¶ 55–60.
228. *Chandran*, Writ Petition (Crl.) No. 112 of 2007, ¶¶ 20–21.
229. *Vadanan*, AIR 2015 SC 2243 (emphasis added).
230. *Id.* ¶ 71.

limits the weight accorded to post-removal settlement, reinforces the legitimacy of foreign proceedings, and signals an absence of acquiescence. Delay, by contrast, tends to shift the welfare inquiry inward; timely action pulls it outward toward restoration of the pre-removal jurisdictional equilibrium.

2. Nature and Depth of the Parent–Child Relationship

Indian courts have treated the *quality of the pre-removal parent–child relationship* as a material welfare determinant, distinguishing between demonstrated shared parenting and mere formal entitlement.

In *Bhattacharya v. State of Karnataka*, the Supreme Court undertook a detailed evaluation of the father's caregiving role prior to the child's removal.[231] The Court recorded that the appellant had provided *"extensive details of his association with the child and the steps which he has taken since the birth of the child to be associated with the upbringing of the child."*[232] The Court further observed that *"the appellant has taken the responsibility for shared parenting while the child was in the US."*[233] The judgment reproduced a tabulated record demonstrating repeated instances where the minor child had *"stayed with the petitioner alone,"* travelled exclusively with him, and remained under his sole care for extended periods. The Court also noted that the father had *"followed their tracks to India and invoked judicial remedies here,"* and that the child had remained in India only *"for a short period."*[234] On this evidentiary foundation, the Supreme Court concluded that *"the welfare of the child would best be served by his accompanying the appellant to the US."*[235]

The reasoning in *Bhattacharya* makes clear that the Court was persuaded not merely by formal custody rights but by documented evidence of active, sustained parenting and personal involvement in the child's daily life.

By contrast, in *Majoo*, the Supreme Court declined to order repatriation of the child to the United States notwithstanding the American proceedings. The Court noted, significantly, that *"even the respondent does not grudge the appellant getting custody of the minor, provided she returns to America with the minor."*[236] The father's position, as recorded by the Court, was that *"all that the respondent wants is that the minor is brought up and educated in America, instead of India, as the minor would benefit from the same."*

The Court was not persuaded that this insistence on geographical upbringing outweighed the child's settled welfare in India. It expressly observed that the minor *"appears to be settled in his environment including his school studies and friends,"* and further that repatriation *"does not appear to us to be an acceptable option worthy of being exercised at this stage."*[237]

---

231. Bhattacharya v. State of Karnataka, Civil Appeal No. 3284/2020 (India), https://indiankanoon.org/doc/36377351/.
232. *Id.* ¶ 16 (emphasis added).
233. *Id.* (emphasis added).
234. *Id.* (emphasis added).
235. *Id.* (emphasis added).
236. *Majoo*, AIR 2011 SC 1952 (emphasis added).
237. *Id.* (emphasis added).

Critically, the Court also recorded that the respondent *"has contracted a second marriage and did not appear to be keen for having actual custody of the minor."* This factual matrix, remarriage, absence of insistence on personal custody, and focus instead on the child being raised in the United States, weighed against directing return. The Court ultimately held that *"[i]nterest of the minor shall be better served if he continued in the custody of his mother."*[238]

Majoo therefore underscores that in the welfare calculus, the Court will look beyond formal custodial claims and examine the substantive orientation of the left-behind parent. Where the record reveals that the parent *"does not grudge"* custody remaining with the taking parent, is primarily insistent that the child be *"brought up and educated"* in a particular country, and *"did not appear to be keen for having actual custody,"* the case for repatriation weakens considerably. The inquiry shifts from abstract jurisdictional entitlement to lived parental engagement. *Majoo* thus marks a clear distinction between a parent seeking meaningful custodial responsibility and one seeking geographical correction, a distinction that can prove determinative under the overarching welfare standard.

3. Facilitative Intent of the Left-Behind Parent as a Welfare-Enhancing Factor

Indian courts have repeatedly considered whether the left-behind parent has demonstrated a genuine willingness to accommodate the taking parent's practical, financial, and legal concerns upon the child's return. While facilitative intent is never dispositive in isolation, it has significantly strengthened the case for repatriation in several leading decisions. The inquiry is not rights-based; it is welfare-based. Undertakings that reduce hardship, coercion, or instability upon return directly inform the welfare analysis.

a. Structured Undertakings to Secure a "Soft Landing"

In *Goel v. State of Delhi*, the Supreme Court upheld a direction for return to the United States after extensive undertakings were furnished by the father to mitigate the mother's concerns.[239] The Delhi High Court, whose directions were substantially affirmed, conditioned return upon detailed financial, residential, and legal safeguards. These included:

- Return at the father's expense
- Provision of separate furnished accommodation with basic amenities
- Payment of living expenses for an initial period
- Coverage of the child's schooling, health insurance, and related expenses
- Provision of transportation
- Payment of the mother's legal expenses where necessary
- Deposit of funds in escrow to secure compliance

The father was further required to undertake that custody would not be altered by force upon return and that future visitation and custody would be

238. *Id.* (emphasis added).

239. Goel v. State of Delhi, AIR Online 2018 SC 71 (India), https://indiankanoon.org/doc/182690117/.

determined by the competent U.S. court. The structure of the order reflects that return was not granted mechanically on comity grounds; it was conditioned upon enforceable safeguards designed to prevent instability or coercion upon arrival. The undertakings were central to the Court's welfare determination.

b. Protection Against Coercive or Penal Consequences

In *Chandran* the Supreme Court, while directing return, recognized that appropriate conditions may be imposed to ensure that the taking parent is not exposed to immediate penal consequences upon arrival in the foreign jurisdiction.[240] The Court emphasized that welfare remains paramount even where the child is directed to return to the country of habitual residence. Protective directions, whether concerning access, interim arrangements, or avoidance of coercive action, are therefore relevant in determining whether repatriation would expose the child to indirect harm.

The decision reflects judicial awareness that the prospect of incarceration, criminal prosecution, or unilateral custody alteration upon return may destabilize the child's environment and thus bear directly upon welfare.

Across these decisions, a consistent principle emerges: facilitative intent does not override the welfare inquiry; it informs it. By neutralizing foreseeable hardship or hostility upon return, the left-behind parent strengthens the argument that repatriation will not expose the child to instability or indirect harm. In a non-Hague framework, such undertakings frequently operate as the practical bridge between comity and welfare.

H. The Speed with Which the Left-Behind Parent Acts— The Consequence of Delay

In *Viswanathan*, the Karnataka High Court refused repatriation to Germany.[241] The wife left Germany with the child on May 16, 2017. The petitioner obtained an order from the German court on May 17, 2017, granting him custody and directing that the child not be taken out of Germany. On June 8, 2017, the Indian family court granted interim custody to the wife and issued a restraining order against the petitioner-husband. On November 7, 2017, the German court recorded an agreement that the petitioner would pursue the custody dispute in India. Between November 2017 and January 2019, the petitioner pursued visitation applications. The writ petition seeking repatriation was filed only on or about May 27, 2022, *nearly five years after the child had been brought to India.*

By the time the matter was heard, the court recorded that "*the son is living in Bangalore for . . . about more than 5 years.*" The court repeatedly emphasized the child's continued residence in India and the consequences of disturbing it at that stage. It noted, "*The son is presently residing with the mother and his grand parents in Bangalore, in an atmosphere which is conducive to his overall growth.*"[242]

240. *Chandran*, Writ Petition (Crl.) No. 112 of 2007.

241. *Viswanathan*, Criminal Appeal No. 1482/2017 (emphasis added).

242. *Id.* ¶ 14(iv) (emphasis added).

It further observed: "At this point of time, if the wife is directed to shift to Germany, the environment of the child would suddenly and abruptly be changed which would disturb the son's daily routine and his education in formative years."[243]

The court also underscored that the Indian family court's interim custody order from 2017 *"is still in force,"* and that the high court *"would not direct repatriation of the son to Germany" "in violation of the aforesaid interim order, which binds the parties."*[244]

The return petition was accordingly dismissed.

In *Khaitan*, the Calcutta High Court declined to direct repatriation of a U.S.-born child to California.[245] Although the father relied heavily on custody orders issued by the Superior Court of California, the chronology of events, and the passage of time before effective relief was secured, shaped the court's refusal to order return.

The brief timeline is as follows: The parties travelled to India on *October 15, 2018*. The father returned to the United States on October 20, 2018. The mother was *"supposed to return to California on 24th February, 2019."* She did not. From May 2019, the child began residing with the mother at Rourkela and was admitted in school there. The father obtained a temporary custody order from the Superior Court of California on July 24, 2019. On September 12, 2019, the foreign court recorded that the child *"is best protected by removal from NEHA KHAITAN and returned to Pranav KHAITAN's sole custody in California."*[246] A decree of dissolution of marriage and grant of complete legal and physical custody followed on June 19, 2020.

The writ petition in India was filed on September 3, 2020. By the time judgment was delivered on *December 21, 2022*, the child had been residing in India *for more than three years.*

The court noted, *"Ishaan was in USA since his birth on 27th January, 2016 till 15th October, 2018. He is, thus, residing in India more than three years."* It further recorded, *"Since the month of May, 2019, he is residing with Neha at Rourkela. He had been admitted in a renowned school in Rourkela and is presently studying there."*[247]

The court also emphasized, *"The period of schooling of the child in India is more than that of his schooling in USA."*[248] And in declining repatriation, it held, *"In the light of all these circumstances, repatriation of the minor to USA on the principle of 'comity of courts' does not appear to us to be an acceptable option worthy of being exercised at this stage."*[249]

Although the father had obtained foreign custody orders within a year of the child's retention, the child continued to remain in India throughout 2019, 2020, 2021, and 2022. By the time the writ was finally adjudicated, the court

243. *Id.* ¶ 14(vi).
244. *Id.* ¶ 14(vii) (emphasis added).
245. *Khaitan*, W.P.A. 6937/2020.
246. *Id.* ¶ 2 (emphasis added).
247. *Id.* ¶ 22 (emphasis added).
248. *Id.* (emphasis added).
249. *Id.* (emphasis added).

was evaluating a child who had spent the majority of his conscious schooling years in India.

The court did not treat the matter as a prompt wrongful removal warranting summary return, repatriation was refused, and visitation rights were structured instead.

Similarly, in *Sasidharan,* the Kerala High Court declined to order repatriation of a U.S.-born child to California.[250] Although the case discusses jurisdiction and comity, the decisive thread running through the judgment is delay—delay in approaching the foreign court and delay in invoking habeas corpus before the high court.

The child was born in the United States on February 16, 2017. The mother and child travelled to India on January 9, 2018, when the child was ten months old. A return ticket had been booked for March 1, 2018. By early March 2018, the mother informed the father that she had decided not to return to the United States. In fact, on February 9, 2018, the mother instituted proceedings for divorce and guardianship before the family court at Thiruvananthapuram. Restraining orders were issued against the father.

Despite knowledge of these proceedings and the child's continued presence in India, the father did not immediately invoke foreign jurisdiction. Instead, he approached the Santa Clara district attorney's office only on September 6, 2018, six months after the expected date of return. California proceedings followed, culminating in orders in 2019, including a writ of habeas corpus dated July 10, 2019. Yet the father approached the Kerala High Court only in January 2020, nearly two years after the child had entered India. By the time the high court rendered judgment on January 21, 2021, three years had elapsed since the child's relocation.

The court expressly treated this delay as fatal to the claim for summary repatriation, and held: "The 'first-strike' principle definitely is not applicable as found in Nithya Anand Raghavan, but the delay of six months in approaching the foreign Court and two years to move this Court, stands against the petitioner."[251]

The court then tied this delay directly to the doctrinal distinction between summary and elaborate inquiry. Citing precedent, it reiterated that summary jurisdiction may be exercised where the court is *"moved promptly and quickly,"* but that where *"a considerable time has passed since the child has been removed and if the child has developed roots in India,"* an elaborate inquiry is warranted.[252] And further, *"The child as of now is found to have developed roots in India."*[253]

However, unlike *Sasidharan,* where the father waited six months before even approaching the concerned U.S. authorities and nearly two years before invoking the writ jurisdiction of the Indian high court, in *Kandavelou* the father initiated matrimonial and custody proceedings in New York within a few months

250. *Sasidharan,* Writ Petition (Crl.) No. 18/2020.
251. *Id.* ¶ 29.
252. *Id.* ¶ 24 (emphasis added).
253. *Id.* ¶ 14 (emphasis added).

of the child's removal in February 2015.[254] The Madras High Court nonetheless refused repatriation, emphasizing that no proceedings were pending when the mother left the United States and that, by the time the matter was decided, the child had been in India for several years with guardianship proceedings already underway. Thus, the case illustrates that prompt foreign action, while relevant, does not automatically compel return, especially where no preexisting restraint order existed at the time of departure and Indian proceedings have since crystallized.

In *Mahuwala*, the Gujarat High Court declined to direct return of the child to the United States.[255] The child had been removed on July 8, 2017. The writ petition was filed on December 11, 2018, about one year and five months later. The court expressly noted, "*It cannot be said that petition is filed promptly and quickly after the child is removed from the custody.*"[256] That lapse weighed against the petitioner. The court ultimately dismissed the petition.[257]

Lastly, in *Shukla*, the child was taken from the United States to India on March 17, 2019.[258] The habeas petition was filed in 2020. The father subsequently obtained an order from the Superior Court of Washington dated December 24, 2020, directing return of the child. The Allahabad High Court declined repatriation.

While the court *did not treat the case as one of extreme delay spanning years*, it emphasized that summary jurisdiction is to be exercised only when the matter is brought before the court in close proximity to the removal. The court further underscored that a writ of habeas corpus cannot be used as a mere mechanism to enforce a foreign custody order: "The remedy of writ of habeas corpus cannot be used for mere enforcement of the directions given by the foreign court against a person within its jurisdiction and convert that jurisdiction into that of an executing court."[259]

I. Age, Voice, and Maturity of the Child

Indian courts routinely interact with children in international removal cases. Yet they have consistently cautioned that the child's preference, even when clearly articulated, is not dispositive. The governing principle remains unchanged: the "*welfare of the child is of paramount consideration.*"[260] Within that framework, age and maturity may either strengthen a refusal to return or be treated as secondary to broader welfare considerations.

This section examines (1) mature child's objection cases where courts declined return, and (2) exceptional cases where courts refused to treat the tender years doctrine as determinative.

254. *Kandavelou*, H.C.P. No. 1631/2015.
255. *Mahuwala*, AIR 2020 Guj 100.
256. *Id.* ¶ 13(a) (emphasis added).
257. *Id.*
258. *Shukla*, Habeas Corpus Writ Petition No. 43/2020.
259. *Id.* ¶ 22.
260. *Raghavan*, Criminal Appeal No. 972 of 2017, ¶ 24 (emphasis added).

1. Mature Child's Preference as a Strong Welfare Indicator

The doctrinal foundation lies in *Raghavan* where the Supreme Court clarified that even in non-Convention cases involving foreign custody orders, Indian courts may refuse return:

> [W]hile examining the issue the Courts in India are free to decline the relief of return of the child . . . if it is satisfied that the child is now settled in its new environment or if it would expose the child to physical or psychological harm or otherwise place the child in an intolerable position or if the child is quite mature and objects to its return.[261]

Thus, a mature child's objection is not an autonomous defense but a welfare factor.

In *Khambatta v. State of Maharashtra*, the petitioner-mother, an American citizen, sought a writ of habeas corpus directing that her two daughters be produced and returned to her custody in the United States, alleging that the father had wrongfully retained them in India in violation of a shared custody order passed by the Vermont court.[262] The parties had married in India in 2001 and subsequently settled in the United States, where their two daughters were born and raised. In November 2018, the Vermont court passed a consent order granting shared parental rights and responsibilities. In August 2019, the father travelled to India with the daughters for what was projected to be a short visit. They did not return. The Vermont court thereafter initiated contempt proceedings and ultimately awarded sole legal and physical parental rights to the mother.

By the time the matter came up for final adjudication before the Bombay High Court, the daughters were *17 and 15 years old*, respectively. They had been residing in India since August 2019 and were enrolled in school there.

The high court emphasized that this was not a case involving children of such young age that they were incapable of forming an intelligent opinion. The court observed: "*The elder would soon attain the age of majority i.e. 18 years and the younger daughter is more than 15 years old, both of them do have the capacity to form their own intelligent opinions.*"[263]

The court interacted with the daughters in chambers. It recorded that they were "*emphatic*" in their desire to reside with their father in India. While acknowledging that the children's wishes were not, by themselves, decisive, the court treated their maturity and stated preference as a significant welfare factor, particularly given that one daughter was nearing majority.

Ultimately, the court held that the mother's status as parent, and even the existence of adverse orders passed by the Vermont court, could not override the paramount consideration of welfare. The writ petition was dismissed, though visitation rights were structured in favor of the mother.

---

261. *Id.*

262. Khambatta v. State of Maharashtra, AIR Online 2021 Bom 567 (India), https://indiankanoon.org/doc/89387267/.

263. *Id.* ¶ 22 (emphasis added).

Similarly, Chava v. Anne arose out of a long-standing marriage solemnized in Chennai in 1999 under Hindu rites.[264] The parties later settled in Virginia, where twin boys were born on April 16, 2008. Both parents subsequently acquired U.S. citizenship by naturalization.

In December 2020, the mother travelled to India with the children on return tickets. They did not go back. The father initiated divorce and custody proceedings before the Circuit Court of Fairfax County, Virginia, and ultimately secured ex parte orders granting him divorce and sole custody. Meanwhile, proceedings were also initiated before Indian courts, including a habeas corpus petition seeking production and return of the children to the United States.

By the time the present civil revision petitions came up before the Madras High Court, the twin boys were *approximately 15 years old* and had been residing in Chennai for more than two years. They were pursuing their education in India and had integrated into social and extracurricular life there. Significantly, the learned single judge independently interacted with the children in chambers. The court recorded their answers in detail. When asked with whom they wished to live, the boys stated unequivocally: "*We want to live with our mother only.*"[265]

They further expressed a clear preference to remain in Chennai and complete their education there: "*As of now, we want to complete our basic education by residing at Chennai, India. There is no difficulty for us in continuing our education from India. . . .*"[266]

The court characterized the children not as "*mere minors*" but as "*matured minors*" capable of forming and articulating an intelligent preference. It observed that the 15-year-old boys were answering "*in a spontaneous manner with clear thoughts*" and that their wishes could not be ignored in the welfare analysis.[267]

The court emphasized that forcible removal would likely cause harm: "*Forcible handing over of the 15 year old twin minor children shall cause physical and psychological harm to the children.*"[268]

While acknowledging prior habeas corpus directions and the foreign custody order, the court reiterated that such orders are only one factor in the welfare inquiry. Ultimately, the high court declined to strike off the Indian matrimonial and domestic violence proceedings and granted interim custody of the twin boys to the mother, pending adjudication on merits.

In narrative terms, *Chava* represents a case at the adolescent end of the age spectrum: the children were not of tender years but old enough to form and articulate a clear preference. The court treated their maturity, continuity of residence, and expressed wishes as central to the welfare analysis, and declined to compel their return to the foreign jurisdiction in the face of their emphatic objection.

Lastly, in *Pradhan v. State of Karnataka*, the petitioner-mother approached the Karnataka High Court by way of a writ of habeas corpus seeking return of her

264. Chava v. Anne, C.R.P. Nos. 3586/2022 (India), https://indiankanoon.org/doc/122633203/.
265. *Id.* ¶ 45 (emphasis added).
266. *Id.* (emphasis added).
267. *Id.* ¶ 71 (emphasis added).
268. *Id.* (emphasis added).

nine-year-old son, Advik Pradhan, to Germany.[269] The parties, both Indian nationals originally from Odisha, had married in 2010. The child was born in 2013.

In 2016, the family relocated to Bangkok for professional reasons, where the child pursued his schooling between 2017 and December 2021. In January 2022, both parents made a conscious decision to move to Germany for career prospects and what the mother described as superior educational standards.

On July 19, 2023, the father left Germany with the child, without the mother's consent. The mother secured an ex parte interim order from the German family court concerning the child's residence and schooling, and thereafter sought his return through Indian proceedings.

By the time the writ petition was heard, the child was *nine years old*. The high court noted at the outset that custody of a male child above five years with the father is lawful under section 6 of the Hindu Minority and Guardianship Act, 1956, and therefore the case was not one of unlawful detention in the strict sense.

Crucially, the court interacted with the child in chambers twice. During the interaction, the child expressed a clear preference to remain in Bangkok with his father. The court recorded, "*Advik was clear in his mind to stay in Bangkok.*"[270]

The judges conducted what they described as a "*long interaction*" with him, in the absence of his parents. They observed that the child was "*a brilliant child with an high intelligent quotient and capable of exercising options wisely.*"[271] The court found that he had "*good comprehension of contemporary affairs in the world and [was] very resolute in his views,*" and that he "*expressed in no uncertain terms that he desired to reside with his father in Bangkok.*"[272]

In contrast, while the mother emphasized the German court's order transferring decision-making authority over residence and schooling to her, the high court treated that order as only a factor to be considered. The court noted that the German order was ex parte and issued without the benefit of interacting with the child.

Applying the settled principle that "*the welfare of the child is of paramount importance,*" the court concluded that the child was happy and settled in his present environment in Bangkok and declined to direct his return to Germany. Custody was permitted to remain with the father, subject to safeguards, including execution of bonds and visitation rights for the mother.

In narrative terms, *Pradhan* is significant for its emphasis on a child who, though not yet adolescent, was treated as sufficiently mature to articulate a reasoned preference. The court's assessment rested not on abstract principles of comity or habitual residence alone, but on a direct, qualitative evaluation of the child's intelligence, emotional state, and expressed wishes. Ultimately, the refusal to order return turned on a welfare analysis grounded in the child's own clearly articulated preference and perceived stability in his current environment.

---

269. Pradhan v. State of Karnataka, WPHC No. 79/2023 (India), https://indiankanoon.org/doc/168486202/.

270. *Id.* ¶ 21 (emphasis added).

271. *Id.* (emphasis added).

272. *Id.* (emphasis added).

2. Tender Years Cases: Carefully Reasoned Exceptions

In the broader landscape of Indian custody jurisprudence, the tender years principle has traditionally carried considerable persuasive force. Courts have frequently emphasized that very young children, particularly infants and young girls, ordinarily require the care, affection, and presence of the mother, and this consideration often weighs heavily in domestic custody disputes. The cases discussed here do not negate that general tendency. Rather, they represent a distinct line of international child-removal decisions in which the Supreme Court, while expressly acknowledging the child's tender age, declined to treat age as determinative and ordered the child's return to the foreign jurisdiction. These decisions therefore operate not as repudiations of the tender years doctrine in the domestic sphere, but as *carefully reasoned exceptions* shaped by transnational welfare considerations.

a. Sahu v. State of Rajasthan

The parties were married in India in May 2016 and thereafter relocated to the United States, where the husband was employed.[273] A daughter, Kiyara Verma, was born in the United States on May 3, 2017, and was a U.S. citizen by birth. Marital discord followed. The wife approached the Norfolk Juvenile and Domestic Relations District Court in Virginia, seeking, inter alia, sole custody. On September 26, 2018, a consent order was passed granting joint legal custody and shared physical custody, and directing, among other things, that the parties surrender their passports (including the child's) to the guardian ad litem if settlement efforts failed.

Within days of that order, the wife left the United States with the child and travelled to India. The Norfolk court thereafter passed an ex parte order granting sole custody to the husband. The husband then invoked the writ jurisdiction of the Rajasthan High Court, which directed the return of the child to the United States. The matter ultimately reached the Supreme Court.

At the time of adjudication, the child was less than three years old. The mother argued that the child was "*only about 2½ years old and moreover being a girl-child requires the care, attention and protection of the mother.*"[274] The invocation of the tender years principle was explicit and central.

The Supreme Court directly addressed the issue of age: "Age of the child—the child is less than 3 years old. She is a girl and, therefore, there can be no manner of doubt that she probably requires her mother more than her father. This is a factor in favour of the wife."[275]

The Court thus acknowledged the intuitive force of maternal preference in early childhood. *However, it refused to elevate age into a controlling principle.* After weighing the child's U.S. citizenship, the fact that the mother herself had invoked the jurisdiction of the Norfolk court, and her violation of a subsisting

---

273. *Sahu*, AIR 2020 SC 577.
274. *Id.* ¶ 7 (emphasis added).
275. *Id.* ¶ 24 (emphasis added).

custody order, the Court concluded, "*As far as the present case is concerned other than the age of the child nothing is in favour of the mother.*"[276]

That statement is doctrinally significant. Age was treated as a factor—indeed, an important one—but insufficient to outweigh the structural welfare considerations pointing toward return. The Court ultimately held that it was in the best interest of the child that custody issues be adjudicated in the United States, and structured directions accordingly.

The decision demonstrates that even in the case of a girl child under three years of age, the Supreme Court did not apply an automatic tender years presumption. Welfare, not maternal preference, remained paramount.

b. Bhattacharya v. State of Karnataka

In *Bhattacharya*, the parties were Indian nationals who had relocated to the United States.[277] Their son, Adhrit, was born on December 25, 2016, in the United States and was a U.S. citizen. In March 2019, the mother travelled to India with the child and subsequently resolved not to return. The father promptly instituted custody proceedings before the Superior Court of New Jersey, which granted him temporary custody.

The father then filed a habeas corpus petition in India. The Karnataka High Court directed repatriation of the child to the United States, subject to certain conditions. The matter reached the Supreme Court, which examined whether the high court's direction of return was in the child's welfare.

At the time of hearing, the child was approximately three and a half years old. The Supreme Court expressly noted, "*The child was born in the US. Undoubtedly, the child is less than four years of age today.*" Despite the child's tender age, the Court undertook a summary welfare inquiry, emphasizing the prompt action taken by the father, the father's association with the child, the child's U.S. citizenship, the short duration of stay in India, and the absence of evidence that return would cause harm. The Court concluded, "*The Court has come to the conclusion that the welfare of the child would best be served by his accompanying the appellant to the US.*"[278]

The Court reiterated its "*overarching duty to ensure and preserve the welfare of a minor child within its jurisdiction.*"[279] Notably, there was no suggestion that the child's age created any presumption against repatriation. Instead, age was subsumed within the broader welfare matrix.

c. Emerging Principle

Taken together, these decisions suggest a calibrated approach rather than a wholesale rejection of the tender years doctrine. First, the Supreme Court continues to recognize that very young children, including girl children under

276. *Id.* ¶ 31 (emphasis added).
277. *Bhattacharya*, Civil Appeal No. 3284/2020.
278. *Id.* ¶ 16 (emphasis added).
279. *Id.* (emphasis added).

three, may have needs traditionally associated with maternal care. Age remains a relevant welfare consideration.

Second, however, age does not operate as an automatic entitlement in favor of the mother. The Court does not treat tender years as creating a presumption that displaces all other factors.

Third, where other considerations weigh strongly in favor of the left-behind parent, such as habitual residence in the foreign jurisdiction, citizenship, subsisting custody orders, prompt recourse to the foreign court, or evidence that return would not cause harm, the Court has shown a willingness to give those factors decisive weight, even in cases involving very young children.

Fourth, in that limited class of transnational removal cases, the presence of tender years has not prevented repatriation where the overall welfare analysis supports return.

The jurisprudence therefore does not abolish the tender years principle in Indian law. Rather, it clarifies that in international custody disputes, age is one factor among many. Where competing structural welfare considerations strongly favor the left-behind parent, courts may decline to allow tender years, standing alone, to control the outcome. Welfare, assessed holistically and contextually, remains the governing standard.

J. Where One Parent Is a Foreign National (Not of Indian Origin)

1. *Hulshof v. State of Maharashtra*

In *Hulshof* the Bombay High Court dealt with the habeas corpus petition of a Dutch mother seeking return of her five-year-old daughter to the Netherlands.[280] The case is significant not merely because return was ordered, but because of the combined weight of three factors: (1) the mother was a foreign national with a subsisting foreign custody determination in her favor; (2) the child was of tender age; and (3) the father's conduct demonstrated disregard of time-bound travel permission and subsequent foreign court directions.

The petitioner-mother is a Dutch national and permanent resident of the Netherlands. The respondent-father is an Indian national. The parties were married in the Netherlands in 2013 under Dutch law. Their daughter was born in December 2018 in the Netherlands and is a Dutch citizen by birth.

The family resided in the Netherlands for the majority of the child's life. The marriage was dissolved by the District Court of East Brabant on April 28, 2023. That judgment addressed parenting arrangements in detail. It determined that the child's *main residence would be with the mother*, while the father was granted structured contact and shared parenting time. The father had initially sought to have the main residence with him, but withdrew that request prior to final determination.

In July 2023, the father applied for substitute consent to take the child to India during summer vacation. The Dutch court granted permission for a *two-week visit only*, from early to mid-August 2023. Round-trip tickets were booked.

280. Hulshof v. State of Maharashtra, Criminal Writ Petition No. 3951 of 2023 (India), https://indiankanoon.org/doc/146226476/.

Before departure, the father applied for and obtained a *new passport for the child,* despite her existing passport already having been handed over pursuant to court directions. The mother alleged that this reflected an intention not to return. The father travelled to India with the child in August 2023. He did not return at the end of the permitted two-week period.

The mother then initiated proceedings before the District Court of The Hague. On November 9, 2023, that court directed that the child be returned to the Netherlands by a specified date and required the father to either bring the child back or hand her over with valid travel documents. The father did not comply.

The mother then approached the Bombay High Court in habeas corpus.

The high court recorded that the child was *just aged 5 years.* It noted that she had spent the majority of her life in the Netherlands in the company of her mother. The court facilitated interaction between mother and child during the pendency of proceedings and observed that the meetings were uneventful and demonstrated clear bonding. The court expressly stated that there was "*good attachment as loving mother-daughter*" between them and emphasized that this was "*very important for a girl child of tender age of 5 years.*"[281] The court therefore did not treat age as neutral. It treated tender years as developmentally significant in the welfare analysis.

Based on the facts that the child was born in the Netherlands, she is a Dutch national, she had resided in the Netherlands for the majority of her life, her stay in India was only for a few months at the time of adjudication, and that she had not yet "set her roots" in India, the court concluded that the natural process of development in the environment of her native country, in the company of her mother, was indispensable for her comprehensive development.

The Father's Conduct: The court did not ignore the circumstances of retention. It noted that the father had obtained limited travel permission for two weeks. He had procured a new passport before departure. He failed to return the child within the permitted time. He did not comply with the Hague court's return order. He had participated fully in Dutch proceedings and accepted their jurisdiction in the divorce and custody determination.

The High court viewed the father's subsequent conduct against this background. The case was not one where the foreign order was obtained ex parte without participation; nor was it a situation where the child had spent years in India and developed deep roots. The retention occurred shortly after a structured custody arrangement had been judicially finalized abroad.

Return Direction: Balancing comity with welfare, the high court exercised its parens patriae jurisdiction and directed that the child be returned to the Netherlands. Safeguards were incorporated to protect the father's contact rights and ensure structured visitation consistent with the Dutch orders.

281. *Id.* ¶ 23 (emphasis added).

2. *Boas v. Union of India*

The pattern seen in *Hulshof* resurfaces, in even sharper relief, in the Punjab and Haryana High Court's decision in *Boas*.[282] Here again, the court was confronted with a foreign national mother seeking the return of a young child to the country of habitual residence after the father had travelled to India pursuant to limited permission and failed to return.

The petitioner in *Boas* was a Brazilian national with permanent residency in Canada. The respondent-father was a Canadian citizen. Their son was born in Canada in February 2021 and is a Canadian national. The family's marital life and the child's upbringing were centered in Ontario. Following marital discord and allegations of domestic violence, the parties separated in early 2024.

On July 2, 2024, the Ontario Family Court permitted the father to travel to India with the child for a short visit of two to three weeks. That permission was conditional and time-bound. It required compliance with specific undertakings, including return within the stipulated period. The father did not return.

The mother approached the Superior Court of Justice (Family Court), Ontario. On November 13, 2024, the Canadian court granted sole and final custody of the child to the mother, directed the father to return the child within seven days, and imposed monetary consequences for noncompliance. The father neither returned the child nor facilitated communication as ordered.

Instead, he remained in India and initiated custody proceedings before a family court in Punjab.

The high court's analysis did not treat this as a routine custody contest between two fit parents. It examined the sequence of conduct. It was brought on record that when the father applied for visa extension in India, he uploaded an earlier Canadian order but did not disclose either the limited July 2024 travel permission or the final November 2024 custody decree. The Union of India confirmed before the court that these later orders had not been revealed. Additionally, while the father's visa had been extended, the child's Indian visa had expired. The continued stay of the child in India was therefore unauthorized.

These circumstances mattered. The court characterized the father's actions as a deliberate defiance of the Canadian court's authority and an attempt to create jurisdictional facts in India. It observed that Indian courts cannot be used as instruments to sidestep valid foreign judicial orders, nor can jurisdiction be attracted through suppression or unilateral retention.

At the same time, the court did not abandon the welfare inquiry. It reiterated that foreign custody orders are not to be enforced mechanically and that the child's welfare remains paramount. However, on facts, there was nothing to suggest that repatriation would expose the child to harm. The child was a Canadian national, Canada was his habitual residence, and the retention in India followed immediately upon a limited travel permission. The court interacted with the child during the proceedings and recorded that he appeared comfortable and emotionally secure in the presence of his mother.

---

282. Boas v. Union of India, Criminal Writ Petition No. 1086 of 2025 (India), https://indiankanoon.org/doc/196289315/.

Importantly, the court made a pointed observation regarding children of tender years. It stated that even where the father may be capable and well-intentioned, especially in cases involving young children, a mother's care, grounded in instinct and emotional bond, cannot be lightly disregarded. In that factual matrix, the child's welfare aligned with the foreign decree.

Ultimately, the court directed repatriation of the child to Canada in the custody of the mother.

Placed alongside the Dutch decision, *Boas* reinforces a discernible judicial response: where a foreign national mother holds a clear and recent custody determination in her favor, the child is young, and the father's retention follows limited travel permission coupled with noncompliance or suppression, Indian courts have shown willingness to order return. The analysis in both cases is framed as welfare-driven, but the father's conduct and the immediacy of the breach appear to significantly influence the outcome.

3. Where the Foreign National Is the Father—A Different Judicial Response

A useful contrast emerges in *M v. State of NCT of Delhi*.[283] In that case, the left-behind parent was a German national father seeking return of his minor daughter to Dubai after the Indian mother brought the child to India on April 10, 2018, on an emergency travel document. The child had been born on March 14, 2013, and was therefore five years old at the time of adjudication.

Unlike *Hulshof* and *Boas*, this was not a case where the foreign national parent held a subsisting foreign custody decree in his favor. There was no prior foreign court determination granting the father sole or primary custody. The parties had been residing in Dubai and had entered into an interim parenting arrangement in November 2017, but no final adjudication on custody had taken place abroad before the child's removal.

The mother's removal of the child was unquestionably unilateral. She obtained an emergency travel document from the Indian Consulate in Dubai on April 1, 2018, on the representation that the child's passport was "lost," and travelled to India on April 10, 2018. The father alleged collusion and misrepresentation. Subsequent proceedings revealed serious irregularities surrounding the child's Indian passport renewal, including nondisclosure of the child's German nationality.

Yet, despite these troubling aspects, the child was not directed to be returned.

The court's interaction with the child proved significant. The child, then five years old, expressed love for both parents and a desire not to choose between them. Although she stated she was happy in Dubai and attending school there, she also expected her mother to be with her if she were to return. The court was therefore not confronted with a simple restoration of a child to a sole custodial foreign parent; rather, it faced a fractured family unit in which the caregiving matrix could not be seamlessly reassembled abroad.

283. M v. State of NCT of Delhi, AIR Online 2018 Del 1593 (India), https://indiankanoon.org/doc/158531205/.

Most importantly, this case lacked the decisive foreign judicial command that existed in *Hulshof* and *Boas*. There was no subsisting, recent foreign custody order directing return. There was no defiance of a time-bound travel permission issued by a foreign court. There was no post-removal foreign decree mandating repatriation. In *Hulshof* and *Boas*, the foreign national mother stood armed with clear, operative custody determinations and the father's retention followed immediately upon limited travel permission coupled with noncompliance. Here, by contrast, the father's claim rested on parental entitlement and habitual residence, not on a breached foreign judicial mandate.

The contrast is difficult to ignore. Where the foreign national parent was the mother, armed with a clear foreign custody determination and seeking restoration of a young child to her habitual residence, Indian courts ordered return. Where the foreign national parent was the father, in the absence of a prior foreign custody decree and in the face of the mother's continued physical care of a five-year-old child in India, the court declined to order repatriation—notwithstanding serious concerns about the manner of removal.

The difference, therefore, does not formally rest on gender. It rests on a combination of factors, but when placed alongside *Hulshof* and *Boas*, the outcome underscores that while the gender of the foreign left-behind parent, standing alone, is not determinative, it may have some bearing in the Indian court's welfare analysis.

4. Where the Foreign National (Non-Indian Origin) Left-Behind Parent Moves Slow

In *Mphaka v. State of Gujarat*, the Gujarat High Court declined to order return of a child aged "*02 years and 09 months*" to his Malawian mother.[284] The petitioner alleged that the father had abducted the child from Malawi and was keeping him in illegal detention in India. She emphasized the child's tender age and argued that a child below three years "*would be better taken care of by the mother rather than the father.*"[285]

The court, however, placed decisive weight on chronology. The child had been brought to India on November 20, 2021. The habeas petition was filed only on June 5, 2023. The court noted this lapse explicitly and refused to treat the matter as one warranting summary intervention. It held that "*[c]ustody of the child by the father, who is a natural guardian cannot be said to be illegal in absence of any order of Competent Court to the contrary.*"[286] Even assuming the removal was without consent, the court observed that "*though such act may appear to be immoral, it is not illegal and by that custody of a child with the father does not become illegal.*"[287]

Unlike *Hulshof* and *Boas*, where the foreign national mothers moved swiftly and the retention followed immediately upon breach of time-bound travel permission, here the lapse of more than a year and a half before invoking habeas jurisdiction materially altered the posture of the case. The court

284. Mphaka v. State of Gujarat, R/Special Criminal App. No. 6714/2023 (India), https://indiankanoon.org/doc/39165655/.

285. *Id.* ¶ 3 (emphasis added).

286. *Id.* ¶ 4 (emphasis added).

287. *Id.* (emphasis added).

declined to exercise extraordinary jurisdiction and relegated the parties to appropriate civil remedies.

Placed alongside the earlier decisions, *Mphaka* underscores that even where the petitioner is a foreign national mother of a child of tender years, delay in approaching the court can significantly weaken the claim for repatriation. *Promptness in action, therefore, appears to be the most critical variable for foreign parents, when weighed against gender or existence of a foreign court order.*

K. Aftermath of Hulshof*: The Supreme Court's Intervention*

In *Hulshof*, the story did not end with the Bombay High Court's carefully structured return order. What followed prompted an unusually sharp response from the Supreme Court of India.[288]

As noted earlier, the Bombay High Court had allowed the mother's habeas corpus petition and permitted her to return to the Netherlands with the five-year-old child. Crucially, however, the high court did not treat the case as a zero-sum custody transfer. It expressly emphasized shared parenting and structured the return order around continuing paternal access. The operative directions required that the father be allowed contact, care, and upbringing rights in terms of the Dutch decree dated April 28, 2023. It further provided that if that Dutch order were terminated, the mother would seek appropriate directions from the Dutch court to revive or restore it, so that the child would not be deprived of paternal support. The high court's judgment was thus consciously balanced: return to the country of habitual residence, but *with robust safeguards for the father's access.*

After the mother and child returned to the Netherlands on February 7, 2024, events took a different turn. The father approached the Supreme Court by way of a special leave petition. During the hearing, it emerged that shortly after returning to the Netherlands, the mother had moved the Dutch court seeking suspension or modification of the existing care arrangement. More significantly, the father's right of residence in the Netherlands was revoked on March 13, 2024. The consequence of that administrative action was that he would be unable to enter the Netherlands, the very country to which the child had been repatriated pursuant to the Bombay High Court's order.

The father argued before the Supreme Court that the high court's directions guaranteeing participatory access had been rendered illusory. Clause (vi) of the Bombay order contemplated that he would give two weeks' notice and be entitled to associate with the child in terms of the Dutch decree. Clause (vii) required that if the Dutch order were terminated, the mother would seek its restoration. The father contended that the revocation of his residence rights, coupled with the mother's steps before Dutch authorities, made compliance impossible.

The Supreme Court did not treat this as a minor postscript.

While it did not disturb the repatriation order, the Court made its displeasure clear. It recorded that the Dutch order of April 28, 2023, continued to hold the field and that the high court's conditions were imposed in parens patriae jurisdiction. Having secured custody and returned to the Netherlands under

288. Survase v. Hulshof, S.L.P. (Crl.) No. 5224/2024 (India), https://indiankanoon.org/doc/182525600/.

the protection of the high court's judgment, the mother was *"duty bound"* to comply with the terms on which custody had been handed over.

The Court observed that the mother's actions were *"not consistent with the express directions of the High Court"* and that it was *"unconscionable"* to increase hostility by preventing the father from contacting the child. The judgment emphasized that the Bombay High Court's decision was a *"balanced judgment"* protecting the best interests of the child and that its conditions could not be treated as optional.[289]

Significantly, the Supreme Court directed that the mother issue a *"No Objection"* to Dutch authorities if the father sought entry into the Netherlands to exercise access rights. It also granted liberty to the father to move the Bombay High Court for appropriate directions, including recalling the judgment dated February 7, 2024, if the conditions were not observed. The Court expressly noted that the high court's jurisdiction was of a continuing nature and that it was not powerless to ensure that the sanctity of its order was maintained.

The tone of the order is notable. The Supreme Court did not question the propriety of repatriation. It did not dilute the comity-based reasoning that had justified return. What it reacted to was the perceived frustration of the access structure that had been central to the high court's reasoning. In effect, the Supreme Court signaled that where an Indian court orders repatriation in reliance upon structured shared-parenting safeguards, those safeguards are integral to the welfare analysis. A parent who invokes Indian writ jurisdiction, secures return, and then takes steps that undermine the conditions of access risks judicial censure and further intervention.

The aftermath of *Hulshof* thus illustrates an important corrective principle: repatriation orders grounded in comity and welfare are conditional in spirit as well as in form. The benefit of return cannot be severed from the obligation to honor the access framework that made return judicially acceptable in the first place.

L. *When Comity Is Weaponized: The Supreme Court's Reaction in* In re Perry Kansagra

If the aftermath of *Hulshof* revealed the Supreme Court's insistence that repatriation orders must be honored in spirit as well as form, *In re Perry Kansagra* represents an even more forceful institutional response.[290] In that case, the Court concluded that its trust had been deliberately abused, not merely by noncompliance, but by calculated misrepresentation in a foreign forum.

The background is critical.

In an international child custody dispute concerning Kenya and India, in October 2020, the Supreme Court had affirmed custody of a minor child, Aditya, to the father, Perry Kansagra (who was a Kenyan national), subject to carefully structured safeguards. The child had been residing in India with the mother. The Court directed that before custody was shifted to Kenya, the father was to obtain a *"mirror order"* from the Kenyan court reflecting the Supreme Court's

289. *Id.* ¶ 15 (emphasis added).

290. *In re* Perry Kansagra, Suo-Moto Contempt Petition (Civil) No. 3/2021 (India), https://indiankanoon.org/doc/131369924/.

directions. The mirror order was not ornamental. It was described as the *"fulcrum"* of the arrangement, the device by which the Indian court would ensure enforceability and protection of visitation rights once the child was relocated.

The father represented that the High Court of Kenya at Nairobi had registered the Indian judgment and that such registration constituted a valid mirror order. On that basis, and in reliance upon solemn undertakings given to both the Delhi High Court and the Supreme Court, custody was handed over to him, and the child was permitted to leave India.

What followed fundamentally altered the Court's perception of the case.

It later emerged that on May 21, 2021, the High Court of Kenya had dismissed the father's originating summons and held that the Supreme Court's judgment was not registrable. In other words, the very foundation on which the Indian Supreme Court had allowed custody to shift, the existence of a mirror order, had collapsed.

This development was never disclosed to the Supreme Court.

Instead, the father continued to assert compliance. In affidavits filed before the Court, he stated that he had no intention of disobeying its orders. At the same time, he failed to facilitate visitation rights, blocked communications between the child and the mother, failed to renew documentation, and ultimately withdrew authorization to his counsel while proceedings were pending.

More troubling still, the father approached the High Court of Kenya seeking declarations that there was no valid mirror order and that the Supreme Court's directions were unenforceable and beyond jurisdiction. He pleaded that compliance would be *"humiliating,"* questioned the Indian court's ascertainment of the child's wishes, and sought a declaration that the Indian orders were incapable of enforcement.

The Supreme Court treated this not as ordinary noncompliance, but as a calculated attempt to secure relief from one court and undermine it in another.

In its judgment recalling the earlier custody orders, the Court observed that the father had persuaded it to pass orders in his favor by projecting the Kenyan registration as a valid mirror order, and then suppressed the subsequent Kenyan decision rejecting registration. It recorded that the mirror order was the *"fulcrum"* on which custody had been handed over, and that the suppression of the Kenyan order constituted a fraud on the Court.

The Court described the conduct as *"defiant and contumacious,"* noted *"concrete material and reason to believe that it was a well-planned conspiracy,"* and held that the custody obtained under such circumstances was illegal and void ab initio.[291] The earlier judgments were recalled. The guardianship proceedings were dismissed. Custody with the father was declared unlawful.

The matter did not end there.

In November 2022, the Supreme Court delivered its sentencing judgment in the suo motu contempt proceedings. It held that the father had committed both *civil and criminal contempt*. The Court found that he had deliberately misled the Court with solemn undertakings he never intended to honor; that he

291. *Id.* ¶ 35 (emphasis added).

had suppressed material developments in Kenya; that he had obstructed the administration of justice; and that by representing before a foreign court that the Supreme Court's orders were unenforceable and without jurisdiction, he had lowered the authority of the Court.

The Court was explicit that this was not merely disobedience, but interference with the administration of justice and a lowering of institutional authority. It invoked its powers under Article 129 of the Constitution and emphasized that contempt jurisdiction extends to punishing those who obstruct judicial proceedings and scandalize or undermine the Court's authority.

The punishment reflected the gravity with which the Court viewed the misconduct. The contemnor was sentenced to imprisonment along with substantial fines. The Ministry of Home Affairs was directed to secure his presence to undergo imprisonment.

The tone of the judgment is instructive. The Court spoke of the *"majesty of law,"* the need to protect the rule of law, and the imperative that parties who approach the Court in custody matters do so with clean hands. It made clear that undertakings given to secure custody cannot be treated as tactical devices. Nor can foreign proceedings be used to neutralize or delegitimize Indian judicial orders after relief has been obtained.

Taken together with *Hulshof*, *Kansagra* underscores an important institutional principle: Indian courts may extend comity, structure transnational transitions, and rely upon undertakings, but they do not respond mildly when those mechanisms are manipulated. When a litigant secures custody on representations about foreign enforceability and then repudiates or undermines those representations abroad, the Court treats the conduct as an attack not only on the opposing parent, but on the authority of the Court itself.

3.7.4. Child Removal *from* India Pursuant to a Foreign Court Order

In *Latha v. Sachin*, the Karnataka High Court was confronted with a habeas petition filed by the mother after the children had already left India and were in Australia with the father.[292] The parties had been living in Australia. Both parents (of Indian origin) and both children were Australian citizens. The marital relationship deteriorated, and the father returned to India with the children in April 2017. A criminal complaint was lodged by the mother in Karnataka, and the police attempted to prevent the father from leaving the country. However, on *April 20, 2017*, the father departed India with the children from Mumbai airport.

Crucially, thereafter, the Family Court of Australia at Parramatta issued an order on August 23, 2017, directing, *"That the children Tanvi Nad born 13 September 2005 and Shaan Nad born 22 June 2008 ('the children') live with the father,"* and, *"That the father have sole parental responsibility for the children."* By the time the high court adjudicated the matter, the children were in Australia pursuant to that order. The high court recorded that the father had *"obtained custody of their children legally from the Family Court, Australia."*[293]

292. Latha v. Sachin, WPHC 64/2017 (India), https://indiankanoon.org/doc/43690976/.
293. *Id.* ¶ 14 (emphasis added).

The court did not treat the case as one of illegal detention within India. It held that habeas corpus is a remedy against unlawful confinement, and that the petitioner, being an Australian citizen and a party before the Australian court, ought to pursue remedies there. The petition was described as "*nothing but misuse*" of writ jurisdiction.

The court was particularly critical of the mother's conduct. It found that she had approached the court "*with unclean hands,*" misused the state machinery for more than a year, and invoked habeas corpus despite knowing that a competent Australian court had already issued custody orders. The petition was dismissed with costs of ₹50,000, the court observing that such misuse of extraordinary jurisdiction could not be encouraged.

A. Entertaining Habeas Corpus Despite the Child Being Outside India

However, there have been cases where Indian high courts have exercised writ jurisdiction even after the child was no longer physically within India. A recent illustration is *Verma v. State Government of NCT of Delhi.*[294] In that case, during the pendency of guardianship proceedings and interim visitation directions, the mother travelled to the United States with the child without seeking permission from either the family court or the high court. She had been directed by a prior order dated July 4, 2024, to bring the child to the Delhi High Court Mediation Centre on specified dates. Instead, she left India on the intervening night of July 26–27, 2024, admitted the child to a school in the United States, and did not disclose her travel in advance.

The Division Bench held that the removal was "*violative of the letter and spirit of the various orders*" of the family court and the high court.[295] It further observed that the mother had not been candid with the authorities and had taken a position before the passport office that there was "*no order preventing her or the child from travelling abroad.*"[296]

Significantly, despite the child being in the United States at the time of hearing, the court rejected the contention that habeas corpus was not maintainable. Relying on *Sahu*, it reiterated, "*It is too late in the day to urge that a writ of habeas corpus is not maintainable if the child is in the custody of another parent.*"[297] The court held that where a child has been moved out of India in violation of subsisting court orders, custody "*cannot be held to be lawful custody and the habeas corpus petition is clearly maintainable.*"[298]

Thus, unlike *Latha*, where the high court declined jurisdiction because custody flowed from a valid foreign order and the children were Australian citizens, *Verma* reflects a different posture: Indian courts may entertain habeas corpus even when the child is abroad, particularly where the departure is in breach of Indian court orders and undermines pending guardianship proceedings.

294. Verma v. State Government of NCT of Delhi, Writ Petion (Crl.) 2808/2024 (India), https://delhihighcourt.nic.in/app/showlogo/100018821728471371020_66413_28082024.pdf/2024.

295. *Id.* ¶ 9 (emphasis added).

296. *Id.* ¶ 10 (emphasis added).

297. *Id.* ¶ 13 (emphasis added).

298. *Id.* ¶ 14 (emphasis added).

B. An Added Nuance: The Unaddressed Territorial Question

As discussed earlier, in *Verma,* the Delhi High Court entertained a habeas corpus petition after the mother had taken the child to the United States during the pendency of guardianship proceedings and in violation of visitation directions. The court's reasoning centered on the legality of custody. It held that where a child is removed in breach of subsisting orders of the guardianship court and prior directions of the high court, such custody *"cannot be held to be lawful custody and the habeas corpus petition is clearly maintainable."*[299] The analytical focus was thus on whether the removal rendered the custody unlawful for purposes of writ jurisdiction, notwithstanding the fact that the child was with a natural guardian.

However, an additional nuance arises. By the time the writ was being adjudicated, the child was no longer within India. The order does not contain a separate or detailed examination of whether the high court's habeas jurisdiction depends upon the child's continued physical presence within its territorial limits. The court proceeded on the footing that removal in violation of its own orders was sufficient to sustain maintainability, without expressly grappling with the territorial dimension.

In that sense, *Verma* is instructive not because it resolves the territorial competence issue in doctrinal terms, but because it reflects a practical willingness to exercise writ jurisdiction even after the child has left India, particularly where the departure itself is alleged to have occurred in defiance of Indian court orders.

3.7.5. The Crux: When Indian Courts Have Ordered Return in Recent Years

A review of recent writ jurisprudence does not suggest the existence of a consistent or predictable return mechanism in India. However, in a limited but notable cluster of recent decisions, Indian courts have directed return where particular factual conditions converged. These cases appear to represent fact-specific exceptions rather than a structural shift in approach.

In *Ganesh v. State of Tamil Nadu,* the Supreme Court ordered return of two children to the United States where they had resided for nearly a decade, were enrolled in school there, and a structured shared parenting arrangement had already been judicially recognized. The removal occurred in breach of that framework. The Court restored jurisdiction to the U.S. forum.[300]

In *Sreekumar v. Union of India,* the Bombay High Court directed return of a five-year-old U.S. citizen whose mother had travelled to India on return tickets and then cancelled them. The court rejected a rigid invocation of tender years and emphasized the child's American citizenship, schooling, and the father's prompt approach.[301]

299. *Id.* (emphasis added).

300. Ganesh v. State of Tamil Nadu, Writ Petition (Crl.) No. 402/2011 (India), https://indiankanoon.org/doc/64568495/.

301. Sreekumar v. Union of India, Criminal Writ Petition No. 2259/2023 (India), https://indiankanoon.org/doc/180036507/.

In *Arunagiri v. Nathan*, the Madras High Court ordered return of two American citizen children who had lived in the United States for 14 years.[302] A Maryland court had already passed a return direction. The high court relied on "most intimate contact" and summary jurisdiction.

In *Brar v. State of Punjab*, return to Canada was ordered where the six-year-old child had spent the overwhelming majority of her life there and had not developed roots in India.[303] The court focused on continuity of environment.

In *Kaur v. State of Punjab*, a four-year-old child was ordered returned to Australia despite her tender age.[304] The presence of an Australian interim order and the child's upbringing abroad were determinative.

In *Gehlot v. State of Gujarat*, return to New Zealand was ordered where there was a fully reasoned foreign guardianship order, long-standing residence in New Zealand, and noncompliance by the father.[305]

In *Pujar v. State of Gujarat*, the Gujarat High Court directed return of an eight-year-old Australian citizen where the Federal Circuit Court of Australia had ordered return and the child had lived his entire life there.[306]

In *Verma v. State of Rajasthan*, a two-year-old child was directed to be returned to Virginia after the mother, having invoked U.S. jurisdiction and entered into a joint custody agreement, left before the next hearing.[307]

In *Kaur v. State of Haryana*, custody was restored to the mother of a four-and-a-half-year-old child who had been living in Australia; although tender age supported the outcome, the child's foreign life remained central.[308]

Across these cases, several common features recur. Return has been ordered where the child's life was demonstrably rooted abroad. Long-term residence, foreign citizenship, enrollment in school, and established social environment weigh heavily. Return has been ordered where a foreign court was already seized of custody and had passed an interim or final direction, particularly where the removing parent had participated in those proceedings. Return has been ordered where the removal occurred in breach of undertakings, limited travel permissions, or consent-based custody arrangements. Return has been ordered where the left-behind parent moved with reasonable promptitude and the child had not yet developed deep roots in India.

302. Arunagiri v. Nathan, H.C.P. No. 654/2021 (India), https://indiankanoon.org/doc/180974371/.

303. Brar v. State of Punjab, AIR Online 2020 P&H 1280 (India), https://indiankanoon.org/doc/69277162/.

304. Kaur v. State of Punjab, AIR Online 2021 P&H 405 (India), https://indiankanoon.org/doc/83360165/.

305. Gehlot v. State of Gujarat, R/SCR.A/3419/2020 (India), https://indiankanoon.org/doc/50036233/.

306. Pujar v. State of Gujarat, R/SCR.A/5043/2019 (India), https://indiankanoon.org/doc/133819987/.

307. Verma v. State of Rajasthan, D.B. H.C.P. No. 229/2018 (India), https://indiankanoon.org/doc/155316994/.

308. Kaur v. State of Haryana, CRWP No. 3251/2022 (India), https://indiankanoon.org/doc/116573596/.

Tender years have not operated as an automatic bar to repatriation. In *Kaur* and *Sreekumar*, children below or around five were returned. Age has been treated as relevant, but not controlling when countervailing factors exist.

The consistent judicial posture in these return cases is not one of blind comity. Courts repeatedly recite that welfare is paramount and that foreign orders are only factors. Yet, in application, welfare is often understood as preservation of the child's established foreign environment unless concrete harm is demonstrated. What emerges from this body of cases is not a Hague Convention framework, but a discernible pattern: when the foreign nexus is strong, the breach recent, and the harm speculative or unproven, Indian writ courts have been willing, even in tender years cases, to restore the child to the forum of habitual residence. That is the crux of the recent return jurisprudence.

These decisions do not represent the normative position of Indian law, nor do they signal the emergence of a structured return regime. They remain fact-specific outcomes within a discretionary writ framework that does not presume repatriation and does not function as a Hague-style mechanism. Importantly, the cases discussed here have been deliberately selected from the period after April 2018, when the Justice Rajesh Bindal Committee formally recommended that India should not accede to the Hague Convention on the Civil Aspects of International Child Abduction. Even in the years following that recommendation, Indian courts have continued to approach return applications through a welfare-centric, case-by-case analysis. The post-2018 return decisions therefore reflect exceptional factual constellations rather than a doctrinal shift toward automatic or presumptive return.

3.7.6. India Without Signing: A De Facto Hague Model—With an Expansive Grave Risk Escape Valve

India insists it has not signed the Hague Convention. Formally, that is correct. Institutionally, however, the writ jurisprudence of the past several years reveals something more uncomfortable: Indian courts are already applying a functional analogue of the Hague return framework, but without the discipline, procedural architecture, or textual constraints of the Convention. The post-April 2018 cases, after the Bindal Committee recommended that India should not accede, make this especially clear.

Under the Hague Convention, the analytical sequence is straightforward:

1. Was there a wrongful removal or retention?
2. Was the child habitually resident in the requesting state?
3. Were rights of custody being exercised?
4. If yes, return must follow unless a limited exception applies—such as:
   - Grave risk of physical or psychological harm
   - Child's objection (if of sufficient age and maturity)
   - Consent or acquiescence
   - Settlement after one year

Now consider what Indian courts have actually done in writ jurisdiction since 2018.

A. Habitual Residence—Without Calling It That

Indian courts routinely examine where the child was born, schooled, socially embedded, and emotionally integrated. They speak in the language of "most intimate contact," "closest concern," and "natural environment." In practice, this is nothing but a habitual residence analysis under a different vocabulary.

In cases such as *Ganesh, Sreekumar, Arunagiri, Brar,* and *Pujar,* courts placed decisive weight on long-term residence abroad, schooling continuity, citizenship, and social integration. These are classic Hague indicia. The inquiry is not framed as "habitual residence," but the substance is identical.

B. Wrongful Retention—Through the Lens of Conduct

Under the Convention, wrongful retention is established by breach of rights of custody.

Indian courts do not use that phrase. Instead, they examine:

- Breach of limited travel permissions
- Violation of consent-based custody frameworks
- Suppression of foreign court orders
- Failure to return within agreed timelines
- Stealthy securing of the child's presence in India

In *Verma, Pujar, Gehlot,* and *Kaur,* the removing parent's breach of undertakings was not incidental, it was central. That is a wrongful retention analysis in all but name.

C. Promptitude—The One-Year Defense in Disguise

Article 12 of the Hague Convention creates a one-year rule, after which "settlement" becomes a defense. Indian courts do not reference Article 12, but they have developed an almost parallel doctrine.

In *Viswanathan, Khaitan, Sasidharan, Mahuwala, Kandavelou,* and *Shukla,* delay of 1.5 to two years was fatal. Courts emphasized rooting, schooling, and acclimatization. The language mirrors the *"settled in the new environment"* defense. Conversely, where the left-behind parent acted *"promptly and without delay,"* summary return was more likely. This is structurally indistinguishable from the Hague one-year framework.

D. Child's Objection—Directly Applied

Indian courts explicitly consider the wishes of children of sufficient maturity. In *Pradhan,* a nine-year-old's intelligent and reasoned objection to return was decisive. In *Chava* and *Khambatta,* mature teenagers' preferences were respected. This aligns squarely with Article 13's mature child exception.

E. Consent and Acquiescence

Indian courts have refused return where the left-behind parent consented to relocation or acquiesced by enrolling the child in local schools. That is precisely the Hague consent/acquiescence defense.

F. Removal Pursuant to Court Order

In *Latha*, return was denied because relocation occurred pursuant to an Australian court order. Hague law does not apply to judicially authorized relocation. The Indian court reached the same outcome.

G. So Where Is the Difference?

The difference lies in the treatment of what the Hague Convention calls the "grave risk of harm" exception under Article 13(b). Under the Convention, grave risk is meant to be narrow. It is not a best interest rehearing. It is not a comparative custody evaluation. It is not a generalized concern about living conditions abroad. It requires a serious, specific, and intolerable risk of harm. And the governing standard, for example in the United States, is that of *"beyond reasonable doubt."*

Indian courts, however, do not cabin the inquiry so tightly. The writ jurisdiction is constitutionally grounded in parens patriae power. The Supreme Court has repeatedly held that the sole and paramount consideration is welfare and best interest, to which all other considerations must yield. That formulation is broader than Article 13(b) of the Hague Abduction Convention.

Where serious allegations of sexual abuse were raised in post-2018 cases, Indian courts declined return without narrowing the inquiry to whether protective measures could mitigate the risk in the requesting state, or whether the allegations remained unfounded. The analysis was not confined to intolerable situations; it extended into credibility assessments and welfare balancing. Similarly, in cases involving domestic violence, Indian courts have been willing to conduct what amounts to a merits review, rather than a threshold risk assessment, before deciding whether return is appropriate. This is the critical divergence.

Under the Hague Convention, the grave risk defense is an exception to return. In India, welfare is the governing principle. The result is that what would be treated as an exception under Hague jurisprudence becomes, in Indian writ courts, a full-spectrum inquiry. The grave risk valve is broader. More elastic. Less disciplined.

H. The Structural Irony

The Bindal Committee feared that signing the Hague Convention would deprive Indian courts of discretion. Yet the post-2018 jurisprudence demonstrates that Indian courts are already:

- Ordering summary returns
- Respecting foreign custody proceedings
- Prioritizing habitual residence
- Applying delay-based settlement reasoning
- Considering child objections
- Recognizing consent and acquiescence

In substance, the architecture mirrors the Convention. The real difference is not in the existence of discretion. It is in its containment.

Hague courts operate within a defined textual structure, with clearly enumerated defenses and a mandate for expeditious resolution. Indian writ courts operate within a welfare-first constitutional mandate that allows the grave risk rationale to expand into a broader best interest reassessment.

That expansion cuts both ways. It permits protection in genuine abuse cases. It also produces unpredictability.

I. The Hard Conclusion

India has not acceded to the Hague Convention. However, recent writ jurisprudence indicates that Indian courts have, in practice, applied a framework that closely resembles the Convention's analytical structure. The courts distinguish between prompt and delayed petitions, give substantial weight to the jurisdiction with the closest factual connection to the child, consider the views of children who are of sufficient age and maturity, and recognize circumstances amounting to consent or acquiescence.

What India does differently, and more broadly, is treat the grave risk analysis as an open-ended welfare inquiry rather than a narrowly circumscribed exception.

In other words: India does not reject the Hague model. It implements a discretionary version of it, one in which the grave risk exception is applied with wider latitude and less structural constraint. That is not a rejection of international norms. It is a domesticated adaptation of them.

3.7.7. UCCJEA Temporary Emergency Jurisdiction Versus Indian Writ Jurisdiction: A Structural Comparison

At a superficial level, the temporary emergency jurisdiction provision under the UCCJEA and the writ jurisdiction exercised by Indian high courts in child custody matters may appear analogous. Both are invoked in urgent cross-border disputes. Both are described as extraordinary remedies. Both may be triggered in situations involving alleged wrongful removal. Beyond that surface similarity, however, the two frameworks diverge in structure, scope, and consequence.

Under the UCCJEA, temporary emergency jurisdiction is deliberately narrow. A court may exercise it only if the child is physically present in the state and has been abandoned, or if it is necessary in an emergency to protect the child (or a sibling or parent) from mistreatment or abuse. The statutory language is precise. The jurisdiction is temporary. It is not a vehicle for determining long-term custody. It exists to stabilize an immediate risk until the court having home state jurisdiction assumes or resumes control. Once the home state court acts, the emergency court must defer. Judicial communication is contemplated. The structure is coordinated and transitional.

Indian writ jurisdiction is conceptually different.

The power of an Indian high court to issue a writ of habeas corpus in custody matters flows from its constitutional parens patriae authority. It is not confined by a statutory definition of "emergency." The inquiry is not limited to abandonment or abuse. Instead, the high court examines whether the custody is unlawful and, more broadly, whether intervention is required in the best interest and welfare of the child. While the Supreme Court has repeatedly characterized habeas corpus as an extraordinary remedy to be exercised sparingly, the doctrinal boundaries are significantly more elastic than those under the UCCJEA.

A central distinction lies in the nature of the jurisdiction exercised. Temporary emergency jurisdiction in the United States is provisional and subordinate to the jurisdictional hierarchy established by the statute. It does not authorize a court to override the home state's authority permanently. By contrast, when an Indian high court entertains a writ petition, it does not automatically relinquish its authority merely because a foreign court has passed an order. The high court may undertake a summary inquiry and direct return. Alternatively, it may conclude that an elaborate inquiry into welfare is necessary and direct the parties to pursue proceedings before a competent guardianship court in India. The jurisdiction is discretionary and can have determinative consequences.

The requirement of physical presence also operates differently in practice. Under the UCCJEA, physical presence of the child in the state is a jurisdictional prerequisite for the exercise of temporary emergency jurisdiction. Without physical presence, the statute does not permit emergency action. Indian writ jurisprudence has traditionally emphasized territorial presence as well, since habeas corpus is directed toward production of the person alleged to be unlawfully detained.

However, recent decisions demonstrate that Indian courts have, in certain circumstances, entertained writ petitions even when the child was no longer physically present within the territorial jurisdiction of the high court. In such cases, the courts did not treat absence as an automatic jurisdictional bar. Instead, the focus shifted to the broader constitutional authority of the court and the legality of the custodial arrangement. This marks a notable departure from the UCCJEA model, where physical presence is indispensable to emergency jurisdiction.

Another significant distinction concerns the scope of inquiry. Temporary emergency jurisdiction under the UCCJEA is not intended to become a substitute for a full custody adjudication. It is confined to immediate protection. Indian writ courts, on the other hand, retain the discretion to move beyond a threshold assessment. While the Supreme Court has cautioned that writ proceedings should not transform into plenary custody trials, high courts may nonetheless evaluate factors such as delay, foreign proceedings, parental conduct, integration of the child, and allegations of harm. The inquiry, though labeled summary in some cases, may extend beyond the limited fact-finding typical of UCCJEA emergency hearings.

Finally, the normative orientation differs. The UCCJEA is embedded in a cooperative interstate and international framework. Its emergency jurisdiction is part of a coordinated scheme designed to avoid competing custody orders. Indian writ jurisdiction is not situated within such a multilateral statutory structure. It is anchored in constitutional power and guided by the paramount consideration of welfare. There is no statutory mandate for judicial communication with foreign courts, nor an automatic obligation to defer upon the issuance of a foreign custody order.

In essence, temporary emergency jurisdiction under the UCCJEA is a narrowly tailored, time-bound mechanism intended to preserve jurisdictional coherence until the appropriate forum acts. Indian writ jurisdiction is broader, constitutionally grounded, and capable, at least in certain cases, of operating even in the absence of strict territorial presence. It is not merely an emergency measure. It is an exercise of parens patriae authority that may either restore the status quo or redirect the dispute into a full custodial determination within India.

The resemblance between the two doctrines is therefore limited to their shared urgency. Structurally and functionally, they operate on fundamentally different premises.

CHAPTER 4

Practical Guidance

4.1. Scope of the Chapter: Practical Guidance

This chapter is about what must be evaluated before a single pleading is filed. In India–U.S. family disputes, early structural decisions frequently determine outcome more than the merits ever will.

Cross-border divorce and custody litigation is rarely driven only by statutory grounds or best interests analysis. Religion may determine the applicable personal law. Domicile may determine whether a foreign decree survives scrutiny under section 13 of the Code of Civil Procedure (CPC). Immigration status may constrain litigation posture in the United States. A pending criminal complaint in India may alter financial leverage overnight. The wrong first filing may harden jurisdiction in a forum that is substantively disadvantageous.

International family litigation between India and the United States is not merely about proving grounds for divorce or prevailing in a custody hearing. It is about structural thresholds: which personal law applies, which court will assume control, which forum's financial philosophy will govern, whether parallel proceedings will be sustainable, and whether a decree obtained abroad will be worth the paper it is printed on.

The purpose of this chapter is to identify, in disciplined sequence, the questions competent counsel must answer before initiating or responding to litigation. These are strategic fault lines. Once crossed, they are rarely reversible.

4.2. Personal Status and Structural Threshold Issues

4.2.1. Whether the Client's Religion Determines Applicable Personal Law

For a U.S. lawyer, this matters for one reason: *it determines what India will treat as a "valid" divorce path if your client ends up needing to rely on a U.S. judgment (or defend against one) in India.* You are not drafting the Indian petition. You are deciding whether your client can safely proceed in the United States without creating a decree that is useless, or worse, strategically harmful, on the India side.

Here is the practical impact. If the marriage is one that India classifies under the Hindu Marriage Act, the Special Marriage Act, the Indian Divorce Act

(Christian), the Parsi Act, or Muslim personal law, you are dealing with different assumptions about what counts as a proper ground, what procedural protections are expected, and what an Indian court will consider legitimate when recognition gets litigated. "Indian law" is not one system; it is multiple statutory tracks plus personal law overlays. So when the client says "we got married in Delhi," that is not enough. You need to know: *under what act the parties got married, and who will argue what later.*

This is also where U.S. strategy can quietly break. If you advise a client to race to a no-fault divorce in the United States without understanding what India thinks this marriage is, you may be walking them into a predictable outcome: they are "divorced" in New York and still "married" in India, and suddenly India becomes the forum for criminal leverage, maintenance leverage, or status litigation. That is not a doctrinal nuance. It is a practical mess, especially for clients who travel, have property, have parents in India, need Overseas Citizenship of India (OCI), or have reputational exposure.

So the U.S. lawyer's first job is not to master every Indian statute. It is to *identify which Indian lane this marriage sits in* so they can anticipate (1) recognition vulnerability, (2) parallel filing risk, and (3) how quickly the other side can weaponize India once the U.S. filing happens.

4.2.2. Whether the Ground for Divorce Matters

A U.S. lawyer dealing with a divorce with Indian elements must pause and ask whether the ground on which their client divorces in the United States will later survive scrutiny in India.

Most U.S. divorces proceed on no-fault grounds. That feels routine. But when recognition becomes contested in India, the question is not simply "were they divorced?" It becomes: was the divorce granted on a ground that aligns with the applicable Indian statute, and was jurisdiction exercised on a basis India will accept?

If the marriage falls under the Hindu Marriage Act or the Special Marriage Act, and the U.S. decree is purely no-fault without findings that correspond to recognized statutory grounds, that gap can become the argument. A hostile spouse may resist recognition, reopen status, or use the decree's structure as leverage in maintenance or criminal proceedings.

So before filing in the United States, the screening question is straightforward: If this decree is challenged in India, what will the attack look like? If the likely argument is that the ground is not recognized, or that there was no meaningful submission to jurisdiction, that risk must be factored into timing, service strategy, and settlement structure.

The point is not that no-fault divorces are invalid. The point is that in India–U.S. litigation, recognition is often strategic, not automatic.

4.2.3. Whether the Client's Nationality/Citizenship Affects Jurisdiction or Diplomatic Posture

Nationality will not usually determine jurisdiction by itself. But it often determines who feels empowered to litigate in India, and who feels exposed.

Real-World Pattern: An Indian citizen married in Delhi relocates to Texas on an H-1B visa. The marriage breaks down. He files for divorce in Texas. She returns to India and initiates proceedings there not necessarily because India has clearer jurisdiction, but because she is an Indian citizen, has family support there, and can litigate at lower personal cost. His U.S. filing does not prevent India from becoming active terrain.

Another Common Scenario: Both spouses are U.S. citizens of Indian origin. One still holds an Indian passport or OCI. The other has surrendered Indian citizenship. When litigation becomes hostile, the spouse retaining Indian nationality is better positioned to initiate or sustain Indian proceedings, including criminal complaints or maintenance actions. Travel asymmetry emerges. One party can enter and litigate freely. The other hesitates.

You also see nationality surface in child disputes. If a child holds Indian citizenship, passport control and exit permissions become more complicated, and arguments about habitual residence and return may be framed differently than if the child is solely a U.S. citizen.

And Then There Is Perception: An Indian national divorcing abroad may face arguments in India that the foreign decree is an attempt to bypass Indian law. A foreign national litigating in India may face subtle pressure framed around "forum appropriateness" or community expectations. These arguments are rarely doctrinal; they are strategic. For U.S. counsel, the screening question is simple: *Does nationality give the other side confidence that India is a viable second forum?* If the answer is yes, assume that it may be used, not because nationality creates automatic jurisdiction, but because it affects access, leverage, and willingness to escalate.

4.2.4. Whether the Client's Domicile Affects Jurisdictional Claims

Domicile is where cross-border cases quietly unravel. A client may have lived in New Jersey for 12 years, own a home there, pay U.S. taxes, and still face an argument in India that the U.S. court exercised jurisdiction on a basis India does not recognize. Indian courts have repeatedly scrutinized whether the foreign court's assumption of jurisdiction aligns with Indian conflict-of-laws principles. Residence alone is not always enough.

You have seen this pattern in practice: A spouse files for divorce in New York on residency grounds. The other spouse appears minimally or defaults. The decree is granted. Months later, proceedings are initiated in India challenging recognition, arguing that the petitioner remained domiciled in India or that the foreign court lacked jurisdiction in a manner acceptable under CPC section 13. The status question reopens. Maintenance exposure resurfaces. Criminal complaints follow. The issue is not abstract domicile theory. It is evidentiary positioning.

Real-World Example: A non-resident Indian (NRI) husband working in California files for divorce there after several years of employment. The wife returns to India during separation. He proceeds on no-fault. She later challenges recognition in India, arguing that the matrimonial home and domicile of origin remained in India and that she never meaningfully submitted to U.S. jurisdiction. The Indian court examines not just where he lived, but the nature of his ties to India, property, voter registration, frequency of visits, and family residence. What felt settled in California becomes live litigation in India. The inverse also occurs. A spouse relocates to India shortly before filing there, asserting Indian domicile to preempt a U.S. action. The other party challenges that move as tactical and temporary. Indian courts look at duration, intent, continuity of residence, and surrounding conduct.

For U.S. counsel, the question is practical: *If this decree is tested in India, what will the domicile narrative look like?* If domicile is genuinely shifted, document it. If ties to India remain substantial, assume they will be used. Domicile arguments rarely win cases alone. They often sustain parallel litigation long enough to create leverage.

4.2.5. Whether the Client's Immigration Status in the United States Will Be Impacted by Litigation

Before you file anything, confirm what immigration posture you are destabilizing. *If your client is on a dependent visa*, divorce may immediately affect lawful status. If your client is the principal visa holder, criminal allegations abroad, even unproven ones, can create *immigration anxiety* that alters settlement leverage. If there is a pending I-130, I-485, or removal of conditions filing, timing becomes critical. Divorce before or after a particular filing stage can materially change risk exposure.

You Have Likely Seen This: A spouse on an H-4 visa initiates divorce proceedings without understanding that status is tied to the H-1B holder. Suddenly, immigration counsel is scrambling. Or a conditional permanent resident divorces before the two-year mark and must shift into a waiver posture with U.S. Citizenship and Immigration Services, increasing scrutiny at precisely the moment litigation becomes adversarial.

There is also the *reputational dimension*. Allegations of domestic violence in India, whether through a complaint under Indian law or otherwise, may not automatically affect U.S. immigration status, but clients often assume they will. That fear can distort negotiation. Conversely, certain findings in U.S. proceedings may have downstream immigration consequences. *The family case does not exist in isolation*. Immigration timelines, visa dependence, naturalization eligibility, and travel freedom should be mapped before strategy is locked in. You are not expected to practice immigration law. You are expected to ask the right question early enough to bring immigration counsel into the room.

4.2.6. Whether Indian Immigration Status or OCI Creates Leverage or Risk

OCI status cuts both ways.

On one hand, holding OCI rather than Indian citizenship *may strengthen a weaker Indian domicile argument* that the client's center of life is no longer India. It can reinforce a narrative of relocation and diminished domicile ties. That matters if forum or recognition becomes contested.

On the other hand, OCI, particularly for a child, can become leverage. OCI renewal for a minor typically requires documentation and, in practice, cooperation from both parents. If the child's OCI card is expiring, or if documentation is incomplete, one parent's refusal to cooperate can create real pressure. A child physically present in India without valid status may be facing regulatory deadlines. That is not theoretical leverage; it is immediate.

There is also the passport dimension. Indian courts have, in contentious matters, directed the impounding of passports or imposed travel restrictions to secure appearance. For an NRI spouse with pending green card proceedings, employment-based petitions, or naturalization timelines, the inability to travel, or the fear of being unable to return, can be destabilizing. The risk is not just inconvenience. It may affect employment continuity and immigration posture in the United States.

So this is not merely about who can travel comfortably. It is about who controls documentation, who can trigger regulatory vulnerability, and whether immigration status, Indian or U.S., can be used as pressure in parallel litigation.

Before dismissing Indian proceedings as peripheral, assess whether status, citizenship, OCI, passport, or visa creates leverage that will alter the balance of the case.

4.2.7. Whether the Client's Gender Will Affect Caregiving Presumptions

For custody, gender still matters more in India than many U.S. lawyers assume. Indian courts formally apply the welfare principle, but in practice, children of tender years are often placed with the mother unless there are strong countervailing factors. It is not labeled as a strict "tender years doctrine," yet its influence is visible in outcomes. If the child is very young, and the mother has been the primary caregiver, a father seeking primary custody in India faces an uphill climb unless there are serious welfare concerns.

That does not mean fathers cannot succeed. They can, especially where caregiving history supports them or where the mother's circumstances create instability. But the starting posture is not neutral in very young-child cases. *For U.S. counsel advising a father,* this matters if India becomes an active forum. Filing strategy should not ignore how a young child's age will be perceived in Indian proceedings.

On the divorce and financial side, the asymmetry looks different. India does not have a matrimonial property division regime comparable to equitable distribution in many U.S. states. There is no automatic 50/50 division of marital assets. Property remains title-driven unless specific claims are made. *From a strictly financial perspective, a higher-earning husband may perceive India as a more favorable forum for asset exposure.*

But that advantage comes with a counterweight. India retains several gender-specific criminal provisions, including cruelty-based offenses, that are available to wives and can be invoked quickly. A husband who files aggressively in India to limit financial exposure may simultaneously face criminal complaints that alter leverage overnight. Even if such complaints are defensible, the immediate pressure, travel risk, reputational exposure, and passport concerns are real. So the gender dynamic is not linear. In custody, the mother of a very young child often begins from a position of structural advantage. In property division, the titled spouse may perceive structural advantage. In criminal exposure, the husband may face significant statutory vulnerability.

Advising without acknowledging all three realities is incomplete.

4.2.8. Whether Race or Cultural Optics Will Influence Litigation Strategy

This is uncomfortable to discuss, but pretending it does not matter is naïve.

A foreign national spouse of non-Indian origin often *has a cleaner domicile narrative*. If that spouse has lived, worked, and built a life outside India, the argument that their center of gravity lies abroad is usually straightforward. In a recognition contest, that clarity can help. Courts are more receptive to a domicile analysis that aligns with lived reality.

But domicile cuts both ways. *Indian law does not require both spouses to be domiciled in India for Indian jurisdiction to activate*. One spouse's continuing Indian domicile, or even a strong assertion of it, can be enough to anchor proceedings. So even where the foreign spouse's domicile story is strong, that does not insulate them from Indian litigation if the other spouse asserts India as the matrimonial base. *When a child is involved*, the practical effect is sharper. If one spouse clearly retains Indian domicile, Indian proceedings may move forward on that basis alone, and the other spouse cannot rely on the absence of Indian domicile as insulation. Once custody and welfare are implicated, the non-domiciled spouse may still be drawn fully into Indian litigation regardless of how clean their own domicile narrative appears.

Cultural framing also operates beneath the surface. Indian courts are deeply familiar with the joint family system, extended caregiving networks, and the social consequences of marital breakdown. A narrative of an Indian wife stranded abroad, isolated from family support, unemployed, or dependent on immigration status can carry weight, especially if the husband has returned to India and positioned himself within a familiar support structure. That narrative may not be written into doctrine, but it appears in affidavits, interim orders, and judicial reasoning. *Conversely, a foreign spouse may be portrayed as culturally detached, less integrated into the child's linguistic or familial environment, or insufficiently connected to the child's roots*. Those arguments do not always prevail, but they are frequently made. Arguments about cultural continuity, extended family access, language, schooling, and home environment take on greater force. A relocation that appears neutral in the United States may be framed in India as severing the child from lineage and family structure. A child raised primarily abroad may be characterized differently than a child who spent formative years within an Indian joint family.

None of this is codified as bias. It is context. The practical question for counsel is not whether courts are cultural. It is whether the narrative of belonging—where the marriage was rooted, where the child's identity is anchored, who appears supported and who appears isolated—will influence how the case is received.

Ignoring those optics does not neutralize them. Anticipating them allows you to prepare for them.

4.3. Forum Strategy and First-Filed Advantage

4.3.1. Whether Filing First in India Provides Jurisdictional Advantage

Whether filing first in India is advantageous *depends entirely on who your client is*, what their personal circumstances look like, and what they ultimately want out of the litigation. *In some cases, filing first in India is exactly the right move.* If your client intends to remain closely tied to India, has property or business interests there, expects parallel proceedings regardless, or believes the financial framework is more predictable for their situation, anchoring jurisdiction early may provide stability. It may also preempt a more aggressive filing abroad.

In other cases, filing first in India is the precise opposite of what the client wants. If the client's life is now firmly rooted in the United States and the goal is to move forward quickly with minimal entanglement, initiating proceedings in India may open doors that are difficult to close. It may expose the client to interim maintenance claims, multiple applications, travel complications, or ancillary proceedings that escalate rather than contain the dispute.

You must also assess collateral exposure. Can the client still be subjected to financial restraints, passport issues, or other sanctions through Indian proceedings? Could extended family members in India be drawn into the conflict or pressured through complaints? Is the client prepared for litigation to unfold simultaneously in two jurisdictions?

The decision to file first in India is not ideological. It is strategic. In some fact patterns, it provides control. In others, it triggers a cascade of consequences that make resolution harder, not easier.

4.3.2. Whether Filing First in the United States Secures Home-State Control

U.S. lawyers are accustomed to the idea of *exclusive and continuing jurisdiction*, particularly in custody under the Uniform Child Custody Jurisdiction and Enforcement Act (UCCJEA). Once a state properly assumes jurisdiction, other states defer.

In India–U.S. matters, that assumption can mislead. Indian courts often view themselves as having continuing and, in practical effect, exclusive divorce jurisdiction over marriages solemnized in India under Indian statutes, provided statutory connecting factors exist. A prior U.S. filing does not automatically divest Indian courts of authority. If the marriage was solemnized in India and one spouse invokes Indian statutory jurisdiction, Indian courts will move regardless of pending U.S. proceedings.

Custody operates differently as well. India does not apply a strict home-state residency rule comparable to the UCCJEA. There is no fixed six-month threshold that forecloses jurisdiction elsewhere. The welfare of the child governs, and if the child is present in India or brought within Indian territory, Indian courts may assume jurisdiction and proceed.

So while a U.S. filing may create exclusive and continuing jurisdiction for domestic U.S. purposes, that exclusivity does not bind India. If India has a statutory hook, parallel proceedings are not unusual. The strategic question is not simply whether filing first in the United States secures control. It is whether it meaningfully prevents India from exercising what it views as its own continuing jurisdiction.

4.3.3. Whether the Child's Habitual Residence Analysis Favors Your Chosen Forum

In U.S. custody litigation with an international dimension, *habitual residence* is the anchor for Hague relief and often (unintentionally) overlaps with the UCCJEA *home-state* concept. Lawyers think in terms of six-month residency thresholds and wrongful removal.

India uses a different vocabulary. The term that often appears in Indian custody proceedings is "ordinary residence." In practice, that concept can reflect what looks like a blended analysis of home-state and habitual residence, but it is not a treaty-based test and it is not rigidly defined. Courts examine where the child has been living in fact, the continuity of stay, schooling, and the surrounding circumstances. The inquiry is fact-driven and welfare-centered.

If a child has been living in the United States for a sustained period, arguments about habitual residence or home-state jurisdiction may be strong for U.S. purposes. But once the child is physically present in India, Indian courts may assess ordinary residence and welfare without being bound by Hague return obligations. Timing becomes critical. The longer a child remains in one jurisdiction, the stronger the narrative of integration. *Delay weakens removal arguments. Prompt action preserves them.*

So the question is not only which forum you prefer. It is whether the child's actual living pattern supports that choice, and how quickly that pattern may shift.

4.3.4. Whether Participation in Foreign Proceedings Amounts to Submission

This is where statutory language and practical reality diverge. *Indian matrimonial statutes expressly use the word "jurisdiction" when identifying the court in which a divorce petition may be instituted.* For example, the statute may permit filing where the parties last resided together as a couple or where the wife is currently residing. To a U.S. lawyer, that structure *may look analogous to venue.* It reads like a geographic allocation rule.

But because the statute frames it as jurisdiction, the consequences are different. If your client believes that *India is no longer the proper forum because a new domicile of choice* has been established abroad, *that objection must generally be raised before the Indian court* itself. There is no automatic dismissal simply because the couple now resides elsewhere.

And that is where the submission risk arises. If the client does not appear, the matter may proceed ex parte. If the client appears to contest jurisdiction, that appearance becomes part of the record. Even if the intention is a limited challenge, *the act of entering the proceedings can blur into substantive participation.* Interim applications may require response. Protective filings may become necessary. What begins as a jurisdictional objection can quickly become ongoing litigation. So, the practical issue is not semantic. It is tactical. *Because the statute labels these provisions as jurisdictional, contesting them usually requires stepping into the forum.* Once that happens, the argument that the client never submitted becomes harder to sustain.

4.3.5. Whether Delay Will Weaken Jurisdictional or Return Claims

In child removal cases, delay is often fatal.

If a child is taken to India and the left-behind parent waits, even for understandable reasons, the legal terrain shifts. Courts begin to look not only at the original removal but at the child's present circumstances. Integration into school, extended family involvement, and day-to-day stability start to weigh more heavily as time passes.

The reasons for delay rarely carry the weight parents expect. Hoping for an amicable resolution, negotiating informally, or assuming that a pending U.S. custody case will control the outcome does not freeze the factual record. Even if the taking parent initiated proceedings in the United States and fully participated there before removing the child, that participation does not prevent Indian courts from focusing on the child's current welfare once the child is physically present in India.

What makes matters significantly worse is when the taking parent initiates a plenary custody proceeding in India soon after arrival. That filing reframes the dispute. Instead of a narrow question about return, the case becomes a full custody adjudication under a welfare standard. The longer that proceeding continues, the more the child's residence in India appears normalized.

From a U.S. perspective, a parent may believe that existing custody litigation or home-state jurisdiction preserves their position. From an India–U.S. perspective, physical presence and the passage of time often drive the analysis.

The practical lesson is simple. If return is the objective, speed matters. Once delay sets in, arguments shift from wrongful removal to settled environment, and recovering ground becomes exponentially harder.

4.3.6. Whether Parallel Litigation Is Financially and Strategically Sustainable

Goes without saying, running cases in both India and the United States is rarely sustainable for long. Two sets of counsel. Two procedural systems. Two streams of interim applications. Travel costs. Time away from work. *Emotional fatigue.* Clients often underestimate how quickly this becomes *financially draining*.

Parallel proceedings also create *strategic instability*, and lead the way to *conflicting orders*. One forum may move faster on interim relief. The other may take a different view of status, custody, or maintenance. The pressure to respond in both jurisdictions increases the risk of inconsistent positions.

There is also collateral exposure. Ongoing litigation in India can affect employment, immigration timelines, and travel freedom in the United States.

Conversely, aggressive U.S. filings can provoke escalation in India. The question is not whether parallel litigation is possible. It is whether your client can realistically sustain it, financially and psychologically, without undermining their long-term goals.

4.4. Service and Parallel Proceedings

4.4.1. Whether Service Will Comply with the Hague Service Convention and Survive CPC Section 13 Scrutiny

When the responding spouse is in India and not cooperating, Hague service is the only formally recognized route. India has objected to Article 10 methods, which means service by postal channels, courier, or direct email will not reliably withstand later scrutiny if recognition is challenged in India.

The mechanics are slow and outside counsel's control. A request must be transmitted to India's Central Authority with properly formatted documents. If anything is incomplete, the request may be rejected or delayed. In some cases, proof of service returns in about six months. In others, it takes significantly longer. *Occasionally, confirmation does not return at all,* leaving counsel in procedural limbo.

U.S. state courts often wait approximately six months before considering substituted service, absent emergency circumstances. After that, courts may permit alternative methods such as email or publication to move the case forward. That may satisfy domestic procedural requirements.

However, the real risk often surfaces in the form of an anti-suit injunction, which is discussed in the next section. Alternatively, if recognition is litigated in India, service becomes a focal point under CPC section 13. An ex parte decree obtained after substituted service that did not strictly comply with the Hague Convention can be attacked as procedurally defective. What solved a timing problem in the United States may create a recognition vulnerability in India.

In practice, some lawyers choose to attempt service by post or private process server in parallel, even though it does not satisfy Hague requirements, *in the hope that the other side will participate without contesting service.* If the responding spouse appears and engages substantively without objecting, the service issue may never mature into a fatal defect. But this is a calculated risk. If the other side defaults and later challenges recognition, non-Hague service becomes the weakest link.

The strategic question is whether speed is worth potential future exposure. In India–U.S. matters, service is not just a procedural step. It is often the foundation on which recognition stands or falls.

4.4.2. Whether There Is Risk of an Anti-Suit Injunction from an Indian Court

At present, the most anticipated escalation in India–U.S. matrimonial disputes is the anti-suit injunction. If one spouse files in the United States, the other may move quickly in India seeking an order restraining the U.S. proceedings. Indian courts, in appropriate cases, have granted such injunctions where they believe continuation of foreign litigation would be oppressive, inequitable, or contrary to Indian statutory policy.

The asymmetry lies in service and urgency. When Indian proceedings are initiated, Hague service into the United States is typically required. Indian courts formally recognize that treaty compliance governs service abroad. Yet in practice, where a litigant frames the matter as urgent, Indian courts may issue interim anti-suit orders at an early stage, sometimes before full Hague service is completed. *The threshold for "emergency" in India can be broader than in New York.* Assertions of matrimonial oppression, financial hardship, risk of inconsistent decrees, or child-related concerns are often sufficient to trigger interim restraint.

This creates a procedural imbalance. Your client may be waiting months to perfect Hague service in the United States. Meanwhile, an Indian court may issue an interim order restraining continuation of the U.S. action.

For clients deeply connected to India, this becomes a catch-22. If they ignore the Indian injunction and continue litigating in the United States, they *risk contempt exposure* in India. If they comply and pause the U.S. proceedings, they lose strategic momentum. In some instances, *injunction orders have named not only the litigant but also counsel associated with the foreign proceedings*, increasing professional and reputational pressure.

The practical response is preventive rather than reactive. *Before filing in the United States, assess whether India is likely to be invoked.* Evaluate whether advance notice, calibrated pleadings, or *coordinated strategy with Indian counsel* can reduce the perception of unilateral advantage. In some cases, *limited communication or carefully structured service* can narrow the window for an ex parte anti-suit application. In others, it may be prudent to anticipate the application and prepare immediate contest on maintainability and jurisdiction in India.

Indian counsel can also explore interim protective steps, including contesting territorial jurisdiction at the threshold, seeking vacation of ex parte restraint, or narrowing the scope of any injunction order.

Anti-suit injunction risk cannot always be eliminated. But it can be anticipated. In India–U.S. disputes, it is no longer a remote possibility. It is often the first countermove.

4.4.3. Whether Emergency Ex Parte Relief in India Can Create Immediate Pressure

Ex parte interim relief in India can generate immediate and disproportionate pressure, particularly on a spouse living abroad. Orders may be issued at an early stage, sometimes before full service is perfected, if the matter is framed as urgent. Assertions of financial distress, risk of inconsistent decrees, or harm to marital status are often sufficient to secure interim restraint.

As discussed in the context of anti-suit injunction risk, interim relief in India can issue quickly and on a broader conception of urgency than most New York practitioners are accustomed to. If an Indian court grants ex parte restraint, the pressure shifts immediately to the spouse living abroad. Compliance may require personal appearance. Noncompliance may invite contempt allegations. Continuing with foreign proceedings may be framed as defiance of a subsisting order.

The consequence is practical, not theoretical. Logistics become difficult. Travel may be constrained. Employment schedules are disrupted. Immigration timelines can be affected if international mobility is impaired or if proceedings escalate. This is why emergency relief risk must be assessed at the filing stage. Once such an order is passed, the conversation moves from strategy to containment.

4.4.4. Whether a Foreign Decree Risks Nonrecognition in India

Recognition is far smoother when both parties participated fully in the foreign proceedings and the decree rests on a ground recognizable under Indian law. A contested decree after proper service, appearance, and adjudication stands on stronger footing than a default judgment.

Irretrievable breakdown of marriage remains a grey area. While Indian courts have, in certain circumstances, granted divorce on that ground in exercise of extraordinary powers, it is not a statutory ground under most personal laws. A foreign decree based purely on irretrievable breakdown can therefore attract closer scrutiny if recognition is resisted.

The *complications increase significantly when custody is involved* and cooperation breaks down. A divorce decree that includes custody findings rendered after full participation is easier to defend. A *one-sided custody determination,* particularly where the other parent did not appear or did not meaningfully participate, is far more vulnerable. *In practical terms,* registering or enforcing a unilateral custody order in India is extremely difficult. Indian courts will independently assess welfare rather than simply adopt a foreign custody outcome.

Cooperation changes the landscape. For instance, if both parties negotiate and include language in a New York order that reflects shared parenting intent, acknowledges jurisdictional facts carefully, and anticipates Indian scrutiny, the likelihood of smooth recognition improves substantially. Drafting matters.

4.4.5. Whether Mirror Orders Are Available in India

India does not have a mirror-order mechanism. There is no automatic recognition or registration process by which a foreign divorce or custody order is simply adopted and enforced. The closest framework is section 13 of the CPC, which governs when a foreign judgment is conclusive in India. That inquiry is not administrative. It is judicial.

For a foreign decree to stand, the court in India may examine whether the foreign court had competent jurisdiction, whether the matter was decided on the merits, whether both parties had notice and an opportunity to participate, and whether the decree offends Indian public policy. *Full participation and cooperation materially strengthen* the case for recognition. A unilateral decree does not. *Indian courts do not automatically enforce foreign custody determinations.* Welfare remains paramount. Even where a foreign court has issued a detailed order, an Indian court may independently assess the child's present circumstances. Registration, in the mechanical sense, does not occur.

The process is time-consuming. It may require fresh proceedings. It may require physical presence. It almost always requires continued cooperation between parties if smooth enforcement is the goal.

Where ongoing cross-border parenting is anticipated, coordinated drafting and parallel protective steps may be necessary. Mirror orders are often discussed as a solution in international practice. In India, that concept operates differently, and reliance on automatic enforcement is misplaced.

4.4.6. Whether Mirror Orders Should Be Secured Before Permitting Travel

In theory, securing a mirror order before permitting international travel sounds prudent. In practice, in highly contested India–U.S. cases, *it is often unrealistic*. If cooperation is already strained, the parent promising to obtain a mirror order in India may have no practical ability to guarantee that outcome. Indian courts do not automatically replicate foreign custody terms, and interim relief may not align with the original order.

There is also risk in making that undertaking. If a parent represents to a U.S. court that a mirror order will be obtained and then fails to secure it, the representation itself can become the basis for contempt allegations or adverse findings. What was intended as reassurance can quickly turn into exposure.

4.5. Child-Centered Risk Assessment

4.5.1. Whether There Is a Realistic Risk of Child Abduction

Primarily, yes. In most contested India–U.S. disputes, once a child leaves the United States for India during active litigation or breakdown, the risk of non-return is real. It does not require dramatic threats or overt declarations. It requires only opportunity, logistical feasibility, and a parent willing to anchor the dispute in India.

Once the child is physically in India, the legal posture changes immediately. Indian courts apply a welfare-based analysis. There is no automatic treaty-based return mechanism. A U.S. custody order does not bind an Indian court. Even if a U.S. court issues a return directive, enforcement in India is uncertain and fact-driven.

The escalation is rarely linear. What begins as a "visit" can quickly become (1) a plenary custody petition in India, (2) interim applications seeking residence orders, (3) requests for travel restraint, (4) parallel maintenance or criminal complaints, and (5) urgent injunctions restraining foreign proceedings (among other things).

Litigating in any foreign country is expensive, time-consuming, and unpredictable, and India is no exception. Outcomes turn heavily on fact patterns, judicial discretion, and interim positioning. Multiple proceedings may run simultaneously. The U.S. case does not pause this dynamic.

There are limited situations where the risk calculus changes. If both parents have deep, ongoing ties to the United States; are genuinely cooperative; the child is older and capable of expressing an independent view; is fully integrated in the U.S. school system; there is no history of domestic violence, coercion, or abuse; employment, property, and future plans are clearly centered in the United States; and there is credible evidence of intent to return, then temporary travel may be manageable.

Absent those factors, the pattern is simple. The child travels. The child does not return. The dispute relocates. This is not about distrust. It is about structural reality once physical control of the child shifts.

4.5.2. Whether Certain Actions or Inactions Create Consent or Acquiescence Defenses

Consent and acquiescence are rarely explicit. They are built from conduct.

Agreeing to sell a jointly owned home or the spouse's vehicle shortly before or after the child travels can later be framed as evidence that the move was permanent or at least anticipated. What may have been a financial convenience can be recast as alignment with relocation.

Failing to maintain regular contact with the child while the child is in India weakens a later claim that the removal was wrongful. Gaps in communication are often cited as indifference or acceptance.

Written correspondence is particularly dangerous. An email agreeing "for now," a message saying "let's see how it goes," or informal *consent to extend a visitor visa* or *renew an OCI card* can be produced later as proof of agreement. Courts read those messages carefully. Casual language becomes evidence.

School admission decisions are frequently decisive. *Even enrollment in what appears to be a short-term or summer program* can be presented as integration into the new environment. If the child is admitted to a regular academic session, the argument becomes stronger.

Open-ended statements cause problems. Phrases like "stay as long as you need," "we'll figure it out later," or "if it works, we can discuss next year" create ambiguity that benefits the relocating parent.

Failure to require concrete safeguards also matters. No written assurance of return. No defined return date. No affidavit. No return tickets. No documentation specifying the temporary nature of the visit. The absence of structure is often characterized as implied consent.

In cross-border disputes, silence and informality are rarely neutral. They are often reconstructed later as agreement.

4.5.3. Whether Passage of Time Will Create a Settlement or Integration Defense

Most certainly yes. It cannot be stressed enough.

India does not operate on a rigid residency threshold before assuming custody jurisdiction. The inquiry turns on welfare and the child's present circumstances. That means any meaningful passage of time strengthens the argument that the child has developed roots in India. Enrollment in school, friendships, language immersion, extended family bonding, routine medical care, extracurricular activities. All of it accumulates. What began as a contested removal gradually becomes a lived reality. Courts are reluctant to unsettle a child who appears stable, even if the original move was disputed. The longer the delay, the harder the return argument becomes.

The only situations where counterarguments have occasionally prevailed are fact-specific and uncommon. For example, where the left-behind parent had been the child's primary and near-exclusive caregiver for years, where the child's life was deeply anchored with that parent, and where the taking parent actively caused the delay by concealing the child's location or obstructing contact. In those limited circumstances, courts have been more willing to discount integration arguments. *But those cases are rare. They require compelling evidence.*

As a general matter, once time passes and roots form, the dispute shifts from wrongful removal to present welfare. And that shift favors the parent in physical control.

4.5.4. Whether Extended Family Support Structures Will Influence Custody Analysis

Yes.

In India, the *presence of a joint family structure is often projected as a stabilizing and culturally rooted environment* for the child. Grandparents and extended relatives are presented as daily caregivers, emotional anchors, and sources of continuity. Courts are accustomed to seeing that framework. The contrast is frequently drawn with what is described as "nanny culture" abroad. The narrative becomes one of a child raised within a multigenerational household versus a child primarily supervised by hired caregivers while parents work long hours. That framing can be powerful, even if it oversimplifies reality.

If the taking parent was not employed in the United States but can demonstrate the ability to obtain employment in India, and can portray themselves as fully available to the child in the interim, that becomes part of the welfare narrative. If they can further show that they are financially more secure in India due to extended family support, shared housing, or lower living costs, the presentation strengthens. The argument becomes that the child will have both parental presence and economic backing in India.

Allegations that the other parent was frequently absent due to professional commitments are commonly raised. Affidavits from relatives are easily obtained. Descriptions of shared caregiving, family involvement, and economic stability can be assembled quickly.

Extended family support does not determine custody on its own. But in Indian proceedings, it is rarely treated as peripheral.

4.5.5. Whether Undertakings or Financial Bonds Should Be Required Before Travel

Yes. If international travel is permitted during a dispute, undertakings and, where appropriate, financial bonds should be considered. Written commitments to return by a defined date, acknowledgment of jurisdiction, agreement to comply with existing custody orders, and security deposits can create at least some deterrent effect.

But they are not foolproof guarantees. In some cases, the taking parent may argue that the required bond is financially oppressive and that inability to furnish it should not deprive the child of exposure to Indian culture or extended family. Courts may be receptive to that framing. In other cases, a determined parent may be willing to forfeit the bond amount if remaining in India is strategically more valuable.

Undertakings themselves are only as strong as enforcement. They can be ignored. They can later be challenged as having been signed under pressure or "acute duress." If litigation escalates in India, those undertakings do not automatically compel compliance there. So while bonds and undertakings are prudent risk-mitigation tools, they must be viewed realistically. They reduce risk; they do not eliminate it.

4.5.6. Whether Travel Restrictions Should Be Reciprocal

Yes. If the parties are entering into a travel stipulation, it is *far more rational* to draft it so that restrictions apply to both parents. *Symmetry reduces the perception that the order is punitive or strategically one sided.* Courts are also more likely to approve and enforce balanced provisions.

Reciprocity minimizes later arguments of coercion. A parent subject to unilateral restrictions may later claim that the agreement was extracted under pressure or was substantively unfair. When obligations run both ways, that argument weakens.

It also reduces the risk of misuse. A one-sided order can be weaponized. A parent may rely on it to permanently restrict international travel, invoke enforcement mechanisms selectively, or initiate ancillary measures that escalate conflict. Balanced clauses narrow that leverage.

Travel stipulations in cross-border cases should aim to preserve stability, not create strategic advantage. Reciprocity helps signal that intent.

4.5.7. Whether the Child's Passport Should Be Surrendered to the Court

Placing the child's passport in court custody or escrow can be a useful protective measure. It creates friction against unilateral travel and signals that the court is monitoring cross-border movement.

But it is not a complete safeguard. If the child holds an Indian passport, the other parent may attempt to secure a replacement or emergency document through the Indian consulate, sometimes by framing the request as urgent. Even where formal procedures exist, the practical risk cannot be ignored.

If the child is a U.S. citizen, surrendering the U.S. passport does not eliminate all exit routes. A passport is not required for land travel to Canada for a minor U.S. citizen in certain circumstances. A birth certificate may suffice. Once outside the United States, emergency travel documents can potentially be sought from the Indian embassy. The point is not that passport surrender is ineffective.

It is that it must be viewed as one layer of protection, not a fail-safe mechanism. In high-risk cases, passport control should be combined with other preventive measures rather than relied upon in isolation.

4.5.8. Whether to Enroll in the U.S. Passport Issuance Alert Program

Enrollment in the U.S. Passport Issuance Alert Program can be useful, but expectations must be realistic. The program provides notice if an application is submitted for a new U.S. passport for the child. That advance warning can give a parent time to object or seek court intervention before issuance.

Its limitations are significant. It does not affect passports that have already been issued and are in circulation. It does not stop travel if a valid passport is already available. It also does not address scenarios where a parent seeks to renounce the child's U.S. citizenship or pursue issuance of an Indian passport instead. It is a monitoring tool, not a travel restriction. It must be considered as part of a broader strategy rather than a solution in itself.

4.5.9. Whether the Child Should Be Placed on a U.S. Prevent Departure List

Ideally, yes in high-risk cases, but with full awareness of its limits.

Placement requires a clear U.S. court order prohibiting the child from leaving a defined jurisdiction. Without that order, federal authorities will not act. Even with it, the mechanism primarily functions through commercial airline systems.

It does not seal every exit. A child could potentially leave by land or water. Certain travel routes may not trigger the same screening mechanisms. Documentation work-arounds are also possible, including use of a foreign passport or emergency travel document where available. For land travel in some contexts, a birth certificate may suffice.

There are also practical enforcement realities. Very young children traveling in a parent's lap are not scrutinized in the same way as independent travelers. The system is designed to intercept known travel through commercial air carriers, not to function as a comprehensive border lockdown. A prevent departure order can meaningfully reduce risk, particularly for international air travel. But it is not absolute, and it should be considered one tool within a broader prevention strategy.

4.5.10. Whether to Allow International Travel During a Pending Dispute

It depends on the relationship between the parties. The more cooperative and stable the dynamic, the more manageable temporary travel may be. Where there is genuine trust, documented history of honoring parenting arrangements, clear return dates, and aligned long-term plans, the risk profile can be lower. The more hostile the situation, the greater the risk of non-return.

If litigation is already underway, communication has broken down, allegations are being exchanged, or one party feels cornered, international travel becomes a structural shift in leverage. Once the child is physically outside the United States, the dispute may migrate with the child.

In most contested India–U.S. cases, the default position is caution. The deterioration of the relationship often correlates directly with the likelihood that a temporary visit becomes something else.

4.5.11. Whether to Seek an Emergency Return Order in the United States or Immediately Proceed in India

The answer, in most serious removal scenarios, is *simultaneous action*. An emergency return application in the United States preserves your record, demonstrates nonacquiescence, and may be critical for immigration or enforcement posture. But stopping there is rarely sufficient once the child is physically in India.

Indian proceedings, particularly those invoking writ jurisdiction before a high court, can take time to mobilize. Logistics matter. Summer vacation periods and peak winter recesses often mean high courts are closed or functioning at limited capacity. Filing windows narrow. Listing delays occur. Even urgent matters may not move at the speed a U.S. practitioner expects.

There is also practical delay in identifying and retaining reliable counsel on the ground. Cross-border coordination takes time. Documents must be transmitted. Affidavits prepared. Strategy aligned. If you wait for one jurisdiction to act before moving in the other, time is lost. And in child removal cases, time shifts leverage.

Simultaneous filing is not about aggression. It is about preserving options before procedural realities in either country slow momentum.

4.5.12. Whether Hague Remedies Are Jurisdictionally Available

Hague is not a principle, it is a treaty mechanism. If the child is in a country that is not a Hague Abduction Convention partner, *there is no Hague "case"* to bring there, no Central Authority process to invoke there, and no treaty obligation on that country's courts to order return on a summary timeline.

So the first screening question is not "Was this wrongful removal?" It is "Where is the child right now, and is that country a Hague Convention country for purposes of return?" If the child is in the United States and was removed from another Hague partner country, Hague relief may be available in U.S. courts under the implementing statute. If the child is in India, Hague return remedies are not jurisdictionally available in India because India is not a Convention country. That one fact changes speed, leverage, and predictability more than any merits argument.

This is also where instinct misleads even experienced lawyers. In a Hague case, the theory is narrow. You do not litigate best interests in the return proceeding. You litigate habitual residence, rights of custody, wrongful removal or retention, and then a limited set of defenses that are supposed to be construed narrowly and decided quickly. That is the design. Even when messy in practice, Hague provides a defined procedural lane. India does not.

Now comes the nuance. Indian child return jurisprudence is eerily similar to Hague defenses in its reasoning. Courts analyze consent or acquiescence, passage of time and settlement, allegations of harm, the child's views, and undertakings. On a surface reading, it can feel Hague-adjacent. It is easy to assume that the mechanism will function similarly.

That assumption is incorrect. The similarity is thematic, not structural. India's mechanism is not a treaty-based summary return proceeding. It is typically some combination of habeas-style relief, guardianship proceedings, or plenary custody litigation governed by the welfare principle. Once you are in that framework, the case is no longer confined to a narrow return inquiry on a clock. It becomes a discretionary, fact-intensive welfare adjudication. Almost any Hague-style argument can be absorbed and reframed within welfare.

The practical consequences are immediate. First, timelines. Hague is built on urgency. India has no comparable statutory obligation to decide within treaty-driven timeframes. If the child remains in India while proceedings unfold, time begins to favor the parent with physical control because integration strengthens with each passing month.

Second, scope. Hague expects courts to separate return from custody merits. In India, once welfare is engaged, the litigation can expand into schooling, stability, extended family support, financial structures, and parental conduct. The return question rarely remains insulated from broader custody considerations.

Third, predictability. Hague practice, while imperfect, operates within a shared treaty framework across partner countries. In India, outcomes turn sharply on fact patterns, timing, and judicial discretion. Two superficially similar removals can produce very different results depending on delay, integration, and how the court frames welfare.

The bottom line is this: if the child is in India, Hague concepts may still inform strategy, but Hague remedies are not jurisdictionally available there. Expect welfare litigation. Expect delay to matter. Expect speed and predictability to differ from what Hague was designed to deliver.

The resemblance in reasoning should not obscure the absence of treaty mechanism. That distinction is decisive.

4.6. Criminal and Allegations Risk

4.6.1. Whether Pressing Criminal Charges in India Will Strategically Help or Escalate

In international parental child abduction scenarios, criminal leverage is often misunderstood. *India does not treat international parental child abduction as a standalone criminal offense where both parents are legal guardians and there is no subsisting court order restricting movement.* In other words, if one parent removes the child in the absence of a clear judicial restraint, there is generally no automatic criminal liability merely for the act of relocation. *That means criminal avenues in pure removal cases are limited.*

In rare situations, a left-behind mother may attempt to invoke criminal provisions if factual circumstances support it, but those scenarios are not the norm. More commonly, it is the left-behind father who seeks remedies after removal, and in many such cases he has no direct criminal option available solely on the basis of relocation.

So the strategic calculus is narrower than clients expect. Criminal complaints in India are typically grounded not in abduction alone, but in allegations of cruelty, domestic violence, dowry-related offenses, or other independent claims. Once those are invoked, the matter shifts from a custody dispute to a criminal proceeding with broader consequences.

The question, therefore, is not simply whether filing a criminal complaint will help. It is whether there is a legally sustainable basis for one at all, and whether initiating that path will meaningfully advance the client's objective or permanently escalate the conflict.

4.6.2. Whether Pressing Criminal Charges in the United States Will Strategically Help or Escalate

This is a *double-edged sword*. In cross-border custody disputes involving India, criminal complaints in the United States are *usually a last resort*. Once law enforcement or a prosecutor takes control of the case, it is *no longer the client's litigation tool*. It becomes a state action. The complaining parent cannot simply withdraw the matter if negotiations resume. *That decision rests with the prosecutor*.

There are also cross-border consequences. Indian courts may react unfavorably if one parent initiates criminal proceedings abroad while parallel custody or matrimonial litigation is pending in India. It can be framed as coercive, tactical, or retaliatory. That perception can influence interim relief and overall tone.

Criminal proceedings in the United States may also trigger immigration complications, travel restrictions, and reputational exposure that outlive the family dispute. Once charges are filed, collateral consequences are difficult to contain.

That does not mean criminal remedies are never appropriate. In cases involving genuine abuse, violence, or credible threats, they may be necessary. But as a strategic move in a custody battle, they often escalate beyond the client's control. The question is not whether criminal law is available. It is whether invoking it will move the dispute toward resolution or push it into a harder, less predictable posture.

4.6.3. Whether the Client Will Face Domestic Violence or Sexual Abuse Allegations in India

In very hotly contested cross-border disputes, this is a very likely development. Allegations of domestic violence, cruelty, or even sexual misconduct frequently surface once custody and jurisdiction become contested. In some cases, those allegations are genuine and must be treated with the seriousness they deserve. In others, they are significantly exaggerated or strategically framed to strengthen leverage in parallel matrimonial or custody proceedings.

From a risk perspective, the likelihood of such allegations increases when one party feels cornered, financially exposed, or disadvantaged in jurisdictional posture. Once raised, these claims alter the litigation landscape immediately. They can justify interim protective orders, travel restraints, maintenance applications, and criminal complaints.

The practical difficulty is that even exaggerated allegations are not easily dismissed at the threshold. Courts often err on the side of caution at interim stages. The existence of an allegation, even before adjudication, can influence custody dynamics and settlement leverage.

The strategic question is not whether the client believes the allegations are false. It is whether the client is prepared for the procedural and reputational consequences once they are made. In high-conflict India–U.S. disputes, this risk should be assumed, not treated as remote.

4.6.4. Whether the Client Should Travel to India During a Hotly Contested Divorce

In many cases, particularly where the client is a man and the dispute is intensely contested, the answer is no.

There are multiple statutory pathways in India through which a husband can be criminally implicated once matrimonial conflict escalates. *Allegations of cruelty, domestic violence, financial harassment, or other offenses can quickly translate into criminal complaints.* Even if ultimately defensible, *the immediate exposure can include police process, court appearances, and travel restrictions.*

It is true that in recent years Indian courts have issued guidelines intended to prevent misuse of certain matrimonial criminal provisions and to curb automatic arrests. That development offers some procedural protection. But it does not eliminate risk. Being named in a criminal complaint is itself a disruptive event.

For NRIs, the risk is compounded. Criminal proceedings abroad can complicate immigration records, background disclosures, visa renewals, and green card processes in the United States. Even unresolved allegations can trigger reporting obligations or create uncertainty in pending applications.

Traveling into that environment during active conflict should be a calculated decision, not an emotional one. Once physically present in India, the client's leverage shifts. Exiting may not be as simple as entering.

4.7. Financial Exposure and Property Consequences

4.7.1. Whether Property Division Rules Differ Radically Between Forums

Yes. Radically.

Most U.S. states operate under equitable distribution or community property frameworks. Marital assets are identified, valued, and divided according to statutory principles. Title is relevant, but not dispositive. Contributions, duration of marriage, earning capacity, and future prospects all factor in. India does not have a comparable matrimonial property regime across personal laws. There is no automatic 50–50 division. Property is largely title-driven. If an asset is in one spouse's sole name, the other does not automatically acquire a half share merely by virtue of marriage. Claims can be made in certain circumstances, but there is no uniform statutory equitable distribution system.

That difference alone can alter forum strategy dramatically. A higher-earning spouse who has accumulated assets in their own name may perceive India as financially less risky. A financially dependent spouse may view the United States as offering broader redistributive relief.

This is not subtle. It is foundational.

4.7.2. Whether Spousal Maintenance Exposure Differs Significantly Between Forums

Yes, and the difference is not just quantum. It is structural. In the United States, maintenance or alimony is typically governed by statutory guidelines or judicial factors, often with duration linked to the length of the marriage. There is a discernible trend toward rehabilitative or durational awards rather than indefinite support, particularly in shorter marriages. Even where discretion exists, there is usually a framework that cabins unpredictability.

In India, maintenance is available under multiple statutes and procedural routes. The quantum is highly fact-driven and discretionary. Courts consider standard of living, earning capacity, financial status, and dependency, but there is no uniform formula. Interim maintenance can be awarded early and may continue throughout lengthy proceedings.

Because India does not have a comprehensive matrimonial property division regime, maintenance is often interpreted broadly. It becomes the principal economic equalization mechanism. Where there is no structured asset division, maintenance arguments may expand to reflect lifestyle parity, housing needs, educational expenses, and long-term financial security.

The risk assessment therefore differs sharply. In the United States, exposure may include significant asset division but often within a time-defined maintenance framework. In India, there may be limited property redistribution but potentially sustained and adjustable maintenance exposure, sometimes across parallel proceedings. For cross-border clients, this structural divergence is central to forum strategy.

4.7.3. Whether Financial Disclosure Standards Differ Materially Across Jurisdictions

Yes. And this difference is more consequential than most lawyers initially assume.

In the United States, structured financial disclosure is foundational. From the outset of matrimonial litigation, parties are typically required to file sworn financial statements, produce tax returns, W-2s, 1099s, bank records, credit card statements, brokerage accounts, retirement accounts, business records, and supporting documentation. Discovery tools are formal, enforceable, and sanctions-backed. Nondisclosure is not merely frowned upon. It is punishable. The system is built on compulsory transparency.

India historically operated within a more flexible and less standardized financial disclosure framework in maintenance proceedings. Affidavits were often not required or varied significantly in detail from case to case. Courts were required to assess maintenance claims on the basis of uneven financial material, with parties frequently disputing the accuracy or completeness of income disclosures. The absence of a uniform disclosure format contributed to inconsistency and delay in adjudication, as courts had to determine financial capacity without a consistent evidentiary baseline.

That is precisely what the Supreme Court attempted to address in Rajnesh v. Neha (2020). In that decision, the Court acknowledged the systemic problem, noting that maintenance applications were frequently delayed and inconsistently decided. It observed that in practice, in a vast majority of cases, applications were not disposed of within prescribed timeframes. Recognizing this structural deficiency, the Court framed national guidelines mandating comprehensive affidavits of disclosure of assets and liabilities.

The Court directed that parties must file detailed affidavits disclosing income, expenditure, movable and immovable assets, liabilities, and dependent obligations in a prescribed format. The purpose was explicit: to introduce uniformity, reduce guesswork, and prevent parties from suppressing material financial information. The Court emphasized that maintenance is to be determined based on the respondent's financial capacity and relevant factors, and that such adjudication requires accurate data.

This was a landmark procedural intervention. It signaled that maintenance determinations cannot rest on broad assertions of poverty or prosperity.

But even post-*Rajnesh,* the enforcement culture differs from that of the United States. First, while affidavits are now required, discovery in India does not operate with the same breadth, immediacy, or sanction-backed rigor as in many U.S. jurisdictions. There is no equivalent of automatic forensic-level exchange at the outset of every matrimonial case. Courts rely heavily on affidavit-based disclosure unless specifically pressed for further production. Second, compliance depends substantially on judicial vigilance. In the United States, disclosure regimes are embedded in procedural rules with built-in enforcement consequences. In India, while courts can draw adverse inferences or impose costs, practical enforcement varies by court, docket load, and counsel engagement. Third, financial opacity is often litigated rather than automatically cured. Disputes over actual income, business ownership, cash components, or family-controlled assets can extend proceedings. The burden frequently falls on the claimant spouse to demonstrate that the disclosed income is understated. The contrast is therefore structural and cultural.

In the United States, the presumption is full financial transparency at the outset, backed by enforceable discovery mechanisms. In India, even after *Rajnesh v. Neha,* disclosure is more affidavit-driven, enforcement is more discretionary, and the adversarial burden of exposing nondisclosure often remains with the opposing party.

This difference matters profoundly in cross-border cases. A client who is accustomed to U.S.-style mandatory, document-heavy disclosure may be surprised by the procedural tempo in India. Conversely, a spouse relying on limited affidavit disclosure in India may face far more intrusive and enforceable scrutiny in a U.S. court.

The two systems are converging in principle. They are not identical in execution.

4.8. Other Considerations

4.8.1. Whether Digital Communications Establish Jurisdictional Admissions

Yes, far more often than clients realize.

Emails, WhatsApp messages, text exchanges, and even casual statements in parenting apps can later be characterized as jurisdictional admissions. A message saying, "we moved back home," "India is better for the kids," or "let's fight it out here" may be cited as evidence of intent to relocate permanently or submit to a particular forum.

Statements about residence, schooling, duration of stay, or agreement to "try things out in India for a year" can undermine later arguments that a move was temporary. Even tone matters. Silence in response to relocation plans can be framed as acquiescence. *Even a casual moving in party invitation over WhatsApp signifying relocation of somewhat permanent nature can trigger issues* depicting intent.

Jurisdictional litigation is built on small facts. Digital correspondence is often the most concrete evidence of those facts. Clients must be told clearly: assume every message may be read in court. Because it will be.

4.8.2. Whether Cross-Border Mediation Is Viable Before Parallel Litigation Escalates

Sometimes yes. Often only early. Cross-border mediation can be effective before parties harden their positions in court. If both sides are still communicating, if there are no active criminal allegations, and if jurisdictional fights have not yet entrenched, mediation may preserve flexibility and reduce cost. The window narrows quickly once parallel proceedings begin.

Once one party files in India and the other in the United States, positions become public. Pleadings are drafted. Allegations are formalized. Interim orders are sought. At that stage, mediation becomes less about problem-solving and more about damage control.

Mediation is most viable when it precedes escalation, not after injunctions, contempt threats, or criminal complaints are in play. Timing determines whether it is a genuine settlement opportunity or a procedural pause in a larger war.

4.9. The Immediate Necessity of Dual Counsel in India and the United States

In serious India–U.S. disputes, early engagement of counsel in both jurisdictions is usually essential. These matters do not unfold in isolation. A filing in New York can trigger an urgent application in India. An interim order in India can shift settlement leverage in the United States. A criminal complaint in one forum can complicate immigration or reputational exposure in the other. The systems interact quickly and often without warning.

Waiting to retain counsel in the second jurisdiction until after escalation has occurred is a common and costly mistake. *At the same time, this is not simply about retaining two lawyers. It is about retaining the right two lawyers.*

In India, many advocates practice broadly across civil, criminal, and commercial work. Far fewer focus deeply on family law. Fewer still regularly handle international family disputes involving cross-border custody, anti-suit injunctions, recognition challenges, or Hague-adjacent arguments. *The procedural posture of these cases is specialized.* High court writ practice is specialized. Managing interim relief and jurisdictional objections alongside foreign proceedings is specialized.

Experience matters, and so do practical inroads. Knowing how listing works, how urgent matters are mentioned, how vacation benches function, and how to move quickly within a particular high court is not theoretical knowledge. It is operational familiarity. Without it, time is lost. The same principle applies in the United States. Counsel must understand not only domestic custody doctrine, but also how orders will be scrutinized abroad, how service must be structured to withstand CPC section 13 review, and how criminal or immigration exposure may intersect with matrimonial litigation.

Dual counsel, properly coordinated, is not duplication. It is structural risk management across interacting systems and avoids "unintended" malpractice issues. When aligned early and thoughtfully, it enables consistent strategy, disciplined admissions, and deliberate sequencing. When delayed or mismatched, it often produces reactive litigation and avoidable exposure.

In cross-border disputes, the margin for procedural error is thin. Coordinated, experienced representation in both jurisdictions is not a luxury. It is foundational.

Index

D

Q

R

S

T

U

W

Y

Z